COM+
Developer's Guide

JOHN PAUL **MUELLER**

Osborne/**McGraw-Hill**

Berkeley   New York   St. Louis   San Francisco
Auckland   Bogotá   Hamburg   London   Madrid
Mexico City   Milan   Montreal   New Delhi   Panama City
Paris   São Paulo   Singapore   Sydney
Tokyo   Toronto

Osborne/**McGraw-Hill**
2600 Tenth Street
Berkeley, California 94710
U.S.A.

For information on translations or book distributors outside the U.S.A., or to arrange bulk purchase discounts for sales promotions, premiums, or fund-raisers, please contact Osborne/**McGraw-Hill** at the above address.

COM+ Developer's Guide

1234567890 DOC DOC 019876543210

Book P/N 0-07-212603-5   and   CD P/N 0-07-212604-3
      parts of
ISBN 0-07-212086-X

Publisher
  Brandon A. Nordin
Associate Publisher and
Editor-in-Chief
  Scott Rogers
Acquisitions Editors
  Wendy Rinaldi
  Ann Sellers
Project Editor
  Carolyn Welch
Acquisitions Coordinator
  Monika Faltiss
Technical Editor
  Greg Guntle
Copy Editor
  Dennis Weaver

Proofreader
  Susie Elkind
Indexer
  Valerie Robbins
Computer Designer
  Jani Beckwith
  Elizabeth Jang
  Liz Pauw
Illustrator
  Robert Hansen
  Brian Wells
  Beth Young
Series Design
  Peter Hancik

This book was composed with Corel VENTURA ™ Publisher.

This book is dedicated to my friends and neighbors,
the Rabuck and the Kintz families.
I couldn't ask for more considerate people to live next to me,
and I hope they'll always think of me as a friend as well.

About the Author...

John Paul Mueller is a freelance author and technical editor. He has writing in his blood, having produced 46 books and almost 200 articles to date. The topics range from networking to artificial intelligence and from database management to heads down programming. Some of his current books include a COM+ programmer's guide and a Windows NT Web server handbook. His technical editing skills have helped over 23 authors refine the content of their manuscripts, some of which are certification related. In addition to book projects, John has provided technical editing services to both Data Based Advisor and Coast Compute magazines. A recognized authority on computer industry certifications, he's also contributed certification-related articles to magazines like Certified Professional Magazine.

When John isn't working at the computer, you can find him in his workshop. He's an avid woodworker and candle maker. On any given afternoon you can find him working at a lathe or putting the finishing touches on a bookcase. One of his newest craft projects is glycerin soap making, which comes in pretty handy for gift baskets. You can reach John on the Internet at JMueller@mwt.net. John is also setting up a new Web site at: http://www.mwt.net/~jmueller/, feel free to take a look and make suggestions on how he can improve it. One of his current projects is creating book FAQ sheets that should help you find the book information you need much faster.

CONTENTS

Acknowledgments xi
Introduction xiii

▼ 1   COM+—The Latest in Component Technology   1
    What is COM+?   2
        The COM+ Difference   3
        A Look at the Big Picture   5
    How COM+ and COM Compare   5
        COM+ Design Goals   5
        Transactions and COM+   6
        Messages and COM+   6
        COM+ Services   7
    The MTS Difference   9
        MTS Service Description   9
        The Role of Resource Pooling in COM+   10
    Where Does MSMQ Fit In?   11

▼ 2   COM Essentials—The Short Version   13
    Creating an Object   15
        In-Process   16

Out-of-Process 17

Component Reuse 33

Calling an Interface Method 34

Understanding IUnknown 35

Understanding the ActiveX Interfaces 36

Using the ActiveX Interfaces 38

Reference Counting 40

Registry Requirements 40

Working with Apartments and Threads 47

Thread Types 47

Apartment Types and Assignments 49

Marshaling Requirements 52

▼ 3   Unique COM+ Features 53

COM+ and Automation 56

Understanding Just-In-Time (JIT) Activation 57

Transaction Processing 58

COM+ Context 59

Understanding Resource Dispensers 60

Understanding the Compensating Resource Manager 61

COM+ Event Sinks 62

COM+ Catalog 62

Object Pooling 63

Role-Based Security 63

Understanding Standard Windows Security 64

How Role-Based Security Differs 86

Understanding Component Load Balancing (CLB) 91

Understanding Load-Balancing Goals 92

How Does Load Balancing Work? 92

Dealing with Downed Servers and Routers 94

▼ 4   An Overview of MTS 95

What Is a Transaction? 96

Understanding Transactions 97

MTS and COM+ 99

Understanding the Transaction Sequence 102

An Overview of MTS Objects 102

Defining the Transaction Events 103

Remote Execution Considerations 104

MTS Load-Balancing Concerns 105

Understanding COM+ Application Reliability 106

COM/DCOM Issues 107

Transactions and Databases   108
    Handling Database Diversity   109
    MTS Database Features   109
    Database Programming with MTS   112
    MTS and COM+   114
Security Considerations   114
Understanding Microsoft Distributed Transaction
    Coordinator (MS-DTC)   115
    MS-DTC in Operation   116
    The Distributed Part of MS-DTC   117

▼ 5   An Overview of MSMQ   119
An Overview of Asynchronous Communication for MSMQ . . .   121
    Routing   122
    Types of Disk Access   124
    Delivery Guarantees   126
    Security   128
    MSMQ and MTS   133
An Overview of Message Queues   136
    Understanding the Message Queue Types   137
    Message Queues for Disconnected Applications   139
The Server View of Messaging   140
    Parts of a Message   140
    The COM View of Message and Queue Manipulation   140
    MSMQ Error Handling   144
Understanding the Active Directory/MQIS Database   148
    Database Installation Requirements and Sizing   149
    Hosting   149
    MSMQ 1.0 versus MSMQ 2.0   151
Performance Issues   152
    MSMQ Internal Performance Problems   152
    Processing Limitations that Affect Application Performance   154

▼ 6   Understanding the Application Types   159
Understanding COM+ Application Differences   161
    Server-Based Components   163
    COM+ Benefits   163
    Attributes, Context, and State   164
    Four Levels of Component Change   166
Understanding the Programming Issues   173
    Performance   174
    Security   175

COM+ Application Types   176
    Server Applications   177
    Library Applications   177
    Proxy Applications   178
    Preinstalled Applications   178
Offline Application Considerations   179
Working with MTS and MSMQ Alone   181

▼ 7   A Transaction Driven Application   183

Installing SQL Server 6.5 Developer Edition   186
Creating a SQL Server Remote Development and Diagnostic Aid   190
Defining the Application   198
    An Application Task Overview   201
    An Overview of the Database   202
    An In-Depth View of the Individual Tables   202
    Creating the Database and Associated Tables   207
    The N-tier View of the Project   221
Creating the Server-Side Components   222
    Creating the Component Shell   223
    Adding the Component Code   237
    Registering and Installing the Component on the Server . .   247
Creating the Client-Side Component   261
    Creating the Component Shell   262
    Adding the Component Code   265
    Creating a Simple Catalog Test Application   269
Creating a Test Application   280
    Creating the Application Shell   281
    Defining the User Interface   284
    Adding the Application Code   294
    Testing the COM+ Application   302

▼ 8   Dealing with Transaction Failure   305

Failure Scenarios   307
    Connected   310
    Disconnected   316
Error-Recovery Methods   319
    Detecting the Source of the Error   319
    Interpreting Error Codes   346
    Dealing with Error Overload   347
    Staging a Recovery   348

▼ 9   Sending Messages and COM Objects   353

An Overview of the Communication Scenario   358
Two APIs   358
Defining the Message Type   365
Understanding the Data Transfer Sequence   366
Creating the Required Queues   366
Creating a Listener/Player Application   369
Creating the Listener/Player Shell   370
Designing the Dialog Form   372
Adding Playback Code   372
Creating a Test Application   379
Creating the Test Application Shell   379
Designing the Test Application Dialog Form   380
Adding the Test Code   382
Testing the Application   386
Checking Out the Message   387
Viewing the Message Output   393
MSMQ Administrative Issues   394
Basics of Queue Management   394
Dead Letter Messages Queue   396
Checking the Event Viewer   396

▼ 10 Working in Disconnected Mode   399

Defining the Application   402
Desktop versus Distributed Development   404
Understanding the Default COM+ Recorder, Listener,
and Player   406
An Overview of Application Data Flow   411
Creating and Installing the Component   413
Creating the Component Shell   413
Adding Some Component Code   417
Installing the Component   418
Creating a Test Application   426
Designing the Application Shell   427
Defining the Dialog Form   429
Adding Some Application Code   429
Testing in Connected Mode   437
Testing in Disconnected Mode   437

▼   Glossary   443

▼   Index   477

ACKNOWLEDGMENTS

Thanks to my wife, Rebecca, for working with me to get this book completed. I really don't know what I would have done without her help in researching and compiling some of the information that appears in this book (especially the glossary). She also did a fine job of proofreading my rough draft and page proofing the final result.

Greg Guntle deserves thanks for his technical edit of this book. He greatly added to the accuracy and depth of the material you see here. In addition, he worked very hard in testing many of the procedures you see in this book—over and over again. I don't know what I would have done without his aid and assistance in figuring out some of the intricacies of COM+.

A special thanks goes to Karen Watterson. She spent many hours looking at my database designs and ensuring the accuracy of my SQL Server information. There were many tweaks made at her suggestion and she did nothing but encourage me during the rather arduous task of writing many of the database elements of this book.

Matt Wagner, my agent, deserves credit for helping me get the contract in the first place and taking care of all the details that most authors don't really think about. I really appreciate the thoughtful and kind way that he dealt with some of the family problems I had while writing this book. Certainly, he made my job much easier than it could have been under the circumstances.

The technical support staff at Microsoft deserve credit for answering the questions that helped fill in the blanks and made the Visual C++ learning experience go faster. Likewise, I'd like to thank the people on the various Internet newsgroups I visited who helped provide insights into C++ programming techniques. Especially important were the tips on how to work with OLE DB and ADO.

Finally, I would like to thank Wendy Rinaldi, Ann Sellers, Carolyn Welch, Dennis Weaver, and the rest of the production staff at Osborne for their assistance in bringing this book to print. I especially appreciate Wendy's patience when things didn't go exceptionally well.

INTRODUCTION

Windows 2000—it's the operating system that many people have looked forward to with an equal mix of excitement and anguish. At the time of this writing, Windows 2000 is still a gleam in Microsoft's eye, but not for long. As the time for the Windows 2000 release approaches, the amount of hype in the media has increased—Windows 2000 is going to be a major upgrade of the Windows operating system. There's no doubt that many companies will upgrade immediately, while others will take a look-and-see approach before making the leap. No matter when your company decides to update, it will eventually do so simply because of the vast number of new features that Windows 2000 provides. From a network administrator's perspective, Windows 2000 is a must-have update for the advantages that Active Directory alone provides. Of course, new security features like Kerberos and Public Key Infrastructure (PKI) will play no small part in the decision for most companies to upgrade.

For the programmer of a large company or the independent developer, the exciting part of Windows 2000 is all the new application programming interface (API) features like media streaming that it'll bring. Of course, the most important of these features is COM+. Obviously, there's also Active Directory and new application-specific APIs to consider as well. In short, programmers will have a lot of new "toys" to play with, many of which will make the job of creating robust enterprise-level applications much easier.

The anguish part of the Windows 2000 equation is the rather steep learning curve that COM+ and these other new technologies promise. For many developers, all that COM+ will promise at first is a lot of long nights reading about the new technology and time spent experimenting with it. (Obviously, the payoff for all of this work is applications that can scale across the network or Internet and, eventually, reduced development time.) Even Microsoft tacitly admits that COM+ will cause many developers problems—they've been trying to get around some of these problems by offering a vast array of developer courses during the entire Windows 2000 beta.

That's one of the reasons this book is so important to you. It helps you understand what COM+ will do for you and how you can ease the learning curve—at least a little bit. We'll explore the world of COM+ and I'll help you break the various technologies that make it up into more manageable pieces. You'll find out that much of the seeming complexity that surrounds COM+ is nothing more than the consolidation of technologies that appear in separate packages today, along with some enhancements that will make COM development as a whole much easier than it is right now.

A lot of books will give you all of the theoretical background that we'll talk about in this book. The thing that makes this book different is the real-world approach that I'll take in demonstrating COM+ to you. Of course, that means working with real-world programming examples that should help you get started using COM+ faster. One of the more important application types in use at the enterprise level is the database—which is the kind of application we'll create first and enhance in various ways. The database example in this book uses multiple tables, and we go through the entire set of design steps required to create both the database and the application that manages it. Obviously, part of this process is going to involve writing a server-side component that not only makes the query process easier but reduces network traffic as well.

COM+ doesn't have to be a Pandora's box of difficult to understand technologies and utilities that thwart your every effort. This book will help you learn about this new and exciting part of Windows 2000. Together, we can learn about everything that COM+ can do to make your desktop and LAN applications scale to the WAN and Internet levels.

WHAT'S IN THIS BOOK

It helps to look at the book contents from a goal perspective—what is this book going to help you accomplish and how? This book has three major goals: to teach COM+ theory, to show how COM+ can be used in both the general and enterprise programming environments, and, finally, to provide fully functional code examples. Chapters 1 through 6 will cover COM+ theory and usage details, while Chapters 7 through 10 will provide the fully functional code examples.

Chapter 1 of the book is designed to acquaint you with COM+. It does this by providing some direct information about COM+ itself and comparing COM+ to its predecessor, COM. A comparison is important because it helps you understand that if you know COM today, the learning curve for COM+ is going to be a lot smaller than you originally thought. There are also two sections devoted to the new features in the COM+ environment: Microsoft Management Queue (MSMQ) and Microsoft Transaction Server (MTS). MSMQ has been enhanced to provide support for things like disconnected applications (a term I'll describe in the chapter), while MTS has been enhanced to provide transaction processing for databases and objects alike.

Chapter 2 provides an essential overview of COM itself. This overview replaces what many books cover in four or five chapters, which means that I haven't taken the time to look at all of the details. This overview won't be enough to teach you about COM, so if you don't know anything at all about COM today, this isn't the book for you. This chapter will provide enough information to ensure both of us have the same understanding about basic concepts. In addition, this overview will serve as a refresher for anyone who has worked with COM before but hasn't done so recently. Finally, this chapter will help you understand what Microsoft has used as a basis for creating COM+. It's important to have a good starting point before we start on the COM+ learning journey that follows.

Chapter 3 is intended as an introduction to specific COM+ features that aren't directly related to either MTS or MSMQ. This is an essential COM+ chapter. The MTS- and MSMQ-related information is covered in Chapters 4 and 5, respectively. What you'll learn in these three chapters is that COM+ is essentially an enhanced and consolidated version of COM, MTS, MSMQ, and DCOM (which is still used to transfer data over the network). These three chapters also include much of the how to and when to use COM+ information. By the time you finish these three chapters, you should have enough theoretical information to at least understand the programming examples that follow.

Chapter 6 is a specialty chapter that discusses important COM+ issues on a practical, rather than a theoretical level. It provides an overview of the kinds of applications that you can expect to create with COM+ that aren't necessarily supported by COM—at least not directly. Yes, COM+ is an extension of COM, but an extension that helps you to do more than ever before with component technology. It's important to understand that COM+ does allow you to create new application types that will reduce the development time required to roll out enterprise-level application suites as a whole.

Chapters 7 through 10 present four fully functional programming examples. I tried to choose examples that demonstrate a wide variety of potential COM+ uses at the medium-sized company to the enterprise level. The examples concentrate on new COM+ uses rather than things that COM+ simply copied from COM. For example, the database example looks at how you can use a server-side component to reduce network traffic. This server-side component makes use of MTS to ensure that all transactions take place as anticipated—including those that really aren't database specific.

INTENDED AUDIENCE

This book is designed for the professional (experienced) programmer. It doesn't differentiate between the consultant or enterprise programmer, although some of the material is definitely enterprise oriented. The developer will need a good knowledge of Visual C++ and at least some experience with COM. I do provide step-by-step instructions for using SQL Server, but an understanding of how database managers (DBMSs) work is required as well. I'm not going to spend a lot of time telling you how a DBMS works, but I will tell you why I've done them in a certain way (some of which seems contrary to common practice today). As a result, the book will provide only an overview of many COM concepts so that it can concentrate on the details of COM+ programming.

Since MTS and MSMQ are relatively new additions to the COM programmer's environment, the coverage of these two topics will be a little more extensive. However, I'm assuming that you'll already have some idea of how to work with these products from the user level. In other words, the book will provide technical details, not user-level information (except as needed by the example programs).

WHAT YOU'LL NEED

COM+ is a new technology, and Microsoft hasn't created a consolidated tool (at least not at the time of this writing) for you to work with it. At a very minimum, you'll need a copy of Visual C++ 6 Professional Edition (Enterprise Edition is required for any database examples), the Windows 2000 Platform SDK, and Microsoft Data Access Components (MDAC) version 2.5. You may also need the COM+ SDK. The need for this product depends on what Microsoft does in the time between when I finish this book and you buy it at the store. Theoretically, the COM+ SDK will be incorporated within the Windows 2000 Platform SDK.

As part of the setup for Visual C++, make sure you install Service Pack 3. This upgrade is very important because Visual C++ will almost certainly freeze if you try to debug an application without installing Service Pack 3 when working with Windows 2000. This upgrade comes with newer copies of Visual C++ 6.0 as part of the package. You can also download it from the Microsoft Visual Studio Web site online. Finally, the service pack will come with your MSDN subscription. Make sure you also install any service packs required for SQL Server or other products used with this book. I explain how to apply the SQL Server updates in Chapter 7 of the book.

You won't be able to use the older versions of the Visual C++ product, in most cases, because I plan to use new features in every example. (Visual C++ 5 may work marginally for some examples, but I won't provide any workarounds for using this product.) I'm assuming that you're using Windows 2000 as your operating system, and none of the examples are guaranteed to work on any other version of the Windows operating system. In fact, I can guarantee that with few exceptions they won't.

NOTE: Many of the concepts you'll learn in this book won't appear in your online documentation. Some of it's so new that it only appears on selected Web sites. You'll find either a tip or a note alerting you to the location of such information throughout the book. In addition, Microsoft made some material available only through selected channels like an MSDN subscription. Other pieces of information are simply undocumented, and you won't find them anywhere except within a newsgroup when someone finds the feature accidentally.

You'll also need a computer running Windows 2000 Professional (or Server) to use as a workstation, and I strongly recommend a second server computer running Windows 2000 Server (you must have at least one machine running Windows 2000 Server for MSMQ support). Both your server and workstation will require enough RAM and other resources to fully support the tools you'll need throughout this book. In most cases, this means you'll need a minimum of a 350MHz Pentium II computer with 64MB of RAM and at least 4GB of hard disk space for your workstation. A server will require additional RAM and hard drive space. Using multiple processors on the server is a plus, but not a requirement.

Even though you could potentially get by with less, you'll find that a lower-end computer will quickly bog down as you try to write code and test it. I did try running the examples on a 300MHz Pentium machine with 128MB RAM and 3GB free hard drive space. The performance was terrible; I could literally watch screen redraws because of the load that Windows 2000 placed on the machine at the time of this writing. Microsoft will likely fix some of these performance problems and others will go away when you use production versus beta code, but it pays to provide a setup that will actually run the examples in a reasonable amount of time.

CONVENTIONS USED IN THIS BOOK

In this section, we'll cover usage conventions. We'll discuss programming conventions a little later when we look at Hungarian Notation and how to use it. This book uses the following conventions:

[<Filename>]   When you see square brackets around a value, switch, or command, it means that this is an optional component. You don't have to include it as part of the command line or dialog field unless you want the additional functionality that the value, switch, or command provides.

<Filename>   A variable name between angle brackets is a value that you need to replace with something else. The variable name you'll see usually provides a clue as to what kind of information you need to supply. In this case, you'll need to provide a filename. Never type the angle brackets when you type the value.

ALL CAPS	There are three places you'll see ALL CAPS: commands, filenames, and case-sensitive registry entries. Normally, you'll type a command at the DOS prompt, within a PIF file field, or within the Run dialog field. If you see all caps somewhere else, it's safe to assume that the item is a case-sensitive registry entry or some other value like a filename.
File | Open	Menus and the selections on them appear with a vertical bar. "File | Open" means "Access the File menu and choose Open."
Italic	There are three places you see italic text: new words, multivalue entries, and undefined values. You'll always see a value in italic whenever the actual value of something is unknown. The book also uses italic where more than one value might be correct. For example, you might see FILE*xxxx*0 in text. This means that the value could be anywhere between FILE0000 and FILE9999.
Monospace	It's important to differentiate the text that you'll use in a macro or type at the command line from the text that explains it. This book uses monospace type to make this differentiation. Every time you see monospace text, you'll know that the information you see will appear in a macro, within a system file like CONFIG.SYS or AUTOEXEC.BAT, or as something you'll type at the command line. You'll even see the switches used with Windows commands in this text. There's also another time you'll see monospace text. Every code listing uses monospaced code to make the text easier to read. Using monospaced text also makes it easier to add things like indentation to the coding example.

Icons

This book contains many icons that help you identify certain types of information. The following paragraphs describe the purpose of each icon.

NOTE: Notes tell you about interesting facts that don't necessarily affect your ability to use the other information in the book. I use note boxes to give you bits of information that I've picked up while using Visual C++, Windows NT, or Windows 95.

TIP: Everyone likes tips, because they tell you new ways of doing things that you might not have thought about before. Tip boxes also provide an alternative way of doing something that you might like better than the first approach I provided.

CAUTION: This means watch out! Cautions almost always tell you about some kind of system or data damage that'll occur if you perform a certain action (or fail to perform others). Make sure you understand a caution thoroughly before you follow any instructions that come after it.

WEB LINK: The Internet contains a wealth of information, but finding it can be difficult, to say the least. Web Links help you find new sources of information on the Internet that you can use to improve your programming or learn new techniques. You'll also find newsgroup Web Links that tell where you can find other people to talk with about Visual C++. Finally, Web Links will help you find utility programs that'll make programming faster and easier than before.

Sidebars

Sidebars will contain additional information that you don't necessarily have to know to write a good program. In many cases, I'll provide material that's related to the current topic, but not related well enough, or perhaps not important enough, to include with the topic at hand. Most sidebars will provide interesting material that an intermediate or advanced programmer will want to use to enhance the applications they create or their own personal productivity. For example, you may find an explanation of wizard configuration issues or a discussion about why a particular add-on product is a good deal for the developer in a sidebar.

You'll also find a variety of margin notes in the book. They describe some bit of information you should remember before starting a procedure or performing other kinds of work. Margin notes also contain useful tidbits like the location of a file or something you should look for in an example program. In most cases, margin notes are simply helpful nuggets of information you can use to improve your programming as a whole.

AN OVERVIEW OF HUNGARIAN NOTATION

Secret codes—the stuff of spy movies and a variety of other human endeavors. When you first see Hungarian Notation, you may view it as just another secret code. It contains all the elements of a secret code, including an arcane series of letters that you have to decode and an almost indecipherable result when you do. However, it won't take long for you to realize that it's other programmers' code that's secret, not the Hungarian Notation used in this book.

Hungarian Notation can save you a lot of time and effort. Anyone who's spent enough time programming realizes the value of good documentation when you try to understand what you did in a previous coding session or to interpret someone else's code. That's part of what Hungarian Notation will do for you—document your code.

An understanding of Hungarian Notation will also help you gain more insight from the examples in this book and from the Microsoft (and other vendor) manuals in general. Just about every Windows programming language vendor uses some form of Hungarian Notation in their manuals. In addition, these same concepts are equally applicable to other languages like Visual FoxPro, Delphi, and Visual Basic. The codes remain similar across a variety of programming languages, even when the language itself doesn't.

So, what precisely is Hungarian Notation? It's a way of telling other people what you intend to do with a variable. Knowing what a variable is supposed to do can often help explain the code itself. For example, if I tell you that a particular variable contains a handle to a window, then you know a lot more about it than the fact that it's simply a variable. You can interpret the code surrounding that variable with the understanding that it's supposed to do something with a window.

The first stage of development for this variable-naming system was started by Charles Simonyi of Microsoft Corporation. He called his system Hungarian Notation, so that's the name we'll use here. There are many places where you can obtain a copy of his work, including BBSs and some of the Microsoft programming Web sites on the Internet. (Many online services like CompuServe also carry copies of Hungarian Notation in its various incarnations.) Simonyi's work was further enhanced by other developers. For example, Xbase programmers use their own special version of Hungarian Notation. It takes into account the different types of variables that Xbase provides. An enhanced Xbase version of Hungarian Notation was published by Robert A. Difalco of Fresh Technologies. You can find his work on a few DBMS-specific BBSs as well as the Computer Associates Clipper forum on CompuServe.

The basis for the ideas presented in this section is found in one form or another in one of the two previously mentioned documents. The purpose in publishing them here is to make you aware of the exact nature of the conventions I employ and how you can best use them in your own code. There are four reasons why you should use these naming conventions in your programs:

▼ **Mnemonic value** This allows you to remember the name of a variable more easily, an important consideration for team projects.

■ **Suggestive value** You may not be the only one modifying your code. If you're working on a team project, others in the team will at least look at the code you've written. Using these conventions will help others understand what you mean when using a specific convention.

■ **Consistency** A programmer's work is often viewed not only in terms of efficiency or functionality but also for ease of readability by other programmers. Using these conventions will help you maintain uniform code from one project to another. Other programmers will be able to anticipate the value or function of a section of code simply by the conventions you use.

▲ **Speed of decision** In the business world, the speed at which you can create and modify code will often determine how successful a particular venture will be. Using consistent code will reduce the time you spend trying to decide what someone meant when creating a variable or function. This reduction in decision time will increase the amount of time you have available for productive work.

Now that I've told you why you should use Hungarian Notation, let's look at how I plan to implement it in this book. I'll use the rules in the following section when naming variables. You'll also see me use them when naming database fields or other value-related constructs. Some functions and procedures will use them as well, but only if Hungarian Notation will make the meaning of the function or procedure clearer.

Rule 1: Prefixing a Variable

Always prefix a variable with one or more lowercase letters indicating its type. In most cases, this is the first letter of the variable type, so it's easy to remember what letter to use. The following examples show the most common prefixes for Visual Basic, Delphi, and C. (There are literally hundreds of combinations used in Windows that don't appear here.) You'll also see a few database-specific identifiers provided here:

a	Array
c	Character
d	Date
dbl	Double
dc	Device context
dw	Double word
f	Flag, Boolean, or logical
h	Handle
i	Integer
inst	Instance
l	Long
li	Long integer
lp	Long pointer
msg	Message
n	Numeric
o	Object
pal	Palette
psz	Pointer to a zero terminated string
ptr	Pointer (or P when used with other variables like psz)
r	Real
rc	Rectangle
rgb	Red, green, blue (color variable)
rsrc	Resource

sgl	Single
si	Short integer
sz	Zero terminated string
u	Unsigned
ui	Unsigned integer or byte
w	Word
wnd	Window

Rule 2: Identifying State Variables

Some variables represent the state of an object like a database, a field, or a control. They might even store the state of another variable. Telling other programmers that a variable monitors the current state of an object can help them see its significance within the program. You can identify state variables using one of the following three-character qualifiers:

New	A new state
Sav	A saved state
Tem	A temporary state

Rule 3: Using a Standard Qualifier

A standard qualifier can help someone see the purpose of a variable almost instantly. This isn't the type of information that the variable contains, but how it reacts with other variables. For example, using the Clr qualifier tells the viewer that this variable is used in some way with color. You can even combine the qualifiers to amplify their effect and describe how the variable is used. For example, cClrCrs is a character variable that determines the color of the cursor on the display. Using one to three of these qualifiers is usually sufficient to describe the purpose of a variable. The following standard qualifiers are examples of the more common types:

Ar	Array
Attr	Attribute
B	Bottom
Clr	Color
Col	Column
Crs	Cursor
Dbf	Database file
F	First
File	File

Fld	Field
L	Last/left
Msg	Message
Name	Name
Ntx	Index file
R	Right
Rec	Record number
Ret	Return value
Scr	Screen
Str	String
T	Top
X	Row
Y	Column

Rule 4: Adding Descriptive Text

Once you clearly define the variable's contents and purpose, you can refine the definition with some descriptive text. For example, you might have a long pointer to a string containing an employee's name that looks like this: lpszEmpName. The first two letters tell you that this is a long pointer. The second two letters tell you that this is a zero (or NULL) terminated string. The rest of the letters tell you that this is an employee name. (Notice that I used the standard qualifier, Name, for this example.) Seeing a variable name like this in a piece of code tells you what to expect from it at a glance.

Rule 5: Creating More Than One Variable

There are times when you won't be able to satisfy every need in a particular module using a single variable. In those cases, you might want to create more than one of that variable type and simply number them. You could also designate its function using some type of number indicator like those shown here:

1,2,3	State pointer references as in cSavClr1, cSavClr2, etc.
Max	Strict upper limit as in nFldMax, maximum number of fields
Min	Strict lower limit as in nRecMin, minimum number of records
Ord	An ordinal number of some type

ABOUT THE CD

I'm sure you'll enjoy all of the examples in the book and will want to make the best possible use of them as you learn about COM+. However, trying to type all of that code by hand can be frustrating, especially when you look at the examples in Chapter 7. Obviously, you need another alternative to typing all of that code, like getting it in electronic form so you don't have to repeat my efforts.

In the past, the source code for the book would have been made available on the Osborne Web site. The source code for this book weighs in at 76MB, which makes downloading the source code a very time consuming and error prone process for those of you with dial-up connections.

The CD for this book is designed with you in mind. It allows you to see working examples of the source code without typing a single line of code or downloading anything. The CD includes compiled versions of every example, in addition to the source code, which should make using the examples that much easier.

Remember that a CD is a real-only device. So, when you copy the files from the CD to your hard drive, the files will also be marked as read-only. You can use Windows Explorer to remove the read-only attribute from the files on your hard drive so that you can make changes to the source code and recompile it as needed.

Please feel free to contact me at JMueller@mwt.net if you have any problems at all with the source code. I want to make this book as easy as possible for you to use and learn from. Be sure to send me your comments as well. I always keep track of reader comments and use them to improve my books. Both positive and negative comments about any book topic are always welcome.

CHAPTER 1

COM+—The Latest in Component Technology

Just in case you haven't figured it out yet, COM+ is a really big feature for Windows 2000. Of course, the problem with being a really big feature is that everyone has a different view of exactly what this really big feature is all about. By now, you've gotten so much hype and so little information about COM+ that you're probably wondering if this technology is even real. It is real, and it's based on existing technology—COM.

This chapter is going to help you understand what COM+ is all about. We'll spend some time wiping away the cloud of misinformation and hype that surrounds this component technology. In fact, the first section of the chapter will answer a very important question, "What is COM+?" We'll take a look at what COM+ is really all about from a programmer's perspective. More than that, we'll also view COM+ from the user perspective so that you can get a better understanding of how COM+ can help the people using your applications.

One of the best ways to learn about a new technology is to compare it to an existing technology, when one exists. COM+ is really an improved version of COM. The second section of the chapter will show you how these two technologies compare. In short, you'll find out what kinds of enhancements COM+ makes to standard COM. You may be surprised by what you find because COM+ really is both different and yet the same as COM.

Microsoft Transaction Server (MTS) is usually associated with database management systems (DBMS). However, transactions aren't limited to database work—you can use them in other places as well. Anytime you want to perform a set of steps with guaranteed results or total failure, MTS is the technology to look at. MTS will allow you to create applications that either perform *all* of the steps required to complete a task or *none* of them. The result is that your system will always end up in a stable state. So, how does MTS relate to COM+? We'll discuss that very question in the third section of the chapter.

The final part of this chapter will look at another enabling technology, Microsoft Message Queue (MSMQ). This is yet another new addition for Windows 2000 (though you could have added it in Windows NT). Just as MTS frees an application from worrying about how much of a transaction has completed, MSMQ frees an application from worrying about the connected state of the computer that it's operating on. We'll see in the fourth section of this chapter just how MSMQ makes COM+ a very unique tool when compared to its predecessor.

WHAT IS COM+?

COM+ is one of the most important new technologies waiting for you in Windows 2000—new, yet old at the same time. I've always viewed components as a sort of programmer's Lego, a building block for creating something useful out of standardized parts. In this respect, COM+ is no different than any component technology you've explored in the past. Creating an application still requires talent, even if the talent is to put building blocks together. COM+ doesn't contain any kind of magic that'll allow applications to appear from nowhere; you still have to put in the time required to create them.

The COM+ Difference

So, if COM+ is still a component technology, what is it offering you? Think of COM+ as a Lego expansion set. Yes, it's still all about building blocks, but now you have new blocks to add to your collection, along with a few motorized parts to make your applications move. In short, COM+ is COM on steroids. It represents Microsoft's latest advance in application development for today's complex programming environment.

COM+ and Connectivity

If you have any doubts about the need for better component technology, just look at the kind of environment programmer's work in today. When I first started writing code, I had to worry about the local machine, and that's it. This local machine was running DOS, which meant it had limited amounts of memory and even fewer instructions to worry about. In the days of DOS, programming was quite simple, but also quite limited. I didn't need a large Lego set; in fact, all I really needed were simple tools to create a single Lego.

Even when I moved to Windows 3.x, the programming environment focused on the local machine, with just a few LAN elements thrown in for good measure. Windows 3.x programming focused on the user's desktop, not on a corporation as a whole. In short, Windows 3.x was simply DOS with graphics from a programmer's perspective.

There's no local, self-contained machine running DOS or Windows 3.x today. When you write an application now you have to worry about how that application will affect the Internet, or a LAN, or some other machine. Computers today are connected together in ways that I couldn't even imagine they'd be when I started programming. The Internet is a major part of many application development efforts; you really can't write an application today without at least thinking about how it'll work in a network situation. In addition, users are no longer happy to store their data locally while on the road. They want to be able to connect to the company's intranet using a virtual private network. The same connection will allow them to update their local data to reflect changes at the office. People today are connected to each other in more ways than one, and applications have to keep pace with the changing needs of these users.

COM+ and the User

In addition to connectivity, people expect more assistance out of applications today. A character mode application like the ones I used to create in DOS just wouldn't work. Those applications were designed with an advanced user in mind. Many users today have just turned on their computer for the first time and have no idea at all of how to run it. In short, the application has to be smart enough to keep the users from shooting themselves in the foot. Applications that are designed to prevent users from hurting themselves are very complex to create. It's not enough to think about the logical considerations; you have to think about the illogical things, too.

There are certain connectivity and ease-of-use issues that COM+ is designed to handle for the programmer. For example, if a user is on the road and needs to enter a new order in the database, can you really expect them to remember some arcane procedure you taught them at the office for working on the road? It's very likely that the user isn't going to remember and that you'll have a mess to clean up when the user gets back to the office. A COM+ application can act the same no matter where the user is. Since the user uses the same procedure all of the time for entering data and the programmer doesn't need to do much more in the way of application programming, everyone's a winner in this scenario.

COM+ and the User Interface

We're still not done with the programmer issues today versus yesterday. There's one additional technological difference that you need to consider. A graphical user interface (GUI) may be wonderful for the user, but I'm not convinced that the programmer gets anything at all out of it other than a major writer's cramp. Getting all of those icons onscreen takes time and lots of code. In the days of DOS, I didn't need much in the way of input. Everything was character driven, so the user interface was often an afterthought after I got the rest of the application working. As soon as Windows 3.x came into the picture, the programmer needed to worry about graphics. The user interface moved from the back burner to the very first thing the programmer had to worry about when creating an application. In short, application programming went from business logic driven to user need driven and finally to data driven. The data you manipulate, and the expertise of the user that you're writing for, determines what an application will look like today.

Component technology has come to the programmer's rescue in a big way when it comes to dealing with a GUI. Instead of writing miles of code to draw every control and handle every event that the user generates, the programmer can now use predefined objects to get the job done. All that the user programmer really needs to worry about is the appearance of a form and the business logic required to make that form work. COM+ extends the kinds of things that you can do with a GUI. Again, we're looking at connected applications that change to reflect current conditions in the company as a whole.

COM+ and the Programmer

Programmers won't ever have the simple programming environment of DOS again. They'll have to face the consequences of working in a world where the PC has really taken over as a primary business tool. COM+ provides the solution to a programmer's problem of creating an application quickly, but with all of the connectivity and ease-of-use issues taken care of.

No one today could create the kinds of complex applications required for Internet use in a GUI environment using straight procedural code—at least they couldn't do so without expending a lot of time. In short, using COM (or some other component technology) is no longer a luxury because you need the component technology to create an application of any kind. It won't be long before COM+ will be a requirement as well because people will have to be connected at all times to their sources of information, and that's what COM+ offers them.

A Look at the Big Picture

By now you should have a clearer idea of what COM+ is from a conceptual perspective. It's a simple-to-use component technology that allows developers to create applications that provide a good user interface and require fewer lines of code. Without a component technology, developers would need to resort to the really terrifying experience of managing every part of every application themselves.

Obviously, COM+ is a lot more complex than what I've just described. For one thing, it relies on other servers like Microsoft Transaction Server (MTS) and Microsoft Message Queue (MSMQ) to accomplish its work. However, it's important when facing a technology as complex as this to get the bird's-eye view first. That's what we've just done; we've looked at the overall effect that COM+ is supposed to provide for you as a programmer.

HOW COM+ AND COM COMPARE

From a component creation perspective, COM and COM+ are about the same. Despite all of the hype to the contrary, you can create a component using either form of the technology. In fact, COM+ is merely an augmentation of existing COM technology when it comes to working with components. The important thing to remember is that COM+ is a true superset of COM, so you lose nothing by using COM+ in place of COM in your applications.

Now that you have some idea of how COM and COM+ are the same, it's time to look at how they differ. The following sections are going to provide you with an overview of these differences. We'll refine this overview as the book progresses. What this overview is designed to do is help you separate the hype of COM+ improvements from changes that'll really make a difference when it comes time to create an application.

COM+ Design Goals

To better understand what you do gain using COM+, it's important to understand some of the goals that the design team had in mind when putting COM+ together. One of the main goals was to make developing components for server use as easy as they are for client use. Before COM+, there were a lot of server-specific issues to take care of like multiple users hitting a component at the same time. COM+ removes a number of the problems that come with a multiuser environment like the one you find on servers. Of course, the end result is to promote distributed application development.

A secondary goal was to make it just as easy to develop enterprise applications as it is to develop workgroup applications. What this means is that COM+ allows you to create components that'll scale to any size. "Load balancing" is a term that you'll hear more and more as companies try to create an environment where a single programming effort will result in components that continue to work as the company grows.

In short, these two goals define part of what COM+ is all about. Unlike COM, COM+ is designed to allow you to create distributed applications that rely on component technology that scales to any size. This COM+ difference will greatly affect how you create applications in the future. In many cases, you'll now create components that applications on the client will use to access data on yet another server.

Let's talk about the client and server situation a little further. COM+ is also part of Microsoft's Distributed interNet Architecture (DNA). Essentially, this is an *n*-tier architecture where various servers perform specific tasks. Those tasks are just part of a whole application. In other words, a single application on the user's machine may actually require the services provided by more than one server. One server might have the components that include the basic business logic for the request, another server might access in-memory databases containing things like a list of the states in the United States, and a third server might provide access to the company's main data store. The whole idea is to create an environment where the user doesn't care which server has what he or she needs to get the job done, just that the job gets done in the most efficient manner possible.

Transactions and COM+

Accomplishing the two goals of distributed application development and component scalability that we talked about in the previous section is easier said than done. Anytime you have two machines talking with each other over a cable (be it a telephone wire or co-axial cable), you have to create some type of protocol for the discussion. In addition, there's a much greater chance for lost data, which means that you need some type of transaction technology in place. Microsoft Transaction Server (MTS) is part of the COM+ universe. MTS is the mechanism by which COM+ guarantees delivery of data from one machine to another. We'll discuss exactly how MTS comes into play in "The MTS Difference" section of the chapter.

Messages and COM+

COM+ also introduces a new concept: disconnected applications. However, it uses an old technology to implement this concept in the form of MSMQ. In the past, an application that required services from the server or wanted to provide input to the server had to maintain a live connection. Obviously, this is impossible for employees on the road, so companies often had to rely on cumbersome technologies of dubious value that forced the employee to use different methods in different situations. In addition to the problem of getting an employee trained to use more than one data entry and management method, there was a problem with getting the employee to use the right method at the right time.

These old technologies also forced the programmer to do more work. Even if the programmer only needed to worry about two data entry scenarios, that's still twice the amount of code and debugging. In essence, the programmer was actually writing the same application twice because of a lack of disconnected application tools.

MSMQ and COM+ have been teamed up to allow a programmer to build logic into the application that doesn't care about the current connected state of the application. Data that an application wants to send to the server gets stored in a local message queue if the application can't establish a connection with the server. When the user does make a connection, the data in the message queue is automatically uploaded for the user.

Resources that the application will require from the server can also be downloaded before the user attempts to break the connection with the server. This will allow the user to request at least a subset of the data from the server, never realizing that there isn't a connection in place for getting the requested information. The only time the user will notice any difference at all is if the data requested is needed immediately and the need to download it from the server wasn't anticipated. Even so, as soon as the user establishes a connection, the requested data can be downloaded in the background.

As you can see, coupling COM+ and MSMQ means that the user will only need to know one application usage procedure. No longer will the administrator have to pull their hair out when the wrong procedure is used for data entry purposes. In addition, the programmer will be able to deliver a working application much faster because there'll be only one set of data access routines to write.

COM+ Services

So far, we've seen that COM+ is an amalgam of various existing technologies. In short, nothing I've said so far is all that new. However, the fact that COM+ provides a wrapper for making all of these technologies work together is a new idea. Microsoft has found that it's not enough to provide disparate services that could allow applications to talk with servers using components rather than some of the older technologies we relied on in the past. Creating a single package for all of these technologies is the way to ensure that programmers will actually use the technologies that Microsoft has provided.

COM+ isn't merely a wrapper for existing services, however. It also provides some unique services that you won't find in any of Microsoft's older offerings. The following list provides you with an overview of what these offerings are. We'll study these features in greater detail as the book progresses (especially in Chapters 2 and 3).

▼ **Events** Applications can receive events generated on the server as if they occurred on the local machine. This means that the server-side components you create will have a direct connection to the client. COM+ allows you to use unicast (event is sent to one event sink), multicast (event is sent to multiple event sinks), and unbound (event occurs when client makes contact) events. The unbound event is particularly useful because it can inform a client about conditions on the server after the client performs an initial login. In other words, every client who logs in to the system will receive the current (dynamic) status of the server that they're logging in to.

■ **Security** COM+ actually relies on MTS for the security of its data in many cases. However, COM+ still has security concerns when instantiated objects on the server need to communicate with a client and there isn't any transaction. In addition, COM+ allows the creation of queued components—essentially a component in a message. Security is a requirement if you don't want another company taking a look at your business logic. COM+ checks security at several levels, including the class itself, any interface requests, and all method calls. These security roles are mapped through Active Directory to the Windows 2000 domain accounts.

- **Component Load Balancing (CLB)**   Large companies very rarely get by with just one server. In the past, the company would divide the users into groups and each group would have their own server. This method worked fine unless one of the servers went down. However, it was very inefficient because one server might have a light load while another struggled to keep up. Load balancing allows everyone to access all of the available servers through a router. The router keeps track of how much of a load each server has and balances new requests accordingly. In addition, the router can move current requests from a failed server to the good ones in the cluster without the user even realizing that a server failure has occurred. (Note that this feature will be provided as a separate download after Microsoft releases Windows 2000, or as part of one of the Windows 2000 server versions.)

- **Queued components**   Clients require updates to the components they hold from time to time, and in some cases will require a new component before they can perform a specific task. In the past, the administrator had to install new components on each machine individually or create cumbersome batch files to do the job. The use of queued components allows each client to automatically update itself in the background. The administrator doesn't need to do much more than install the component on the server and send the proper broadcast message.

- **In-Memory Database (IMDB)**   Did you ever wait for what seemed like hours for a simple request to arrive from the server? I'm not talking about a search of the Internet for all occurrences of "War and Peace." I'm talking about something like a state name based on a ZIP code entry at the top of a form. Accessing a database on disk is slow; accessing the same database in memory is much faster. A planned COM+ add-on will allow you to create in-memory databases that contain small tables of static data that the user will require access to a lot. This feature was originally planned for inclusion with Windows 2000, but is now planned as a separate product for later release. IMDB may appear with a new name and with enhanced features that will allow it to work as a standard database that resides in memory instead of on disk. Microsoft's original reason for removing this product from Windows 2000 is that the beta version of IMDB worked too differently from a standard DBMS and caused developer confusion.

- **Compensating Resource Manager**   This particular service is used with legacy applications. It actually builds a framework around the old server application so that clients can access the application using all of the new features that COM+ provides. The main goal of this service is to allow you to maintain your investment in established applications, yet allow the old application to interact with other resources on the server. Of course, this feature comes at the cost of performance, so upgrading your components to COM+ is one of the things you should consider.

▲   **Administration**   COM+ uses a Microsoft Management Console (MMC) snap-in to provide administrative services for your server-side components. This snap-in allows you to manage all COM components and allows you to administer all of the new services that COM+ provides. This snap-in also provides a programming interface that allows you to install, configure, and automatically deploy your COM+ components. It relies on Active Directory's catalog to store the attributes for each of the components installed on the server. The COM+ component attributes include transactions, security roles, and activation properties.

THE MTS DIFFERENCE

MTS is an important part of COM+. This section of the chapter is going to provide you with a very brief overview of MTS. We'll talk about the two most important aspects of MTS: the services it provides and the purpose of resource pooling. In Chapter 4, we'll look at MTS in greater detail and define its part in the grand scheme of things a bit better. Obviously, there's a lot more to know about MTS from both a management and a programming perspective.

MTS Service Description

As previously mentioned, COM+ relies on MTS to perform specific services that ensure data gets delivered from one machine to another. These services not only ensure that the data gets delivered, but that both the sender and the receiver are sure of the integrity of the data. The following list provides an overview of the services that MTS provides for COM+:

▼   **Transactions**   A transaction is a single group of instructions that have to be carried out to complete a task. Either a transaction is completed or it's rolled back so that the application environment is the same as it was before the transaction started. MTS frees the programmer from managing transactions. All the programmer needs to do is specify that a given set of instructions constitutes a transaction.

■   **Resource pooling**   Today's servers have huge quantities of memory and hard disk space that components can use to complete tasks. However, given the complex environment in which components are often placed, trying to manage resources is a difficult task to say the least. MTS also features automated resource management. Not only does resource pooling free the programmer from micromanaging system resources, but it also ensures that each component gets the resources it needs.

■   **Security**   Getting data from one point to another and ensuring that it gets recorded properly won't do much for you if someone breaks into the connection between the client and server and corrupts the data. As a result, security's one of the more important features that MTS provides.

▲ **Administration**   Managing your MTS setup so that you can get optimum performance from your server is an important task. Microsoft provides a Microsoft Management Console (MMC) snap-in that makes MTS management easier. In addition, using an MMC snap-in reduces the administrator's learning curve since all administrative tools in Windows 2000 now use the MMC interface.

As you can see, MTS provides a lot more than just transaction management, though that is its main function. The other services that MTS provides merely augment the main function of making sure that data gets from one point to another without interruption and that all of the operations formed on that data are completed successfully, or not at all. Without these services, COM+ as a whole would fail because data security is a primary requirement to creating distributed applications.

One of the services that doesn't appear in our list is serialization. This particular feature of MTS ensures that both data and commands arrive at the database in the same order that they were created on the client, even if the network protocol used to transfer the packets of information doesn't guarantee any order of delivery. This means that you won't need to worry quite as much about the features provided by the underlying network protocol—at least not when it concerns the order that your data will arrive in.

The Role of Resource Pooling in COM+

One of the MTS services requires special mention. Resource pooling is one of the more important reasons to use MTS because resource pooling is a requirement for efficient transactions on a large scale. A smart resource-pooling scheme wouldn't just allocate and deallocate system resources. Allocating and then deallocating resources takes time that could be used for other purposes. Marking resources that are already allocated for use would allow for reuse and get rid of some of the inefficiencies of transaction management. In fact, MTS does provide four different levels of resource status. It uses the notion of enlisting a resource for use and then using it. Each of the four levels of resource status is described in the following list:

▼ **Resources in Unenlisted Inventory**   This is a resource that's available for assignment to any object or transaction. All resources start in this state and remain that way until they're needed by an application for processing purposes.

■ **Resources in Enlisted Inventory**   Transactions may involve more than one object. If one object no longer needs a resource, the resource can be set aside for use by another object in the same transaction. This resource status allows a transaction to maintain control over a resource until none of the objects contained within it require the resource any longer.

■ **Resources in Unenlisted Use**   An object that owns a resource that isn't part of a transaction owns that resource in an unenlisted state. This particular resource status also gets used if an object is operating within a transaction, but the resource is marked as not being transactional.

▲ **Resources in Enlisted Use**   There are three conditions that must exist before this resource status gets used. The resource must be assigned to an object. The object instance must be part of a transaction. Finally, the resource dispenser must successfully enlist the resource as part of the transaction.

At this point, you have an idea of why resource pooling in MTS is important. It allows MTS to allocate, deallocate, and manage resources efficiently. Resource pooling also promotes resource reuse so that the server doesn't waste time allocating a resource that was just used by another object in the same transaction. Considering the fact that COM+ is all about objects, wise object resource management is a requirement for successful implementation of the COM+ component strategy.

WHERE DOES MSMQ FIT IN?

MSMQ is the messaging arm of the COM+ strategy for Microsoft. It allows applications to do things that would have been impossible in the past. One of the ways in which MSMQ aids in application development is communications. COM+ requests and responses are sent and received as messages. This means that all COM+ really needs is a message queue to put the message in. MSMQ places such queues on both the server and the client, then provides a method for transferring data in these queues between the two machines without the user's assistance. The server and the client don't really need to connect directly as long as they pick up their messages.

Some programmers find this particular issue confusing because we're all used to looking at synchronous real-time communication. It helps to look at this messaging arrangement in the same way you that look at email on the Internet. You can have a conversation with an associate using email without directly contacting that associate. The use of email allows both of you to communicate ideas and learn new ways of doing things. Likewise, disconnected applications can use the MSMQ queues to hold a conversation with the server. Obviously, there has to be some way to exchange the information between the queues. Again, it's easy to look at Internet email as a means of understanding how MSMQ works. Even though you can answer your email offline, you eventually need to get online to upload the responses you create to the ISP's server. The same thing happens with a disconnected application using MSMQ.

Microsoft had to provide four features in MSMQ to make it a useful technology. The following list describes these four features and tells you why they're important:

▼ **Delivery guarantees**   Unless MSMQ guarantees delivery of messages, there is no way to ensure that the server or client will actually receive query responses. Without a guaranteed communication, your application would be unreliable. In sum, a guarantee of delivery, no matter how long such delivery takes, is a requirement to create a robust reliable application that ensures the user will get the same results whether connected or disconnected from the server.

- ■ **Routing**   The programmer may not have any idea of exactly how the user will connect to the server. The user might require a dial-up connection over a modem one day and a direct network connection the next. As a result, it's up to the MSMQ to ensure that messages get from the client to the server and vice versa. Routing these messages is an important part of MSMQ's background processing on behalf of the user.

- ■ **Connectionless**   The whole reason to use MSMQ is so that you can build disconnected applications. Today's user needs a reliable method of accessing and updating server information without learning more than one technique of doing so. Disconnected applications reduce both application development time and user training time. In addition, the application is inherently more reliable because there are fewer points of failure. A single way of doing things means that there is a set procedure in place that the user can always rely on.

- ▲ **Security**   Like everything else in a distributed application, your data must remain secure. In this case, MSMQ provides the means for ensuring that messages are kept secret. Data on both the client and server must remain encrypted so that prying eyes don't gain access to your company's data by looking through the messages that MSMQ stores on the hard drive.

MSMQ actually contains three discrete components including the message queues, a Queue Manager, and the application programming interface (API) used to request data from the Queue Manager. We'll talk about these components in detail in Chapter 5. For the moment, all you really need to know is that the client and server never access the messages that MSMQ stores directly. All access is through the API using the Queue Manager.

There's a fourth MSMQ component that you also need to be aware of that has little to do with the actual handling of the messages. It's the MSMQ Information Service (MQIS). This database holds the definitions for MSMQ sites, machines, queues, and users. The actual database is implemented using SQL Server, which is why Windows 2000 provides a "limited" version of SQL Server as part of the package. You won't find MQIS on every machine, and definitely not on any client. MQIS is a central repository of data and is therefore found on just a few servers (at least one) on the network.

As you can see, MSMQ is designed to work locally, on a LAN, or at the enterprise level without any changes in code on your part. The idea is a simple one: using messages to transfer both data and objects from one place to another. The implementation is equally simple. All you really need is a mailbox on each disconnected machine and a background task to deliver the mail. In short, MSMQ is designed to make application development for COM+ a lot easier than writing enterprise-level applications from scratch.

CHAPTER 2

COM Essentials—The Short Version

It's important to know what you're doing and why you're doing it. The Component Object Model (COM) represents years of work on the part of Microsoft to develop a component technology. Essentially, components are like building blocks. They allow you to create a new application using modules instead of writing individual lines of code. Obviously, you need to glue all of these modules together and define how they'll work; but, in the long run, you should still end up writing less code than you'd normally have to write to produce today's complex applications.

In this chapter, we'll talk about the theory behind COM. I'm assuming that you already have some knowledge and you only need a refresher course in COM technology. We'll begin with the simplest part of COM: the object. COM supports several object types, each of which is used in different situations. This first section will look at the various object types and answer questions like those related to component reuse.

Using objects comes next. We'll talk about one of the main components of COM objects: the interface. Essentially, an interface represents a method for bundling functions that the user can access when working with your object. Obviously, there's a lot of work that goes on behind the scenes, and we'll cover quite a bit of it in this section.

WEB LINK: COM, Distributed COM (DCOM), and COM+ are important parts of Microsoft's component strategy for both Windows and the Internet. It's important to know where you can get help when you need it. There's a general COM Web site at http://www.microsoft.com/com/.

Part of the reason that people use objects instead of other forms of precompiled code is dynamic linking. The code and data you need isn't loaded until actually requested by the application. It's important to understand how this process works, especially later when we get into remote technologies like DCOM and COM+.

The registry has become the central repository of information for all of the settings that Windows requires to operate. Objects are no exception to the rule. Somewhere along the way, you'll add entries to the registry so that Windows can find, configure, and use your object. Some of the tools that Visual C++ provides hide these details from you, which is just fine in most cases because the entries you need to make are mundane and repeatable. However, it still pays to know what your object is adding to the registry so that you can check for errors in these settings later.

The final section of this chapter attacks the topic of apartments and threads. I decided to include these sections because the topic of apartments and threads sends many programmers screaming. This section will help clear up the mass of misinformation that many programmers have to wade through in order to gain the few nuggets of information they really need. No, this section isn't a full-blown conceptual description of how apartments and threads work. It's more of a practical discussion that provides you with just what you need to know to really understand what's going on with the objects you create.

CREATING AN OBJECT

Let's begin this discussion with a quick definition of an object, since this term is used in a variety of ways and the meaning of this term can vary depending on whom you talk with. An object is an amalgamation of code and data. Everything needed for the object to work is contained with this code and data.

Objects consist of three programmer-accessible elements: properties, methods, and events. Properties define the object's configuration. For example, most visual objects include one or more color related properties that allow you to define the color aspect of the object's appearance. Methods define the kinds of tasks that the object can perform. Programmers normally use methods to tell the object to do something, check on the object's status, or modify property values during runtime. Events are generated as the result of some change in object status. For example, when a user presses a button, an event is generated. In some cases, events are internally generated, such as the event generated when a countdown timer finishes counting down.

One other principle that you need to consider when working with objects is the idea of a container. A container is simply a portion of an application that can hold an object. Another name for an application that contains an object container is a client. The client requests a service from the server (the object). There are several different ways a container can be used to hold an object. We'll discuss those methods later in this section of the chapter. All you really need to know for now is that an object requires a container to perform useful work and the container requires the services that an object can provide. These two application elements live in a symbiotic relationship where both elements benefit.

The component you write using Visual C++ includes the code and data descriptions that will eventually be used by Windows to create an object. The component isn't an object—it's merely a description of an object. A component can be used by Windows to create any number of objects, which may differ slightly because of differences in property settings. For example, a single component can define multiple button types, but a single button object will always be a specific kind of button. In short, an object is a single instance of a component. That's why the process of creating an object using the description found in a component is called instantiation.

Obviously, not all objects are created equal. There are different ways to instantiate an object that helps define how the object will interact with the calling application. COM objects can be grouped by the way they load. Either the server will load in the same memory and address space as the client application, or it'll load outside of that client as a separate process with its own memory. That's the most basic difference between in-process and out-of-process servers—where and how they load. The first two sections that follow will examine the relationship between in-process and out-of-process servers in more detail.

TIP: One of the easier ways to differentiate an in-process and an out-of-process server is by their file extension. In-process servers normally use a DLL or OCX extension, while out-of-process servers normally have an EXE extension.

In addition to loading methods, there are ways to categorize components by the way they allow you to reuse the code they contain. For example, the basic button component allows a good deal of code reuse. Every button created in Windows is essentially a copy of the basic button with some features added. Code reuse allows one programmer to benefit from another programmer's work. You start out with a generic case of an object and create a more specific object that meets certain needs. Code reuse is one of the reasons that programmers like using object technology, like COM, so much. The third section that follows will talk about code reuse issues in more detail.

In-Process

Of the two component memory models, the one used by in-process servers is the easiest to understand and work with. A good example of an in-process server is an ActiveX component—you add it to your application using the development language's IDE. Most ActiveX components have some type of visual interface and you set their properties using property pages that get exposed in a variety of ways depending on the development language's IDE.

In-process servers also include the DLLs used to display foreign data within an application. You'll find listings of these types of components within the file association entries in the Windows Registry (HKEY_CLASSES_ROOT is the main area for this type of data). The DLLs used for displaying various types of foreign data, on the other hand, are normally accessed directly from the code in your application. In short, in-process servers, for the most part, are part of the application you create from the very beginning of the design process.

A new category of in-process server includes the Microsoft Management Console (MMC) snap-ins used in Windows 2000. MMC itself is simply a container used to hold the snap-ins. The snap-ins are DLLs that allow a network administrator to monitor and configure various elements within Windows 2000. As you can see, in-process servers cover a fairly broad range of application-specific categories, but not nearly the range covered by out-of-process servers (as you'll see in the next section).

NOTE: In-process servers are normally contained in DLL files, so some developers call them DLL servers. It's important to remember that OCX files are essentially renamed DLL files in this case. On the other hand, since out-of-process servers are normally stand-alone applications, they reside in EXE files and are called EXE servers by some developers.

When an application calls upon the services of an in-process server, the object that Windows creates resides within the application memory space. This means that the application has direct access to the object. It's easy to see how an in-process server and a container communicate. After all, they're in the same address space, which makes passing data back and forth relatively easy. All that the container needs is an address for the required interface and a list of methods to work with.

All in-process server calls are local. What this means to the programmer is that you don't need to take some potential out-of-process server problems into account. For example, your in-process server will never get disconnected because of a bad network connection. This makes the process of troubleshooting errant components much easier. On the other hand, the inability to use in-process servers from a remote location also reduces their flexibility—you're limited to using the resources on the local machine.

The ability to make local calls and use addresses between server and client makes in-process servers faster and easier to program than out-of-process servers. There are no address or data translations that need to take place. An in-process server represents the most efficient way to work with component technology, despite several limitations we'll discuss in the next section of the chapter. The application programmer interacts with the object just like any other part of the program.

While it's important to understand there are in-process servers from a COM perspective, we won't spend a lot of time working with them in this book. The main event for COM+ is the out-of-process server that we'll discuss in the following section. With that in mind, this chapter won't cover in-process servers in much more detail except in the way they affect the operation of applications in general and their differences with out-of-process servers.

Out-of-Process

Out-of-process servers come in a very wide variety of shapes and sizes. For example, any COM component that resides on a server, yet provides services to a workstation, is an out-of-process server. So, any component used with DCOM is an out-of-process server, as are those used for Microsoft Message Queue (MSMQ) and Microsoft Transaction Server (MTS). In short, the most common use of out-of-process servers right now is within the realm of remote execution where an application makes use of resources on another machine.

Don't get the idea, however, that out-of-process servers are limited to remote execution scenarios—this just represents the latest in a series of out-of-process server uses. Out-of-process servers are also used in a number of application scenarios where data integrity and multiple threads of execution are both important considerations. For example, graphics libraries often use the out-of-process server approach. The library starts up in a separate process to ensure that its data remains secure.

TIP: Some people find it easy to confuse an out-of-process server with an application that supports OLE. The first is a component, the second is a container. Components can't execute on their own—they need the services of a container. This is equally true whether the component is an in-process server or an out-of-process server.

An out-of-process server relies on a proxy/stub mechanism to accomplish its work. The proxy gets installed in the client's memory space. As far as the client is concerned, it's still talking with a local server. In reality, though, it's talking with the server's proxy. The proxy stands in for the real object, which is executing in a separate process. Likewise, the stub gets installed in the server's memory space. As far as the server is concerned, the container is installed in local memory. The operating system takes care of any communication required to transfer information from the proxy to the server and from the stub to the container. Since the proxy/stub mechanism is fixed, the data transfer can take place safely.

Out-of-process servers don't share the ease of programming or the speed advantages enjoyed by in-process servers. The very fact that an out-of-process server resides outside of the application's memory space means that all addresses must be translated, a time-consuming task to say the least. However, the out-of-process server is protected from direct access by another process by the operating system. In other words, while any address that the container might get from the server would be useless, both enjoy the security and reliability that separate process execution can provide.

There are actually two forms of out-of-process server calls: local procedure call (LPC) and remote procedure call (RPC). Looked at simply, the difference between the two is that an LPC occurs on a local machine while an RPC occurs on a remote machine. When a container calls on the services of an out-of-process server that requires the use of RPC, it could run into a myriad of problems including disconnections and delays.

WEB LINK: Microsoft didn't create the RPC specification. It was created by the Open Software Foundation. You can find out more about the Distributed Computing Environment (DCE) RPC specification at http://www.opengroup.org/, http://www.osf.org/, or http://web1.osf.org/. There's also a good overview of how RPC works at http://www.ja.net/documents/NetworkNews/Issue44/RPC.html.

It's time to look at more specific information about how an out-of-process server works in general. The DCOM connection is one of the most common out-of-process server uses. In addition, DCOM is one of the more all-encompassing connection types because it relies on the use of an RPC connection between the client and the server. With this in mind, we're going to take a detailed look at how DCOM works in the following sections. However, it's important to remember that this information also details how out-of-process server connections work in general.

NOTE: Another reason that this information is so very important is that it forms the basis of what we're going to work with throughout the rest of the book. You must know this information because DCOM forms the basis of the COM+ technologies that we'll study as the book progresses. Both MTS and MSMQ rely on RPC to create new application types like the disconnected application. In short, without the historical context of DCOM to fall back on, the process of learning COM+ will take a great deal more time.

Typical Out-of-Process Connections

One of the main things you need to worry about when working with a remote access protocol like DCOM is precisely how the connection will take place. After all, without a good connection, many other considerations are rendered moot.

This section of the chapter answers several questions. First, we'll look at how the connection actually works—at least from an overview perspective. Second, we'll look at the question of how DCOM keeps the connection from becoming so mired in detail that the user gets tired of waiting for something to happen. Third, we'll look at some load-balancing concerns—it's essential to know how DCOM scales as the load on one or more components in an application increases.

HOW DOES THE CONNECTION WORK?   In this section, we'll take a bird's-eye view of how DCOM creates and manages a connection between the client and server. It's important to understand how this connection works so that you can troubleshoot problems in your own applications. Figure 2-1 contains a block diagram of the flow of data from the client to the server. The following list describes each of the diagram elements:

▼ **Client**   Originates requests to the server for resources and support.

■ **OLE32**   A DLL containing the methods used to create an instance of an object (along with a wealth of other functionality). There are five methods available for remote object creation: CoCreateInstanceEx(), CoGetInstanceFromFile(), CoGetInstanceFromStorage(), CoGetClassObject(), and CoGetClassObjectFromURL().

■ **Service Control Manager (SCM)**   Creates the initial connection between the client and server. The SCM is only used during object creation. This feature gets implemented by the TransportLoad() method in the RPCLTSCM.DLL file.

■ **Proxy**   The server's presence within the client's address space. The proxy, which is actually a table of interfaces, is created and managed by the operating system at the request of the COM runtime. It allows the client to think that the server is local, even though the server is actually located on another machine. Windows uses a method like CreateProxyFromTypeInfo() found in the RPCRT4.DLL file to create the proxy.

■ **COM runtime**   Operating system elements that host objects and provide client/server communication. The COM runtime is part of any COM-related scenario—both in-process and out-of-process, local and remote.

■ **Security provider**   The security provider logs the client machine into the server machine. Windows 2000 provides support for several standard security providers for both Internet and local network use. These providers include NT LAN Manager (NTLM, the standard Windows NT security protocol), Kerberos, Distributed Password Authentication (DPA, which is used by CompuServe and MSN), secure channel security services like Secure Sockets Layer (SSL)/Private Communication Technology (PCT), and third-party Distributed Computing Environment (DCE) providers. Some security providers will also ensure that all data transferred between the client and server is protected in some way—usually through the use of encryption.

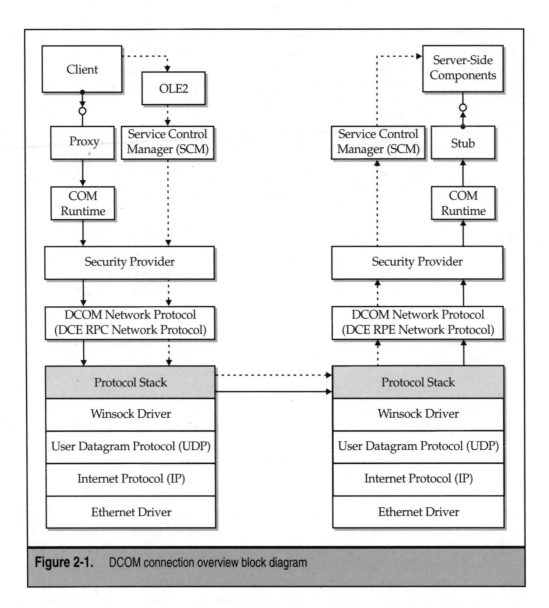

Figure 2-1.   DCOM connection overview block diagram

■ **DCOM Network Protocol (DCE RPC Network Protocol)**   Defines a protocol
  for creating a connection with a remote server for the purpose of using
  objects. In addition to implementing a component protocol, this block contains
  all of the elements to implement the object remote procedure call (ORPC)
  specification at an application level. This particular component is known by
  several different names in the Microsoft documentation, the most popular of
  which is DCOM wire protocol. We'll discuss the DCOM Network Protocol in
  detail later in this chapter.

■ **Protocol stack**   Actual network communication requires more than just one protocol—there are network-related protocols to consider as well. The protocol stack consists of all the protocols required to create a connection between the client and server, including network-specific protocols like TCP/IP. Figure 2-1 shows a typical protocol stack consisting of a Winsock driver, a UDP, an IP, and an Ethernet driver. Not shown is the Ethernet network interface card (NIC) actually used to create the physical connection between the client and server.

■ **Stub**   The client's presence within the server's address space. The stub is created and managed by the operating system at the request of the COM runtime. As far as the server is concerned, it's working with a local client. Windows uses a method like CreateStubFromTypeInfo() found in the RPCRT4.DLL file to create the stub.

▲ **Server**   The COM object that the client has requested services and resources from.

There are actually two communication paths shown in Figure 2-1. The first path (the dotted line) is used to create an instance of the object. The second path (solid line) is used for normal communication between the client and the server. Creating a line of communication between a client and server normally follows these steps:

1. Client issues one of the five object creation method calls that we discussed earlier in the section (the OLE32.DLL bullet). The call must include both a class ID (CLSID) and a server name (along with any information required to log on to the server). As an alternative, the client can issue a standard call that OLE32.DLL will resolve to a remote location based on a registry entry, or the client can use monikers.

2. OLE32.DLL calls upon the client-side SCM to create a connection to the server machine since it can't service the call locally.

3. The DCOM network protocol creates the required packets to send information from the client to the server.

4. The server-side SCM creates an instance of the desired server-side component and returns a pointer of the object instance to the client.

5. The server-side SCM calls upon the COM runtime to create a stub for the component to interact with.

6. The client-side SCM calls upon the COM runtime to create a proxy for the client to interact with.

7. The SCM returns a pointer to the proxy to the client.

8. Normal client- and server-side component communications begin.

CONNECTION-ORIENTED DATA FLOW OPTIMIZATION   Sometimes, the development and placement of a component depends on just how much communication is taking place. Consider a situation when a client needs access to the contents of a database. You could place a component directly on the client machine that would access the Database Manager, gain access to the required data, then format it for the user. However, this design would require a lot of network communication because the client would need to constantly communicate with the Database Manager and send or receive the data.

Splitting the component in two would allow you to reduce the amount of data traversing the network. One component on the client machine could send data requests and format the incoming data. A second component on the server could make the data requests and deliver only the required information to the client. Using this approach would significantly reduce network traffic, enhance both client and server efficiency, and make the user more productive all at the same time.

DCOM does perform some connection manipulation on its own. One of the most important changes that DCOM will implement automatically is connection optimization. For example, if you have a server-side component that's manipulating a database using ODBC, DCOM will more than likely copy the component to the client, then get out of the picture. Since the connection to the database is through ODBC, neither the client nor the Database Manager notice any difference in the performance of the component. However, since DCOM is out of the picture, the component executes more efficiently. Obviously, this is a very specific kind of connection change and is only implemented when the client will see a significant performance gain.

LOAD-BALANCING CONCERNS Load balancing is another connection-related problem. Normally, you'll begin with all of the server-side components required for an application loaded on a single machine. As people get added to the application user's list, you may have to move some components to their own machine to avoid overloading a single machine. Breaking the component into smaller pieces may relieve some server stress as well. However, at some point even a well-designed component may overload a single server. At this point, you need to balance the component load across multiple servers.

NOTE: We'll talk about more than one type of load balancing within the book as a whole. This section is an introduction to load balancing within the realm of DCOM. We'll cover load balancing in a lot more detail in Chapter 7. Windows 2000 has a great deal to offer when it comes to load balancing, especially if you're using the newer technologies that involve COM+.

DCOM supports two types of load balancing: static and dynamic. Static load balancing occurs when you assign specific users to specific servers. Older versions of Windows normally rely on registry entries to enforce the assignment of user machines to a specific server. Fortunately, administrators can use the Win32 remote registry functions to make any changes.

Another method to statically load balance DCOM connections is to use a database containing usernames and the servers they're assigned to. While this method does allow the administrator to make reassignments quickly, it also means adding some processing overhead to the connection and complexity to the application. The processing overhead comes into play in several ways—the most important of which is the time required for the client to look up the appropriate server prior to requesting component services. In addition, the client has to be rewritten to use the database, which may make the application unnecessarily complex and inflexible.

Yet another method of overcoming problems with static load balancing is to use a referral component. In this case, the client is designed to request the component's services from the referral component at the outset, so no extra programming is required. Once the referral component receives a request, it automatically makes the connection for the client, reducing the amount of overhead from using this technique. The obvious downside of this form of static load balancing is that you need to write a special referral component.

As we'll see in Chapter 7, Active Directory is the storage medium of choice for Windows 2000 developers. Instead of placing the DCOM entry in the registry, it appears in the Active Directory centralized storage. The actual storage location is called the COM+ Catalog Manager and it unites the COM and Microsoft Transaction Server (MTS) registry entry methods. Obviously, this second method allows the administrator to make all required configuration changes from one location to a store that's always online, rather than to multiple registries, some of which may be offline because the associated machine is turned off. In addition, this second method allows the administrator to assign a specific user to a specific server, rather than assigning a machine to the server.

TIP: Both developers and administrators will be able to interact with the COM+ Catalog using the COM+ Explorer. In addition, Microsoft is developing a series of new COM interfaces that will allow the developer to interface with the COM+ Catalog directly.

Two of the major problems with static load balancing are that you need a predictable load and administrator intervention to implement it. In other words, static load balancing would probably work fine for an order entry system where the same number of users would log in each day. It probably wouldn't work well for an Internet site where the number of users could vary by a large amount over the period of a few hours.

Dynamic load balancing can also rely on the referral component technique described earlier. However, in this case, the referral component would take factors like current server load, past user request history, and current network topology into account when assigning a user to a machine, rather than assign the user based on a static list. Using this technique means that the referral component would require more time to get the job done, but that the network would process requests more efficiently once the connection was made.

There are several problems with this approach. For one thing, the complexity of the referral component is greatly increased. Instead of just directing the user's request to another component, the referral component now has to make some decision as to which server to select. In addition, this technique relies on a database for storing user request history, the availability of server statistics (which must be refreshed for each request), and the availability of network topology data. In other words, dynamic load balancing is much harder to implement because you're essentially replacing the network administrator with some software.

Balancing a load at connection time doesn't necessarily mean that the load will remain balanced either. True dynamic load balancing needs to incorporate some type of reconnect strategy. As the load from a user on one machine increases and the load from a user on another machine decreases, it might be necessary to reconnect them to different servers to keep the load on both servers balanced. Unfortunately, DCOM doesn't provide any built-in functionality to implement a reconnection strategy, which means the developer will need to create yet another component that monitors the current situation and makes reconnection recommendations as necessary.

Implementing a reconnection strategy is complicated by the requirement of the component to retain state information for the client. The component and client would both need to decide that the current state information is no longer required, then request a reconnection before the next method invocation. As you can see, building a reconnection strategy is extremely complex, making the prospect of adding yet another server to the network quite appealing. The complexity of the problem is most likely one of the reasons that Microsoft didn't implement a reconnection strategy as part of DCOM itself.

There's another load-balancing strategy for DCOM that relies on the new COM+ capabilities built into Windows 2000. This method assumes that you have a lot of users to manage and that the application you've created adheres to Microsoft's new Distributed interNet Applications (DNA) architecture.

Implementing the COM+ form of load balancing is relatively easy. The first thing you'll need is an application cluster, which is a set of up to eight machines that are capable of running the requested component. Once you have the application cluster machines loaded with the server-side components that you want to use, you'll need to add a load-balancing router to the picture. The load-balancing router sends client requests to one of the machines in the application cluster.

The client application won't access the application cluster machines directly. What will happen instead is that client requests will get sent to the load-balancing router. The load-balancing router will use an algorithm to determine which application cluster machine is least busy, then route the request to that application cluster machine. Of course, the question that the load-balancing router will need to answer is what criteria to use for determining application cluster machine load. The default algorithm uses a response time algorithm to determine which machine to use. You can, however, write your own load-balancing engine that determines which application cluster machine is least busy. For example, you may determine that the number of available resources is a better way to determine which application cluster machine has the lightest load if your component requires a lot of resources to execute. We'll see how the newer COM+ strategy works in Chapter 7.

The bottom line from a developer perspective is that you'll write your application to direct all server-side component requests to the load balancing router. If the configuration of the network changes, it won't matter because the load-balancing router will still accept all component requests. As you can see, using the COM+ methodology for balancing the component load on several servers is the easiest to implement, as long as you have the required hardware and all of that hardware is running Windows 2000.

NOTE: The current MTS method for creating components in a load-balanced environment is to create the reference early and hold on to it as long as possible. This approach ensures that the client will get the resources required to complete execution of a given task and that MTS operates as efficiently as possible. The new approach for COM+ is to create components only when necessary and to release them as early as possible to free resources. Obviously, these two approaches are completely opposite of each other, which means you may have to rewrite some of your older applications to take advantage of the latest COM+ technology.

A Detailed Look at the DCOM Network Protocol

The first thing we'll need to talk about in this section is what the term "DCOM network protocol" means. The DCOM network protocol is a superset of the Open Systems Foundation (OSF) distributed computing environment (DCE) remote procedure call (RPC) network protocol. Essentially, the DCOM network protocol defines the methodology for allowing COM to work across two machines and making it appear to both client and server that there's only one machine involved. By this point, you should understand that DCOM is simply COM that works across two machines and that there has to be a network infrastructure with required protocols involved to enable that communication.

NOTE: Once you've done a little reading, you'll find out that DCE is actually composed of several components, only one of which is RPC. There are also the Cell and Global Directory Services (CDS and GDS), the Security Service, DCE Threads, Distributed Time Service (DTS), and Distributed File Service (DFS) components. In addition, DCE isn't a stand-alone protocol; it's designed to allow an operating system vendor to include its services within an operating system. This is precisely what Microsoft has done with DCOM by basing DCOM on DCE RPC.

The following sections will help you better understand the DCOM network protocol and where it fits in the scheme of things for you as a programmer. We're not going to cover every last detail of this protocol since there are entire volumes on the topic. Instead, I'll cover the highlights of DCOM network protocol as a whole and what makes it different than the protocol that it's based on, DCE RPC.

MANY NAMES, SAME FUNCTIONALITY Trying to nail down what the term "DCOM network protocol" means can prove frustrating unless you know where to look. Unfortunately, while there are a lot of Microsoft-generated drawings and presentations out there with DCOM network protocol written on them, searching the various resources that Microsoft provides will shed very little light on this technology. What you really need to look for is the DCOM wire protocol.

The DCOM wire protocol standard defines the kind of packets that get put on the wire between the client and the server. (Obviously, there are other network protocols required to actually create the connection between client and server, as shown earlier in Figure 2-1.) The DCOM wire protocol standard defines the format of these packets and what the client and server should expect to see in them. In other words, the DCOM wire protocol specifies how the information gets physically transferred from one machine to the other.

DCOM network protocol goes by yet another name, object RPC (ORPC). The ORPC moniker shows the close relationship between DCOM and DCE RPC. This particular name for the single technology that we've been talking about throughout this chapter is the most common one you'll see. The "object" part of ORPC points to the fact that Microsoft has extended RPC to support remote handling of objects. In fact, they have added several additional data structures—the most important of which is the interface pointer identifier (IPID)—that we'll discuss as the chapter progresses. These additional data structures allow DCOM to request remote instantiation of an object from a server.

The whole point of this particular part of the discussion is that you'll need to do a little digging if you really want to find out every detail about DCOM. For the remainder of this section, I'll refer to the whole array of DCOM communication names and specifications as DCOM network protocol. However, it's also important to know that there are other names you'll find this technology listed under.

WEB LINK: Microsoft has prepared a complete specification for the DCOM Wire Protocol. Reading this specification will give you a better idea of precisely how DCOM transmissions are supposed to work. You'll find the specification at http://msdn.microsoft.com/library/specs/distributedcomponent-object-modelprotocoldcom10.htm. One of the best places to find out more about DCE RPC is at http://www.opengroup.org/publications/catalog/c706.htm. This site contains an overview of DCE, a copy of the DCE specification, and a wealth of other information you'll find useful when learning about how DCOM works. If you have questions about DCE that you'd like help with, there's a newsgroup you can go to at comp.soft-sys.dce. There's also an interesting presentation of how DCOM works within the DCE environment. You'll find it at http://www.opengroup.org/dce/proggrp/meetings/july98/FrankHayes/.

THE IRemoteActivation INTERFACE   Like many other object technologies, DCOM network protocol relies on an interface to encapsulate the methods required to create, maintain, and eventually sever a connection between client and server. In this case, we're not talking about a COM interface, but an RPC interface named IRemoteActivation. The IRemoteActivation interface is exposed by the Service Control Manager (SCM) on each machine (see Figure 2-1). The SCM is physically located in the RPCSS.EXE file and isn't associated with the SCM that Windows 2000 uses to manage services.

Interestingly enough, IRemoteActivation contains only one method, RemoteActivation(), which activates the COM object on a remote machine. RemoteActivation() makes up for a lack in a pure DCE RPC implementation by allowing remote activation of the server by the client. In a pure DCE RPC implementation, you must run the server first, then allow the client to access it remotely. It's instructional to look at the arguments that the client passes to the server using the RemoteActivation() method and what the server passes back to the client. Table 2-1 shows the input arguments, while Table 2-2 shows the output arguments for RemoteActivation().

Argument	Description
hRpc	RPC binding handle used to make the request.
ORPCthis	A data structure that contains the version of DCOM that the client is using, one or more flags that indicate the presence of additional data, the causalty ID (CID) of the client, and an array of special extensions. The client's major version number is compared to the server's major version number. If the major version numbers don't match, the server sends back an error message result rather than the desired object. A server can have a higher minor version number than the client. The CID is actually a globally unique identifier (GUID) used to link the method calls between two or more machines. For example, if machine A requests that machine B activate a component, and machine B has to request that machine C activate a component first, then the calls are causally related and DCOM will generate a CID for them. The CID will remain in effect until the original call machine A created is satisfied by a return call from machine B. Currently, there are only two special extensions that you'll find in use in this structure. The first is for error information, while the second is for debugging purposes. We won't discuss these special extensions because of their special-purpose nature.
Clsid	Class ID of the object that the client wants to create and activate on the server. This argument is typically used if the application calls CoCreateInstanceEx(), CoGetClassObject(), or CoGetClassObjectFromURL().
pwszObjectName	A pointer to a wide character string containing path and executable filename information for the object that the client wants to create. This argument is typically used if the application calls CoGetInstanceFromFile().
pObjectStorage	A client-side interface pointer to an object that supports the IStorage interface. The server will use this interface to determine which object to instantiate. This argument is typically used if the application calls CoGetInstanceFromStorage().

Table 2-1.   RemoteActivation() Input Arguments

Argument	Description
ClientImpLevel	Constant value taken from RPC_C_IMP that determines the client's default impersonation level.
Mode	This argument is normally set to MODE_GET_CLASS_OBJECT when instantiating a new object. The Mode argument gets passed to the server's IPersistFile::Load() method if either the pwszObjectName or pObjectStorage arguments contain a value.
Interfaces	Contains the number of interfaces that the client is requesting.
pIIDs	A list of interface identifiers (IIDs) that the client wants. One of the more common IIDs is IID_Unknown for the IUnknown interface.
cRequestedProtseqs	Number of protocol sequences specified in the RequestedProtseqs argument.
RequestedProtseqs	An array containing a list of the protocol sequences that the client wants OXID binding handles for.

Table 2-1.   RemoteActivation() Input Arguments *(continued)*

NOTE: Not every argument in either Table 2-1 or 2-2 is required. A RemoteActivation() call typically includes only the arguments required to satisfy the object creation request. For example, if you include the Clsid argument, then you won't normally need to include the pwszObjectName argument as well.

As you can see from Tables 2-1 and 2-2, the interaction between the client and server is very straightforward and there isn't much more information required than what you'd provide for a local object instantiation. The big difference is how the call is handled by the SCM. As a matter of fact, you'll never need to worry about creating a RemoteActivation() method call unless you begin to work with DCOM directly. If you issue a standard CoCreateInstance() call and OLE32 finds that the object doesn't exist on the local machine, it'll create the required DCOM call for you based on the information provided in the CoCreateInstance() call and on any registry entries it finds.

Argument	Description
OPRCthat	This parameter appears at the head of every protocol data unit (PDU) for COM methods. It contains a list of flags that defines the presence of other data and an extension array used for special purposes.
pOxid	The object export identifier (OXID) for the object that the server has just created for the client. This is the binding information that the client will need to connect to the interface specified by the interface pointer identifier (IPID).
ppsaOxidBindings	Contains the endpoint and security bindings required to reach the OXID. In most cases, the SCM is the endpoint, which resides at a well-known port address for each of the major protocols. For example, the SCM port for UPD and TCP is 1066. The endpoint is a UNC-based string instead of a port number when named pipes are used.
pipidRemUnknown	The IPID of the OXID's IRemUnknown (remote unknown) interface. This is the equivalent of the COM IUnknown interface, but for a remote rather than a local machine.
pAuthnHint	Constant value taken from the RPC_C_AUTHN list. It provides a hint to the client about the minimal level of authentication that the server will accept.
pServerVersion	The version of DCOM supported by the server. The client and server must support the same major version number of DCOM. In addition, the server's minor revision level must be equal or greater than that of the client or an error will occur. If the server's minor version number is greater than that of the client, then the server automatically scales its level of DCOM support to match that of the client.
phr	The HRESULT of the activation operation. This is the COM object's instantiation return value to the client, and shouldn't be confused with the value returned by the server itself for the operation as a whole.

Table 2-2.   RemoteActivation() Output Arguments

Argument	Description
ppInterfaceData	An array of interface pointers. This array will contain one entry for each interface requested using the pIIDs argument and in the same order. Each interface pointer is actually a data structure consisting of two elements. The first element contains the size of an object reference data structure. The second element is the object reference data structure itself (we'll discuss this data structure in the section that follows). There are three kinds of object reference data structures: standard, handler, and custom. All three of these structure types begin with a signature, flags, and a GUID for the interface pointer. The end of the structure is object reference data structure type specific.
pResults	An array of HRESULTs for each <Object>::QueryInterface() method call performed on the server while gaining access to each of the IIDs requested by the client. This array won't include an object instantiation HRESULT value, since that HRESULT is returned in the phr argument.

Table 2-2. RemoteActivation() Output Arguments *(continued)*

TIP: The DCOM network protocol transmits method arguments using the network data representation (NDR) format. The NDR format determines how the various values get marshaled into data packets for network transmission. Knowing how the DCOM network protocol formats data allows you to do a few things that you couldn't normally do, like use a network sniffer to see how packets get transmitted from one machine to the next. There's one extension to NDR for DCOM so that NDR can support interface pointers. The MInterfacePointer data type (the object reference data structure mentioned in Table 2-2) doesn't contain a pointer to a vtable contain functions—it's merely an object reference. One of the more interesting things about the MInterfacePointer structure is that it begins with a signature field that spells MEOW when you look at the data stream in ASCII. Some programmers have speculated that this is actually an acronym for Microsoft Extended Object Wire, but Microsoft hasn't documented it as being so. One thing is certain: You can always tell when you're looking at an object reference in a network sniffer if you see the word MEOW at the beginning.

OBJECT REFERENCES   From the preceding sections, you now know that the main purpose of all these data transfers between the client and server is to provide the client with access to a specific instance of an object interface using the object reference. Each interface requires a separate object reference that the client uses to access the methods that the interface contains. Object references are passed back to the client using the ppInterfaceData array (MInterfacePointer data type).

There are two main types of object reference data structures (OBJREF_STANDARD and OBJREF_HANDLER) and one ancillary type (OBJREF_CUSTOM). Each of these data structures includes a signature (MEOW), a flag specifying the kind of object reference, and a GUID containing the interface identifier. Each of the object reference data structure types also contains specialized data. The data contained in the main object reference types can be broken down as follows:

▼ **Standard object reference** A data structure containing a reference to the object that was created on the server.

■ **Dual string array** A data structure containing two strings. The first string contains the information the client needs to bind to the object on the server. The second string contains security information the client will need to access the object on the server.

▲ **Handler class ID** This is only applicable to the OBJREF_HANDLER object reference data structure. It contains the GUID for the handler code.

Let's look at the standard object reference in more detail. This is a data structure consisting of five elements: flags, the number of reference counts associated with the object, the OXID for the server that owns the object, the object identifier (OID) of the object that implements the interface, and the IPID. The flags are used to define special settings for the object reference. The only flag that you'll ever need to worry about when working with DCOM directly is SORF_NOPING, which tells DCOM that the object interface doesn't need to be pinged to keep it alive. The cPublicRefs field, which contains the number of reference counts associated with the object, reduces network traffic by allowing a single call to replace multiple IUnknown::AddRef() calls.

The Network Name Difference

It's important to understand all of the theory behind how DCOM works; however, at some point you have to start working on the practical aspects of implementing DCOM. Obviously, you can create a low-level connection that manipulates DCOM itself, but for the most part, you'll never need to do so. In fact, creating a DCOM connection can be as easy as creating an alternative type of registry entry (which requires no changes to your code) or adding the name of a network resource as part of your object instantiation call.

There are a variety of ways to create a DCOM connection. The most common method is to issue a special call from within your application to create the call. All five of the following function calls include a method for requesting the name of a network resource where the object will get instantiated. (Notice that CoCreateInstance() isn't included in this list since it lacks the means to define a precise server name.)

▼ CoCreateInstanceEx()

■ CoGetInstanceFromFile()

■ CoGetInstanceFromStorage()

■ CoGetClassObject()

▲ CoGetClassObjectFromURL()

The method argument that you're interested in for the first four calls is pServerInfo, which is a data structure of type COSERVERINFO. This data structure contains several elements that describe the connection to the server, as shown in Table 2-3. The CoGetClassObjectFromURL() method relies on the szCodeURL argument to point to the server containing the object that you want to instantiate.

What happens if you don't want to create a special code to create a connection? DCOM also allows you do use a standard CoCreateInstance call by creating a special registry entry. Using this technique allows you to create a client application that will work on any machine; it won't matter whether the component is local or remote. Creating the required HKEY_CLASSES_ROOT registry entries for remote activation of a component is a two-step process, as shown here:

1. Create an HKEY_CLASSES_ROOT\APPID\<Application Identifier GUID> entry for the remote server like this:

   ```
   "RemoteServerName"="<DNS Name>"
   ```

2. Create an HKEY_CLASSES_ROOT\ClsID\<Class Identifier GUID> entry for the component like this:

   ```
   "AppID"="<AppID GUID>"
   ```

Parameter	Description
pwszName	A pointer to a string containing the name of the server in wide character format.
pAuthInfo	COAUTHINFO data structure pointer containing access information for the server. This data structure has to contain the information required to access the server, such as the user's name and password. Setting this argument to NULL will force DCOM to use the default security provided by the user's account.

Table 2-3. COSERVERINFO Data Structure Description

The application identifier (AppID) concept was originally introduced for security reasons. All of the COM objects that share the same AppID will also get the same security levels when accessing the server. However, the AppID also allows you to avoid redundant registry entries by allowing all of the components that reside on a single server to share one AppID. This makes the administrator's job easier when a group of components moves from one server to another.

Fortunately, you don't have to worry about modifying the registry entries directly (unless you want to do it as part of the application installation process). Microsoft provides the DCOM Configuration Tool, which makes the required changes for you once you've provided the correct level of information. Unfortunately, using this tool means modifying each user's machine individually and installing the required support on the user's machine. As a result, we won't look at the DCOM Configuration Tool since its usefulness to the programmer of large projects is decidedly limited.

At this point, you might think that modifying the user's local registry entries would cause problems for a large organization even if Microsoft has provided a tool to perform the task for you. The answer to this need is Active Directory. Windows 2000 provides you with the capability of creating registry entries in a central location that the user will download as part of the process of logging in to the domain. What this means is that you'll create the required DCOM entries on the server and everything else will happen automatically. Changes will require a single change on the server as well, which should greatly ease the administrator's burden. Obviously, you must run Active Directory to gain this ease-of-usage benefit.

Component Reuse

Component reuse takes many different forms, but there are two main forms called "containment" and "aggregation" (at least by Microsoft). Anyone who has ever created a component has likely used a base component as a starting point. This constitutes a form of component reuse in that you're using a base component as a starting point for a new component, rather than building the component from scratch. However, the method that you use for gaining access to the base component changes the way that you create the new component.

The form of component reuse that Visual C++ programmers use is called aggregation because you're taking code that you've created and adding it to existing code to create a whole component that has some of the same properties as the parent. This is what happens when the programmer subclasses an existing component, changes some of the properties, methods, and events supported by that component by overriding them, then compiles the result to create a new component. Aggregation has the advantage of creating very small components that contain only the code required to make the component work. However, this kind of component suffers from complexity—you must know how the base component works before you can subclass it to create a new one. In many cases, the added complexity increases development time.

A second form of component reuse is very familiar to Visual Basic programmers. You place a copy of a component on a Visual Basic form, which acts as a container for the resulting runtime object. In this case, you're not creating an aggregate—there isn't a single component, but several distinct components working together toward a specific end. Containment, the name for this second form of component reuse, allows the developer to create a composite supercomponent, which is really more of an application than a component by definition. A developer can create this type of component relatively fast and only needs to know enough about the base component to use the features that it provides that are common to the new component. In addition, this kind of component can actually contain several base components, making it a very flexible solution. Unfortunately, these components can quickly become quite large, and because there are bits of code that aren't used by the new component, unforeseen interactions can take place, increasing the amount of time required to debug the new component.

TIP: As with many Microsoft programming technologies, those describing the two main forms of component reuse have several different names. An easier to remember and understand way to refer to these two forms of component reuse is "source" and "binary." Containment is a form of binary component reuse because you create an object to accomplish it. This is the method commonly used by Visual Basic, which doesn't support source component reuse. Visual C++ programmers are more familiar with source component reuse. It depends on having the source for a parent component available and then using that code as a starting point for a new component. This is how aggregation works. You subclass the code (also known as inheritance) for an existing object and use it as the starting point for a new component.

CALLING AN INTERFACE METHOD

All COM objects use interfaces. At its core, an interface is nothing more than an array of pointers to the methods provided by your ActiveX control or other COM components. An interface provides a reliable, language-independent method for accessing the methods and properties within an object. In fact, some programmers have been known to describe a simple ActiveX control as a COM component that implements the IUnknown interface. However, to be useful, an ActiveX control has to implement more than the IUnknown interface.

You'll use interfaces to provide every piece of information about your ActiveX control and how it operates. Using interfaces allows anyone to use an ActiveX control and ensures that the control itself remains safe from the vagaries of data corruption. Of course, this assumes that the interface is created correctly and that the control adheres to Microsoft specifications.

NOTE: It's very important to remember that all forms of COM rely heavily on the registry. As a result, you may see component problems that have nothing to do with your code, but with faulty registry entries. Make sure you look for every potential cause of errors when debugging an errant component. While the various Visual C++ wizards do a terrific job of creating the registry entries required to support your component, there are times when it pays to take a look at what entries were made and why. Chapter 5 has full details about the contents of the registry and what you can expect when looking for various types of registry entries. Make sure you pay special attention to the CLSID key description, because this is where your component entries will appear in the registry.

The following three sections are going to look at three important aspects of COM as they relate to ActiveX, which is the basis of our discussion later for other types of components. In the first section we'll look at IUnknown, which is the basic interface that any COM or COM+ component must support. Once we get past IUnknown, however, it's time to look at both standard and required interfaces for various types of controls. We'll cover these topics in the two sections that follow the IUnknown discussion.

Understanding IUnknown

Working with COM components is all about communication of some type. You want to create some code that's easy to reuse because it can communicate with the client using it and adapt, if necessary. ActiveX control communication consists of a client, a server, and an interpreter named COMPOBJ.DLL between them. Essentially, these three objects are the basis of what we'll discuss throughout the book because they encompass the three objects that most people work with.

That's not all there is to know about the communication, though—an ActiveX control (a COM component of any kind for that matter) needs to provide a standard interface to make it useful. When an application instantiates a copy of an ActiveX control (the component object), it receives a pointer to a list of functions. That list of functions is housed in what's termed an interface. To make it easier for you to understand what an interface is (at least in the context of an ActiveX control), think of it as a set of semantically related functions implemented as part of a component object. You'll normally see an interface as an array of functions defined in the OLE2 headers for your programming language.

An interface can perform a variety of tasks. For example, you might add a data operation interface like GetData or SetData. The more complex an ActiveX control, the more interfaces it requires to perform its task.

There's one interface called IUnknown that every ActiveX control must provide. It's the basis of all other interfaces—every other interface inherits from this basic interface. This is the interface that gets passed back to your application when you instantiate a copy of the control as a component object. Within this interface (and every other interface supported by an ActiveX control) are the three function calls listed here:

▼   **QueryInterface()**   This function allows the application to determine what interfaces the object supports. If the application queries an interface and the ActiveX control supports it, the application receives an array of pointers to the functions supported by the interface. Otherwise, the application receives a null pointer.

■   **AddRef()**   This function creates a new relationship to a component object interface. Using this function creates another pointer to the array of function pointers supported by the interface. A component object maintains a reference count of the number of relationships that it has established. The component object only gets unloaded from memory when the reference count is 0.

▲   **Release()**   This function allows you to destroy the relationship between an application and an ActiveX control. It decreases the reference count by 1. If the component object's reference count is 0, then this function call also requests the destruction of the component object.

The presence of IUnknown means that your application can communicate with any component object it encounters. If your application recognizes the interfaces that the component object supports, it can communicate with that object at a fairly high level. For example, an ActiveX control provides very specific interfaces that your programming environment will know about if it supports them. If your application only recognizes a few of the interfaces, it still might be able to communicate with the component object, but at a much lower level.

There are a lot of interfaces that the OLE2 specification already supports for specific kinds of component objects. The Microsoft OLE2 SDK provides a full synopsis of all of these component object types and the interfaces that they're required to support. We'll also cover a few of the ActiveX-specific requirements throughout this book. However, just because Microsoft hasn't defined a particular interface doesn't mean that you can't define it yourself. The specifications we'll talk about throughout this book, and those that you'll learn from other sources, are the minimum interfaces that you can implement. Nothing says that you can't implement more interfaces, then publish an API that tells how to use them. That's the beauty of using COM—you can extend it as needed to meet specific requirements.

Understanding the ActiveX Interfaces

Interfaces encompass the idea of standardized access, which is the main goal of using component technology to build applications. Not only do components allow you to reuse code, but they also allow you to do so using standard methods that don't rely on an in-depth knowledge of the inner functioning of the component itself.

Microsoft publishes standards that allow everyone who creates an ActiveX control to create something that everyone can use. These standards enforce the idea that the interface will follow a specific set of rules when providing information about the control that it supports. So, at a higher level, an interface is also a standard—an ideology about how things should work.

No matter how you view interfaces, they're a fact of life for anyone who creates ActiveX controls. You must create specific interfaces that do certain things for the control to work properly. However, there's another part of the picture to consider. Remember that an interface defines the relationship between the client and the server, so both the client and the server have something to say about the interface requirements.

Visual C++ supports a variety of ActiveX control types—everything from a full control to one that's optimized for working with Internet Explorer alone. The interfaces you need to provide for the component to work with a specific environment depends a great deal on the environment itself. In other words, a component designed for Internet Explorer use may have different needs than one designed for use with applications in general.

With the client, server, and environmental needs in mind, we'll look not only at required interfaces in this section, but also at the interfaces required to work in a specific environment. Table 2-4 provides a comparison of various ActiveX control environments and the interfaces they require. Note the special I<Class> entry in the list. This particular interface is different for every component because it contains the elements specific to that component, including both methods and properties. Obviously, this table shows the minimum number of interfaces and you could easily extend the I<Class> entry to include several interfaces if needed by your particular application.

NOTE: The Composite and Lite Composite ActiveX control environments are based on CCom-CompositeControl class instead of CComControl class. The CComCompositeControl class allows the control to contain other Windows controls and to host multiple controls in a single control. In addition, the HMTL and Lite HTML ActiveX control environments implement two IDispatch interfaces. The first interface interacts with the control itself. The second interface is designed to handle user interface events, methods, and properties. The second interface includes one default method, OnClick().

Interface	Full	Lite	Composite	HTML	Lite Composite	Lite HTML
I<Class>	X	X	X	X	X	X
IDispatch	X	X	X	X	X	X
IPersistStreamInit	X	X	X	X	X	X
IOleControl	X	X	X	X	X	X
IOleObject	X	X	X	X	X	X
IOleInPlaceActivateObject	X	X	X	X	X	X
IViewObjectEx	X	X	X	X	X	X
IViewObject2	X	X	X	X	X	X
IViewObject	X	X	X	X	X	X
IOleInPlaceObject-Windowless	X	X	X	X	X	X
IPersistStorage	X		X	X		
IQuickActivate	X		X	X		
IDataObject	X		X	X		
IProvideClassInfo	X		X	X		
IProvideClassInfo2	X		X	X		

Table 2-4. Interface Support Required for Various ActiveX Control Types

NOTE: There are many other interfaces that ActiveX controls have to support to obtain certain levels of functionality. For example, if you want to support events in your ActiveX control, then you'll need to provide an IConnectionPointContainer interface. There are some cases when you'd need to provide interfaces in addition to the one that you want to support. For example, the IConnectionPointContainer interface also requires you to implement the IEnumConnectionPoints, IConnectionPoint, and IEnumConnections interfaces. Another common supplementary interface is ISpecifyPropertyPages, which tells the container application that your control includes at least one property page. The property page itself will need to support the IPropertyPage or IPropertyPage2 interface.

Using the ActiveX Interfaces

The previous section talked about the interfaces you were required to provide given a specific ActiveX control environment. Now that you have a little better idea of which interfaces are required where, let's talk a little about what those interfaces are for. The following list provides a brief description of each major ActiveX control interface:

- ▼ **IDataObject**   This interface defines everything needed to transfer information between two objects, including the data format and the method used to transfer the information. If there's more than one format that the data can appear in, this interface will provide an enumerated list of available formats. This is also the interface that provides information about data rendered for a specific device (making it unsuitable for devices that don't conform to a specific standard).

- ■ **IDispatch**   There are two methods for accessing the methods and properties provided by an ActiveX control. IDispatch provides an indirect method that relies on a type library for implementation purposes. This interface is always used as part of a dual-interface control. A dual interface isn't necessarily a requirement by Microsoft standard. However, most developers implement a dual interface today to allow their control to work with more than just the language that it was developed in. IDispatch is a late bound interface.

- ■ **IPersistStreamInit**   Making sure that a control's data remains intact between uses is important (otherwise you'd have to reconfigure your applications every time you used them). You'll use this interface to make sure that any stream data required by your control is persistent or saved between sessions. This is a replacement for the older IPersistStream interface. The main difference between the two interfaces is that IPersistStreamInit also includes initialization code in the form of the InitNew() method, which initializes a control to a default state.

- ■ **IOleControl**   Communication is key with ActiveX controls. The overall purpose of this interface is control communication between the client and server. The normal purpose of this interface is to provide keyboard information. For example, a client could ask about the control's keyboard behavior and whether it provides full or partial support for control key combinations.

- **IOleObject**   This is the most essential of all interfaces for an ActiveX control since it provides both basic control functionality and communication features. Along with this interface, a control must provide support for both IDataObject and IPersistStorage for every embedded object that it supports. IOleObject contains a wide variety of methods designed to enhance control functionality. There's a minimum of 21 interface-specific methods along with the 3 standard methods (QueryInterface(), AddRef(), and Release()), for a total of 24 methods in a standard IOleObject interface. Of the 21 interface specific methods, 6 can be ignored by returning E_NOTIMPL (error not implemented) if you don't require the functionality they provide: SetExtent(), InitFromData(), GetClipboardData(), SetColorScheme(), SetMoniker(), and GetMoniker(). Three of the methods—DoVerb(), Close(), and SetHostNames()—require a full control-specific implementation.

- **IOleInPlaceActivateObject**   Some types of ActiveX controls require a method for communicating with the container frame and documents. Normally, you'll find this interface used when a control needs to support MDI or other complex application environments. This particular interface allows visual editing of the control in certain application types like a programming language IDE.

- **IViewObjectEx, IViewObject2, and IViewObject**   All three of these interfaces have one thing in common: they allow the ActiveX control a certain measure of autonomy in displaying itself without passing a data object to the container. Not only does this speed up the drawing of the control, but it ensures there's a minimum of drawing problems. The caller can request specific types of drawing features. For example, it can choose between a full or iconic display of the object. The IViewObject2 improves on IViewObject by returning the size of the drawing required to represent the object when using a specific presentation. You'd normally use this interface when working with compound document containers. The IViewObjectEx interface includes all of the features of IViewObject2. It improves on IViewObject2 by adding flicker-free drawing for nonrectangular objects, hit testing for nonrectangular objects, and control sizing. You'd use this interface to implement irregularly shaped controls.

- **IOleInPlaceObjectWindowless**   Use this interface to allow a windowless control to receive window messages and to participate in drag-and-drop operations.

- **IPersistStorage**   Storing your data objects from one session to the next is an important part of making the control react the same way each time you use it. This interface provides a structured storage medium where each object has its own storage area within the container's storage medium. You must implement this interface along with IOleObject and IDataObject to make the control work within an embedded environment.

- ■ **IQuickActivate**   Performance is often a factor when working with ActiveX controls, especially if the user has already spent time waiting for the control to download from the Internet. This interface allows the control and container to combine load-time or initialization-time handshaking into a single call, greatly improving control performance.

- ■ **IDataObject**   This interface works with the control's data. It allows the container and client to exchange information and also provides the means for one object to notify the other of data changes. The data transfer methods supported by this interface allow objects to specify the format of the data or enumerate the available data formats. The client can also specify that data is rendered for a specific device.

- ▲ **IProvideClassInfo and IProvideClassInfo2**   Use this interface to access a control's coclass entry in its type library. The IProvideClassInfo2 interface is simply a faster version of the IProvideClassInfo interface. It also provides an ancillary method, GetGUID, which returns the object's outgoing IID for its default event set.

Reference Counting

Reference counting is an important part of component technology. You don't want to destroy an object, then release the memory it used before all references to that object are also deleted. On the other hand, you don't want to keep an object around that no one is using. An object requires memory and system resources that you'll only want to maintain while the object is in use. As a result, there has to be some way of keeping track of whether the object is in use or not. That's where the reference counting mechanism comes into play.

The IUnknown interface includes two methods called AddRef() and Release(), as does every other interface that you'll ever use. These two methods allow you to increment the reference counter (AddRef()) or decrement the reference counter (Release()) as needed. When the reference count within the object goes to 0, then Windows knows that no one is referencing the object anymore and the object can be released.

REGISTRY REQUIREMENTS

There's an important task that every COM component must perform. You must register the components you create within the registry before Windows will know that they're present and in a usable state. Normally, this task is accomplished for you automatically with code contained within the component itself. Visual C++ adds this code as part of creating the component shell.

All of these component registry entries appear in the HKEY_CLASSES_ROOT hive of the registry. This hive is responsible for maintaining file association, OLE1, and OLE2 information for Windows. Since there are out-of-process servers associated with specific file extensions, the combination of all three elements in one hive is important for making component access relatively easy. In addition to OLE, the HKEY_CLASSES_ROOT hive is home to all of the COM and COM+ entries. Figure 2-2 shows the typical HKEY_CLASSES_ROOT organization. Notice that the main division in this hive is between file extension associations and the OLE1 registry entries used to service them. These OLE1 entries usually include a pointer to a OLE2 entry in the CLSID key that contains, among other things, a pointer to an out-of-process server or an application designed to service the file extension.

I'm not going to bore you with an in-depth discussion of this entire hive since we're really only concerned with the OLE2 entries that make our component visible to Windows. You'll find the visual element entries for OCXExmpl (the example component that I created) under the HKEY_CLASSES_ROOT\CLSID key. Each of the 128-digit numbers here (known as globally unique identifiers or GUIDs) represents a specific component class. It's important that you don't assume that each GUID represents a single component

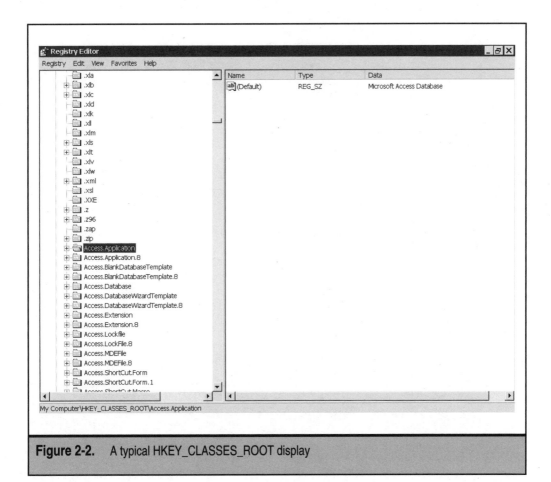

Figure 2-2.   A typical HKEY_CLASSES_ROOT display

since some components use more than one GUID for various purposes like property pages. Figure 2-3 shows a typical GUID entry for a component. In this case, we're looking at an in-process server, named OCXExmple, that I designed using the MFC ActiveX Control Wizard. It's a special kind of pushbutton, so I haven't included much in the way of extras for this component—what you're seeing is a very typical minimal entry for an in-process server. However, even this simple component includes a property page for changing the control's appearance. Figure 2-4 shows the property page GUID for the example component. In other words, this single component uses at least two GUIDs to service the component itself.

NOTE: Remember that Figures 2-3 and 2-4 show typical entries. The actual number of entries for a component will vary and not every component supports all of the registry entries shown here. In fact, depending on how you write your component, you can add custom registry entries that we won't discuss in this section of the chapter.

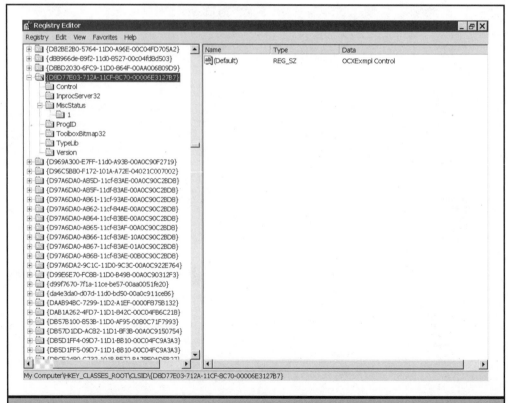

Figure 2-3. Each CLSID entry in the HKEY_CLASSES_ROOT hive represents a single component class

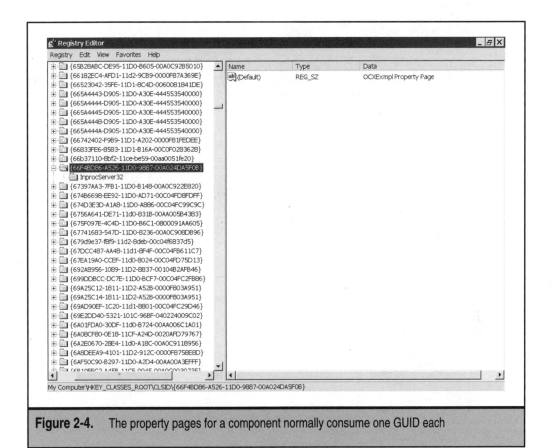

Figure 2-4. The property pages for a component normally consume one GUID each

Let's talk about the property page in Figure 2-4 first since it's the easier of the two entries to understand. All we have is two keys—the first is shown in Figure 2-4. It contains a plain language name for the property page. The InprocServer32 key contains the path to the DLL file (an OCX, in this case) that will service property page requests.

Figure 2-3 contains the keys normally associated with a control. This includes the name and GUID for the control as the main key. The GUID that appears in the AppID value also appears within the AppID key of the HKEY_CLASSES_ROOT hive, which as you'll remember from our DCOM discussion is one of the criteria for setting up remote access for this control from a remote location. Notice that the control entry also includes an InprocServer32 key that serves the same purpose as the one for the property page. However, in this case the key also contains a value that specifies the threading model of the component. Like any other Windows application, this DLL has a program identifier entry. However, since there's no user interface for a DLL outside of a container, all that the program identifier entry in the registry will do is provide a human-readable name for the control. The ToolBoxBitmap32 key contains the location of the icon used to display the component within a toolbox and the number of the icon within that file to use. For example, the location of the component in this case is OCXExmple.OCX and the number of the icon that we want to use within that file is 1. The TypeLib key contains the GUID for the type library information for the component. The type library describes the characteristics for the component for an IDE (we'll see how this works later in this section). Finally, the Version key contains the version number of the control.

There are other keys that you need to know about in the HKEY_CLASSES_ROOT hive when it comes to the operation of the OCXExmpl component. For example, there's the matter of interfaces to consider. If you'll remember from our previous discussions, an interface represents a convenient method for bundling functions. The OCXExmpl component actually contains two different elements: those used by the application to talk with the component, and those used by the component to generate events. Figure 2-5 shows both of these elements as they appear in the HKEY_CLASSES_ROOT\Interface key. The first is for the component interfaces, and the second is for the component event interfaces.

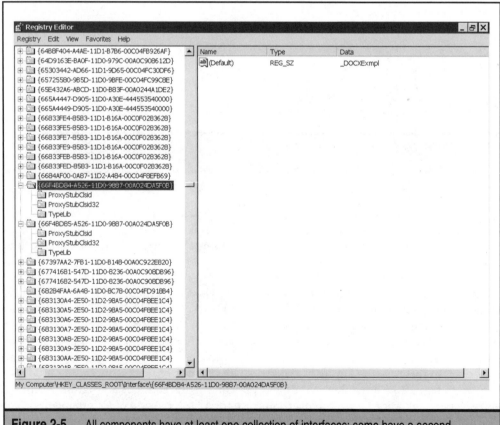

Figure 2-5.   All components have at least one collection of interfaces; some have a second interface devoted to event handling, as shown here

The organization of these two interfaces is the same, so I'll describe them generically. The first key that you'll see for an interface is the name of the interface. This is generally the same name that you assigned to your interface when you wrote the component. The two ProxyStubClsid keys identify the GUID of the proxy/stub handler for the interface. Refer to our discussion of DCOM (especially Figure 2-1) again if you don't know how the proxy/stub mechanism works. The TypeLib key performs the same task as the key of the same name for the component. It points to the GUID of the type library, which contains a description of the interface functions.

We've been talking quite a bit about the type library. The type library contains a description of the component that's used by certain IDEs like the one provided with Visual Basic. This is the same description that appears in the IDL file you create (or allow Visual C++ to create automatically for you) when writing a component. Like the other elements of our component, the type library has an entry in the registry as well. Figure 2-6 shows a typical example of a type library entry (the one for the OCXExmpl component) as it appears in the HKEY_CLASSES_ROOT/TypeLib key.

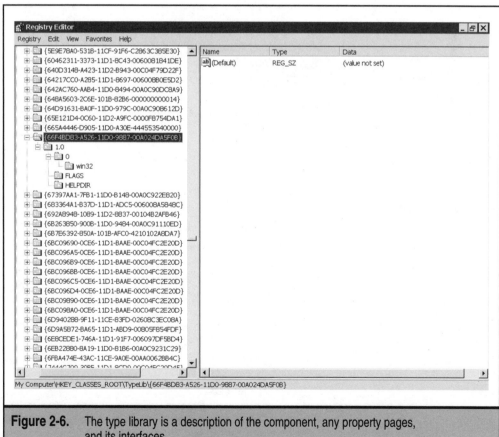

Figure 2-6.   The type library is a description of the component, any property pages, and its interfaces

The first thing you should notice about this key is the 1.0 key below it. This key identifies the version of the component that we're working with. As more of the same type of component with different version numbers appear, you'll see other version number keys appear in the type library key entry as well. This makes it easy for applications and program development products to compare component versions. The Win32 key contains the path to the component file itself, while the HELPDIR key contains the path to the help file associated with the component. The FLAGS key contains a number that defines the flags used to govern the interpretation of the component's data.

You don't have to go through all of this work to find out the majority of the information we just covered for your component. The OLE/COM Object Viewer shown in Figure 2-7 will provide this information as well. Note, however, that there's a lack of coverage for some component entries. For example, you'll find it difficult at best to figure out the GUIDs for any property pages associated with the component. This requires a search of the registry, just as we've done here.

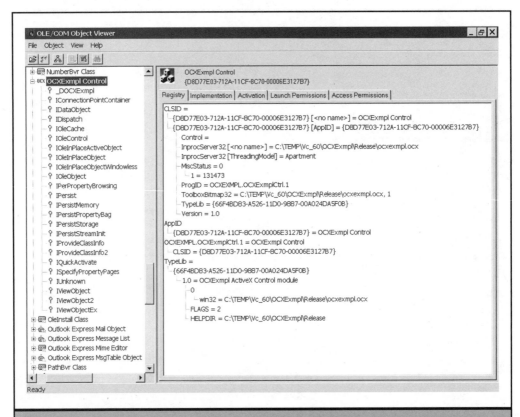

Figure 2-7. The OLE/COM Object Viewer is a standard part of the Visual C++ package and enables to learn more about the components you create

Obviously, the OLE/COM Object Viewer provides an easier to use interface than the Registry Editor does, so it's the first place you should look when hunting down the registry entries for a component. Notice that the OLE/COM Object Viewer also performs a partial interpretation of the type library for you. The list of interfaces is derived from a reading of the type library contents. However, this list only includes the component entries—event entries aren't listed. As you can see, the combination of the OLE/COM Object Viewer and the Registry Editor does give you a very complete view of your component and how it works.

WORKING WITH APARTMENTS AND THREADS

Components can be classified in a lot of different ways. All of these classifications may seem confusing at first, but knowing the particulars of how one component compares to another helps in creating applications that can use those components efficiently. In addition, you'll find that knowing how to compare components can help you make the decision of which component to use when more than one component can fulfill a specific purpose within your application. In fact, these comparisons can help you weed out poorly designed components that won't work with your application at all.

This section of the chapter looks at three different considerations that help you categorize components in two new ways: by apartment types and by the threading technique they use. In the first section we'll look at the various kinds of threads that you can create. It's important to know how these thread types differ so that you can detect whether a component will actually use threading efficiently to improve overall component (and as a result, application) performance. The second section will look at the question of an apartment and what it means to component design. Finally, we'll look at the marshaling (data transfer and conversion) requirements when working with components.

Thread Types

As far as Windows is concerned, there are threads and the processes that contain them and nothing else. However, from an MFC perspective, there are actually two kinds of threads: UI and worker. Both are threads that can perform a single sequence of execution within the application. The difference comes in the way that these two kinds of threads are implemented and used. The following sections talk about these two thread types and how they're used.

TIP: You can use the Win32 CreateThread() function to create a thread that doesn't rely on MFC. The advantage of doing so is that you eliminate some overhead normally encountered using the MFC libraries. In addition, this method conserves memory. The downside, of course, is that you can't use any of the capabilities that MFC provides. In most cases, you'll find that CreateThread() works best for worker threads that perform simple repetitive tasks.

Worker Threads

Worker threads are normally used for background tasks that require no or minimal user interaction. They're implemented as a function that returns a UINT result and accept one argument of the LPVOID data type as shown here:

```
UNINT MyThread (LPVOID pParam)
{
    return 0;
}
```

A worker thread normally returns a value of 0, which indicates that it successfully completed whatever task it was designed to perform. You can return other values to indicate either errors or usage counts. However, the calling application has to be designed to retrieve the exit value using the GetExitCodeThread() function.

Another way to end a worker thread and generate an exit code is to use the AfxEndThread() function. Using this function will stop thread execution and perform any required cleanup prior to exiting to the calling application. The calling application would still need to use the GetExitCodeThread() function to retrieve the exit value provided to the AfxEndThread() function. The exact meaning of any exit codes is up to you, so the calling application will need to be designed to work with a specific thread function before it'll know what an exit code means.

The pParam argument can contain any number of 32-bit values. However, passing a pointer to a data structure has several benefits that you may want to consider. For one thing, using a structure allows you to pass more than one argument to the thread. In many cases, a single argument won't be enough to provide the thread with everything needed to perform useful work, so a structure is the only way to get around the single input argument requirement. In addition, using a structure allows the worker thread to pass information back to the caller. All that the worker thread would need to do is modify the contents of a structure member during the course of execution.

UI Threads

As the name suggests, UI threads are normally created to provide some type of user interface functionality within an application. You'll derive the UI thread from the CWinThread class instead of using a function, as with the worker thread. Obviously, this means that implementing a UI thread is more complex than a worker thread, but you also get more flexibility.

NOTE: Terminating a UI thread is much the same as terminating a worker thread. However, a UI thread requires a little special handling if you want the caller to retrieve the exit code for the thread. First, you need to set the m_bAutoDelete data member to FALSE, which prevents the CWinThread object from deleting itself. Second, you'll need to manually delete the thread and release any memory that it uses. As an alternative, you can always duplicate the CWinThread handle that you receive during thread creation using the DuplicateHandle() method. In this case, you'll want to create the thread in the suspended state, duplicate the handle, then start the thread using the ResumeThread() method.

There's only one CWinThread class method that you must override when creating a new UI thread, although there are several others that are commonly overridden as well. The InitIntance() method is the one method that you must override because it's the first one called after the thread is created. The InitInstance() method should contain all of the code required to initialize your thread. Obviously, this means displaying a main dialog box for the thread, if necessary.

The ExitInstance() method will normally get overridden only if you need to perform some thread cleanup or postprocessing. The only place that you can all this method from is the Run() method (should you decide to override it as well). ExitInstance() performs the default tasks of deleting the CWinThread object, if m_bAutoDelete is TRUE. It's always the last method called before the thread terminates.

Of the other methods available to you, the only other methods that you may need to override are OnIdle(), Run(), PreTranslateMessage(), and ProcessWndProcException(). The OnIdle() method handles any idle time processing for the thread. For example, OnIdle() would get called if the application displayed a dialog box and the user wasn't doing anything with it. Run() controls the flow of activity within the thread—this includes the message pump. PreTranslateMessage() filters messages before they're sent to either TranslateMessage() or DispatchMessage. Finally, the ProcessWndProcException() method handles any unhandled exceptions thrown by the thread's message and command handlers. However, you'd normally want to handle these exceptions within the handler rather than wait until it reaches this point of the thread.

Apartment Types and Assignments

Apartments have often evoked primal emotions of sheer terror in programmers, and for good reason—they're poorly understood in most cases. This section of the chapter won't answer every question you have about apartments, but it'll provide an overview that should help in at least understanding what they do and what your role is in working with them.

In the previous section of the chapter we began a discussion of threads and how they affect your application. Now we must look at the bigger picture of a process as well. A process is a single memory area within the workstation that's used to execute one or more threads of instructions. Every time you start a new application, you also begin a new process. Applications can have multiple threads of execution, but they're always associated with one, and only one, process.

The use of processes and threads to define the execution and data management environment of an application begs another question. Not all applications are designed to handle threads the same, so how does COM allow a client programmed to execute code in one way to interact with a component designed to use another methodology? It helps to understand the scope of the problem by looking at the four different execution environments normally found within Windows:

▼ **Legacy** Older code that wasn't designed to allow either multithreading or reentrancy will often fail if the client attempts either of these operations. In short, the code is restricted to access by a single client at a time and in such a way that none of the code is reentered. In addition, this code won't allow for any of the performance benefits for multithreading.

■ **Windows limited** There's a class of application that can't use threads efficiently because of limitations in Windows itself. There are, of necessity, limitations in the way that threads and windowing primitives relate. So, even though this kind of code may support the idea of reentrancy (the ability of the code to handle multiple client requests at the same time), it doesn't support multithreading.

■ **Developer time limited** In some cases, especially those that involve large-scale applications, there's little time for the developer to worry about how the code handles the problems of both reentrancy and multithreading. The idea is to get the code finished in the shortest time possible and ready for implementation. In many cases, it's this kind of situation that gives rise to particular classes of COM problems that can be solved only through the use of apartments.

▲ **Thread safe** The final execution environment is one in which the developer has time to write hand-tuned code that's both multithreaded and allows reentrancy. This type of code makes the fullest possible use of the execution environment, but may run into significant problems when working with code written for the other three environments. In short, this code may actually be too optimized for its own good.

Now that you understand the various execution environments, it should be easier to understand how apartments come into play. An apartment is a way of grouping code written for like execution environments. That way, code written for a single thread of execution without any reentrancy won't crash when multiple clients need to access it. Likewise, modern code that's designed to make use of both multithreading and reentrancy won't need to be rewritten to make use of the methodologies employed in older code.

COM implements several predefined apartment types and handles various execution environments consisting of concurrency (multithreaded versus single threaded) and reentrancy requirements. An object belongs to one, and only one, apartment, but one apartment may hold multiple objects. Apartments are also created for a specific process. So, a single apartment always resides in just one process, but a single process can contain multiple apartments. The use of apartments allows a single application to contain components with vastly different concurrency and reentrancy requirements, yet still function properly.

So, how does COM relate to threads? An application can create a thread whenever it wants to, and that thread may begin execution immediately. However, if the thread wants to use COM, then it must first initialize COM. This means entering a specific apartment within the application using the CoInitializeEx(), CoInitialize(), or OleInitialize() functions. (Of these three functions, only CoInitializeEx() allows you to specify which type of apartment to enter—the other two calls assume you want to enter a single threaded apartment.) A thread may only work with the objects within that apartment. In short, a thread may be restricted from accessing memory that an object occupies, even if that memory is fully visible and accessible to the thread. This explains why you can receive an RPC_E_WRONG_THREAD error message within a thread, even if you do everything successfully that COM requires from a coding perspective. When a thread completes its work within an apartment, it must exit using either CoUninitialize() or OleUninitialize().

TIP: Failing to call either CoUninitialize() or OleUninitialize() before you terminate a thread that uses COM will delay the reclamation of resources. A thread must also exit an apartment before it can enter an apartment of a different type. (Any attempt to change apartments without exiting the initial apartment first will return an RPC_E_CHANGED_MODE error.)

If you'll remember from our discussion of the registry, every component defines the threading model within the GUID that describes the control itself as part of the ThreadingModel value of the InprocServer32 key. The ThreadingModel value determines the type of apartment that the component will be placed into. Windows 2000 supports five different apartment-threading values, as shown in the following list:

▼   **Free**   Multithreaded Apartment (MTA)

■   **Neutral**   Thread-Neutral Apartment (TNA, only available in Windows 2000)

■   **Both**   MTA or Single Threaded Apartment (STA)

■   **Apartment**   STA (as a separate thread)

▲   **Not specified**   STA (in the main thread of execution)

Let's discuss the two apartment models that have been around for a while, STA and MTA. Every application that requires an MTA only has one. Any object that's listed as MTA will reside in this apartment—any thread marked as MTA will be able to access any MTA object within the application. In short, a single object is expected to handle requests by more than one thread at a time—a requirement for some types of applications, like those used for Web servers, where more than one user requires access to the object at once. All threads and objects that are marked as MTA are assumed to be both multithreaded and thread safe (allowing reentrancy).

STAs introduce a few restrictions into the mix. The first is that an STA contains one, and only one, object. This ensures that once a component is instantiated, the resulting object doesn't share memory space with any other object, which could result in corruption. The second restriction is that one, and only one, thread can enter the apartment to interact with the object inside. The reason for this restriction is obvious. A single threaded object can only handle the requests of one thread at a time, which means that COM must protect the object from access by more than one thread. Ensuring that only one thread can enter the apartment at a time is the easiest way to accomplish this task. As a result of these restrictions, a single process could contain multiple STAs—one for each STA object that the application instantiated.

Microsoft has introduced a new apartment type for Windows 2000 that's specifically designed to meet the needs of COM+ developers. Like the MTA, there's at most one TNA within a process. One of the things that differentiates TNA from the other two apartment types is that it contains objects only—no threads are allowed within this apartment. Instead of executing within the TNA, when a thread requests access to a TNA object, it receives a lightweight proxy that switches to the object's context without the penalty of a thread switch. MTA threads can request this access directly, while STA threads will need to create a new thread-neutral object.

TIP: As of Windows 2000, components without a user interface, such as those used for MTS and MSMQ, should be marked as thread neutral. On the other hand, you'll still need to mark components with a user interface as STA (ThreadModel=Apartment) because of the way that Windows supports handles to windows. Windows issues specific handles to specific threads. This means that not every thread can use the same handle, which limits the reentrancy of the code and data within an object that supports a user interface.

Marshaling Requirements

Both out-of-process and in-process servers must implement the IMarshal interface, which provides the means for moving data between container and server. Normally, this requirement is taken care of for you through the MIDL compiler that works with the IDL/ODL files we've discussed throughout the chapter. In other words, the description of the interfaces for your COM server (ActiveX component throughout most of the chapter) is enough to provide an IMarshal implementation.

Obviously, implementing IMarshal for an in-process server is going to be a lot easier than an out-of-process server because of the memory issues involved. While it isn't hard to move an integer from the server to a container, what do you do about structures? Since the memory pointed at by the structure isn't accessible to the container, the entire structure has to be copied, which can present problems. Now, what happens if the server passes a pointer to a structure? It's no longer a matter of copying the structure from the server to the container—the marshaling mechanism can only pass the pointer provided by the server, then use that pointer to allow the container to gain access to data stored in the server memory space as needed.

As you can see, the whole topic of marshaling can become quite complex, especially when it comes to an out-of-process server implementation. Fortunately, the default implementation of the IMarshal interface is enough—the only time you'd need to override it is for performance considerations.

CHAPTER 3

Unique COM+ Features

COM+ is one of the most anticipated additions to Windows 2000 besides Active Directory. Many people view this as a new feature that will cure many of the component technology woes that companies currently face. However, it's important to realize that COM+ offers features in addition to, not instead of, the current Microsoft component technology. Despite what Microsoft's marketing machine might ask you to believe, COM+ is a continuation of current Component Object Model (COM) technology.

Of course, the continuity feature of COM+ has certain benefits for the developer. For one thing, the investment that you've made in existing technology is still protected. You'll find that you still require essentially the same tools to create a component-based application and that an application designed for COM runs about the same as it did in the past. In short, COM+ is really just COM the next generation.

Consolidation might be a better word to use for COM+ than new. COM+ takes what amounts to three disparate technologies and mixes them together. When you work with COM+, what you're really seeing is the effect of working with COM, Microsoft Transaction Server (MTS), and Microsoft Management Queue (MSMQ), with some other technologies like DCOM thrown in for good measure. That's right, DCOM is still at the root of data transfer over the network.

So, why add a "+" to COM at all? There are some new features in COM+ that you need to know about to use it effectively. Describing those features is the whole purpose behind this chapter. We'll look at the new pieces that Microsoft has put into COM to make it a better integration tool. Part of the consolidation effort is to allow you to work with the various COM+ elements in a way that's invisible to both the developer and the end user. It doesn't pay to consolidate something if all of the component parts are still completely visible and require individual access.

The first section of the chapter will discuss the new automation features in COM+. The latest COM offering does some things for you automatically that you normally had to do manually in the past. For one thing, the past problem of a component holding on to system resources is gone. A component holds on to system resources long enough to complete the task that you've assigned now, then releases those resources immediately. Better resource handling means that your server will work more efficiently and could reduce the need for immediate upgrades. In addition, the fact that COM and MTS are now integrated means that you'll spend less time worrying about how to make transactions work. Finally, COM+ components use what's known as a context. Essentially, a context helps determine how the component interacts with the client and reacts to client requests.

There are two sections of this chapter that actually work side by side. The first member of this pair is the resource dispenser. In addition to the efforts of individual components, Windows 2000 takes a proactive approach to resource management. A resource dispenser ensures that each component receives only the resources that it actually needs and only for the time it needs them. Then, rather than completely deallocating the resource, the resource dispenser returns it to a pool that's used to supply the needs of other components. This resource pool strategy greatly reduces the time to allocate and deallocate resources, which means that an application uses fewer processor clock cycles handling housekeeping chores.

The next section of the chapter will look at the Compensating Resource Manager (CRM), which is the other part of the resource management pair. Normally, you'd be required to create a resource dispenser for your application. Depending on the complexity of your application, the resource dispenser might not have a lot of work to do. COM+ gets rid of the extra programming requirement by providing a default resource dispenser known as the CRM. This COM+ feature allows your application to work with the DTC without requiring you to create a special resource dispenser. All of the "magic" required to perform this task is in the special interface you add to your component. CRM accesses this interface and allows your component to vote on the outcome of a transaction based on the results of the individual transaction within the component. In short, you get all of the features of a full resource dispenser implementation, without any of the work. The CRM also takes care of any recovery requirements for a failed transaction based on the log entries it makes, which means that you get automatic error recovery without any additional work.

The fourth section of the chapter talks about COM+ event sinks. An event sink is a receptor for events. When an event occurs on the server, the associated event sink receives the event message, then reacts to it. In short, this feature really isn't new, but it's handled in a different way for COM+. Remember that COM+ incorporates many remote execution techniques based on older technologies like DCOM. As a result, the event that occurred may not have happened on the local server—the client, or even a server that's currently handling a part of a larger application request, may have generated it.

The fifth section of the chapter covers a topic that should excite any programmer who has had to deal with the vagaries of type libraries. Instead of creating a component description in a separate file that your application may or may not understand, COM+ includes the concept of a component catalog. The component catalog is essentially a special-purpose database that holds descriptions of components registered on the server. An application can download these descriptions to find out more about the component and how to interact with it. In short, you no longer have to worry about where the TLB (type library) file is; your application can download the required information from a central store.

In the sixth section of the chapter, we'll look at the topic of object pooling and resource objects. Object pooling is a follow-on to the pooling currently used by Microsoft Data Access Components (MDAC). When working with MDAC, an application can create a connection to the database, then return it to the connection pool when finished. The connection isn't destroyed, so it takes less time to get a needed connection from the pool and reuse it than to create a new connection. Object pooling works the same way, but with all kinds of objects, including database connections. Using object pooling makes an application much more efficient. Resource objects are special components that support object pooling. There are several requirements for creating resource objects, but the most important is that they support the IObjectControl interface.

Role-based security is the topic of the seventh section of the chapter. Windows 2000 uses role-based security because it's the most efficient way to handle user access in large-scale network environments. Think of roles as a more flexible extension of groups. You create a list of the various company roles (like manager), then assign one or more roles to each user. A role defines who the user is by what tasks he or she performs. In other words, role-based security doesn't assume a user should have access to an object simply because they belong to a certain department; the user has to perform a task that requires access to the object in order to meet the security requirements.

The final section of the chapter is going to cover a feature that may or may not be available when you first read this chapter, Component Load Balancing (CLB). This feature was originally supposed to ship with Windows 2000, but Microsoft chose to ship it as a separate item and only with the higher-end servers. However, this feature is so important that I decided to cover it anyway. Essentially, CLB allows Windows 2000 to automatically balance a component load between several servers. For example, you might have a database component loaded on four servers because of the amount of usage the component receives. How does an administrator determine which server a user gets assigned to? In the past, the best an administrator could do was statically assign a user to a specific server and hope for the best. Unfortunately, this meant that some servers had a large load while others sat idle. CLB changes all that. Now a user request for component access is assigned to the server best able to handle it dynamically. The user ends up with the best access time possible and the company doesn't need to upgrade their servers as often because each server gets used to its fullest potential.

COM+ AND AUTOMATION

COM programmers spent a lot of time managing parts of their applications that the user probably assumed were automatic or never saw at all. Part of the problem was the fact that Microsoft had so many technologies that could work with COM but were offered as separate packages. Of course, the two main pieces of this picture are MSMQ and MTS, both of which are now offered as part of the Windows 2000 operating system. Earlier I talked about the fact that COM+ isn't so much new as it is consolidated. The consolidation factor is what allows COM+ to do more of the behind-the-scenes work for you automatically. In short, the developer's main benefit from using COM+ is less work because COM+ is doing more of the work for you.

This section of this chapter is going to look at three pieces of the automation puzzle. The first piece is just-in-time activation. This technology allows the server to use resources more efficiently by keeping components active only while they're needed. When a client holds a component reference that isn't used for a long time, the server deactivates the component until needed in the future. The next time the client makes a request, the component is automatically reactivated.

Another part of the puzzle is transactions. Transactions ensure that each client request is handled at least once, but only once. This is an especially important feature when it comes to databases, when entering data more than one time could cause data damage. We're going to work with transactions a lot throughout the book, so this section will provide a simple overview. If you want something in-depth, check out the theoretical coverage in Chapter 4 or our first transactional example in Chapter 7.

The final section is going to provide you with an overview of COM+ domains and context, both of which help you as a developer better understand how a particular instance of a component is being used. Viewing components in context allows you to perform more processing, with fewer checks. It also helps out in the automation department by allowing COM+ to do more for you, especially in the area of security. If you want to learn more about the specifics of COM+ security, check out the section entitled "Role-Based Security" in this chapter.

Understanding Just-In-Time (JIT) Activation

Server resources are always in demand by someone. Because of this, standard COM programming techniques often include getting a resource and then holding on to it until the component no longer needs the resource. This means that a resource might be tied up for long periods without any use. The new COM+ methodology is to gain access to a resource, then return it to the resource pool as soon as possible to ensure that other applications have the resources they need. Obviously, there are still a lot of the older COM applications out there that don't use this new strategy, so it's very likely that many of the resources on the server are still being wasted. That's where just-in-time (JIT) activation comes into play.

Using JIT activation means that even if a client holds on to a component reference, Windows 2000 can still use physical resources required by that component until they're needed again by the application. Windows 2000 monitors all of the components that are marked as JIT enabled. When a certain time period has elapsed without any method calls, the component deactivates, and the resources that it's using are returned to the resource pool. As far as the application is concerned, the component is still active and the reference to it is still valid. The next time the application makes a method call to the deactivated component, Windows 2000 will reactivate it and allocate the resources that it requires. This entire process occurs in the background without any programmer input. The user is completely unaware of what has taken place.

So, if the new technique is to release resources when no longer needed, how can JIT activation help the COM+ developer? COM+ is designed to make distributed applications easier to write. As a result, a component might not be activated on the local server—it might actually get activated on a remote server. This means that every client call will go through multiple servers and tie up those resources on those intermediate servers until the remote server can provide access to the requested component. Obviously, it doesn't take many of these requests to degrade overall network performance (because of the increased number of network calls) and the performance of several servers. JIT activation is also a help in the case when you want to reduce the number of client calls to a minimum.

At this point, you may be wondering if you have any control over JIT activation at all, other than turning it off or on. Microsoft provides the IObjectControl interface to allow you to interact with components manually. This interface is used for both object pooling (described later in the chapter) and JIT activation. Two of the methods, Activate() and Deactivate() allow you to perform JIT activation tasks on the component manually.

Adding these calls will allow you to make the entire resource allocation process even more efficient.

A third IObjectControl method is CanBePooled(). This method is used with object pooling to tell Windows 2000 whether the object can be pooled or not. An object must return TRUE to the CanBePooled() method call to get sent to the object pool, rather than being destroyed when deactivated by Windows 2000. Using object pooling makes the process of activation and deactivation much faster.

Transaction Processing

Transaction processing usually engenders visions of database management and financial data of various types. In fact, that's how transaction processing originally started. People in the banking industry need to know that the data they enter into a database is actually recorded once, but only one time. Think of the havoc that would result if some transactions were recorded three or four times!

However, financial institutions aren't the only ones who require the use of transactions. A hospital or other critical care facility also needs to know that data is recorded properly. In short, MTS was originally designed to meet the needs of an entire group of people who needed absolute data integrity. There are just some places when anything less is an invitation to disaster.

NOTE: Just to give people the feeling of "new" in Windows 2000, Microsoft has decided to assign new names to several products that you may have used in the past. The products perform essentially the same tasks; just the names have changed. Most of the functionality provided by MTS is now found within the confines of the Distributed Transaction Coordinator (DTC), which actually started out as part of SQL Server. MSMQ is now called by the term Queued Components or Message Queuing, depending on which MSMQ facet that you're working with. In many cases, you'll see these terms mixed together when looking at the Microsoft documentation, so don't be too surprised if things look a tad confusing. Just to keep the book from getting confusing, I'll normally refer to MTS and MSMQ by their old names. The only exception will be if I'm talking about a dialog box or other Windows 2000 feature that uses the new terminology, or if the new term is actually more appropriate for some reason. For example, if I'm talking about how to configure MTS for using with a component, I'll likely use DTC throughout the discussion since this is a new use for an old product.

Of course, data isn't the only kind of object that requires close monitoring, especially in the Windows 2000 distributed application environment. What happens if a component you need gets corrupted in transit from the server, or if two copies of that component are sent at different times? In the first case, the client application could simply stop working. In the second case, you could get some really strange results because an uninitialized component could overwrite the one that your application has initialized.

As you can see, transactions are a very necessary part of the COM+ picture. Both data and code require some sort of monitoring to ensure that the object that gets sent to a client is the one that actually arrives. We'll see more about how transactions work as the book progresses.

COM+ Context

Every COM+ component is created with a special set of properties known as *context*. The context identifies the instance of this component and is associated with only one COM apartment. Multiple objects can be associated with a single context—normally when these objects are requested by the application. In addition, one apartment can contain multiple contexts. The idea behind the context is to get the component a point of reference, some idea of where it is in the grand scheme of application execution. By examining the context in which it's running, a component can perform special processing as needed.

TIP: You may have originally known the contexts used by COM+ as MTS context wrappers. In Windows 2000, MTS context wrappers have been extended to encompass all COM activity. As a result, you won't see the term MTS "context wrappers" used, but they're still present in another form.

COM+ also deals with the context of a component. It uses the properties contained within the context to provide runtime services. In addition, the context affects the component's runtime environment. When working with COM+, you'll interact directly with the context properties to indicate certain types of application and environmental changes to the operating system. For example, if you're working with a transactional component, you'll use the context to vote on the outcome of the transaction.

Every COM+ object has access to the IObjectContext interface. We'll look at this interface in depth in Chapter 4 when we look at MTS. There are six methods directly associated with MTS that allow you to vote on the outcome of a transaction: CreateInstance(), IsInTransaction(), SetAbort(), SetComplete(), EnableCommit(), and DisableCommit(). The IsCallerInRole() method is used with role-based security to examine the caller's current role—their ability to use various methods within your component. The IsSecurityEnabled() method allows you to determine if MTS security is currently set on. The only time that MTS security won't be set on is if the object is running in the client process. The main reason you want to check this particular value is to ensure that security is enabled. Checking this value also allows you to determine where the component is running (on the client or server). In addition to the IObjectContext interface, there are several additional interfaces associated with the component context as listed here:

▼ **IObjectContextInfo**   Allows you to retrieve specifics about the current context, including the transaction ID, activity ID, and context ID. You'll also use the IsInTransaction() method of this interface to determine if your component is currently part of a transaction. The GetTransaction() method will allow you to obtain the ITransaction pointer for the current transaction (if there is one).

■ **IContextState**   Provides the current context status information and allows you to define your component's vote in a transaction. There really isn't a time when you'd need to implement this interface. However, the GetMyTransactionVote() method will allow you to determine the status of your vote on a transaction. The GetDeactivateOnReturn() method will allow you to determine the current state of the "done" bit for the component—the bit that defines when the component has completed its processing.

- ■ **IObjectContextActivity**   The only method in this interface retrieves the activity ID for the current component context.

- ▲ **ISecurityCallContext**   We'll cover this interface in detail in the role-based security section of the chapter. This interface is primarily responsible for allowing a component to determine its current security status. For example, you'd use the methods in this interface to determine what roles are assigned to the current user, which allows you to decide when a user should have access to particular methods in your component.

Normally, you'll use the context properties to determine the state of your component, how it was activated, and who activated it, so that you can determine the best course of action when servicing a method request. There are, however, two special events that require more detailed consideration of the context: activation and interception. Activation occurs when a component is first created or reactivated from the object pool. During activation, a new context is created for the component or the component uses an existing context—normally when called upon to service an exiting client through another object. Interception occurs when a cross-context call is made. The context of the caller is adjusted to match that of the called component. The two objects have different runtime requirements, specified by their contexts. That's the point of using contexts—to allow objects to run in the environment best suited to their needs. The use of interception allows two objects to interact in a way that doesn't violate the context in which they're executing.

UNDERSTANDING RESOURCE DISPENSERS

Resource dispensers do exactly what their name implies—they dispense the component resources that applications require. Any COM+ component can use resource dispensers to manage the various objects required by the component. Windows 2000 supplies a default set of resource dispensers, but you also have the option of building your own. For example, many database managers include both a Resource Manager and one or more custom resource dispensers.

TIP: The moment that a resource dispenser is invoked, the component becomes transactional. The component doesn't need to do anything else to start MTS or work with it. All component transactions in Windows 2000 are declarative, which means that the participating components don't require any special coding. All transactions also conform to the OLE Transactions specification implemented by the Microsoft Distributed Transaction Coordinator (MS DTC), which we'll talk about in several other places in the book.

The resource dispenser works with nondurable data, the type that's stored in memory and lost when the computer is shut down or rebooted. None of the components handled by the resource dispenser are persisted. In short, the resource dispenser allows Windows 2000 to manage a rather large pool of temporary objects that get used for a wide variety of purposes by a number of applications.

There's a wide range of object types that a resource dispenser can work with. The resource dispenser doesn't just work with standard components. It handles all kinds of objects, even objects that you normally wouldn't think required any kind of management. You'll normally find the resource dispenser working with items like database connections, network connections, socket connections, memory blocks, memory structures, queues, threads, and other forms of nondurable objects.

So, how does a resource dispenser work? The client starts to make resource requests of a resource manager like SQL Server. As the number of requests increase, SQL Server creates one of more resource dispensers. The resource dispensers, in turn, create a resource pool to contain objects that aren't needed any longer by the application. When the application finishes using an object like a database connection, the object is placed in the resource pool instead of being destroyed. Using the pool reduces the amount of time to get rid of the object that's no longer needed and the time required to "create" a new object when the applications requests one.

UNDERSTANDING THE COMPENSATING RESOURCE MANAGER

The Compensating Resource Manager (CRM) is the part of COM+ that performs compensating resource management for applications in conjunction with the Distributed Transaction Coordinator (MTS for those of you who don't like new terminology). Remember that Windows 2000 allows you to manage objects other than the database connections and other database-related objects originally managed by MTS. You can now manage all kinds of different object types, both code and data.

We've already discussed the idea behind a resource manager as part of the resource dispenser discussion. Essentially, a resource manager handles the durable objects in a transactional component, while the resource dispenser handles the nondurable (memory only) objects. SQL Server is an example of a resource manager, while the ODBC driver that allows access to SQL Server is an example of a resource dispenser.

Generally, the objects engaged in a transaction have no idea whether the transaction succeeded or failed. The component author assumes that either the transaction succeeded and Windows 2000 won't need to do anything else or that the transaction failed. In case of failure, the transaction is rolled back and a new transaction started. In either case, the component really doesn't need to know the outcome of the transaction.

There are, however, instances when a component will need to do some work in case the transaction fails. For example, when working in a database application, a component may have to request that the errant transaction get rolled back. Since the component is normally deactivated at transaction boundaries to ensure that transaction isolation is maintained, it needs some way to perform this post-transaction activity. That's where the compensating portion of the CRM comes into play. A CRM, then, is a special type of resource manager that allows your component to perform some remedial work in the case of a transaction failure.

The CRM is a nontransactional object. In other words, it can't participate in the transaction. When you think about it, this makes sense since the transaction is already complete and there isn't anything for the CRM to vote on—the transaction has failed and it's time to perform some remedial task.

You'll create the CRM as part of your component's startup code and register it with the system-provided log manager called the CRM Clerk. The CRM Clerk records the information about the CRM and logs any activity that the component performs. This log is the basis for the CRM's remedial action—it allows the CRM to see just where the transaction failed and perform any work required to roll the transaction back.

A basic CRM is composed of two parts: CRM Worker and CRM Compensator. The CRM Worker is the part that's active during the prepare phase of the transaction's two-phase commit. This is the part of your CRM that works with the CRM Clerk to create the durable log entries on disk that will be used to roll back an errant transaction. The CRM Compensator is activated during the commit phase of the transaction. This is the only piece of your component that actually gets to see the outcome of the transaction. If the transaction succeeds, the CRM Compensator normally releases any resources that it holds along with any that are held by the component. Otherwise, the CRM Compensator uses the contents of the log to ensure that the transaction is rolled back, without affecting the tasks performed by other transactions.

All CRMs rely on the ICrmCompensator interface. This interface provides methods that allow the CRM to create log entries, commit a transaction, or abort a transaction. There are also methods that determine when each phase of the transaction begins and ends—two for the prepare phase and two more for the commit phase.

COM+ EVENT SINKS

There really isn't much new here except the name and how this technology applies to your components. For any COM component, an event sink receives event notifications. Once received, the component normally performs some action in response to the event. COM+ event sinks originally referred to the events generated by MTS. The new name simply reflects a change in the range of things that MTS is doing now that MTS is fulfilling a broader range of tasks and is more component oriented. In short, an event sink still does the same thing as it did before.

COM+ CATALOG

When you want to purchase something from a mail order store, you look at the catalog, get a part number, call the company, and order the part that you want. The same thing happens at an application level with COM+. The COM+ Catalog provides a complete list of all of the components registered with the server and their configuration data. In most cases, this configuration data includes COM+ application attributes, class-level attributes, and computer-level attributes. The COM+ Catalog is physically stored in REGDB—which is a registry database as the name implies. You'll normally directly interact with the COM+ catalog through the Component Services MMC snap-in.

Obviously, you can also access the COM+ Catalog through your application. The purpose of the catalog, in this case, is to provide an abstraction layer that hides some of the vagaries of accessing component configuration information. The COM+ Catalog is accessed through the ICOMAdminCatalog interface, which provides methods for accessing the collection as a whole or individual components (called applications in this case). The individual component access includes things like the version number of the component. You can also install, import, export, start, and stop individual applications.

The ICOMAdminCatalog interface provides other "macro" type capabilities. For example, there are special methods that allow you to work with more than one application at a time. This macro capability extends to registering more than one component event class at a time, a real time-saver when working with complex components.

There are also some utility type methods supported by the ICOMAdminCatalog interface that may or may not be usable on your server. For example, since Microsoft is distributing Component Load Balancing as a separate product, there isn't any way to know if you'll have this service installed on your machine. There are, however, methods for starting and stopping this service if it's installed. One service-related task that will always be available is the ability to back up and restore REGDB, the central repository of COM+ configuration data.

OBJECT POOLING

I've spent half the chapter jumping around the topic of object pooling. This is actually a very easy concept to understand. Consider the amount of code required to instantiate an object versus the code required to change that object's properties. It doesn't take a rocket scientist to figure out that changing properties is far less code intensive than creating a new object. That's really what object pooling is all about. Instead of creating new objects every time you need one, then destroying that object when you're done with it, object pooling allows you to save the object for reuse later.

ROLE-BASED SECURITY

Security is a very important issue, especially now that crackers have starting popping up in just about every corner of the computing universe. The proliferation of ActiveX controls, Java applets, scripts of various sorts, macro programming in applications, and unforeseen programming errors in major products have all conspired to take security out of the hands of the administrator and put them in the hands of those who would do harm to your company. Does this sound just a tad paranoid? Perhaps it is in a way, but in other ways it really isn't far off the mark.

Windows 2000 provides a variety of ways for you to reduce your security risk, but I wouldn't go so far as to say you could rest easy at night. If you write applications that invoke all of the security features of Windows 2000, and if the network administrator configures the various object rights on the network correctly, then the risk of intrusion is minimized—but not removed completely. In short, security is a constantly evolving process of configuration management, monitoring, and software upgrades.

Fortunately, Windows 2000 comes with a lot of security tools in its arsenal. The following sections are going to describe two elements of that security array. The first is the standard object-based security that has been around since Windows NT and greatly improved in Windows 2000. Object-based security assigns specific access requirements to a specific object, which must then be met by a user who wants to access that object through the use of a token. The second is the newer role-based security that you'll be using with many of the components we create in this book. In this case, objects are assigned to specific roles, as are users who need to access them. The role is job oriented. To gain access to an object, the user needs to perform a task that requires that object. It's important to realize that both of these technologies work side by side to ensure your network remains safe.

NOTE: This chapter will make use of two terms for people who break the security of Web sites or networks. The first term, hacker, refers to someone who's performing a low-level task, like checking the security that a company provides, at the invitation of the company. In addition, hackers don't do any damage to the network or associated data. The second term, cracker, is someone who breaks into a Web site or network for malicious reasons like stealing data, damaging the network or its data, or installing programs such as viruses.

Understanding Standard Windows Security

Windows 2000 provides a level of security that almost verges on paranoia for an operating system. It allows you to set security in a variety of ways, including both the familiar user and file levels. You can also create groups and assign security by using groups instead of individuals. In addition, you can monitor every aspect of the security system using various alarms and log files. Windows 2000 excels in the way that it actually monitors system activity. Not one event goes without some kind of scrutiny. In fact, the simple act of passing information from one process to another undergoes some level of scrutiny by Windows 2000.

As for applications, the level of security that Windows 2000 provides is a two-edged sword. On the one hand, there aren't too many things that an application can do to break security. In most cases, Windows 2000 will simply terminate an errant application before any kind of security breach can occur. On the other hand, such stringent security actually breaks some older applications that work fine when using less stringent forms of Windows like Windows 95/98. In essence, the security that Windows 2000 provides can actually affect the compatibility your machine can provide. Fortunately for the COM+ developer, the kinds of applications that are normally affected by the stringent security provided by Windows 2000 aren't a concern, so we won't address this issue in any more detail.

The overabundance of security that Windows 2000 provides is a big plus for Internet users and sites. In fact, many Web site developers wish that Windows 2000 provided even more stringent security than it does now. It's the level of native security that makes Windows 2000 an excellent platform for a Web site. In addition, you can improve on most of the standard features provided by a Web site if you go to the added trouble of writing code to use the features that Windows 2000 provides. What this means, in most cases, is creating components that you can access through an ASP script, in addition to the normal security configuration method. (Another way to accomplish the same goal is to create an ISAPI Filter that monitors the security of your system, which is a technique we won't cover in this book.) Even if you can't prevent a cracker from breaking your security, you can at least track what he or she is doing to keep damage to a minimum. In addition, knowing where someone did break in is one way to improve security in the future.

TIP: A famous hacker once said it's not a matter of if, but when, someone will break into your Web site or network—tracking security events will allow you to detect security failures before they become a problem. In some cases, you may even want to perform a security audit of your network by employing the services of a consulting company with hackers in their employ. Hackers and crackers often use the same tools and methods to break into your network—the difference is that the hacker is there to help you improve your security.

Understanding Security Holes

So, why would you want to go to all the effort of building additional Windows 2000–specific security into your component or application? For one thing, it's unlikely that the security setup for your LAN is perfect. You need to ensure that every piece of every application provides the required level of security or there will be holes in the security measures for your LAN. One of the most common sources of security problems in corporations today is the user who doesn't understand the business rules regarding security. Adding Windows 2000–specific security to both the application and associated components helps you overcome some types of user knowledge problems, or at least alert the user that they're doing something outside of company guidelines.

Of course, very few companies are an island anymore. You don't have just your LAN to worry about; you also have the Internet to worry about. Even if you don't open your Web site to the public, there are going to be ways for people outside your company to break in and cause havoc on your network. The Internet opens all kinds of potential cracker opportunities. It doesn't help that there are holes in the current API specifications for Internet security and in the implementation of those specifications by various applications. In some cases, these security holes aren't in the API itself, but in some of the creative solutions people used in the past to make the Internet work. In essence, problem solving in the past created security back doors in the present.

No matter what the source of the security hole is, you can be sure that some cracker is just waiting to find it on your system. Exploiting well-known security holes is one of the major tools of the cracker trade. It's not just accounts that you need to either disable or monitor (like Guest), it's the way that applications are designed. Even Java, which uses the sandbox approach for security, has had holes in it. Recently, crackers were able to use these holes to convince the Java Virtual Machine (JVM) that it needed to erase a file on the user's machine. While some of the security holes are small and difficult to gain access to, the fact remains that there's a hole in your security that a cracker can use to damage your network.

Microsoft has been the object of much trade press scorn in the recent past. Of course, a good amount of this attention is because Microsoft is one of the biggest players out there and, as a result, receives more than its fare share of attention. Crackers have found holes in everything from Internet Explorer to Microsoft Office. There are even holes in the supposedly secure infrastructure of the Internet Component Download service—the method used to download ActiveX components from the Internet. The following list tells you about three of the holes in the Internet Component Download service (although it's almost certain that more holes exist):

▼ **HTML <A HREF> tag**   There are ways to download and run an EXE file using the <A HREF> tag. The current method used by Internet Explorer 3.x/4.x/5.x to keep this problem in check is to have the HTML parser use the URL moniker directly to download the code. It then calls on WinVerifyTrust, which is part of the Internet Component Download service, to check code validity. Is this method 100-percent safe? No, because you're using something other than the standard procedure to verify the contents of a file. In this case, you're relying on the HTML parser. Microsoft's suggested fix for this problem is to refuse permission when asked if you want to download ActiveX controls, and that you should scan any EXE files that you download before opening them. However, the option still exists to bypass both of these suggestions, making it possible for a novice user to infect your network with a virus before you have any idea of what's happening.

■ **Scripts**   Right now scripts are totally free of any kind of security check. There's no way to verify who created the script or what it might do to your machine. More important, there isn't any way to verify what information the script might retrieve from your machine. Microsoft is working right now to create some kind of script certificate. However, even with Internet Explorer 5.x, their advice is to simply turn off script processing if virus attacks through a malicious script is a concern. Once script certificates become a reality, the browser can call WinVerifyTrust to check a script before running it.

▲ **Full applications or other complex download situations**   Internet Explorer does a good job of checking specific kinds of downloads right now. For example, downloading an OCX initiates a WinVerifyTrust sequence. What happens if the download parameters fall outside the limited scope of things checked by Internet Explorer? For example, a user might want to download and install Doom or some other game program. The installation sequence might include unpredictable actions such as making registry entries and rebooting the machine. Internet Explorer can't handle that situation at the moment. Microsoft plans to make future versions of Component Download more robust so that it can handle such events. In short, no matter how secure you think your network is today, there are lots of holes that crackers can use to gain access to it.

WEB LINK: Part of your protection strategy is going to include testing multiple browsers to see how they react—especially if you're creating a public access Web site. As a programmer working with multiple products, you still have to keep track of all the Web sites you visit on a regular basis for ideas. Newer versions of both Internet Explorer and Netscape Communicator allow for a certain amount of importing and exporting of application data. However, if you're using an older version of these browsers, a product called NavEx allows you to create copies of your Internet Explorer Favorite Places folder as Netscape bookmarks and vice versa. You can download it at http:// mach5.ocs.drexel.edu/navex/, http://www2. w-link.net/Software/, or http://www.pcworld.com/fileworld/ file_description/frameset/0,1458,4008,00.html.

NOTE: We'll also look at holes in other types of security technology (especially those that aid in Internet security) in this chapter. For example, Tables 3-1 and 3-2 are full of new specifications designed to plug the holes in the technology we use today. SHTTP, S/WAN, and other technologies like them wouldn't be needed if security didn't present a problem. There's even a new version of MIME called S/MIME to make sure that no one reads your mail.

Obviously, this list points out just three holes in one Windows service. Now, consider how many services are running on your workstation and associated server. Even if every one of those services has just one hole, the potential for a breach of security is immense. Crackers make use of security holes to breach your network security, but you can add security to the components and applications you create to either track that access or block it altogether. As you can see, closing holes and filling chinks in your security setup is important if you want to maintain the data your company has worked so hard to get. In short, you need to know what security features Windows 2000 provides as your first step to understanding how to plug holes in the security of your system.

One of the first steps in understanding how Windows 2000 can help you enhance the security of your network as a whole is to look at the basic security features offered by the operating system itself. Every security feature (like drive mapping) that Windows 2000 has to offer can be accessed using an application. What many programmers seem to forget is that you can also access those features using an ActiveX control. What this means to you as a COM+ developer is that you need to add security features to the components you create that will prevent various types of unauthorized access. Obviously, your first line of defense is to determine the identity of the user requesting access to the component, and then limit the availability of component features to those that the user actually requires.

You can implement these Windows 2000 security features in very simple ways. For example, creating an ActiveX control to display a logon dialog box actually accomplishes two things in any application, especially those that can be accessed outside of your company through connections to the Internet. First, it allows you to verify the identity of that particular user and match their access to the application. A cracker will have a pretty tough time getting past the logon dialog box without the right password. Second, you can tell the server to log every secure access—remember that Windows 2000 gives you the capability of monitoring everything. If someone does manage to break into your system, you'll at least know which account was used. Having an account name will allow you to assess the level of damage the cracker could inflict based on the security level of the person whose account was broken into.

An Overview of Security Standards

Security standards are an important part of your company's safety net. The previous section alerted you to the fact that there are holes in your security net that come from a variety of sources, including the operating system and off-the-shelf applications that you rely on to conduct business. All of those problems are real, but you don't have to face them alone. Standards groups are working even as you read this to come up with methods for protecting data. All you need to do is learn the methods that these groups come up with for managing security on your network.

The advantages to using standards-based security are twofold. First, you won't have to reinvent the wheel and create everything from scratch. Second, your security methods will mesh with those used by other sites, reducing the user learning curve and making it possible for you to use tools developed for other programmers. (There's a rather dubious third advantage—that you'll have some idea of where security breaches might appear and can build components to monitor for them until the associated standards committee defines a fix for the problem.)

There are actually two levels of security standards that you need to think about. The first includes the internal security that Windows 2000 provides. This is your first line of defense against local security threats that exist on your LAN or WAN. These security measures are equally important for Internet use. Table 3-1 provides you with a good overview of these security standards.

WEB LINK: If you want to find out the latest information on where the world is going with security standards (particularly the Internet), take a look at http://www.w3.org/Security/. This page of general information won't provide everything you need, but it'll give you places to look and links to other sites that do provide additional material. Developers will want to get the commercial view of security at http://www.rsasecurity.com/. The RSA site covers a pretty broad range of topics, including the current status of efforts by MasterCard and VISA to create secure credit card transactions. This site is also the best place to start if you want to add new physical security technologies to your applications, such as smart cards. You can also find out the current status of IETF efforts by viewing the document at ftp://ftp.isi.edu/internet-drafts/1id-abstracts.txt.

Once you get past internal security requirements, you need to address those that always occur outside of your company—namely the Internet. Let's take a quick look at the various types of Internet security standards that either have become fact or should be emerging soon. Table 3-2 shows the standards or standards drafts that were available at the time of this writing. You may find even more available by the time you read this.

Standard	Description
DSI (Digital Signature Initiative)	This is a standard originated by W3C to overcome some limitations of channel-level security. For example, channel-level security can't deal with documents and application semantics. A channel also doesn't use the Internet's bandwidth very efficiently because all the processing takes place on the Internet rather than at the client or server. DSI defines a mathematical method for transferring signatures—essentially a unique representation of a specific individual or company. DSI also provides a new method for labeling security properties (PICS2) and a new format for assertions (PEP). This standard is also built on the PKCS7 and X509.v3 standards. You can find out more about this security component at http://www.w3.org/DSig/Overview.html.
Internet Protocol Security Protocol (IPSec)	IETF recently created the IP Security Protocol Working Group to look at the problems of IP security, such as the inability to encrypt data at the protocol level. It's currently working on a wide range of specifications that will ultimately result in more secure IP transactions. You can find out more about this group at http://www.ietf.cnri.reston.va.us/html.charters/ipsec-charter.html.
The Kerberos Network Authentication Service (V5) IETF RFC1510	This is an approved IETF specification that defines a third-party authentication protocol. The Kerberos model is based in part on Needham and Schroeder's trusted third-party authentication protocol and on modifications suggested by Denning and Sacco. As with many Internet authentication protocols, Kerberos works as a trusted third-party authentication service. It uses conventional cryptography that relies on a combination of shared public key and private key. Kerberos emphasizes client authentication with optional server authentication. You can find out more about this service at http://info.internet.isi.edu/in-notes/rfc/files/rfc1510.txt. In addition, you may want to look at the general page at http://www.andrew.cmu.edu/user/chuang/security.html.

Table 3-1.   Windows 2000 Internal Security Standards

Standard	Description
PCT (Private Communication Technology)	The IETF is working with Microsoft on this particular protocol. Like SSL, PCT is designed to provide a secure method of communication between a client and server at the low protocol level. It can work with any high-level protocol such as HTTP, FTP, or TELNET. You can find updates about this emerging security technology at http://www.lne.com/ericm/pct.html.
SSL (Secure Sockets Layer)	This is a W3C standard originally proposed by Netscape for transferring encrypted information from the client to the server at the protocol layer. Sockets allow low-level encryption of transactions in higher-level protocols such as HTTP, NNTP, and FTP. The standard also specifies methods for server and client authentication (although client site authentication is optional). You can find details about SSL at http://home.netscape.com/security/index.html.

Table 3-1. Windows 2000 Internal Security Standards *(continued)*

WEB LINK: Tables 3-1 and 3-2 tell you about a lot of the security-related standards being created by the IETF. Most of the IETF RFC documents can be found at http://www.ietf.org/rfc/. You can also find a list of the current IETF working groups at http://www.ietf.cnri.reston.va.us/html.charters/. These working groups help create the standards used on the Internet.

It's a surprising fact that vendor standards are probably the fastest growing area of the Internet right now besides browser technology (which seems to be growing so fast that even the beta testers have a hard time keeping up). You'll also notice that the majority of standards listed in Tables 3-1 and 3-2 aren't from Microsoft or some other company—they come from one of two groups: the IETF (Internet Engineering Task Force) or a group known as W3C (World Wide Web Consortium). IETF has been around for a long time. It's one of the very first groups to work with the Internet. Be prepared to read a lot about the W3C group as you delve into Internet security issues (and to a lesser extent other standards areas such as HTML tags). It's the one responsible for newer standards of every kind when it comes to the Internet. For example, Microsoft is currently trying to get W3C to accept the <OBJECT> tag and other ActiveX-related HTML extensions.

The security standards in Table 3-2 represent the Internet end of the security picture. It's important to keep this fact in mind. All that these standards really cover is the connection between the client and server. You can still add other security measures at the client,

Standard	Description
Distributed Authentication Security Service (DASS) IETF RFC1507	DASS is an IETF work in progress. It defines an experimental method for providing authentication services on the Internet. The goal of authentication, in this case, is to verify who sent a message or request. Current password schemes have a number of problems that DASS tries to solve. For example, there's no way to verify that the sender of a password isn't impersonating someone else. DASS provides authentication services in a distributed environment. Distributed environments present special challenges because users don't log on to just one machine—they could conceivably log on to every machine on the network. You can find out more about this standard at http://www.wu-wien.ac.at:8082/ rfc/rfc1507.hyx/$$root. It also pays to look at the list of other security standards at http://afs.wu-wien.ac.at/usr/edvz/gonter/rfc-list.html.
Generic Security Service Application Program Interface (GSS-API) IETF RFC1508	This is an approved IETF specification that defines methods for supporting security service calls in a generic manner. Using a generic interface allows greater source code portability on a wider range of platforms. IETF doesn't see this specification as the end of the process, but rather the starting point for other, more specific, standards in the future. However, knowing that this standard exists can help you find the thread of commonality between various security implementation methods. You can find out more about this standard at http://www.wu-wien.ac.at:8082/rfc/rfc1508.hyx/$$root. It also pays to look at the list of other security standards at http://afs.wu-wien.ac.at/usr/edvz/gonter/rfc-list.html.
Generic Security Service Application Program Interface (GSS-API) C-bindings IETF RFC1508	This is an approved IETF specification that defines methods for supporting service calls using C. It's one of the first specific implementation standards based on RFC1508.

Table 3-2.   Current Security Standards for the Internet

Standard	Description
JEPI (Joint Electronic Payments Initiative)	A standard originated by W3C, JEPI provides a method for creating electronic commerce. Transactions will use some form of electronic cash or credit cards. Data transfers from the client to the server will use encryption, digital signatures, and authentication (key exchange) to ensure a secure exchange. This is an emerging standard—some items, such as transport-level security (also called privacy), are currently making their way through the IETF. You can find out more about this standard at http://www.w3.org/ECommerce/Overview-JEPI.html.
Privacy Enhanced Mail Part I (PEM1) Message Encryption and Authentication Procedures IETF RFC1421	This is an approved IETF specification for ensuring that your private mail remains private. Essentially, it outlines a procedure for encrypting mail in such a way that the user's mail is protected but the process of decrypting it is invisible. This includes the use of keys and other forms of certificate management. Some of the specification is based on the CCITT X.400 specification—especially in the areas of Mail Handling Service (MHS) and Mail Transfer System (MTS). You can find out more about this standard at http://www.cs.ucl.ac.uk/research/ice-tel/osisec/documentation/pem.html. There's also a more generic site you may want to check out at http://www.cs.ucl.ac.uk/research/ice-tel/osisec/documentation/.
Privacy Enhanced Mail Part II (PEM2) Certificate-Based Key Management IETF RFC1422	This is an approved IETF specification for managing security keys. It provides both an infrastructure and management architecture based on a public-key certification technique. IETF RFC1422 is an enhancement of the CCITT X.509 specification. It goes beyond the CCITT specification by providing procedures and conventions for a key management infrastructure for use with PEM. You can find out more about this standard at http://www.si.hhs.nl/~henks/comp/crypt.html.

Table 3-2.   Current Security Standards for the Internet *(continued)*

Standard	Description
Privacy Enhanced Mail Part III (PEM3) Algorithms, Modes, and Identifiers IETF RFC1423	This is an approved IETF specification that defines cryptographic algorithms, usage modes, and identifiers specifically for PEM use. The specification covers four main areas of encryption-related information: message encryption algorithms, message integrity check algorithms, symmetric key management algorithms, and asymmetric key management algorithms (including both symmetric encryption and asymmetric signature algorithms). You can find out more about this standard at http://www.si.hhs.nl/~henks/comp/crypt.html.
Privacy Enhanced Mail Part IV (PEM4) Key Certification and Related Services IETF RFC1424	This is an approved IETF specification that defines the method for certifying keys. It also provides a listing of cryptographic-related services that an Internet site would need to provide to the end user. You can find out more about this standard at http://www.si.hhs.nl/~henks/comp/crypt.html.
Secure/Multipurpose Internet Mail Extensions (S/MIME)	This is a specification being promoted by a consortium of vendors, including Microsoft, Banyan, VeriSign, ConnectSoft, QUALCOMM, Frontier Technologies, Network Computing Devices, FTP Software, Wollongong, SecureWare, and Lotus. It was originally developed by RSA Data Security, Inc., as a method for different developers to create message transfer agents (MTAs) that used compatible encryption technology. Essentially, this means that if someone sends you a message using a Lotus product, you can read it with your Banyan product. S/MIME is based on the popular Internet MIME standard (RFC1521). You can find out about standard MIME at http://www.oac.uci.edu/indiv/ehood/MIME/. There's a whole list of S/MIME specific resources at http://www.rsasecurity.com/standards/smime/resources.html.

Table 3-2.   Current Security Standards for the Internet *(continued)*

Standard	Description
Secure/Wide Area Network (S/WAN)	S/WAN is only a glimmer in some people's eyes at the moment. It's an initiative supported by RSA Data Security, Inc. The IETF has a committee working on it as well. RSA intends to incorporate the IETF's IPSec standard into S/WAN. The main goal of S/WAN is to allow companies to mix and match the best firewall and TCP/IP stack products to build Internet-based virtual private networks (VPNs). Current solutions usually lock the user into a single source for both products. You can find out more about S/WAN at http://www.rsasecurity.com/rsalabs/faq/5-1-3.html.
SHTTP (Secure Hypertext Transfer Protocol)	This is the current encrypted data transfer technology used by Open Marketplace Server, which is similar in functionality to SSL. The big difference is that this method only works with HTTP. The Web Transaction Security, or WTS, group of the IETF was recently formed for looking at potential specifications like this one. You can find out more about this standard at http://www.ietf.org/html.charters/wts-charter.html.
Universal Resource Identifiers (URI) in WWW IETF RFC2396 (and others like RFC1630)	URI is an IETF work in progress. Currently, resource names and addresses are provided in clear text. A URL (Uniform Resource Locator) is actually a form of URI containing an address that maps to a specific location on the Internet. URI would provide a means of encoding the names and addresses of Internet objects. In essence, to visit a private site, you'd need to know the encoded name instead of the clear text name. If you'd like to learn more about URIs and how they compare to URLs, check out the W3C Web site at http://www.w3.org/Addressing/.

Table 3-2.   Current Security Standards for the Internet *(continued)*

the server, or both (like the ones shown in Table 3-1). Most of these standards don't cover Internet add-on products such as firewalls, either. Your company can add these additional security features and at least make it more difficult for someone to break into its system.

Making Windows 2000 Security Work for You

So far we've explored some of the Windows 2000 security challenges (in the form of security holes) and the standards that are hopefully going to fix those problems. However, we still haven't looked at the main event, the Windows 2000 Security API. This is the part of Windows 2000 that will allow you, the programmer, full control over how the applications and components that you create will handle security. Now it's time to look at how you can actually implement those security features in the real world. In other words, it's time to take a look at the nuts and bolts of working with security in Windows 2000. There are actually nine different types, or levels, of security we'll explore in this chapter. The following list defines each type:

▼ **Built-in security**   Windows 2000 comes with a certain level of security as part of the operating system. Every object has some type of security associated with it under Windows 2000, and we'll look at how that security is implemented. Using object-level security means that there's little chance than anyone could access any part of the operating system or its data without the proper authorization. Of course, little chance doesn't mean there's no chance at all—it always pays to assume your security is less than perfect.

■ **Authenticode**   This is part of Microsoft Internet Explorer. It verifies that the components you download from the Internet haven't been tampered with in any way and assures a certain level of component accountability (by displaying the author's name and other information to the user). Essentially, this is the same thing as component signing. Authenticode supports three different types of digital certificate including: 128-bit digital signatures generated locally, industry standard Public Key Cryptography Standards (PKCS) #7 and #10 formatted digital signatures, and X.509 version 3 digital certificates.

■ **Cryptography Application Programming Interface**   Some types of security rely on layers of protection to work. In other words, if a cracker were to break through one layer of protection, another layer would exist to prevent further access. That's just what the Cryptography API (also called CryptoAPI) is all about: it's a layer of protection added to all the layers that currently exist. It serves to keep someone from further penetrating your security.

■ **Digital signatures/certificates**   A digital signature works as its name implies. The sender of a document or executable file signs it. You know that the work is genuine by examining the signature. You'll use a series of private and public keys to implement this level of security.

- **Distributed Password Authentication (DPA)**   This is a shared secret authentication method originally started by some of the larger online services like CompuServe and MSN. It allows a user to use the same membership password to access a number of Internet sites when those sites are linked together as a membership organization. In essence, this methodology replicates some of the same features that users can get when using the same password to access multiple servers on a local network. DPA relies on the Microsoft Membership Service for membership authentication and server-specific access information.

- **Kerberos**   This is Microsoft's primary replacement for the Windows NT LAN Manager (NTLM) security currently used to ensure that your data remains safe when using Windows. Kerberos version 5 is a relatively new industry standard security protocol devised at MIT that offers superior security support through the use of a private-key architecture. This protocol supports mutual authentication of both client and server, reduces server load when establishing a connection, and allows the client to delegate authentication to the server through the use of proxy mechanisms. Kerberos connects to an online Key Distribution Center (KDC) and the Directory Service (DS) account to obtain session tickets used for authentication purposes.

- **Private Communication Technology (PCT)**   This is a special level of Internet security that Microsoft and the IETF are working on together. The short version is that PCT will enable a client and server to engage in private communication with little chance of being overheard. This level of security depends on digital signatures and encryption methodologies to do its work.

- **Public Key Infrastructure (PKI)**   This protocol allows two sites to exchange data in an encrypted format without any prior arrangement. The default method for initiating the exchange is to create a Secure Sockets Layer (SSL) connection. The main difference between this technology and others on the market is that it relies on a public-key system of certificates to ensure secure data transfer. The latest specification for SSL is SSL3, which the IETF is calling Transport Layer Security (TLS) protocol. A newer addition to the mix is Private Communication Technology (PCT). PCT still uses public-key encryption, but there are some distinct advantages to using it that we'll discuss later in this section. One of the benefits of using PKI is that there's no online authentication server required since the certificate is issued by a well-known certification authority (normally a company like VeriSign when the technology is used publicly).

- ▲ **Windows 2000 authentication over HTTP**   Many people are under the mistaken assumption that security has to be convoluted or overly complex to work. In some cases, it's the simple solution that provides the best answer.

Authentication can take two forms under Windows 2000 when looked at from the Internet perspective. First, you could simply ask for the user's name and password, and then check that information against an access list on the server. There are two ways of doing this: the basic method that's used during a standard login and Windows 2000 Challenge/Response. The latter method relies on the client to supply the required user name and password based on the current session settings. In other words, the client supplies the information that the user used to log in to the machine in the first place. The other method is equally simple. It relies on an existing technology called Secure Sockets Layer (SSL). SSL relies on encryption and digital certificates to do its work. If you're really paranoid about security, you can even combine these two security methods—they're not mutually exclusive.

Built-In Security Features

Windows 2000 is about the most overengineered operating system on the market today when it comes to security. If you have any doubt as to the importance of security with Microsoft, just look at some of the qualifications that Windows 2000 presents. You can use that capability to your advantage. For example, you could make use of those advanced capabilities within component or grant access to specific application features over the Internet. In short, Windows 2000 provides some sort of security for every need, at least some of which is based on current security standards.

Of course, just how you use the security features of Windows 2000 depends on user and application location. The Internet imposes restrictions because some security elements are out of your control. You'll have to use a lot of restraint when granting access to application features over the Internet because you don't want to damage your security net. In addition, it's impractical to use some features from the Internet because they just aren't important. (Other security features do take the place of the local security features—look at Tables 3-1 and 3-2 to get some ideas on how standards-based security works.)

Whether you're creating a component for Internet, local, WAN, or LAN use, you'll find that a good understanding of the underlying network security architecture is essential. For example, you need to decide whether a client-side or server-side component is better given the architecture of the client machine. Windows 95/98 doesn't provide the same level of security that Windows 2000 does, so you'll find yourself doing without added security under Windows 95/98 at times. However, when Windows 95/98 does provide a security feature, it uses the same setup as Windows 2000, so one security module will work with both of them. (In other cases, you'll definitely want to use a separate module for Windows 2000 to make better use of its enhanced security capabilities—see the following note for details.) The problem for the developer is ensuring a consistent level of security while reducing network traffic. Client-side components tend to reduce network traffic because the client is assigned more of the work, while server-side components tend to be more secure because the server operating system usually provides more robust security features.

Windows 2000 natively uses object-based security. So just what does object-based security entail? The first thing you need to do is define the term "object." Windows 2000 and Windows 95/98 both use the term "object" rather loosely. It's true that a lot of objects are lurking beneath the surface, but you may find that they don't fit precisely within the C++ usage of the term. In general, in the next few sections, we'll look at an object as the encapsulation of code and data required to perform a specific security task. In other words, each security object is a self-contained unit designed to fulfill a specific role. (In many places in both Windows 95/98 and Windows 2000, Microsoft chose to use the full C++ version of an object mainly because it implemented the required functionality as part of MFC. However, when reading either the Microsoft documentation or this chapter, you shouldn't depend on the definition of an object to mean a strict C++ object—think of objects more in the COM sense of the word.)

Knowing that everything is an object makes security a bit easier to understand—at least it's a starting point. However, objects themselves are just a starting point. Users are the other part of the security equation. An object is accessed by a user, so security in Windows is a matter of comparing the object's protection to the user's rights. If the user has sufficient rights (rights that meet or exceed those of the object), then he or she can use the object. The Windows documentation refers to an object's level of protection as a *security descriptor*. This is the structure that tells the security system what rights a user needs to access the object. Likewise, the user has an *access token*, which is another structure that tells the security system what rights a user has in a given situation. "Token" is a good word here because the user will give Windows 2000 the token in exchange for access to the object. (Think of the object as a bus, with Windows 2000 as the driver and the user presenting the required token to board.) Figure 3-1 shows both of these structures.

This is the shortest look you can take at security under either Windows 95/98 or Windows 2000. Simply knowing that there are security objects and user tokens will go a long way toward helping you make sense out of the Windows security API calls. In the following sections we'll take a more detailed look at precisely what a token is and how it works. We'll also look at the security descriptor. You don't absolutely have to know this information to implement security using ActiveX if your only interest is the Internet, but knowing it can help you design ActiveX controls of a more general nature and wider appeal.

UNDERSTANDING ACCESS TOKENS   You'll find that there are two of ways of looking at a user's rights under Windows; both are related to objects in one form or another. The user's access token has a security identifier (SID) to identify the user throughout the network—it's like having an account number. The user token that the SID identifies tells

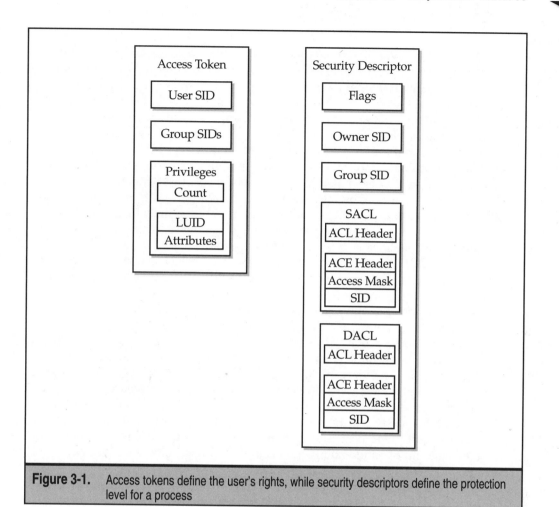

Figure 3-1. Access tokens define the user's rights, while security descriptors define the protection level for a process

A Case for Using Object-Based Security

From a COM+ viewpoint, the security picture is wide open. There are actually two kinds of security that you can implement when working with COM+: object-based (traditional) and role-based (Windows 2000 specific). The choice you make between these two technologies will greatly affect how you handle component design—at least from a security perspective. Role-based security allows you to define access down to the method level based on the role that the requesting user fulfills within the organization. Normally, defining security to the method level is all that you really need to do. However, there are some circumstances when you'll need to do more with a component than role-based security allows.

When working with object-based security, you need to decide at design time how a component that you create will be used so that you can add the requisite security features. Many developers have only the Internet on their mind today, but companies have a much broader range of uses for components than just the Internet. There's no rule saying that you can't create a component designed specifically for use as part of an application. We'll see in Chapter 7 that components can be used on a LAN or WAN to access a database as part of an *n*-tier application. Components could be the answer to applications normally used by a network administrator (or other qualified person). Microsoft Management Console (MMC) may be causing a lot of problems right now because administrators aren't used to using it, but the component nature of the snap-ins that MMC uses will eventually make administrative tools more secure and easier to use. In fact, just about any component can take on multiple personalities if you want it to. You could even add the capability to detect the control's current location or perhaps add a special location field as part of a property page setup. Someone could choose a subset of features for Internet use, another set of features for LAN use, and still another set of features for local use.

About now, many of you are asking what kind of administrator would need to access security but wouldn't use the tools furnished by the NOS to do so. Windows 2000 actually provides a lot of very easy-to-use tools, so adding a lot of functionality isn't worthwhile in the minds of some programmers—at least, not when a component is used at the local level. We'll see in the "How Role-Based Security Differs" section of the chapter that it isn't always necessary to add special security features to your component, even if there are some special security needs, but there are times when even role-based security won't take care of every security need. I mention role-based security here because this new Windows 2000 feature has greatly reduced the amount of hand-coding you need to do for security, but it hasn't eliminated the need for hand-coding completely.

Let's take a look at one of the situations where you'd need to implement some type of internal component security. Consider what would happen if the person administering the application isn't a network administrator—someone with the training to work with the NOS itself. Say that person is a workgroup manager or other individual who doesn't need to see the whole network picture, but just requires enough information to maintain the application he or she is responsible for managing. You'll find yourself in that situation a lot more often than you might think. Large companies with a lot of small workgroups frequently fall into this category. The network administrator doesn't have the knowledge needed to administer the application correctly, but doesn't want the workgroup manager crawling around the network either. Role-based security might answer this need, but then again, it might not. The problem is that you can't really define a single role that addresses the needs of all of the workgroups within the company—at least not with any amount of certainty. Whether you need to implement internal security or use role-based security depends on just how well you can define the role of the person using the component. Sometimes the simple answer isn't the best one—there are times when adding separate security is an essential part of the component development process.

what groups the user belongs to and what privileges the user has. Each group also has a SID, so the user's SID contains references to the various group SIDs that the user belongs to, not to a complete set of group access rights. You'd normally use the User Manager utility under Windows 2000 to change the contents of this access token.

So, what's the privileges section of the access token all about? It begins with a count of the number of privileges that the user has—not the groups that the user belongs to, but the number of special privilege entries in the access token. This section also contains an array of privilege entries. Each privilege entry contains a locally unique identifier (LUID)—essentially a pointer to an object—and an attribute mask. The attribute mask tells what rights the user has to the object. Group SID entries are essentially the same. They contain a privilege count and an array of privilege entries.

TIP: Now would probably be a good time to look at the Windows API help file provided with your copy of Visual C++ to see what kind of SID- and token-related API calls you can find. Examples of SID-related calls include CopySID() and AllocateAndInitializeSID(). You'll also find that the OpenProcessToken() and GetTokenInformation() calls are essential to making security work correctly with any language you use.

USING ACCESS TOKENS   Let's talk briefly about the token calls that the Windows API provides, since they're the first stepping-stones that you'll need to know about when it comes to security. To do anything with a user's account—even if you want to find out who has access to a particular workstation—you need to know about tokens. As previously stated, tokens are the central part of the user side of the security equation. You'll almost always begin a user account access with a call to the OpenProcessToken() call. Notice the name of this call—it deals with any kind of a process, user or otherwise. The whole purpose of this call is to get a token handle with specific rights attached to it. For example, if you want to query the user account, you need the TOKEN_QUERY privilege. (Your access token must contain the rights that you request from the system, which is why an administrator can access a token but other users can't.) Any changes to the user's

Observing the Flow of Access Rights

One of the things that you need to know as part of working with some kinds of objects is that object rights flow down to the lowest possible node unless overridden by another SID. For example, if you give a user read and write rights to the \Temp directory on a hard drive, those rights would also be applied to the \Temp\Stuff directory (unless you assigned the user specific rights to that directory).

The same idea of access flow rights holds true for containers. Assigning a user rights to a container object like a Word document gives the user the right to look at everything within that container, even other files that appear within the container in most cases. As you can see, it's important to track a user's exact rights to various objects on your server through the use of security surveys, since you could have inadvertently given the user more rights than he or she needs to perform a certain task.

account require the TOKEN_ADJUST_PRIVILEGES privilege. There are quite a few of these access rights, so we won't go through them all here.

Once you have an access token handle, you need to decide what to do with it. If you decide you want to change a user's privilege to do something, you need the LUID for the privilege you want to change. All of these appear in the WINNT.H file with an SE_ attached to them. For example, the SE_SYSTEM_PROFILE_NAME privilege allows the user to gather profiling information for the entire system. Some SE values aren't related to users (for example, the SE_LOCK_MEMORY_NAME privilege that allows a process to lock system memory). You get the LUID for a privilege using the LookupPrivilegeValue call. Now you can combine the information you've gotten so far to change the privilege. In general, you'll use the AdjustTokenPrivileges call to make the required change.

Querying the user's account (or other access token information) is fairly straightforward. You use the GetTokenInformation call to retrieve any information you might need. This call requires a token class parameter, which tells Windows what kind of information you need. For example, you'd use the TokenUser class if you wanted to know about a specific user. You'll also need to supply an appropriate structure that Windows can use for storing the information you request—which differs based on the token class you request.

UNDERSTANDING SECURITY DESCRIPTORS   Now, let's look at the security descriptor. Figure 14-1 in Chapter 14 shows that each security descriptor contains five main sections. The first section is a list of flags. These flags tell you the descriptor revision number, format, and ACL (access control list) status.

The next two sections contain SIDs. The owner SID tells who owns the object. This doesn't have to be an individual user; Windows allows you to use a group SID here as well. The one limiting factor is that the group SID must appear in the access token of the person changing the entry. The group SID allows a group of people to own the object. Of the two SIDs, only the owner SID is important under Windows. The group SID is used as part of the Macintosh and POSIX security environment.

The final two sections contain ACLs. The security access control list (SACL) controls Windows' auditing feature. Every time a user or group accesses an object and the auditing feature for that object is turned on, Windows makes an entry in the audit log. The discretionary access control list (DACL) controls who can actually use the object. You can assign both groups and individual users to a specific object.

NOTE: There are actually two types of security descriptors: absolute and self-relative. The absolute security descriptor contains an actual copy of each ACL within its structure. This is the type of security descriptor to use for an object that requires special handling. The self-relative security descriptor only contains a pointer to the SACL and DACL. This type of descriptor saves memory and reduces the time required to change the rights for a group of objects. You'd use it when all the objects in a particular group require the same level of security. For example, you could use this method to secure all the threads within a single application. Windows requires that you convert a self-relative security descriptor to absolute format before you can save it or transfer it to another process. Every descriptor you retrieve using an API call is of the self-relative type—you must convert it before you can save it. You can convert a security descriptor from one type to another using the MakeAbsoluteSD and MakeSelfRelativeSD API calls.

An ACL consists of two types of entries. The first entry is a header that lists the number of access control entries (ACEs) that the ACL contains. Windows uses this number as a method for determining when it's reached the end of the ACE list. (There isn't any kind of end-of-structure record or any way of determining a precise size for each ACE in the structure.) The second entry is an array of ACEs.

> **CAUTION:** Never directly manipulate the contents of an ACL or SID, since Microsoft may change its structure in future versions of Windows. The Windows API provides a wealth of functions to change the contents of these structures. Always use an API call to perform any task with either structure type to reduce the impact of changes in structure on your application.

So, what is an ACE? An *ACE* defines the object rights for a single user or group. Every ACE has a header that defines the type, size, and flags for the ACE. Next comes an access mask that defines the rights that a user or group has to the object. Finally, there's an entry for the user's or group's SID.

There are four different types of ACE headers (three of which are used in the current version of Windows). The *access-allowed* type appears in the DACL and grants rights to a user. You can use it to add to the rights that a user already has to an object on an instance-by-instance basis. For example, say you wanted to keep the user from changing the system time so that you could keep all the machines on the network synchronized. However, there might be one situation—such as daylight savings time—when the user would need this right. You could use an access-allowed ACE to give the user the right to change the time in this one instance. An *access-denied* ACE revokes rights that the user has to an object. You can use it to deny access to an object during special system events. For example, you could deny access rights to a remote terminal while you perform some type of update on it. The *system audit* ACE type works with the SACL. It defines which events to audit for a particular user or group. The *currently unused* ACE type is a system alarm ACE. It allows either the SACL or DACL to set an alarm when specific events happen.

> **TIP:** Now would be a good time to look through the Windows API help file to see what types of access rights Windows provides. You should also look at the various structures used to obtain the information. Especially important are the ACL and ACE structures. Look for the ACE flags that determine how objects in a container react. For example, check out the CONTAINER_INHERIT_ACE constant that allows subdirectories to inherit the protection of the parent directory.

USING SECURITY DESCRIPTORS Understanding what a security descriptor is and how the various structures it contains interact is only one part of the picture. You also need to know how to begin the process of actually accessing and using security descriptors to write a program. The first thing you need to understand is that unlike tokens, security descriptors aren't generalized. You can't use a standard set of calls to access them. In fact, there are five classes of security descriptors, each of which uses a different set of descriptor calls to access the object initially. (You must have the SE_SECURITY_NAME privilege to use any of these functions.)

▼ **Files, directories, pipes, and mail slots**   Use the GetFileSecurity and SetFileSecurity calls to access this object type.

NOTE: Only the NTFS file system under Windows 2000 provides security. The VFAT file system provides it to a lesser degree under Windows 95/98. You can't assign or obtain security descriptors for either the HPFS or FAT file systems under either operating system. The FAT file system doesn't provide any extended attribute space, one requirement for adding security. The HPFS file system provides extended attributes, but they don't include any security features. Of all the file systems described, NTFS is the most secure. However, never assume that any file system is completely secure. There are utility programs on the Internet that will read the contents of an NTFS file partition even if the user hasn't logged in properly to Windows 2000.

■ **Processes, threads, access tokens, and synchronization objects**   You need the GetKernelObjectSecurity and SetKernelObjectSecurity calls to access these objects. All of these objects, even the access tokens, are actually kernel objects. As such, they also have their own security descriptor for protection purposes.

■ **Window stations, desktops, windows, and menus**   The GetUserObjectSecurity and SetUserObjectSecurity calls allow you to access these objects. A *window station* is a combination of keyboard, mouse, and screen—the hardware you use to access the system. *Desktops* contain *windows* and *menus*—the display elements you can see onscreen. These four objects inherit rights from each other in the order shown. In other words, a desktop will inherit the rights of the window station.

■ **System registry keys**   This object type requires use of the RegGetKeySecurity and RegSetKeySecurity calls. Notice that these two calls start with Reg, just like all the other registry-specific calls that Windows supports.

▲ **Executable service objects**   The QueryServiceObjectSecurity and SetServiceObjectSecurity calls work with this object. For some strange reason, neither call appears with the other security calls in the Windows API help file. You'll need to know that these calls exist before you can find them. An executable service is a background task that Windows provides—such as the UPS monitoring function. You'll find the services that your system supports by double-clicking the Services applet in the Control Panel.

Once you do gain access to the object, you'll find that you can perform a variety of tasks using a generic set of API calls. For example, the GetSecurityDescriptorDACL call retrieves a copy of the DACL from any descriptor type. In other words, the descriptors for all of these objects follow roughly the same format—even though the lengths of most of the components will differ. One reason for the differences in size is that each object will contain a different number of ACEs. The SIDs are different sizes as well.

The next step in the process of either querying or modifying the contents of a security descriptor is to disassemble the components. For example, you could view the individual ACEs within a DACL or a SACL by using the GetACE API call. You could also use the owner and group SIDs for a variety of SID-related calls (we discussed these calls in the access tokens sections of the chapter). Suffice it to say that you could use a generic set of functions to manipulate the security descriptor once you obtain a specific procedure. In essence, any security descriptor access will always consist of the same three steps:

1. Get the descriptor.

2. Remove a specific component.

3. Modify the contents of that component.

To change the security descriptor, you reverse the process. In other words, you use a call like AddACE to add a new ACE to an ACL, then use SetSecurityDescriptorSACL to change SACL within a descriptor, and finally, save the descriptor itself using a call like SetFileSecurity (assuming that you want to modify a file object).

ACEING SECURITY IN WINDOWS   Once you start thinking about the way Windows evaluates the ACEs in the DACL, you'll probably discover a few potential problem areas— problems that the Windows utilities take care of automatically, but that you'll need to program around in your application to derive the same result. (The SACL has the same potential problem, but it only affects auditing, so the effect is less severe from the standpoint of system security.)

Windows evaluates the ACEs in an ACL in the order in which they appear. At first, this might not seem like a very big deal. However, it could become a problem in some situations. For example, what if you want to revoke all of a user's rights in one area, but his or her list of ACEs includes membership in a group that allows access to that area? If you place the access-allowed ACE first in the list, the user would get access to the area—Windows stops searching the list as soon as it finds the first ACE that grants all the user's requested rights (or an ACE that denies one of the requested rights). Granted rights are cumulative. If one ACE grants the right to read a file and another the right to write to it, and the user is asking for both read and write rights, Windows will view the two ACEs as granting the requested rights.

TIP: Remember that Windows will stop reading the ACEs once it has satisfied a user request for access. Always place all your access-denied ACEs in the list first to prevent any potential breach in security.

You also need to exercise care in the ordering of group SIDs. Rights that a user acquires from different groups that he or she belongs to are cumulative. This means a user who's part of two groups, one that has access to a file and another that doesn't, will have access to the file if the group granting the right appears first on the list.

Obviously, you could spend all your time trying to figure out the best arrangement of groups. As the number of groups and individual rights that a user possesses increases, the potential for an unintended security breach does as well. That's why it's important to create groups carefully and limit a user's individual rights.

OTHER SECURITY CONCERNS   There are two other concerns when you look at security under Windows 95/98 or Windows 2000: data protection and server protection. The first deals with a client's ability to access data he or she isn't supposed to when accessing data through a server. (I'm not talking about a file server here, but some type of DDE or other application server.) Think about it this way: What if a client didn't have rights to a specific type of data, but accessed the data through a DDE call to a server that did have the required rights? How could the server protect itself from being an unwilling accomplice to a security breach?

Windows provides several API calls that allow a server to impersonate a client. In essence, the calls allow a server to assume the security restrictions of the client in order to determine whether the client has sufficient rights to access a piece of data or a process. For example, a Word for Windows user might require access to an Excel data file. The user could gain access to that file using DDE. In this case, the server would need to verify that the Word for Windows user has sufficient rights to access the file before it sends the requested data. A server might even find that the client has superior rights when he or she uses this technique. The bottom line is that the server's only concern is for the protection of the data, resources, and environment that it manages.

This set of API calls supports three different types of communication: DDE, named pipes, and RPCs. You need to use a different API call for each communication type. For example, to impersonate a DDE client, you'd use the DDEImpersonateClient call. There are some limitations to the level of impersonation support that Windows currently provides. For example, it doesn't currently support TCP/IP connections, so you'd have to resort to using other methods to verify that a user has the proper level of access rights in this case.

The other security concern is protecting the server itself. What prevents a user who calls Excel from Word for Windows from doing something with Excel that damages the server itself? Ensuring that security concerns are taken care of isn't difficult to do with files and other types of named structures, since the file server automatically attaches a security descriptor to these objects. (A DDE server like Excel wouldn't need to do anything, in this case, because the file is under the control of the file server.) However, many of the DDE or application server's private objects aren't named and require special protection. Windows also provides API calls to help a server protect itself. For example, the CreatePrivateObjectSecurity call allows the server to attach a security descriptor to any of its private objects—say, a thread or other process. The security descriptor would prevent anyone other than the server from accessing the private object.

How Role-Based Security Differs

So far we've looked at the traditional object-based security provided by Windows 2000. If you were creating a standard application, object-based security would be the end of the story. In fact, if you're developing components that will be used on Windows NT and Windows 2000, it's still the end of the story. Only when you're working with COM+ under Windows 2000 exclusively do you get the enhanced benefits of role-based security.

Let's take a more detailed look at this new Windows 2000 feature. The following sections will help you understand how role-based security fits into the COM+ component programming scenario. It's important to understand how role-based security will benefit you, so that's the first thing we'll talk about. Role-based security can be used in addition to or in lieu of authentication, which is the topic of the next section. Once you have some idea of what the requirements are for using role-based security, we'll take a look at the main interface that you need to know about, ISecurityCallContext.

Role-Based Security Advantages

While object-based security works fine, in many cases it also has some severe limitations that force a developer to either ignore security issues or perform a lot of hand coding. The most important limitation of object-based security is granularity. You set the security of the entire object, and a user's access to that object is based on an individual or group access token. Role-based security gets around the granularity problem to an extent by allowing you to set security at the method level. In addition to allowing you greater flexibility in setting how much access a user gets to a component, role-based security provides these benefits:

▼ **Configuration**   Normally, you'll use the Component Services administrative tools or scripts to configure the component to use role-based security. However, you can also set certain types of security as part of your component's initialization process. (Normally, you won't add any code to the component to allow the administrator full flexibility to create a security configuration that meets company needs.)

■ **No extra coding**   COM+ automatically takes care of all of the security details for you if you can get by with method-level security. In addition, you'll need to add the ISecurityCallContext interface to your component. Obviously, the reduced coding requirement also translates into a smaller design specification— there aren't any security requirements at either the interface or component design levels.

TIP: COM+ doesn't prevent you from adding code to your component to control role-based security, it only makes it possible to create the component without adding the code. If you add code to your component to enforce role-based security, the component is using programmatic security control. On the other hand, if you allow the administrator full control over security and don't add any code, then the component is using declarative security.

■ **Easier to understand**   Basing security on roles allows administrators to do a better job of configuring component security. You can still add groups or individual users to a role, the difference is one of perception. It's easier to assign a user or group access to individual methods within a component based on the tasks that the user or group is expected to perform.

■ **More flexible**   Unlike hard-coded security features, role-based security is configured outside of the component. This means that there are no coding changes required when the needs of the company change. Instead of changing component code (with the requisite debugging and testing), an administrator can make a change that will take just a few seconds to complete.

▲ **Detailed auditing**   We've already looked at the issue of auditing several times in this section of the chapter. The main reason you want good auditing capability is to ensure that you can track the activities of anyone who breaks into your system. Role-based security allows you to audit security at the method level, rather than the object level. This means that you get a better picture of exactly what a cracker was trying to do with a component and allows you to better assess what remedial action to take.

TIP: This chapter looks at role-based security from a theoretical perspective. In many cases, the administrator may not have any idea of how role-based security works or how it can affect component security, which means that you may need to provide instructions on how to configure the component you create. We'll look at the mechanics of working with role-based security when it comes time to install components on the server in Chapter 7.

Role-based security can also provide some protection that object-level security doesn't really cover. Normally, a user's credentials are checked at the application level. What this means is that the user is granted access one time. The resulting access token is used for all other resource access. In the world of monolithic applications, where a single server provides everything the user will need, this kind of security check is fine. However, what happens if the original application calls a component on one server, and then the component on that server needs the services of a second component on a second server? The user's access to the first server is verified as part of the application startup, but what about access to the second server? As you can see, there's a chance for a security breach between the two servers—another one of those security holes mentioned earlier in the chapter.

Windows 2000 offers something called a *security boundary*—you can force the security checks at either the process (application) or the component level. What this means is that you can reassess the user's credentials every time another component request is made. This ensures that no security breach between servers occurs. In addition to finer control of security, component-level access means that the current security information is included as part of the context information sent to your component during a call. In sum, when you enforce component-level security, the component can use security as one of the methods for determining how to answer a user request, making the component more flexible and better able to respond to changing network conditions. Of course, like everything else, there's no free lunch. The use of a component-level security check comes at the cost of reduced application efficiency and means that the user will spend more time waiting for the application. In addition, there's a small increase in network traffic as well, which may become a problem in networks that are already hard pressed for enough bandwidth to perform company-required tasks.

NOTE: COM+ library applications always use component-level security. You can't enable process-level security for library applications because they always rely on roles, which means checking security at the component level.

Dealing with Authentication and Roles

Authentication and role-based security aren't mutually exclusive. You can create components and install them in such a way that one or both methodologies are used to verify the user and the level of access they have to a component. However, it's important to understand that the verification process happens differently depending on how you configure the component. The following list is designed to help you understand how authentication and role-based security can work hand in hand:

▼ **Authentication Enabled and Role-Based Security Used**   Authentication occurs at the process level. Any users who can't be authenticated don't make it to the component level. Once at the component level, role-based security allows them to access zero or more methods within the component based on the role that the user has been assigned. If a user is authenticated to use the component, yet doesn't have a role assigned, the entire process still fails and the user request is rejected. This is the default COM+ security setup.

■ **Authentication Enabled and Role-Based Security Not Used**   A user is only authenticated at the process level, not at the component level. If the authentication succeeds, the user gains access to everything the component has to offer. This is the default setting for Windows NT 4.0. It's also the settings that any COM component that you migrate to Windows 2000 will use unless the administrator specifically sets role-based security or the developer adds role-based security to the component.

■ **Authentication Disabled and Role-Based Security Used**   Even though Windows 2000 still goes through the motions of authenticating the user, the authentication process is essentially short-circuited. The only user access verification taking place is through role-based security. You'd use this methodology when standard Windows 2000 authentication isn't flexible enough to account for the various roles that a user may fulfill or most of the component's resources are in the public domain. For example, you may want to allow everyone to perform lookups within your parts catalog database, but you may want to restrict access to edit and delete features.

▲ **Authentication Disabled and Role-Based Security Not Used**   This is the "I don't care" security setting. By disabling both security check levels, you're allowing everyone access to all resources that the component has to offer. In most cases, you'll only use this setting for components that are completely in the public domain. For example, you might use this setting for components that handle mundane tasks for your public Internet site. Obviously, such a component has to be rigorously tested for any security holes and you need to limit component access to network resources.

Understanding the ISecurityCallContext Interface

The ISecurityCallContext interface provides access to the security data for a particular component in a particular context. What this means to you as a developer is that you determine what role the current user is in and what their rights are. The fact that this interface is for a particular context means that you can only work with the request associated with this particular instance of the component. In addition, you won't be able to gain information about the component as a whole.

This interface is normally accessible to your COM+ component if the administrator enables role-based security, but you won't always need to use it. The only time you'll need to use it is when you decide to handle security within the component, rather than allow the administrator to handle security as part of the component's configuration. You'll get an E_NOINTERFACE error message if you attempt to obtain a pointer to the interface when role-based security is disabled, so it's pretty easy to figure out when you can use this interface within the component.

You'll normally use the ISecurityCallContext interface to find out specific kinds of information about the current component context. All of this information is contained in the security call context collection—essentially an array of information about the currently executing instance of your component. Here's a list of the information that you can obtain from the security call context collection:

▼   Number of callers

■   Minimum authentication level

■   Callers

■   Direct caller

▲   Original caller

In addition to the security call context collection information, the ISecurityCallContext interface allows you to determine if a caller or user is in a specific role. This is the kind of information you'd use to either grant or reject a request for access to specific methods within the component. You can also determine if role-based security is enabled for this component (versus being available on the server).

Now that you have a little better idea of what the ISecurityCallContext interface can do for you, let's look at the available methods. Table 3-3 provides a list of the methods that you'll use most often.

Method	Description
get_Count()	Returns the number of properties available in the security call context collection.
Get_Item()	Retrieves the value for a specific item within the security call context collection. Obviously, the item you specify must be within the range of available properties, so you should use get_Count first to determine how many properties are available.

Table 3-3.   ISecurityCallContext Method Summary

Method	Description
Get__NewEnum()	Obtains an iterator for the security call context collection.
IsCallerInRole()	Determines if the direct caller is in a specified role. This method won't list all of the roles that the caller is in; it merely allows you to determine if the caller is a member of the role you specify. You can use this method to determine whether a caller should have access to a specific method or resource within the component.
IsSecurityEnabled()	Determines if role-based security is enabled for this instance of the component. The method won't determine if role-based security is enabled for other instances of the component. You already know that role-based security is available on the server since any effort to obtain a pointer to the ISecurityCallContext interface will fail if the server doesn't support role-based security.
IsUserInRole()	Performs essentially the same task as IsCallerInRole, but for a specific user. The difference between the caller and a user is that the caller is the one currently using the component. The user call can refer to any user who has access to the server—not necessarily the user making the current call.

Table 3-3. ISecurityCallContext Method Summary *(continued)*

UNDERSTANDING COMPONENT LOAD BALANCING (CLB)

There's a problem with Microsoft's current component strategy—it's not very scalable to the needs of large corporations or large Internet loads. What if the application you create won't run on a single server for everyone in the company no matter how efficient you make it? For that matter, think about what would happen if your e-commerce site suddenly stopped running because of the load being placed on it by Christmas shoppers. This event has already happened to some companies. In short, components don't scale very well now to meet a wide load range or varying loads. At this point, you need to worry not only about tuning the application, but tuning the way it works across multiple servers. It turns out that the ability to scale is one of the major reasons to use COM+. Your application may really have to run across multiple machines, but using COM+ allows the user to think that their version of the application is always running on the same machine. The technology that I'm referring to is Component Load Balancing—the ability to assign users to the server most able to serve their component requests.

NOTE: CLB isn't included as part of Windows 2000, but it is an important part of COM+. Microsoft decided to remove this feature from the operating system and provide it as a separate product. This section of the chapter is based on the version of CLB that Microsoft originally provided with Windows 2000, and later provided as a separate download to beta testers. This is a theory-only section that will help you understand how CLB relates to COM+ as a whole. You shouldn't use this information to write applications—make sure you get the currently released version of CLB and use it as the basis for writing your applications.

The following sections are going to look at some of the issues you'll face when working with multiserver applications. The first section will deal with the goals that load balancing is trying to achieve. In the next section, we'll look at the theory behind the inner workings of load balancing. Finally, we'll look at an issue that many of us have had to deal with too often: downed servers. COM+ actually provides some techniques for getting around this problem.

Understanding Load-Balancing Goals

Enterprise applications have to service a lot of users that may or may not be within easy access of the server. The same application that allows a salesperson to take orders over the phone has to deal with salespersons on the road and even in different countries. In fact, with the emergence of the Internet, the salesperson may not even be human—it might be the software at the other end of a buyer's query. So, the first goal of load balancing is the ability to scale an application so that it can run on one or more servers equally well.

Salespersons on the road and users who make contact with your company over the Internet have one thing in common: They're both using a dial-in connection that could fail at any time. Recent articles in all of the trade presses have made it clear that companies need some type of fault tolerance for online applications. Some users are actually considering not using the Internet anymore because of poor service in the past, and you don't even want to think about the loss of a large sale because the salesperson couldn't get in touch with the company database. The second goal of load balancing is to create applications that can not only tolerate server failures, but can make those failures transparent to the client (as much as possible, at least).

Finally, the COM+ load-balancing strategy is designed to make it easier to work with complementary technologies. Obviously, Microsoft hasn't managed to take over the world yet, so it's important that the enterprise-level applications you create work with the products that other companies produce.

How Does Load Balancing Work?

In the past, a client would contact a server directly to access the contents of a database or to make a new database entry. There are two problems with this approach. The first problem is that the client needs to know a specific server name and, potentially, its location. Obviously, if you're running an application across multiple servers, this could present a problem to both the network administrator and the application programmer.

COM+ takes a different approach to the whole problem of access. Instead of accessing a server, the client accesses a router. The router then uses its knowledge of the available servers to connect the user to the server with the highest availability and the smallest processing load. The router receives constant feedback about server availability through a response time tracker, which makes it easier for the router to figure out which server to use. Obviously, since every client is accessing the same router, they don't need to know the location or name of the server that they're using. Everything takes places in a dynamic environment.

NOTE: As of this writing, a load-balancing setup contains one router and up to eight servers (called an application cluster). The combination of COM and MTS allows these machines to work together in such a way that the user gets the fastest possible response from the distributed application. Obviously, there are going to be applications that require more than eight servers and perhaps more than a single router for management purposes. Microsoft will likely expand the load-balancing capabilities of Windows 2000 sometime in the future.

Don't get the idea that load balancing will affect an entire application. You might have part of the application installed on the server, another part installed on the user machine, and still another part installed on a back-end server for database access. Load balancing takes place at the class level. You have to specifically mark a class as a candidate for load balancing, then install it on the server. When the client calls on the component containing the class, Windows 2000 will see that the class is supposed to be load balanced and handle it appropriately.

There are some hurdles you'll need to overcome when creating load-balanced COM+ classes. Since server resources are at a premium, you should use this technique for short-lived classes only. For example, a class that makes a database query passes the results back to the user, then destroys itself falls into this category. In addition, the class can't assume that it will be invoked on a specific machine. This means it can't rely on resources found on a specific machine (such as files). Clients will need to observe the short-lived state of the load-balanced class as well. In other words, the client portion of your application should create an instance of the object, use it, then release it as quickly as possible.

The load-balancing router actually contains two discrete services linked together through shared memory. The first is the Load Balancing Service, while the second is the Service Control Manager (SCM).

The Load Balancing Service contains a complete list of the load-balanced components in an in-memory database. The whole purpose of this service is to maintain the load-balancing router tables for the SCM. As the network administrator or developer installs or removes components, the changes get reflected in the load-balancing router tables.

When a client makes a DCOM call to the load-balancing router, it's the SCM that actually receives the request. The SCM looks up the component in the load-balancing router table, then makes a DCOM call to one of the servers in the application cluster to fulfill the request. The server in the application cluster creates an instance of the request object, then passes the proxy for it directly to the client. At this point, the server and the client are in direct communication—the router is no longer needed.

It's at this point that the Load Balancing Service comes back into play. It makes a request of the responding server to get response time statistics. These statistics get entered in the load-balancing router table, which will allow the router to choose the correct application cluster server to respond to the next component request.

Dealing with Downed Servers and Routers

The router is the primary handler of downed servers. Part of the information in the load-balancing router table marks a server as up or down. The router knows when a server has gone down because it no longer responds to statistic requests from the Load Balancing Service portion of the router. When this occurs, the server is marked as down in the load-balancing router table. The router will also assign another server to handle the requests that the down server was handling. In this way, the user isn't even aware that the server has gone down and another server has taken its place.

A downed router is the real problem in this scenario since it represents a single point of failure. You can configure the router as a Microsoft Cluster Server (MSCS) resource. In essence, you'd create a virtual machine composed of several servers, greatly reducing the probability that the router would go offline. It's unlikely that all of the servers in a cluster will go offline at the same time.

CHAPTER 4

An Overview of MTS

icrosoft originally marketed Microsoft Transaction Server (MTS) as a separate product, but today you'll find MTS as an integrated part of Windows 2000. More specifically, MTS is an essential part of COM+, which is really a combination of MTS and COM (with special additions like the new apartment type that we discussed in Chapter 2). In short, now you'll get all of the benefits of MTS alone or as part of COM+ within an integrated solution.

The original version of MTS was designed to ensure that database transactions were completed as anticipated. Transactions are important in database management systems (DBMS) because you want exactly one entry in the database when the user makes a corresponding entry at their workstation. Just as a missed entry would result in data loss, an extra entry would result in a corrupt database that delivers incorrect query results.

MTS is now used to ensure that more than just database transactions remain secure. As part of COM+, it ensures that data transfers of all types are safe and secure. In addition, MTS is now used to ensure the safe transmission of objects from one point to another, which means that not only is data more secure, but code as well. The addition of MTS to COM makes COM+ more reliable than many other component technologies on the market today because you can ensure that one, and only one, component event occurs in any given situation. Of course, there are always trade-offs when you increase the reliability of a product, as we'll see as the chapter progresses.

This chapter is designed to help you understand where MTS fits within the overall Windows 2000 scheme of things. We'll also look at the MTS-specific role within COM+. In addition to the theory of how MTS works, we'll look at some real-world issues like security and interoperability. In sum, when you finish this chapter, you should have a good overall view of MTS and a better idea of why COM+ is such an advance in component technology.

WHAT IS A TRANSACTION?

MTS is all about data and object protection and the services required for managing both data and object protection. It really won't do much more for you than that. However, considering the cost of failed data transmissions and the amount of work they can cause, getting data and objects from one point to another safely is essential. MTS uses secured transactions to accomplish its task. Management is accomplished through the use of the Component Services Microsoft Management Console (MMC) snap-in with Windows 2000. (We'll look at MMC usage issues for MTS in the "Working with the Component Services MMC Snap-In" section of Chapter 8.)

TIP: According to Microsoft's latest statistics, COM is running on 150 million systems worldwide, some of which have been using COM since it was introduced as OLE2 in 1991. These systems will greatly benefit from COM+ because this new methodology packages the various COM-related technologies together and makes them easier to work with. Even though all of the MSMQ, MTS, and COM+ material in this book was current at the time of writing, COM+ is a new technology that will mature as time passes. In short, you need to keep up with Microsoft's latest developments in order to make full use of this exciting new technology. You can find out more about COM+ by viewing Microsoft's COM+ Web site at http://www.microsoft.com/com/tech/complus.asp. One of the more interesting downloads at this site, as of this writing, is a presentation that was given at Tech-Ed 99 that contains Microsoft's vision for COM+ now and in the future. You can find out more about the MTS specific part of the COM+ picture at http://www.microsoft.com/com/tech/MTS.asp. You'll want to visit this site to get the latest SDKs and MTS-related white papers. Finally, if you need help with your MTS project, look at the MTS newsgroups starting with microsoft.public.microsoft.transaction.server. In most cases, these newsgroups can help you solve both usage and programming problems you might experience with MTS.

Using transactions is the short definition of MTS; it's time to look at MTS in a little more detail. The following sections describe various theoretical elements behind using MTS as a component deployment strategy. I've divided the discussion of transactions into two parts. The first part will look at transactions in a generic Windows 2000 way. It's important to understand that despite Microsoft's desire to create a cohesive package, MTS is both a separate technology and a part of COM+. You could, for example, use MTS to create and manage database transactions without relying on the features that COM provides. The second part will look at the MTS contribution to COM+. We'll explore the question of how MTS changes the way that COM works in order to create the more secure and reliable technology combination that Microsoft refers to as COM+. It's essential to understand the relationship between COM and MTS before we embark on the programming examples later in the book. (Obviously, we'll also look at how MSMQ fits into the picture in the next chapter.)

Understanding Transactions

The first question you need to answer is "What is a transaction?" There are a number of different definitions for this term floating around in the trade press, many of which are contradictory. Let's begin by looking at the one thing that most people agree on: A transaction is a way of packaging data and commands and then ensuring they reach their destination successfully. In other words, when you submit a form to the database and use a transaction to do it, you can be sure that either all of the data in the form will get added to the database or none of it will. In short, a transaction is insurance that your database (or other application) won't get erroneous data placed in it—even if it means losing the data for a single transaction (which is normally an entire record for database applications).

MTS is the Windows 2000 component that ensures the data or objects (MTS can encapsulate anything, not just data, within a transaction) you transfer from one machine to another will arrive in good shape and that they'll be fully executed. Execution may include a variety of things, even though most programmers look at transactions as being data oriented and used only within a database management context. A good way to remember what MTS transactions are all about is the acronym ACID. The following list provides an overview of what ACID is all about:

▼   Atomicity   All of the updates required to complete a transaction are grouped together. Either the entire package of updates succeeds and the change becomes durable, or the package fails and all of the updates are removed.

■ Consistency   The transaction is a correct change of the system state. It preserves the state invariants, which means that you won't get unexpected results from the transaction once complete.

■ Isolation   Concurrent transactions can't see each other and the results from one transaction won't affect other transactions running at the same time. Obviously, this is an extension of the principle of encapsulation for objects. Think of a transaction as a form for an object—all of the updates are encapsulated in such a way that the outside world can't see them.

▲ Durability   You could also term this bullet as "fault tolerance." A transaction should be able to survive some level of failure. These failures might include obvious problems like server system failures or unexpected problems like communication failures.

ACID describes MTS in its perfect state, which is what Microsoft would have you believe is always the case. However, there aren't any foolproof technologies for the PC; you have to plan on some level of failure even if you use transactions. It's at this point that some people differ on exactly what a transaction fault tolerance means. For the purposes of this book, a transaction also infers the capability to roll back the addition of data or the execution of commands until the transaction reaches a point of stability, the point at which the last set of operations completed successfully. In addition, the data must be in a known good state (i.e., no incomplete records or damaged entries). A transaction never completes until the receiver accepts the data or commands. The second that the data or commands are accepted, the transaction is complete and the transaction event is over.

Of course, transactions are complicated by a number of environmental factors. For example, in a client/server setup the number of failure points are relatively limited, but you still need to worry about LAN connections and all that such connections imply, as well as the reliability of the software itself. In the modern n-tier application world, a transaction may involve a number of clients and servers, any of which could fail. There are also more connection types to think about, some of which aren't under the originator's control. For example, a failure of a telephone connection could result just as easily from a loss of control by the long-distance supplier as it could the company employee or network administrator. Because of the number of intermediate processing points and communication methods involved in an n-tier application, MTS views transaction completion as the point at which the original request is completed. If the original request fails, then all intermediate transactions are rolled back. This means that all of the machines involved in the series of transactions required to answer an original request must maintain state information until that original request is completed.

Another environmental factor that complicates matters for today's programmer is the Internet. Consider the fact that this media is both unstable and prone to connection losses. In short, an Internet-enabled application needs to consider transactional failures that aren't caused by the application or any associated components, but by the Internet itself. A connection failure could still cause the transaction to fail even if all of the required application code works as anticipated. MTS helps application programmers handle this kind of failure by maintaining connection information for the programmer. In addition, the use of MSMQ can make the state of the connection a moot point, as we'll see in Chapter 5.

Some people also insist that transactions infer some type of data recovery. In other words, the receiver will notify the sender that the data or command wasn't accepted for whatever reason. While error recovery is a very important thing to have, especially when it comes to database managers, you'll find that some transaction methodologies won't allow for any form of recovery. If the data is lost, then it's gone. It's up to the sender to ensure that the data actually got added to the database or that the commands were executed on the server. Transactions under MTS do have a level of data recovery, although it's uncertain how robust that data recovery is and exactly what it'll protect. In most cases, you'll want to be sure that you include some type of data recovery mechanism within your application in addition to whatever Microsoft provides for you when it comes to critical data.

MTS and COM+

As of this writing, Microsoft would have you believe that MTS and COM+ are so closely tied as to make them impossible to understand apart from each other. Actually, it helps to look at the two technologies together, but as separate entities. In fact, if you want the clearest possible view of MTS and COM+ in a nutshell, COM+ is superset of MTS and standard COM combined. The following sections describe this view of MTS and COM+ in more detail.

Understanding the MTS and COM+ Goals

Microsoft has certain goals when it comes to both MTS and COM+. Until now, many programmers have avoided COM because they considered it too complex. Creating components is an error-prone and time-consuming process. The fact that there are so many different ways to create components just makes matters worse. For example, when working with Visual C++, you have a choice of using ATL (small components, with a long development time and problematic feature implementation) or MFC (fast development time, but the components rely on the MFC libraries, which are both large and unreliable). So, the first major goal of COM+ is to make components both easier to use and easier to create. MTS and MSQM allow developers to use a simplified programming model, although it still requires some finesse to create any component.

Critics have long complained that Windows NT (the predecessor of Windows 2000) doesn't scale very well. A lack of scalability means that you can have a server that works fine with a small load, but the capacity to do work diminishes quickly as load is applied in the form of additional tasks. The same criticism has been leveled at COM. As soon as you add the ability to service more than one request at a time, the complexity of the component increases almost exponentially. COM+ is designed to enhance application component scalability through the use of transactions, multiple servers, and load balancing.

Component technology as a whole is designed to reduce maintenance problems in several ways. The most important consideration for this chapter is that MTS makes it possible for a developer to create components that will make applications truly modular. The business logic that's incorporated within a component only gets tested once, instead of within every application. In addition, MTS allows you to enhance the security of the data that's being manipulated by the component, further reducing potential problems.

Finally, one of the main reasons to use MTS is to ensure that the components you create are always available. Placing the components on the server means that the user doesn't have to have a local copy of the component to get some work done. Loading the component on the server makes it available to everyone at the same time. In addition, bug fixes and updates are no longer a chore since only the server needs to be updated instead of every machine on the network.

Putting Components in Context

Part of the difference between COM and COM+ is the idea of "context." You can create a component that has no context at all (which is how most components that use MTA are created today), but that means you really don't have a good idea of how that component is being used by the client. The object exists and is being used by a client, but the operating system doesn't know much about the object except that it's using some resources. The inability of the operating system to assist with component management means that the developer must incorporate logic within the component to handle a wide variety of failure conditions, many of which are generic to all components. (We looked at part of the answer of how COM+ and Windows 2000 accomplish the task of providing the features of a MTA in a context-oriented environment in the discussion of the new TNA in the "Working with Apartments and Threads" section of Chapter 2.)

Placing the component within a context tells the operating system which services this component is going to require so that the operating system can balance the needs of all components within the system. In addition, the context adds attributes to the component that you'd normally need to hard-code during the programming process. Obviously, one of the major contexts for any component that needs to provide reliable data transfer is a transactional context that defines how transactions are handled given a certain set of default conditions.

At this point, you may be thinking that COM+ components require a lot of additional work to invoke the services that they require. However, the opposite is true. The context for the component defines what services the component will require. Interceptors, which are part of the operating system, will look at this context and set the required services up for the component when the client calls it. On return, the interceptors again look at the context and determine what kind of cleanup the component will require since it's finished using these services. In sum, COM+ uses an attribute-based programming model, which differs from the API-based programming model that was used by COM alone.

The portion of MTS that handles resource management is the Compensating Resource Manager (CRM). The CRM associates an action, abort logic, and complete logic with your component and sets the resources aside required to complete these tasks. For example, you might create a component that processes order forms. The action might be to accept the form from the client, look up the status of the requested items, and then return this status information to the client. As you can see, an action consists of one or more objects that execute on one or more servers on behalf of a single client. The abort logic might be to send an error message to the client instead of the order status, while the complete logic might be to place the order in the order database (pending client approval). In short, the component would always perform the same task, but you could independently change the result of the outcome of that task to meet changing company needs.

NOTE: You're currently locked into the context and interceptors that Microsoft provides as part of Windows 2000. The eventual goal is to allow the programmer to define both the context and which interceptors are used. This, in turn, will allow the programmer to define special services in addition to those normally provided by the operating system. Unless you're creating a third-party product, however, you probably won't need this kind of functionality for most applications.

Working with MTS and COM+ Services

Obviously, the goals that Microsoft has set for MTS and COM+ are going to be difficult to achieve without some type of infrastructure. Windows 2000 includes additional COM+-related services that allow you to create and deploy components quickly. Many of these new services are found within MTS and MSMQ (with MTS providing the lion's share of the new services). The result is that you'll spend more time working with the business logic for your application and less time worrying about mundane tasks associated with developing just about any component.

Even though Microsoft stresses the MTS and COM+ connection, there's actually a lot more to this technology than simple transactions. In fact, we'll look at the majority of these technologies somewhere within the book. Just to summarize what kind of technologies we're talking about, the following list provides an overview of all of the services that you'll find within COM+ 1.0:

▼ Server Components (MTS)

■ Transactions (MTS)

■ Security (MTS)

■ Administration (MTS)

■ Queued Components (MSMQ)

▲ Events

As you can see, at least half of the services that are associated with COM+ also have something to do with MTS. Microsoft has literally merged the COM and MTS development teams in order to produce COM+. So, what you're seeing in Windows 2000 is the work of both of these teams. This combination of development teams means that COM+ and MTS may eventually be indivisible, even though they're now two separate products working in a cooperative environment. Let's spend a little more time talking about the MTS-specific contributions to COM+.

Microsoft has worked hard to make writing servers easy. For the most part, writing a server is now like writing any other component. We'll talk about the particulars of writing servers in our first MTS programming example in Chapter 8.

The MTS portion of COM+ does offer transactional services, as mentioned earlier in the chapter. You can set the transactional attributes within the component itself, or as property values after you install it on the server. However, I didn't mention two important features that MTS provides.

The first new MTS feature is AutoComplete, which allows an operation to complete even if the connection is prematurely broken provided there's enough information to do so. AutoComplete can also be used if your client leaves the component normally and the component simply lacks the code required to complete the transaction itself. Normally, you'd have to provide a SetComplete() method within your component to perform this task.

The second new MTS feature is AutoAbort, which means that a transaction is automatically rolled back (or whatever other abort logic you've provided) the instant that the connection is lost. Again, you'd normally implement this logic within the component using the SetAbort() method.

NOTE: There are other contributions that MTS makes to COM+ in addition to these transaction-specific items that we'll cover as the chapter progresses. For example, you'll find that MTS actually helps with security concerns. We'll talk about this particular issue in the "Security Considerations" section of the chapter.

UNDERSTANDING THE TRANSACTION SEQUENCE

The entire idea of creating a transaction infers that there's some sequence of events that takes place in moving data or an object from one place to another when working with COM+. In other words, there's a process that occurs, rather than an isolated set of events as happened in the past. Sequences are a big advantage of using COM+ because they allow you to trace how something happened through the use of log entries. This section of the chapter is going to look at the issue of a transaction sequence in more detail. That actually means looking at two issues when you think about a COM environment. First, we'll need to look at the objects that MTS uses to manage the transaction sequence. Second, we'll need to look at the transaction sequence itself as implemented by the MTS objects.

An Overview of MTS Objects

Like any other COM technology, MTS relies on specific component interfaces. In the case of an object that deals with transactions, you'll need to implement the IObjectContext interface. The whole purpose of this interface is to tell MTS when a transaction has started, when it's completed, and what the results of the transaction are so that MTS knows what to do next. You can also accomplish these tasks using attributes as mentioned in the previous section, so even though you need to implement the IObjectContext interface, you don't have to call on it within your component's code if you don't want to.

The main purpose of many IObjectContext interface calls is to provide success information to MTS. There are actually four different IObjectContext methods that you can call to provide MTS with feedback on the level of success that a particular transaction has. In addition, there are three methods used to determine the current context status. The following list provides you with an overview of these methods:

▼ SetComplete()   The transaction completed as originally anticipated. MTS can mark the transaction as successfully completed. The IObjectContext object is automatically deactivated upon return to the method that first entered the transaction context.

■ SetAbort()   All or part of the transaction has failed. MTS will need to mark the transaction as a failure and roll back any updates that the component may have made. The IObjectContext object is automatically deactivated upon return to the method that first entered the transaction context.

■ EnableCommit()   The transaction isn't complete. However, all of the updates in the transaction have been successfully made, so MTS can commit them. Since the transaction isn't complete, the IObjectContext object remains active even if it returns to the method that first entered the transaction context.

■ DisableCommit()   The transaction isn't complete. In addition, some or all of the requested updates are still pending, incomplete, or failed. MTS can't commit the updates in their current form. Since the transaction isn't complete, the IObjectContext object remains active even if it returns to the method that first entered the transaction context.

■ IsCallerInRole()   Allows you to determine if the direct caller of your component is in a specified role. This method is really handy for determining how your component should react in a given situation. For example, you could determine whether the calling component is in a typical user or a manager role, then act accordingly when processing information.

■ IsInTransaction()   Determines if the calling component is executing within a transaction. You can use this method to determine how to process a request. In addition, it allows you to look for configuration errors. For example, an administrator might configure a component that really requires a transaction to work without one.

▲ IsSecurityEnabled()   Normally returns true unless the component is running in the client's process. MTS always uses security to run components. You can use this method to detect client-side component requests that aren't secure (and are therefore potential security breaches).

Defining the Transaction Events

At this point, you understand that MTS relies on the feedback provided by a single interface, IObjectContext, to monitor the state of a transaction. However, understanding the interface still doesn't explain the transaction sequence. There are events that occur during the transfer.

One of the problems with understanding how MTS works is that transactions are usually surrounded by quite a bit of code. The average programmer is going to find it difficult at times to figure out what the component author is doing when looking at a completed component. In most cases, a transaction consists of five well-defined steps that you'll always need to implement no matter how complex the rest of the component code is. Those steps are as follows:

1. Create an object context object.

2. Tell MTS that you're beginning the transaction by obtaining an object context using the GetObjectContext() method.

3. Perform any work required to complete the transaction. Track all of the updates that you make. Even if the component doesn't deal with a database, it'll have some type of data transformation work to do. For example, even a computational component will accept raw data as input and provide one or more results as output.

4. Compare the results that the component has obtained with the results that the component was supposed to provide.

5. Provide MTS with feedback. The SetComplete() method tells MTS that the transaction was a success. Part of an error-handling routine would be to tell MTS (using the SetAbort() method) that the transaction was a failure.

Remote Execution Considerations

Part of the problem of working with COM+ is that this is a technology designed to work with more than one machine. The sequence of events that we discussed in the previous section may not pertain to just one machine, which means we need to find a way to execute code from a remote location. One of the first things that seasoned COM programmers will note about using MTS and COM+ is that you can't choose a remote platform to execute your code on using the traditional COSERVERINFO data structure that's normally supplied to CoCreateInstanceEx(). The GetObjectContext() call doesn't provide an argument for accepting the COSERVERINFO data structure. So, the question is how MTS determines which remote host to use to service the call.

The answer is relatively simple and more flexible than what COM provides—MTS uses a Catalog Manager to determine the remote execution host. You can configure the catalog used by the catalog manager using either a configuration interface or within the component itself with the MTS catalog interfaces. In short, the programmer can leave the decision of where to execute a component to the administrator, who will configure the component using a standard methodology instead of a custom configuration program. We'll take a more in-depth look at the various catalog management features that Windows 2000 provides to the administrator as part of working with an example component in Chapter 8. For right now, all you really need to know is that there's a catalog and that it's configurable outside of the component environment, which makes COM+ much more flexible than COM.

Visual C++ programmers have access to a number of MTS catalog interfaces. The following list provides you with an overview of the interfaces you'll need to know about to perform both high- and low-level maintenance tasks with the component:

▼ ICatalog   Allows you to connect with specific servers and access the collections they contain. This interface also allows you to retrieve version information for the collection.

■ ICatalogObject   Provides access to a specific object and its properties. You can use this interface to change values. There are also methods for obtaining the object name and key values.

■ ICatalogCollection   Provides access to a collection of objects. There are methods for creating, deleting, modifying, and enumerating objects within the collection. You can also use the resulting object to access related collections.

■ IPackageUtil   Use this interface to import, export, or shut down a package within the Packages collection. Microsoft has replaced the term "package" with "COM+ Applications." If you compare MTS Explorer and the Component Services snap-in, you'll notice this change immediately. We'll discuss the exact nature of COM+ applications in the next section of the chapter.

■ IComponentUtil   Contains a set of methods for importing or installing a component into a collection. You can work with the component by GUID or by name.

■ IRemoteComponentUtil   Allows you to access components on a remote server by name or GUID.

▲ IRoleAssociationUtil   Use this interface to associate a role with a component. You can access the component by GUID or by name.

MTS Load-Balancing Concerns

Knowing that the transactions you create are secure, that the use of a catalog makes the configuration of transaction sequences relatively simple, and that the event sequence is clearly defined is a very good start to making COM+ a technology that's extremely reliable. However, it does little to answer the second concern about Microsoft technologies that we have discussed throughout the book—scalability. While the list of catalog interfaces is very impressive, it still may not answer the question of why you can't choose a specific server to work with your component. Another part of the COM+ equation is load balancing.

Load balancing is taken care of through a combination of a cluster of servers that contain the components you need and a router that determines which server is best able to meet the need given the current network demand and server load. Theoretically, all you should need to do is request services from a specific server and COM+ will automatically choose the best server out of a cluster to answer the request. Once the server is chosen, the router isn't even part of the picture. The load-balancing mechanism provides a direct connection between the client and the server running the component. In short, the need to access a specific server based on load is no longer a real need—all you really need is the ability to request services from a "generic" server and let COM+ do the rest. We'll cover load balancing in detail in Chapter 7. However, it's important to remember that load balancing also affects the ability of MTS to complete transactions in a reliable and timely manner.

UNDERSTANDING COM+ APPLICATION RELIABILITY

MTS components are usually loaded on the server as part of a COM+ application. (The term "COM+ application" replaces the term "package" that was used for MTS alone.) In other words, everything that both the client and server need in order to perform a specific transaction type is placed in one location for easy access. A user application can access one or more COM+ applications to provide a full range of services to the end user. When you look at the Component Services MMC snap-in, what you'll see are four levels of application hierarchy: COM+ application, component, interface, and method. We'll see how this works in the real world in the examples that follow in Chapter 8 and beyond. However, for now it's more important to consider a few packaging requirements that will help keep your transactions easy to manage and administer.

The first problem that you'll encounter when working with COM+ applications is how to maintain fault tolerance. By default, MTS places all of the components in a COM+ application in the same server process. The problem with this approach is that a failure by one component will affect all of the other components in the COM+ application. In short, a COM+ application may experience multiple transaction failures because one component experienced problems.

The obvious solution to this problem is to place all of the components in separate server processes. That way, a failure of one component won't necessarily affect the operation of any other component. However, the problem with this approach is that the speed of the transactions will slow because each transaction has to cross process boundaries and server resources will get wasted.

It helps to understand that a COM+ application helps keep all of the components required for a particular transaction type together. Applications may require more than one type of transaction to get the job done. As a result, one of the more efficient ways to handle fault tolerance is to group associated components into separate processes along transaction lines. That way, a failed component will affect only one of many possible transactions, allowing the application to partially succeed at least. This solution reduces the impact of using multiple processes on execution speed and incurs a minimal penalty on system resources as well.

The second potential problem is activation. There are three potential places to activate a component: the creator's process, another process on the same computer, and a process on a remote computer. The following list discusses all three activation points:

▼   *Creator's process*   The safest place to activate the component is in another process on the same computer. This approach does incur some performance penalties, but if the component fails, the main application might still recover from the failure.

■ *Another process on the same computer*   Activating the component within the creator's process is definitely the most efficient way to do things and ensures the highest possible performance (with an equally high risk). Another problem associated with using the creator's process for component activation is that you won't be able to make use of declarative security—an important MTS feature.

▲ *Process on a remote computer*   In most cases, you won't want to activate the component on another computer for several reasons. The most important reason is that MTS provides remote activation mechanisms using the Remote Computer and Remote Component folders in the MTS Explorer. Considering the likelihood of serious problems, never directly activate a component on another machine.

The final COM+ application design problem you need to consider is security isolation. Security is a major problem on any network. Maintaining security means being able to identify that the object requesting access to a resource actually has the required credentials to do so. Declarative security allows you to do just that. When you deploy a component in MTS Explorer, you assign it a security role. This security role gets mapped into Windows 2000 group and user security. In short, each component acts as a security checkpoint to ensure that the user requesting a specific service is allowed to do so. (Fortunately, the user doesn't have to keep entering his or her password during this process—the identity of the user is checked using their token. We'll discuss MTS security in more detail in the "Security Considerations" section of the chapter.)

COM/DCOM ISSUES

We haven't fully explored COM+ in this chapter—we've only explored one part of what this new technology is all about. However, considering the major role that MTS does play in COM+ as a whole, it's time to take a look at one issue that most developers are likely concerned about—backward compatibility. How will the changes that COM+ makes to the programming environment affect your investment in older COM and DCOM technologies? What will you need to change in your code to make COM+ a reality on your network, rather than just a new add-on that got bolted on to an existing system?

Part of the problem with COM and DCOM of old is that they weren't designed with today's computing environment in mind, and for a simple reason—that environment didn't yet exist and it's unlikely that anyone could have guessed that it would exist. The use of WANs and the Internet has significantly changed the face of computing. Users who work using laptop computers while on the road have added another element to the picture. Finally, the ability and need to work equally well from local and remote locations has changed the face of computing. It's no wonder, therefore, that COM and DCOM are unsuitable for many of today's programming tasks.

Another issue that affects COM alone is how it causes Windows to interact with components. For example, the COM+ method of resource management is to gain access to a resource, use it, and then release it right away. The reason that COM+ can take this approach is that it uses various forms of resource pooling. When dealing with a database, COM+ will pool the database connections, which means that the memory the database connections use never really gets released until the connection isn't needed anymore by any component. The COM method of working with resources is to gain access to the resource, then hold it until no longer needed. This means that every component currently executing has access to resources that it's not really using—those resources are in reserve in case the component needs to use them later. In short, COM is less efficient than COM+ in both speed and usage of system resources like memory.

MTS and COM together will double or even triple memory and processor cycle usage for a given component because a component will now allocate resources for the component itself and the transaction as well. On the other hand, transactional components under COM+ barely increase memory or processor cycle usage because of the effect of early release combined with resource pooling. However, don't get the idea that you're getting something for free. Yes, resource pooling and other COM+ features will make MTS more efficient overall, but these enhancements come at the price of a larger initial investment in both memory and processor cycles to build that resource pool and a loss of efficiency for background task performance when the server is idle.

DCOM intensifies the resource management problems of COM by increasing network traffic as well. Now you not only have local resource management, but the management of resources at a remote location as well to worry about. In short, DCOM makes a bad situation worse.

Hidden in this discussion of problems with both COM and DCOM when compared to COM+ in a transaction environment are potential problems with legacy code. The component you own today will likely require some new code to work well with COM+. Just the differences in resource management will force some coding changes. Add to these changes the differences in how transactions are managed and you begin to understand that while the basic theory behind components hasn't changed, some implementation details have.

TRANSACTIONS AND DATABASES

As stated earlier in the chapter, Microsoft's original purpose for creating MTS was to make databases more reliable. Anyone who's spent much time working with databases realizes that not all database management systems (DBMSs) are created equal. Access certainly isn't the same type of DBMS as SQL Server is—they're used for different purposes. The following sections of the chapter will help you better understand how MTS handles transactions when it comes to database management.

TIP: Microsoft Management Queue (MSMQ) supports transactional messages. What this means to the developer of COM+ applications is that you can now create database applications that support transactions even if the client doesn't have a permanent connection to the server. In short, the client application always appears to have a connection to the server, even when the user is on the road. All of the database updates occur automatically and in the background when the user reconnects the client machine to the network. So, not only does COM+ provide better reliability and resource management than COM alone, you also gain access to a new class of application that frees the user from the fetters of required network connections.

Handling Database Diversity

MTS attempts to mitigate many of the differences between DBMSs by providing database support through open database connectivity (ODBC). What this means to you as a developer is that there are actually two classes of database support in MTS: ODBC-compliant and other. The ODBC-compliant databases will provide a relatively similar level of support. The other category includes direct support for products like IBM DB2 and Oracle. You need to perform tasks associated with these two DBMSs in special ways. We won't discuss DBMSs that don't support ODBC in this chapter since I'd probably need an entire book to tell you about them on a case-by-case basis. Table 4-1 tells you about various popular DBMS and the level of support they provide.

MTS Database Features

So, what does MTS do for ODBC-compliant databases other than the obvious data security element? The following list provides you with some ideas, although this list isn't necessarily complete:

▼ *Database connection pooling* The reason for using database connection pooling is efficiency. Using connections from a preallocated pool reduces the time required to create the connection because the resources required for the connection are already allocated. When an application makes a database connection request, a preallocated connection is used from the pool. Likewise, when the database connection is severed, the connection is returned to the pool.

■ *Automatic transaction enlistment* Reduced coding is the reason that this feature is so great. Normally, when you want to create a transactional connection to a database, you have to enlist the connection into the application's current transaction. MTS takes care of this matter for you automatically, which reduces the amount of code required to create the application and the chance of error.

DBMS Name	Level of Support	Notes and Comments
Computer Associates (CA) Ingres II	Future	As of this writing, CA had not yet released their new Unicenter TNG product that would allow full MTS support. You can read about the intended level of support and get company contact information at http://www.cai.com/press/97may/option.htm.
IBM DB2	Full	You'll need to install version 2.0 or above to get full support. However, you'll also need to install DB2 Connect Enterprise Edition version 5 or above. There are other restrictions you need to know about, many of which are discussed at http://www.software.ibm.com/data/db2/db2tech/db2mts.htm.
Informix	New	As of this writing, Informix is working on a beta ODBC driver for their database that will allow full MTS support. You can read an announcement about the intended level of support at http://www.informix.com/informix/press/1999/msftcom.htm.
Lotus Notes	None	This vendor has made no plans to support MTS as of this writing.
Microsoft Access	Partial	This product doesn't support distributed transactions and there are no plans to support them in the future. The main reason for a lack of support is that this DBMS doesn't externalize distributed transactions.

Table 4-1. Levels of MTS Support in Various DBMS

DBMS Name	Level of Support	Notes and Comments
Microsoft FoxPro	Partial	This product doesn't support distributed transactions and there are no plans to support them in the future. The main reason for a lack of support is that this DBMS doesn't externalize distributed transactions.
Microsoft SQL Server	Full	You'll need to install SQL Server version 6.5 or above to get full support.
Oracle	Full	You'll need to install version 7.3.3 or above to get full support. However, there are restrictions in the types of data you can access. In addition, you'll need to use a special ODBC driver for database access. There are other restrictions you should read about on the Microsoft Web site or as part of your MSDN subscription.
Oracle RDB	None	This vendor has made no plans to support MTS as of this writing.
StarQuest StarSQL Pro	Partial	This product doesn't support distributed transactions. It does, however, support access to a wide variety of mainframe DBMS, including many of those supported by DB2. You can find out more about this product at http://www.starquest.com/.
Sybase PowerBuilder	Future	PowerBuilder version 7 is supposed to support MTS. You can find out more about this product at http://www.sybase.com/.
Tandem NonStop SQL	Future	A future version of NonStop SQL will offer full MTS support. You can find out more about this product at http://www.tandem.com/.

Table 4-1. Levels of MTS Support in Various DBMS *(continued)*

■ *Transparent database access*   One of the benefits of using MTS is that you gain transparent access to databases on a number of platforms, including Windows NT/2000, UNIX, IBM AS/400, IBM MVS, and Tandem. Microsoft is also working on other platform support, as shown in Table 4-1. MTS makes it possible to transparently access database resources on a wide range of platforms through the use of an ODBC DSN, which specifies the name and location of the database.

▲ *Distributed transactions*   The ability to create a transaction that spans servers, platform types, and even DBMS product is essential in today's programming environment. MTS allows the programmer to create a single atomic transaction. All of the changes required to update the database are either made or rolled back. It doesn't matter where those changes are located or why the transaction failed. What this means to you, as a programmer, is that you can create complex enterprise-wide transactions that ensure the entire company's database resource is kept up-to-date. A change that appears in one location within the company is guaranteed to appear in all other locations if you make these changes using a single transaction.

Database Programming with MTS

MTS doesn't require you to jump through hoops to create an application. Microsoft provides the means to use most of their existing technologies with MTS without any coding restrictions, including ADO, RDO, ODBC, and DAO version 3.5 and above with ODBC Direct installed. You can also use the MFC ODBC classes. However, in this case, there's a restriction that you must observe. The code you create must use the CDatabase::OpenEx() method in place of Open(). In addition, the database connection must have the noOdbcDialog option set. The reason you can't use DAO by itself is that Access (or any other DBMS) will display a dialog box at the server asking the user for additional information if the provided ODBC connection data is incomplete or incorrect. Displaying a dialog box could cause the application to appear to hang if it gets displayed at an unattended server or if it doesn't have desktop access. In short, MTS and dialog boxes asking for additional information won't work together simply because there may not be anyone to fill the dialog box in and click OK.

There's one other topic that programmers needs to know about when it comes to working with MTS. Depending on the size of your application, you may want to monitor performance and other statistics to ensure that the application is working as expected. Unfortunately, there isn't any easy way to monitor the performance of MTS within an application without the complex programming required to implement MTS Event Sinks. To implement these sinks, you must have the MTS SDK. So, if statistics are going to be an important part of your application, you'll need to add the MTS SDK to your list of things to get. However, this deficiency points out another problem that you'll face using this technology—MTS is still a new and untested environment. As the book progresses, we'll look at examples of how to put together MTS applications. Whenever possible, we'll look at potential problem areas and the requirements for additional programming tools. In sum, make sure you take the time to fully plan your application out with the extra requirements that MTS incurs in mind.

ODBC drivers don't automatically support MTS. There are several criteria that these drivers must meet before they're considered compliant. One of the more important criteria is that the ODBC driver must be thread safe and not require thread affinity. The reason for these two requirements is that MTS allows access of the ODBC drivers by more than one client at a time, which means that from a COM perspective, the ODBC driver is executing within an MTA (as describe in the "Apartment Types and Assignments" section of Chapter 2). Needless to say, the ODBC driver will also need to run on Windows 9x or Windows NT/2000 so that it can be accessed by MTS running on the same machine. This is all that's required for a DBMS that doesn't support transactions. If the DBMS also supports transactions, then the ODBC driver must provide support for the SQLSetConnectionAttr (SQL_ATTR_ENLIST_IN_DTC) call so that the DBMS can be enlisted within the MTS transaction. In addition, the DBMS must support XA or OLE Transactions standard for transaction coordination purposes.

> **TIP:** Microsoft is doing a great deal of work to ensure that vendors will support MTS with future releases of their products. In many cases, this support includes obvious aids like technical briefings and free MTS prerelease versions. Vendors can also ask for assistance from the MTS development team, get their product tested using a standard test suite, and use the MTS SDK to reduce the amount of coding required to create items like the resource dispenser or ODBC driver.

There are a lot of databases that don't support ODBC. At least two of those databases, Oracle and DB2, provide MTS support. The burden on the vendor for such support is much greater because all of the support code has to be included within the DBMS itself. MTS requires non-ODBC DBMSs to include four pieces of COM support before it can interact with them. Three of these requirements affect the DBMS resource dispenser, while the fourth requirement is to support either the XA or OLE Transactions standard for transaction coordination. Resource dispenser requirements include database connection pooling, which makes the resource dispenser more efficient at handling connections. The resource dispenser must be thread safe and not require thread affinity. Finally, the resource dispenser should automatically enlist the database connection in the component's current database transaction. As you can see, this list nearly matches the list of MTS features we talked about earlier in this section.

> **NOTE:** We discussed the topic of resource dispensers in depth in the "Understanding Resource Dispensers" section of Chapter 2. In short, a resource dispenser is a special component that manages resources like database connections for the DBMS. It also automatically enlists the Resource Manager to participate in the current transaction. However, you'll need a more complete understanding of how resource dispensers work before you'll fully understand why the resource dispenser is such an important part of the MTS transaction mechanism.

MTS and COM+

One of the things that differentiates a COM+ transaction from standard MTS is the way that the transaction is handled. Before COM+, any component that was marked transactional automatically initiated a transaction when accessed. COM+ only creates a transaction when the component actually performs a task that requires transaction support, such as opening a database connection or requesting data from another component that also supports transactions. If the component never does anything that requires a transaction, then COM+ will never create a transaction.

What this means is that COM+ allows the server to use resources more efficiently. The most important efficiency boost is to restrict transaction support to only those situations when you actually need it. In addition to saving processing cycles used to support the transaction, reducing transaction support time also reduces memory costs and network traffic. Overall, you should see a fairly significant boost when using COM+ to service database-oriented MTS transactions.

NOTE: Some types of MTS component access never result in a transaction, even if the component is marked transactional. These kinds of access include using the QueryInterface(), AddRef(), Release(), IDispatch::GetIdsOfNames(), and ISupportErrorInfo() methods. In short, even when using standard COM, your code needs to perform some type of transaction-related task before MTS will create a transaction.

SECURITY CONSIDERATIONS

Security is a major problem for just about every area of computing today. It's important to protect your data at all times and at every point of processing. There are two levels of security to consider when it comes to MTS. We looked at the first level of security in the "Understanding Standard Windows Security" section of Chapter 3. It's important to understand that the security you grew to understand when working with Windows NT is still there in Windows 2000. Of course, the security provided by Windows NT in the past isn't really up to performing all of the tasks that Windows 2000 is performing today. One of the areas where the old method of handling security falls short is MTS. Remote, transaction-oriented communications require security that's more robust than what Windows provided in the past.

TIP: Windows 2000 provides a completely different management interface, new tools, and new security features. It pays to spend time working with these new capabilities to see how they affect the execution of a component. Unfortunate as it may seem, while all of these new features are designed to make the MTS environment more secure, a lack of understanding of how they work may actually open breaches in security that a cracker could use to infiltrate your company. In short, practicing with all of these new features is just as essential as understanding the theory behind how they work. As a developer, you'll need to understand how interface issues will affect the way you design and implement new COM+ components.

MTS lets you to create a secure environment, yet reduces the complexity of doing so by using the same technologies used to implement security in other areas of Windows. The following list outlines some of the ways that Windows 2000 makes working with transactions in COM+ much more secure:

▼ *Role-based security*   Microsoft is using a role-based security model to augment the security capabilities that Windows provided in the past. What this means is that you assign a user to one or more roles that profile his or her rights to the component. For example, a typical user role might have one set of rights to the component, while an administrator role would have other rights that might include those of the typical user.

■ *Method-level security*   Component security is also implemented at the method level now. This means that one method within a component can actually have a higher security setting than other methods associated with the same component.

■ *Context-oriented rights*   The rights assigned to a component flow with the context for the component. If you give a user a certain level of access to the component as a whole, then that access is provided at the method level as well unless you specifically assign the user a different set of rights at that level.

■ *Object flow rights*   Rights flow from one object to the next. This is an obvious addition since the user would require access to all of the components required to complete a particular transaction. Fortunately, you can override this default behavior to ensure that access to sensitive components is properly regulated.

▲ *New security management tool*   The final MTS contribution is administrative handling of components. In the past, the components would have been managed using some special-purpose utility. Microsoft has decided to use MMC for all administration in Windows 2000. You'll actually manage your components using a COM+ administrative snap-in for MMC named Component Services. This management tool is based on the MTS management tool used in the past. We'll look at this tool in Chapter 8 after we create a simple component that we'll use for the example purposes.

UNDERSTANDING MICROSOFT DISTRIBUTED TRANSACTION COORDINATOR (MS-DTC)

Transactions are about an all or nothing scenario. Either all of the changes to a database take place or none of them do. From a developer perspective, the transaction amounts to a series of events bundled together in a cohesive whole. However, from the COM perspective, a transaction isn't quite so simple. A transaction requires the coordinated efforts of one or more components to be complete. In the following sections, we'll look at some of the things that need to take place to ensure that transactions take place as anticipated.

MS-DTC in Operation

Think of a transaction in this way. You're buying a house. Not only must you sign the paperwork, but the selling party must sign all of the paperwork as well. An escrow officer verifies that both parties participating in the transaction duly sign each piece of paperwork. The transaction is complete when all parties complete the signing process and the escrow officer has verified that everything is correct.

Now let's apply this example to MTS. In the world of MTS transactions, one or more components, also known as Resource Managers, participate in a transaction overseen by the MS-DTC, which is also known as a Transaction Manager. MS-DTC ensures that all parties in a transaction agree that the transaction should take place. In addition, MS-DTC ensures that all participants in the transaction perform their required tasks. If any of the parties disagree about the transaction or the nature of the transaction, or fail to perform their specific duties in the transaction, then the transaction is invalid and the MS-DTC rolls the transaction back.

In the "An Overview of MTS Objects" section of the chapter, we talked about the mechanics of creating a transaction. When the transaction begins at the request of the initiating application, the MS-DTC creates an object that represents that transaction. The application then asks each Resource Manager involved in the transaction to perform some required work. When the work is complete, the application signifies that it either wants to complete the transaction or abort the transaction by calling the appropriate method of the transaction object.

At this point, MS-DTC gets involved with the transaction again. MTS performs what's known as a "two-phase commit." During the first phase, the MS-DTC queries all of the resource managers involved in the transaction and asks if they're ready to commit the data involved in the transaction. If all Resource Managers agree that they're ready to commit, then MS-DTC transmits a commit message to all Resource Managers. The Resource Managers are then asked if the data committed successfully. If the data did commit successfully, then the transaction is complete. MS-DTC will roll back the transaction if at any time any Resource Manager fails to respond favorably (or at all).

WEB LINK: There are other forms of transaction management from other vendors. MS-DTC isn't unique when it comes to either transaction management or performing a two-phase commit. The main difference between MS-DTC as it's implemented in Windows 2000 and by other vendors is that the Windows 2000 component is designed to work with a wide variety of data and object types in addition to databases. The International Standards Organization (ISO) has created a standard called Open Systems Interconnect-Transaction Processing Format and Protocol (OSI-TP FAP) that will allow Transaction Managers from different vendors to interoperate, which could theoretically extend the range of Transaction Managers. The standard numbers for this protocol include ISO/IEC 9804, 9805-1 and 10026-3. The problem is that this standard is fairly generic and doesn't extend beyond databases. As a result, you won't find support for OSI-TP within MS-DTC. You can find out more about ISO and order the documents associated with this standard at http://www.iso.ch/welcome.html.

The Distributed Part of MS-DTC

So far, we've looked at the transaction in a generic way. The discussion could have focused on a single computer or a whole group of computers working within a network environment. However, there are some things that need to take place in a network environment that you don't necessarily need to worry about when working with a single computer. For one thing, computers in a network are physically separate and could be running different operating systems (at the very least, different versions of Windows).

Each machine involved in a distributed transaction has its own local Transaction Manager that's part of MS-DTC. The local Transaction Manager takes care of all of the local transactions, but really can't be held responsible for network transactions. In fact, when more than one machine is involved in a transaction, all of the local Transaction Managers cooperate to ensure that the transaction completes as anticipated. In short, all of these local Transaction Managers form a single virtual MS-DTC.

When an application or Resource Manager makes a request for a transaction that involves another machine from the local Transaction Manager, the local Transaction Manager tags that request as an outgoing request. The receiving machine's Transaction Manager tags the request as an incoming request. The two Transaction Managers then form a relationship known as a commit tree, copies of which are stored on each machine involved in the transaction. Any Transaction Manager within the commit tree can abort an errant transaction. However, now there's an additional level of cooperation that must take place. Each Transaction Manager in the commit tree must be informed about the aborted transaction and respond to the abort request before any Resource Managers or applications are informed.

At this point, you can guess that there must be another element at play within MS-DTC and there is—the Global Commit Coordinator. There's one global commit coordinator that resides on the initiating machine. It's the object at the very root of the commit tree and ensures that all of the Transaction Managers stay in sync. The global commit coordinator's only task is to ensure that the outcome of a transaction is never in doubt. Either all of the Transaction Managers commit to a transaction or they all abort it.

CHAPTER 5

An Overview of MSMQ

L ike Microsoft Transaction Server (MTS), Microsoft Message Queue (MSMQ) is a new addition to Windows 2000. However, unlike MTS, MSMQ isn't officially a part of COM+. MSMQ is actually a separately maintained part of the operating system and you have the choice of installing it alone or in conjunction with COM+. In short, the first question we have to pursue in this chapter is why you should even care about MSMQ, especially when reading a book that's supposed to be about COM+.

While it's true that MSMQ is a separate product, there are many cases when you do need to care about the functionality it provides, even when working with COM+. In Chapter 4, we looked at several of these situations. For example, in the "Working with MTS and COM+ Services" section of that chapter, we talked about how MSMQ is required to provide queued component services for COM+. In the "Transactions and Databases" section of Chapter 4, we talked about how MSMQ is an integral part of the picture for database applications that support transactional data exchange. So, while MSMQ is at the periphery of COM+, for the COM+ developer it represents an essential technology—something you need to know about to create certain classes of applications.

We're going to cover a lot of ground in this chapter, including some information about how to use MSMQ on a stand-alone basis. The first section of the chapter is going to introduce you to MSMQ. We're going to look at some basics like how MSMQ works from a conceptual perspective. This overview will provide you with some idea of how MSMQ works internally and what it can do for your applications. We'll also cover four essential MSMQ features in depth: delivery guarantees, security, routing, and how MSMQ interacts with MTS.

In the next section of the chapter, we'll talk about the message queue types. There are queues for both the independent client and the server, and it pays to know how they're put together. We'll also talk about the various queue objects that you'll need to know about and how to create them. MSMQ is all about working with queued information, so this is a very important subject to know.

From a COM+ perspective, MSMQ allows one new capability that you won't be able to replicate in other ways—the disconnected application. The ability to create queued components is unique to MSMQ. The next section of the chapter will help you understand why MSMQ application queues are so important. We'll also talk about how the operation of these queues differs in connected and disconnected modes—yet appears to work the same to the user.

The next section of the chapter is where we'll finally start looking at some actual programming concerns, rather than pure theory. This is the section where we'll look at MSMQ from the server's perspective and talk about what you'll need to gain access to server features. We'll talk about the various COM objects that work with MSMQ, as well error handling and other development considerations.

At this point in the chapter, you should have a good idea on how MSMQ itself works, but there's another part of the picture that we need to discuss in detail: The MSMQ Information Service (MQIS) database. The next section of the chapter does just that. (MSMQ 1.0 uses MQIS, while MSMQ 2.0 uses Active Directory for storing configuration data, but the principles are the same, so we'll cover both versions of the product together.) We'll begin with an overview of what the MQIS database is all about, then move into how MSMQ and SQL Server work together to store your application's data. You'll also learn some usage details like installation requirements, sizing, and hosting. Finally, we'll look at how MSMQ version 1.0 compares with the 2.0 version. Much of the Microsoft documentation still refers to the 1.0 version, and it's important to understand the differences between the two versions so that you know how to interpret any additional documentation you need to work with MSMQ.

Performance and other potential problems is the subject of the last section of the chapter. I'm not going to paint a gloomy picture of MSMQ, but I do feel that it's important for you to understand that there are limitations to this technology. MSMQ should be a new tool in a toolbox filled with programmer tools, not the only tool you own.

WEB LINK: It's possible that not all of you will use Visual C++ to access MSMQ. While I won't be covering other compilers in the book (please see the "What You'll Need" *section in the Introduction to this book for details), some of you will probably want to use other development products with MSMQ. Fortunately, Microsoft provides help for users of other C++ language products at http://support. microsoft.com/support/kb/articles/Q191/5/34.ASP.*

AN OVERVIEW OF ASYNCHRONOUS COMMUNICATION FOR MSMQ

In Chapter 4, we spent a lot of time talking about DCOM and how it works. In some ways, MSMQ works similar to DCOM. What you're doing is creating a connection between a client and a server for the purpose of information exchange. However, instead of creating a direct connection using a network protocol like DCOM does, MSMQ uses queues as an intermediary destination for the data that flows between the client and server. These queues are used to hold messages, which is the method that MSMQ uses in place of the packets normally used by networks to transfer data.

WEB LINK: There are a number of good places to look for information about MSMQ on the Internet. One of the main sources of detailed programmer-specific information is the MSDN Web site at http://msdn.microsoft.com/library/sdkdoc/msmq/msmq_overview_4ilh.htm. You'll more than likely need to register for this Web site before you're granted access the first time, but there isn't any cost for using it.

The advantage to using the message as a basis for transferring information is that the client and server don't need to exist at the same time. In other words, a user can open their application without checking for server availability first and they won't even notice if the server is available once the application is open. A salesperson could record an order now, then allow MSMQ to automatically upload it to the server later without modifying the methods that he or she would normally use. MSMQ makes the delivery in the background without any interaction on the part of the user. The orders that the salesperson creates while the connection to the server is severed are stored in a local queue as messages. Each message will normally represent a single order's data, although there really isn't a limit on how you can format the messages. A message could hold more than one message or only part of a large order.

The disadvantage of using messages as the basis for data transfer is that there's some additional overhead. Obviously, there are more layers of processing now, which means that direct connect scenarios actually run a bit slower. In addition, there's a little additional coding and setup time for the developer when using MSMQ. However, the advantages far outweigh the disadvantages, as we'll see as the chapter progresses.

TIP: The easiest way to figure out if you should use MSMQ for a particular situation is to consider convenience over processing horsepower. Using MSMQ means trading some of the processing capability of your server for some convenience in entering data. Put another way, you need to ask yourself whether management is more inclined to spend money on another server or if they'd rather spend that money on training. MSMQ makes it possible to create applications that always work the same; it doesn't matter where the user is or even if they're connected to the network. Applications that work one way are easier to use and therefore reduce training costs.

Now that you have a better idea what MSMQ is all about from a very generic perspective, let's look at it in more detail. The following sections are going to talk about various architectural aspects of MSMQ. We'll begin by looking at how messages work. This first section will answer the question of how a message gets from the client to the server. In the next section of the chapter, we'll talk about the types of disk activity you can expect when using MSMQ from a general perspective. The whole purpose of this section is to explore the three physical MSMQ elements: message store, recovery data, and transaction logs. The next section will take a very brief look at the idea of delivery guarantees. A technology that can't guarantee delivery of the data that it's responsible for transferring isn't very useful. This section will look at what you can expect from MSMQ when it comes to delivering messages. A third section will look at data security, which is an important consideration in today's computing environment. It seems that I read about yet another virus every day in the various trade press subscriptions that I own. Finally, we'll take a little deeper look into the relationship between MSMQ and MTS. In this last section, we'll answer the question of how MSMQ and MTS can work together to guarantee delivery of messages.

Routing

So how does a messaging application differ from DCOM? The data is most likely the same, which means that your business logic will be the same. However, the delivery method is different. We're now using the idea of messages to transfer data and a queue to hold those messages (a queue is a sort of a mailbox for messages). As a minimum, there's a queue on the server that holds all of the messages that the server components will process. Each active component on the server has a separate queue. These components will pick messages up from their queue whenever processing on the current message is complete.

In addition to the server queue, some clients will have another queue for local message processing. The local queue gets emptied into the server queue anytime there's a connection between the client and the server. In short, messages can be viewed as the packets that would normally get carried between client and server on a network. Obviously, this is a simplification of a more complex process, but it does help to start out with this perspective of the functioning of MSMQ and the messages that it uses.

The obvious advantage for using MSMQ in place of DCOM is the ability to perform disconnected application handling. The local client queue allows the client to continue processing information even when there's no direct connection to the server for handling the messages. (You'll need to configure the client for independent use.) Using a local client queue allows the user to continue working as if the connection existed and without performing any special procedures to transfer the resulting messages from the client to the server when a connection is made. MSMQ handles all of the message transfers in the background without the user's knowledge. Figure 5-1 shows the relationship between the client and the server, and the kinds of queue setups that you can expect.

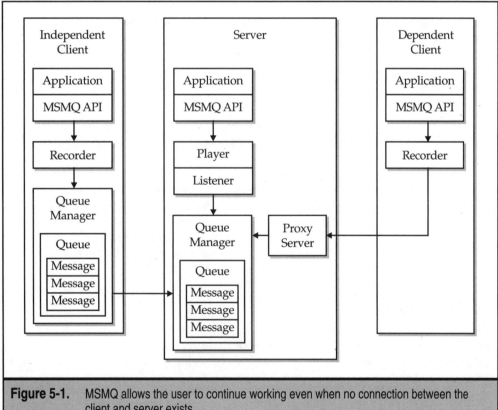

Figure 5-1.   MSMQ allows the user to continue working even when no connection between the client and server exists

Notice that there are actually two client types: dependent and independent. The main difference between the two is that the independent client also provides its own queue, while the dependent client relies on a direct connection to the server. Obviously, you can't use a dependent client setup for a laptop computer that you intend to use on the road because the dependent client lacks a queue. However, a dependent client setup will work for a desktop machine that's located in the same building as a server or on a WAN with a reliable connection. Using a dependent client setup reduces the disk requirements for using MSMQ and can result in a slight performance boost because the messages are only placed in one queue rather than two.

There are three elements required for establishing and maintaining a message flow between the client and server: recorder, listener, and player. The recorder takes the client output, creates messages, then places those messages in either the local message or sends them to a proxy server on the server. MSMQ takes the message that the client creates and places it in the server's queue. When the listener sees a message in the server's queue, it removes the message and gives it to the player. Finally, the player takes the message and turns it into data for the server. You can look at this process as the same one that goes on with an answering machine in your home. When someone calls and finds that you're not home, they leave a message by talking to the answering machine instead of you directly. The answering machine stores the message using any number of methods. When you get home, an indicator on the answering machine tells you that you have one or more messages. Pressing a button on the answering machine normally plays the messages back for you, allowing you to determine who has called in your absence. As you can see, the idea of disconnected communication isn't new. MSMQ represents a new implementation of an existing idea.

TIP: Some programming purists may take exception with the example I've used in this section to show how MSMQ works. However, from a modeling perspective, this is how MSMQ works, even though the inner workings of this technology are much more complex. I find it very helpful to look at COM using real-world examples, like an answering machine, because such analogies make a difficult technology easier to understand. As Microsoft continues to increase the complexity of this technology, most programmers are going to need to find a way to relate COM back to the real world it's supposed to model. So, what would your analogy for MSMQ be? Taking the time now to relate the various COM+-related technologies we'll discuss in this book to real-world models that are easy to understand will save you considerable time later when it comes time to look at code.

Types of Disk Access

MSMQ is a relatively complex product for something that moves messages from one machine to another. Obviously, it's the content of these messages that makes the job that MSMQ performs so difficult. Security and other concerns all work together to increase the amount of disk traffic to transfer just one message. So, what forms of disk traffic will you see when using MSMQ? You can classify the data into three main categories. The following list provides a quick overview of disk access types:

▼ **Message store**   The messages moved from one point to another.

■ **Message recovery data**   The source data required to create another copy of a message should the original data transfer fail.

▲ **Transaction logs**   A list of the messages transferred between machines. The logs normally contain the information needed to track breaches of security and to assist in recovery of a message store should one of the servers fail.

If you have a relatively large setup, you can actually see a performance gain by placing each of these disk activities on a separate drive. You'll use the MSMQ Control Panel applet (the name of this applet may change to Message Queuing by the time you read this) or the MSMQ MMC snap-in to set the locations for these three types of disk activity. Here's what the Storage tab of the Message Queuing Properties dialog box (accessible through the MSMQ Control Panel applet) looks like.

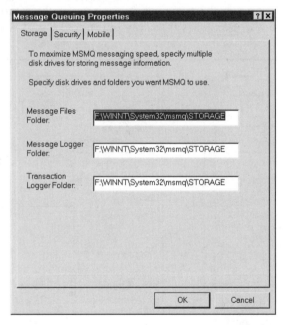

Don't confuse the storage of messages with the storage of MSMQ configuration information. The messages, recovery information, and log entries aren't stored within MQIS (MSMQ 1.0) or Active Directory (MSMQ 2.0). Messages will always appear on the local hard drive at the base location that you select. No matter which version of MSMQ you're using, the size of your message store is limited to 2GB. This isn't 2GB of messages—it's 2GB total, which includes any housekeeping data required to manage the message store. This 2GB total also includes memory-mapped files (which are automatically flushed to disk when marked transactional or as recoverable items—memory-mapped files marked as express aren't flushed to disk).

Delivery Guarantees

In Chapter 4, we talked extensively about transactions. There are actually two kinds of transactions you can create when working with MSMQ: internal and external. An external transaction requires the explicit cooperation of MTS, while an internal transaction relies on the native capabilities of MSMQ. In most cases, you're going to find that the internal transaction type is faster and has fewer limitations. This section of the chapter describes the internal transaction type. We'll look at external transactions in more detail in the MSMQ and MTS section of the chapter.

There are two kinds of internal transaction types to choose from. You can use the MQ_SINGLE_MESSAGE option to send a single message using a transaction with the MSMQMessage.Send() method. If you need to send more than one message using a transaction, then you'll want to begin by creating an MSMQTransaction object. Both of these queue types behave the same, so we can discuss them as a single entity.

It turns out that MSMQ applications use a minimum of three transactions for every data transmission, even if it appears that only one transaction takes place. Figure 5-2

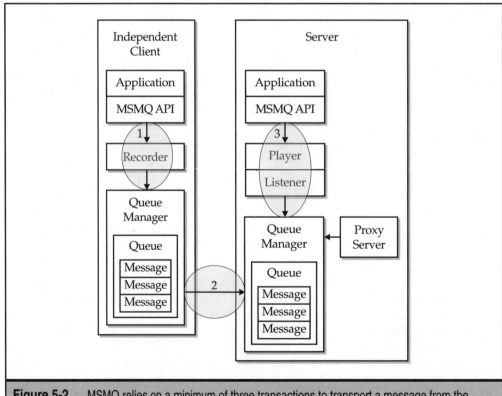

Figure 5-2.   MSMQ relies on a minimum of three transactions to transport a message from the client to the server

shows the three transactions when working with an independent client using an internal transaction. The first transaction occurs between the client application and the local queue. MSMQ creates a second transaction when it takes the message from the local queue and places it in the server queue. That's where the third transaction begins. As soon as the server removes a message from the queue, it creates a third transaction that tracks the message's progress on the server.

This three-transaction approach makes it a lot less likely that an update will fail due to communication problems, which, in turn, makes the application more reliable. In addition, since there's a special MSMQ transaction for delivering data from the client to the server, you can be sure that each message will get successfully transmitted only one time, but that it will get transmitted at least one time.

When working with MSMQ components, there are two ways to deliver your message: fast or reliable. The fast method (also known as express delivery mode) sends the message from machine to machine using memory alone, while the reliable method (either recoverable delivery mode or transactional delivery mode) flushes each message to disk before sending it on to the next machine. The main difference between fast and reliable is disk access. The disk access time may make the message delivery slower, but it also means that you can retrieve another copy of the message should it get lost between two computers or if a server failure occurs. MSMQ assumes that you want fast over reliable, so it normally uses the MQMSG_DELIVERY_EXPRESS option for your messages. If you want to use the slower, more reliable method, you'll want to use the MQMSG_DELIVERY_RECOVERABLE option instead.

Whether you use the fast or reliable message delivery methods, the kind of queue you use is also important. Internal transactions require transactional queues. You can't send a transactional message to a normal queue and vice versa. MSMQ always requires you to determine what kind of queue you want to create during the creation process as shown here.

All you need to do is check the Transactional option in the Queue Name dialog box to make the queue a transactional queue. Obviously, this means that you have to decide whether you want to use transactions during the initial setup of your project or face the possibility of re-creating the queues your application requires later.

Security

Security is a very touchy issue today for a number of reasons. For one thing, there are more threats to security today than ever before. However, that's not the only problem you need to worry about when it comes to security. A lack of knowledge on how various security strategies are implemented is another problem. Lack of standardization is yet another problem. The bottom line is that security is still more of an artistic pursuit and less of a scientific pursuit than it should be. The following sections of the chapter are going to help you understand how MSMQ handles a variety of security concerns.

An Overview of MSMQ Security

As with any other area of security on your server, MSMQ doesn't provide very much in the way of automatic controls. It's up to you to configure the level of security that you want MSMQ to have. MSMQ does provide message security (as we'll see later), but just how good that security is going to work depends a great deal on how you intend to use MSMQ and the sensitivity of the information transferred. As of this writing, MSMQ provides security in three essential ways, as listed here:

▼ **Security context**   MSMQ defaults to using the user's Windows NT/2000 security context for gaining access to the server. This means that the MSMQ component is limited to doing the same things that the user is limited to unless you specifically set the security otherwise. In short, this prevents the user from gaining unauthorized access to server resources using an MSMQ back door. Unfortunately, this can be a two-edged sword. You'll need to determine what risks you'll encounter giving the user enough rights to get the work done on the server that MSMQ has to do without giving them too many rights. In some cases, it might actually be better to set component security higher than what the user normally has to limit the user's direct access to the server.

■ **Security administration control**   As with the rest of Windows NT/2000, MSMQ uses access control lists (ACLs) to determine who has what rights to which objects. There are several ways to change the ACL for component or message objects, depending on how you administer the MSMQ setup. You can change the security information programmatically using the MQSetQueueSecurity() and MQGetQueueSecurity() functions. When working with MSMQ version 1.0, you also have access to security through MSMQ Explorer, which we won't look at in this book. Windows 2000 uses an MSMQ snap-in for MMC, which we'll use in this book for managing security.

▲   **Digital certificate use**   Messages can be encrypted using the digital certificate supported by both the client and server machine. Windows 2000 supports a wide variety of encryption technologies, the most standardized of which is Public Key Infrastructure (PKI), which relies on X.509 digital certificates. You can also use user or machine digital certificates generated locally or by a public provider like VeriSign to encrypt the messages. The two security context functions you'll work with when using MSMQ are MQGetSecurityContext() and MQFreeSecurityContext(). An application obtains the security context, which includes a digital certificate, as part of a PROPID_M_SECURITY_CONTEXT data structure. The MSMQ runtime automatically attaches this certificate to a message before sending it using the MQSendMessage() function.

NOTE: This section of the chapter has talked about various MSMQ functions in detail. There are also COM objects that you can use to perform the same tasks. We'll talk about these objects in "The Server View of Messaging" section of the chapter. For example, you'd use the MSMQMessage.AttachCurrentSecurityContext() method to attach a digital certificate to a message using the COM approach. It's a good idea to know both methods so that you have the flexibility of using whichever approach makes the most sense in your current situation.

Needless to say, these precautions don't help much if the application you build doesn't actually check for security. Windows 2000 validates requests to peek or access a queue against the queue ACL when the requesting application issues a MQOpenQueue() function call. The ability to send a message to a particular queue is validated at the target machine (the server).

NOTE: We talk more about how your data is secured throughout the rest of the chapter. This section looks at MSMQ security concerns in general. For example, there are some MQIS-specific concerns when it comes to certificates that MSMQ version 2.0 doesn't need to worry about. The "MSMQ 1.0 versus MSMQ 2.0" section of the chapter addresses this concern in more detail. Notes also appear throughout the chapter that address specific component requirements and the needs of MQIS itself. Security is a complex topic, so make sure you spend some time learning about it both in general and how it affects certain aspects of MSMQ in detail.

Obviously, MSMQ objects are also secured at three levels: site, machine, and the queue itself. Security is checked for both GetProperty and SetProperty access. However, the default setting of allowing anyone to get properties may not be suitable for your application, so you need to ensure that you set at least this level of security as part of application installation. In addition, the default set property access of only the queue creator may be too restrictive, depending on how your application is configured. You may need to allow special access by the application or by the user. In short, while there are security features available for MSMQ, it's up to you to ensure that they're properly configured.

Understanding Message Security Over a Network Connection

No matter how well you protect access to the components used to implement MSMQ and the directories that contain MSMQ data, there's still one link that could cause problems: the network connection between client and server. Securing components and directories doesn't do anything for the data itself. The data is still unencrypted and completely readable by anyone with the proper access. MSMQ plugs this hole in security by encrypting messages transferred between the client and server using a symmetric key. Using symmetric encryption means that the same key is used to encrypt and decrypt the data within the message. In short, the data encryption and decryption keys aren't unique to the individual machine or user.

The symmetric key has to be sent along with the message because each message uses a unique key, so MSMQ encrypts the symmetric key as well. In this case, a public key for the target machine (usually a digital certificate) is used to encrypt the symmetric key. The target machine must use its private key to unlock the symmetric-key encryption, so this part of the data encryption process is unique for a particular machine or user. Figure 5-3 shows the data encryption process in action.

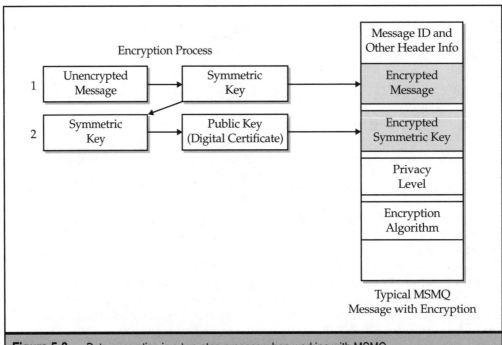

Figure 5-3. Data encryption is a two-step process when working with MSMQ

CAUTION: No matter how you encrypt the message body for transmission across the network, MSMQ retains a clear text copy of the message in the local queue until the queue is emptied. In other words, don't rely on message encryption alone to protect the messages on your server. You need to use a combination of message encryption, user and group rights, and directory security settings to ensure that MSMQ messages remain secure.

There are two key fields below the encrypted message and associated symmetric key. The first is the privacy level, which is specified using the PROPID_M_PRIV_LEVEL property value (stored in the MQMSGPROPS data structure). There are actually four privacy levels that you can associate with a message. If you don't specify a value within the PROPID_M_PRIV_LEVEL property value, then MSMQ assumes that you don't want to encrypt the message (a value of MQMSG_PRIV_LEVEL_NONE). The following table describes each privacy level and how it applies to the two versions of MSMQ that are currently available (Windows 2000 defaults to using MSMQ version 2.0).

Privacy Constant	MSMQ Version	Description
MQMSG_PRIV_LEVEL_BODY	1.0/2.0	40-bit encryption of the message body.
MQMSG_PRIV_LEVEL_BODY_BASE	2.0 only	40-bit encryption of the message body.
MQMSG_PRIV_LEVEL_BODY_ENHANCED	2.0 only	128-bit encryption of the message body.
MQMSG_PRIV_LEVEL_NONE	1.0/2.0	No message encryption takes place. The message is sent in clear text.

Of course, indicating that you want a message encrypted doesn't tell MSMQ how to encrypt it (what algorithm to use for the encryption process). To do that, you'll add an encryption algorithm property (PROPID_M_ENCRYPTION_ALG) to the MSMSGPROPS data structure. The default setting of CALG_RC2 performs block encryption of the message body, while a second value of CALG_RC4 performs stream encryption of the message body. When using block encryption, MSMQ breaks the message up into 64-bit blocks and performs the encryption on the resulting blocks.

TIP: There's a wealth of cryptographic algorithms to choose from when working with Windows 2000 including Secure Sockets Layer (SSL) level 3 encryption (CALG_SSL3_SHAMD5), RSA public-key signature algorithm (CALG_RSA_SIGN), and RSA public-key exchange algorithm (CALG_RSA_KEYX). MSMQ didn't support these other algorithms at the time of this writing, but it wouldn't be too surprising to find out that Microsoft added support for them by the time you read this. To ensure that your MSMQ messages get the best possible encryption, it pays to keep up-to-date with current Microsoft offerings in new encryption algorithms.

MSMQ also supports custom encryption for the message body. However, there are some very stringent limitations on custom encryption, such as not being able to send messages over the Internet. Normally, you won't have to worry about custom encryption anyway since MSMQ does provide access to 128-bit encryption. In short, the need for custom encryption would be for very sensitive data that might require more physical security than the Internet could provide. With this in mind, we won't spend any time talking about custom encryption techniques within the book.

Authentication Principles

Authentication, the process of ensuring that a message is from the person that you actually expect to receive a message from and that the message hasn't been tampered with, is a major tenet of any security scheme involving encryption. After all, how good is the encryption technique if you can't detect intrusions by outside parties? There are three forms of message tampering to consider: messages from outside parties masquerading as messages from a known entity, message content altering, and message content reading. In addition to these three forms of covert message tampering, there are also problems like message damage due to flaws in the transmission media to consider. In sum, you need to be able to verify the source and content of a message with 100-percent certainty all of the time or an encryption method is relatively worthless.

MSMQ uses a common technique of creating a hash value from message elements and then combining it with the target machine's private key (usually a digital certificate) to create a signed hash value. The signed hash value is then compared to the hash value of the sending machine's digital certificate. If the two values compare, then the message is authentic; otherwise, someone has either tampered with the message or the message was corrupted in some way during transmission. In either event, the contents of the message aren't trustworthy and the contents are ignored. The data that the message contained will have to be resent. The following list tells you about the message elements used to create the hash value:

▼ Correlation ID

■ Application specific data

■ Message body

■ Message label

■ Response queue

▲ Administration queue

A message that passes authentication isn't automatically placed in the queue, however. The sender's certificate and security identifier (SID) must appear within the target machine's MQIS (for MSMQ 1.0) or Active Directory entries (MSMQ 2.0). Only after this entire verification process completes to the target machine's satisfaction does the message move into the receiver's queue and become available for processing. While this may seem like a lot of work to verify a single message, consider the consequences of not making absolutely certain that a message is sent by a reliable source.

Authentication, like encryption, isn't a requirement for MSMQ. If you want to require message authentication, then the MQMSGPROPS data structure associated with the message must contain a PROPID_M_AUTH_LEVEL property value that's set to MQMSG_LEVEL_ALWAYS before authentication will take place. In addition to setting the message properties correctly, the sender of the message must have a certificate registered with MSMQ. The certificate is used as part of the authentication process. Normally, the certificate is one that was issued to a specific user or machine. However, there are also internal certificates available for the purpose of creating an authenticated message.

NOTE: There isn't any way to determine if a message inside a queue failed authentication. Either the message didn't request authentication, or it passed authentication. Messages that fail authentication aren't placed inside the queue—they're automatically rejected to ensure that no security violations of the queue take place. The only way to verify that a message passed authentication is to query the sender. If the sender requested authentication and the message appears in the receiver's queue, then the message passed authentication. You can check authentication requests by looking at the PROPID_M_AUTHENTICATED property value of the MQMSGPROPS data structure. This value must return MQMSG_AUTHENTICATION_REQUESTED (for MSMQ 1.0 applications, use a value of 1) to verify that the sending application requested authentication.

One of the precautions you need to take when writing an MSMQ application is to ensure that the sender and receiver of a message are designed to use the same level of authentication. If you set the receiving queue to require authentication, yet the sender is set to not require authentication, then the message will be rejected by the receiving queue. Both the sender and receiver must be set to either require or not require authentication before message authentication will work properly. Remember, configuring the receiving queue to require authentication doesn't automatically force the sender to add authentication to the message.

MSMQ and MTS

As previously mentioned, MSMQ and MTS can work together to create an external transaction. MSMQ actually supports two transaction types: internal and external. The internal transaction relies on features provided by the MSMQ transport to ensure delivery, while the external transaction relies on MTS. We talked about the internal transaction type in the "Delivery Guarantees" section of the chapter—this section will talk about the external transaction type. The issue of which transaction type to choose is one of speed versus reliability and flexibility. An internal transaction runs faster but provides fewer features than an external transaction. The external transaction is more reliable and allows for fuller participation by all of the services that a server has to provide.

WEB LINK: We've looked at a number of different techniques for using MSMQ so far in the chapter, and it could get confusing trying to figure out which techniques to use for a given situation. If you'd like to see how one company used MSMQ to solve its message delivery problems, then look at the MedVision, Inc., case study at http://technet.microsoft.com/cdonline/Content/Complete/Analpln/Cs/medvison.htm. (Microsoft TechNet has other MSMQ case studies as well. This is simply an example of one of them.)

So, how does an external transaction using MSMQ and MTS together work? Figure 5-4 gives you an idea of what to expect. A sending application creates a transaction using MTS. The ActiveX control responsible for the transaction uses MQSendMessage() to

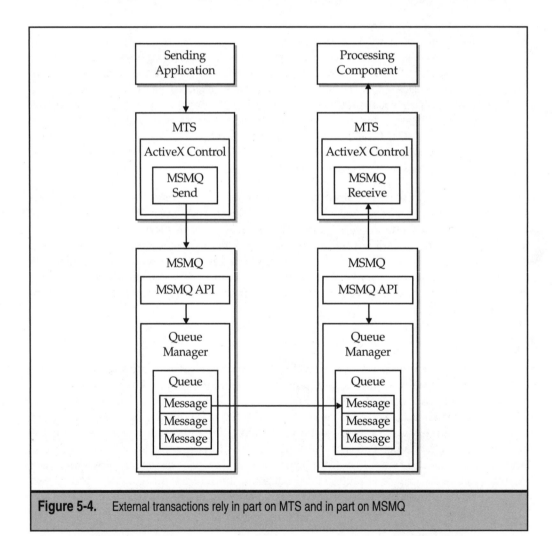

Figure 5-4. External transactions rely in part on MTS and in part on MSMQ

transfer the message to MSMQ. At this point, the MTS participation in the send side of the message is over. MSMQ takes care of sending the message from the local queue to the server queue using an internal MSMQ transaction. At this point, an ActiveX control on the server side MTS setup sees that there's a message in its queue. It creates a transaction, gets the message out of the queue using the MQReceiveMessage() function, then delivers it to the component responsible for processing the data within the message. (The same component could work with the queue and process the data—they're shown separately here because of the difference in function.) At this point, the MTS participation on the server-side message reception is over. Note that we're still using three transactions to transfer the message, just as we did in Figure 5-2. The difference this time is that instead of using MSMQ for all three transactions, MTS takes care of the two local transactions.

Of course, this leads to the question of what we've gained using this method. Remember that an internal MSMQ transaction isn't accessible by Resource Managers. Only MSMQ can see the transaction, which means that your opportunities to work with the transacted message en route are severely limited. Using MTS gives us the flexibility required to add Resource Managers and resource dispensers into the picture (see Chapter 4 for more details on the inner workings of MTS). In short, the main reason to use an external MSMQ transaction is to gain flexibility and perhaps some reliability because MTS is in the picture.

The way that MTS interacts with MSMQ is also an important consideration. MTS uses an all or nothing approach to message groups. Either all of the messages required for a transaction are sent or none of them are. The same holds true for message dequeuing— either all messages are dequeued (removed from the queue) or none are. What this means to you as a developer is that you can create message packages using external transactions that are guaranteed to arrive in order and all together (at least for a single machine).

CAUTION: The way that MTS and MSMQ interact could also cause a problem that you'll only see when working with external queues. A bad message sent by the initiating application could cause a transaction failure on the receiving side. The receiving application will request that the sending application transmit the data again. If the sending application hasn't been fixed, the same message will get sent again. In short, the faulty message could create an endless loop. To keep this problem from happening, you must include application logic that detects messages that will never have a chance of succeeding and terminates the endless transaction loop.

Besides speed and reliability differences, there are other differences between internal and external MSMQ transactions. One of the more important differences from a security standpoint is isolation. MTS transactions run at a serializable isolation level. This means that no one else can see the transaction—it's totally hidden from anyone but the client and server. An MSMQ transaction runs at the read committed isolation level. This means that there are certain circumstances when a listener or other component can see more than just the current transaction. In short, it's a small breach of security, but still a significant one.

Another potential problem is that other Resource Managers can't use internal MSMQ transactions. For example, if you wanted to create a transaction that would encompass both MSMQ and SQL Server, you'd need to use an external transaction because SQL

Server can't participate in an internal transaction. Of course, the lack of resource management coordination also means that internal transactions use less memory than a similar external transaction would. Even a small savings can mean a significant difference when your server is processing hundreds (or even thousands) of transactions every hour. In short, the choice is one of resource management versus transaction flexibility in this case. The flexibility that MTS provides comes at the price of system memory and performance.

AN OVERVIEW OF MESSAGE QUEUES

All other considerations aside, message management and propagation are the two reasons to use MSMQ. Getting data or objects from one point to another using a message as a transport mechanism will be one of your main programming considerations when using MSMQ. Since even the best server in the world will have a backlog of messages at times, it makes sense that there be an area on disk to store them. That's where the message queue comes into play. A message queue is essentially a storage container for messages that an application hasn't been able to process yet. A secondary purpose might be short-term storage until the user has time to archive the data or objects that the message contains.

TIP: Don't confuse the queues used with MSMQ with the queue used as a programming construct. Even though MSMQ queues can work like the programming construct, the use of cursors makes them work more like a SQL database. It's actually a better idea to look at a queue as a storage container—as we do in this section—because it really is something different from the programming construct queue type or a database file.

The sections that follow will help you understand message queues in two ways. First, there are specialized message queues that are used to store various message types. Using more than one queue allows Windows to separate and categorize the messages, making them a lot easier to handle. Using queues also avoids any confusion about which messages belong to a particular application. In short, just as you wouldn't mix cereal with flour in your pantry, you don't mix administrative messages with those that belong to an application. In both cases, we use special containers.

The second section is going to look at the disconnected application. The disconnected application is the next new application on the horizon. Many companies have people working at home or on the road now. Since our society depends on the ability to share information, it's no longer acceptable for these off-site employees to lose access to the company network. Using disconnected application technology allows you to create a situation where it appears to the user that the machine is still connected to the network, even if it isn't. Of course, there are limitations to everything—the user can expect to continue taking orders as normal, but it's not reasonable to expect full and complete access to the company customer database because that data won't be available on the local machine.

Understanding the Message Queue Types

Throughout the chapter, we'll address the topic of queues in several ways. There are two kinds of queues supported by MSMQ: application and system. The application queue is created by the application and is used for messages, administration, reports, and responses. Systems queues are created by MSMQ. There are two types: dead letter and journal. These queues are spread out over several folders, as shown in Figure 5-5.

TIP: You'll find MSMQ management features spread throughout several MMC snap-ins in addition to the Message Queuing Control Panel applet. This makes it inconvenient to perform certain types of MSMQ tasks—at least until you know where to find a specific portion of the MSMQ infrastructure. The three main management functions you need to remember are MSMQ configuration, queue management, and component setup. You'll find MSMQ configuration in the Message Queuing Control Panel applet. The queue management features are found in the Computer Management MMC snap-in. Finally, components are installed and managed using the Component Services MMC snap-in.

Notice that Message Queuing is located under Services and Application in the Computer Management MMC snap-in. MSMQ doesn't create any default message queues,

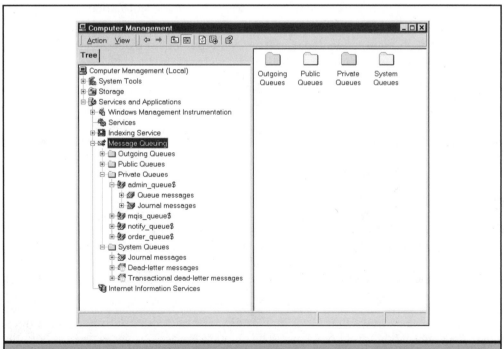

Figure 5-5.   MSMQ creates several default queue folders, in addition to a few default queues

which would be located in the Public Queues or Private Queues folders, or response queues, which would be located in the Outgoing Queues folder. There are, however, default administration, notification, dead-letter, and journal queues. The following list describes the various queue types in more detail:

▼ **Message**   This is the main queue type used by applications. An application creates a queue and then uses it to read or write application-specific messages. You must create a message queue for your application before you can use MSMQ.

■ **Administration**   An application can create and maintain an administrative queue in addition to a standard message queue. The administrative queue is used by the system for acknowledgement messages. These messages indicate that a message sent by the application was received, retrieved, or both by the receiving application.

■ **Report**   A queue used to track the progress of messages as they move from one server to the next. MSMQ uses report queues to communicate with the application. This is a read-only queue.

■ **Response**   Your application will use this queue to respond to other applications. When another application sends a message that requires a response, this is the queue you'll use to transfer that information.

■ **Dead letter**   A system-level queue that's used to store messages that can't be delivered. Transactional messages are kept in a separate dead-letter queue from nontransactional messages.

▲ **Journal**   This is a system queue that's used to track messages that have been retrieved from their destination queue.

Queues can also be public or private. Public queues are available for anyone to use and are tracked by Active Directory/MQIS. Private queues are normally used for one-to-one communications like a response from a server on a client machine. We'll be talking more about these queues as the chapter progresses.

WEB LINK: Sometimes reading the documentation isn't enough, so you need to get help from fellow programmers. Microsoft has provided nine newsgroups for MSMQ as of this writing. The first two newsgroups help you with MSMQ and IIS: microsoft.beta.iis4.msmq and microsoft.public.iis4.beta.msmq. The other seven newsgroups cover specific MSMQ development and usage concerns like deployment, interoperability, networking, performance, programming, security, and setup. You'll find all of these groups in the microsoft.public.msmq folder.

Figure 5-5 also shows that some queues are further divided into two subsections: queue messages and journal messages. The Queue Messages folder is used to hold the messages that your application will actually work with during execution. The Journal Messages folder is used to hold a variety of message types, but all of them record the queue's status in some way. For the most part, you won't need to work with these messages within an application, but may need to work with them for administrative purposes.

Message Queues for Disconnected Applications

As previously mentioned, there are two types of MSMQ clients: dependent and independent. A dependent client must have a connection to the server and can't act on its own in any way. On the other hand, an independent client can perform work with or without a connection to the network. Just how invisible the network connection appears to the user depends on what programming techniques the developer used. As long as an independent client doesn't request data from the network while in disconnected mode, the issue of having a connection is invisible to the user.

So, what makes the independent client so different? When you install MSMQ on a workstation as an independent client, Windows installs some additional software and MSMQ creates local queues as part of the configuration process. We saw how this worked in Figure 5-1 (along with the associated discussion text).

At first, it may seem like observing a few access limitations and ensuring that you don't request data from the server might be all that's required to make your application work in disconnected mode. However, there are also some API calls that you either need to avoid or ensure that you use in such a way that the application will fail gracefully in disconnected mode. It's easy to detect when a queue operation fails because of the lack of a server connection—the function call will time out after at most five minutes, then return an error value of MQ_ERROR_NO_DS. Fortunately, most of these calls aren't critical to normal application operation. The following list tells you what these API calls are:

- ▼   MQLocateBegin
- ■   MQLocateNext
- ■   MQLocateEnd
- ■   MQPathNameToFormatName
- ■   MQSetQueueProperties
- ■   MQGetQueueProperties
- ■   MQSetQueueSecurity (public queues only)
- ■   MQGetQueueSecurity (public queues only)
- ▲   MQGetMachineProperties

There are some disconnected operations that are queue type specific. Most applications will work with public queues, so we'll talk about them first. Any remote queue data that you do want to use while in disconnected mode must be acquired and cached locally. This is an obvious restriction since the queue won't be accessible once the connection with the server is broken. You can, however, still write data to a remote queue and the application will retain full access to local queues, even in disconnected mode, which should reduce the problems you'll encounter.

Private queues are the other type of queue that you'll use in your application. Remember that private queues default to allowing full access by the creator of the queue alone. This means that the creator of the queue will have to obtain the queue's globally unique identifier (GUID) before the connection with the server is severed, then pass that GUID to other applications that need it. Like public queues, any application can submit messages to a remote private queue. These messages are stored locally, then passed to the queue when a connection is reestablished. Your application will also have full access to any local private queues.

THE SERVER VIEW OF MESSAGING

I played around with a few titles for this section and finally decided on the one shown. An MSMQ application requires an understanding of three different elements: the structure of a message, the hierarchical arrangement of the queues, and the use of either API functions or COM objects to manipulate both messages and queues. Most of the MSMQ "action" takes place, therefore, at the server, no matter where that server is located. In this section, we're going to look at the server view of MSMQ; we'll talk about message construction and the methods available for manipulating both queues and messages. (We talked about queue construction earlier in the chapter, so make sure you read the section entitled, "Understanding the Message Queue Types" before reading this section.)

Parts of a Message

For the most part, except for the content of a message, most of the pieces that go into the construction of a message are initialized to a specific value. We've talked about a few exceptions to this rule as the chapter has progressed, but you can probably count the number of these items using one hand. Unfortunately, a basic message won't work for all situations—you need to know how to change the message properties to achieve a specific result. In short, you need to know how messages are put together for those situations where the default settings won't work.

So, what does a message contain? All messages are objects that contain the same number of properties, although you won't necessarily use all of the properties all of the time. Table 5-1 contains a description of the various message properties that you'll use most often.

The COM View of Message and Queue Manipulation

Windows 2000 actually provides two methods for working with MSMQ. You get to choose between the API access method used by previous versions of MSMQ or the newer COM component route. Either route will allow you to create, delete, and work with queues. In most cases, the decision about using either API calls or COM components is a matter of personal taste. However, the big advantage to using COM components is that you can use them with a variety of languages. For the most part, you're limited to using Visual C++ when working with the MSMQ API (although there are ways to get around

Property	Description
Additional Queue Information	
Ack	Defines the kind of message that MSMQ places in the Acknowledgment queue. The default setting doesn't place any messages in the Acknowledgment queue at all. You can also choose options that will place messages in the Acknowledgment queue based on when the message is received by the queue or retrieved by the listener.
AdminQueueInfo	Specifies the name and location of the Acknowledgment queue.
DestinationQueueInfo	Tells MSMQ where you want the message sent. This is a read-only property that's set by MSMQ after you've specified a destination using a method argument.
Journal	Determines whether MSMQ stores a copy of the message in the system journal.
ResponseQueueInfo	You can set MSMQ to provide a response when it receives your message. This property determines the location of the Response queue on the client machine. We'll talk about this property more in the Performance Issues section of the chapter.
Trace	Determines if the message is traced as it travels from machine to machine. The tracing messages are placed in the Report queue.
Data	
Body	Contains the message that you want to transfer from one machine to another. This message is stored as a byte array, which means that you can transfer a wide variety of data types including objects and strings. You'll definitely want to consider the method used to pack data because you'll need to unpack it later.
BodyLength	Defines the size of the message body.

Table 5-1. MSMQ Message Properties

Property	Description
Miscellaneous	
AppSpecific	Allows you to add application-specific information to the message.
Class	This is a read-only property set by MSMQ that specifies the message type. A message can be a standard MSMQ message, a positive or negative acknowledgement, or a report.
CorrelationId	An application-generated number that relates this message to all other messages sent during a given time frame. It allows the application to sort the messages when they arrive at the receiving queue.
Id	A read-only property that contains the MSMQ assigned identification number for the message.
Label	An application-specific moniker for the message. This property can be used for a variety of purposes, but is normally used for displaying a message header in human-readable format.
Priority	The priority determines the importance of the message when compared to other messages. MSMQ uses values from 0 to 7, with 0 being the highest. The default priority setting is 3. Transactional messages are automatically given a priority of 0 by MSMQ.
Security	
AuthLevel	Tells MSMQ whether you want the message authenticated when it arrives at the queue.
EncryptAlgorithm	Defines the algorithm used to encrypt the message prior to transmission. A higher level of encryption provides greater security, but also increases the size of the resulting message.
HashAlgorithm	Determines the hash algorithm used to authenticate a message.
IsAuthenticated	A read-only property that tells whether MSMQ authenticated the message.

Table 5-1. MSMQ Message Properties *(continued)*

Property	Description
PrivLevel	This property tells MSMQ whether the message is private or public. There are three levels of privacy: 40-bit, 40-bit enhanced, and 128-bit message body encryption. The last two levels of encryption are only available when using MSMQ 2.0, which means that you can use them only with Windows 2000.
SenderCertificate	Represents the message sender's security certificate within a byte array. The security certificate is used to authenticate the message.
SenderId	Provides the identity of the person who sent the message. This read-only property is set by MSMQ when the message is sent unless you specifically declare that the message won't be authenticated.
SenderIdType	Defines the type of sender identification: none or a standard sender ID (SID).
SourceMachineGuid	Contains the globally unique identifier (GUID) for the sending machine. This is a read-only value that's automatically added by MSMQ.
Time Tracking	
ArrivedTime	A read-only property that specifies when the message arrived at the queue.
MaxTimeToReachQueue	Defines the amount of time that the message has to reach the queue.
MaxTimeToReceive	Defines the amount of time that the listener has to remove the message from the queue for processing.
SentTime	Contains the time that the message was sent by the client. This is a read-only value that's automatically added by MSMQ.
Transactions	
Delivery	Defines how you want the message delivered. See the "Understanding Transactions" section of Chapter 4 for more details.

Table 5-1. MSMQ Message Properties *(continued)*

this limitation). On the other hand, some programmers feel more comfortable using the MSMQ API because they're more familiar with standard C++ syntax.

NOTE: We've covered many of the API functions that you'll need to know. This allowed you to see how the API function was used in context and also provided you with an overview of the more commonly used API function calls. This book is concentrating on COM and COM+, so we won't spend very much time looking at these API calls in use or covering them in additional detail.

Since the COM components are newer, somewhat easier to work with, and much more flexible than the API calls, we'll concentrate on using the COM components for the remainder of the book. For the most part, there's a direct correlation between MSMQ API function call classes and the COM alternatives. Table 5-2 talks about the various MSMQ-related COM components and how you'd use them in an application.

MSMQ Error Handling

Like anything else, there are situations when the default error handling isn't going to take care of your message queue. For example, a user may inadvertently generate a message with incomplete information and no amount of rework will fix the message so that it can be processed later. Since the message is handled as part of a transaction and there's no

Component	Description
MSMQApplication	Allows you to perform two machine-related tasks. First, you can obtain the ID of the machine using the MachineIdOfMachineName() method. Second, you can register a certification that will be used for security purposes using the RegisterCertification() method.
MSMQCoordinated-TransactionDispenser	Creates an external transaction that relies on MTS to perform the work. The output from the one method associated with this class, BeginTransaction(), is a MSMQTransaction object, which you can then use for sending and receiving messages within a transaction. We'll talk more about the dynamics of transactions in the "Understanding Transactions" section of Chapter 4.

Table 5-2.   MSMQ COM Component Summary

Component	Description
MSMQEvent	Provides an event-handling capability that allows you to monitor various MSMQ events, then react to them within a listener (or other) component. This component allows you to monitor messages arriving at the queue, errors that occur while a message is being delivered to the queue, and messages that don't arrive at the queue before their time-out timer expires. Using the MSMQEvent component allows you to write a single component that can be associated with any number of queues to handle common message-related tasks.
MSMQMessage	Contains all of the methods and properties normally required to work with new messages. You'll use this component to send messages, as well as to gain access to a security context for the message. The properties associated with this component allow you to completely define all message characteristics including the administration and response queue locations. You can also define encryption and delivery options. We'll look at more message-related features as the chapter progresses.
MSMQQuery	Use this component to ask Active Directory about public queues. The single associated method, LookupQueue(), accepts a data structure that allows you to define the parameters of your search. The results of the search are returned in an MSMQQueueInfos object.
MSMQQueue	Allows you to work with queues. This component contains methods for receiving messages, peeking at the contents of the queue, closing the queue, and resetting the queue. A special method, EnableNotification(), allows you to set up event-driven message processing for the queue.

Table 5-2.   MSMQ COM Component Summary *(continued)*

Component	Description
MSMQQueueInfo	Use this component to perform queue management tasks. You can create a new queue, open or delete an existing queue, or refresh or update queue properties for the queue. This component also provides access to a wealth of queue-related properties like privacy and priority levels, creation time, transactional state, time of the last modification, and maximum queue size.
MSMQQueueInfos	An object returned by the MSMQQuery object that allows you to search through a list of public queues meeting certain search criteria. This component relies on two methods, Next() and Reset(), to manage the position of a cursor within the list of queues. The current queue is returned as an MSMQQueueInfo component that contains properties identifying the selected public queue.
MSMQTransaction	An object returned by a call to the BeginTransaction() method of either the MSMQTransactionDispenser or MSMQCoordinatedTransactionDispenser components. The three methods of this component allow you to commit, abort, or initiate a new transaction. You'll normally use this object as part of a MSMQMessage.Send(), MSMQQueue.Receive(), or MSMQReceiveCurrent() call.
MSMQTransactionDispenser	Creates an internal transaction that relies on MSMQ to perform the work. The output from the one method associated with this class, BeginTransaction(), is an MSMQTransaction object, which you can then use for sending and receiving messages within a transaction. We'll talk more about the dynamics of transactions in the "Understanding Transactions" section of Chapter 4.

Table 5-2.   MSMQ COM Component Summary *(continued)*

client to consult with to determine how to handle the errant message, an aborted message will simply end up at the top of the message queue again. In short, your application could end up in an endless loop trying to process a message that can't be processed.

MSMQ provides a mechanism for dealing with messages that abort in the form of retry queues. What you're really doing is moving the message from the active queue to a background queue for processing later. This means that current messages don't get held up waiting for the errant message to process. Of course, you'll eventually need to handle the messages in the retry queue. At this point, there are three ways to handle errant messages, as listed below:

▼ **Fix the message**   Sometimes the message lacks an important bit of information that you can add to make it process correctly. All you need to do, in this case, is fix the erroneous information and move the message back to the normal processing queue from the retry queue. In cases when there's a configuration issue (for example, the user lacked sufficient rights), an administrator could manually fix the problem and then move the message from the retry queue to the normal processing queue.

■ **Gather diagnostic information and delete**   There are situations when no matter what you do to the message, it won't work. In this case, you need to gather as much information about the message as possible, then delete it to prevent the message from becoming a problem for the rest of the system. Obviously, you'll want to generate an event log report using the diagnostic information you've gathered. This will alert the network administrator to potential problems with the MSMQ setup. In addition, you might need to generate an error message for the user so that he or she knows that the message failed. In some cases, you may be able to regenerate the message by having the user reenter the information. Finally, you might need to alert the component developer (for an in-house developer) so that the component can be updated and possibly repaired.

▲ **Generate a compensating message**   This is a situation when the message can't complete because of outside influences. For example, you may have an order entry system that relies on a customer entering a credit card number for payment purposes. The card may be full or out-of-date, or perhaps the customer entered the name incorrectly. A compensating message would allow you to send a request for additional information to the customer, fix the message, then place it back into the normal processing queue. As an alternative, you might generate an error message and simply back the transaction out, effectively deleting the entire transaction from the system.

Implementing this error-handling capability requires a number of component configuration changes. The most important configuration item is specifying a queuing exception class for the component. This class has to implement the IPlaybackControl interface, which contains two methods: FinalClientRetry() and FinalServerRetry(), along with any interface methods that the component normally provides. This exception-handling component gives you the opportunity to take care of message problems. If you decide that the message can't be fixed, then you'd call FinalClientRetry() or FinalServerRetry() to place the message in the dead message queue (just like the dead-letter office for the post office, messages enter but don't leave in most cases). We'll talk more about how exception handling works when we install a component later in the chapter.

UNDERSTANDING THE
ACTIVE DIRECTORY/MQIS DATABASE

MSMQ needs a place to store information about the various queues, sites, machines, and user settings. Depending on your system setup and which version of MSMQ you have installed, you'll use one of two methods for storing this information. The first, MQIS, is generally MSMQ 1.0 specific. MQIS relies on SQL Server as the data storage manager. The second, Active Directory, is generally MSMQ 2.0 specific.

The reason I say that there's only a general association between the version of MSMQ that you use and the method used to store the information is that there are situations when you may not use the standard method. For one thing, MSMQ 2.0 is designed to work in mixed environments. This means there may be MSMQ 1.0 machines that need to work with machines using MSMQ 2.0. These MSMQ 1.0 machines will still use MQIS, not Active Directory, to read and store settings. So, in a mixed environment, you'll also have a mixed storage methodology.

Active Directory is Windows 2000 specific. Since MSMQ 2.0 is already designed to work in mixed environments, it's possible that Microsoft will update Windows NT 4 to use MSMQ 2.0 as well. In this case, since there won't be any Active Directory support, MSMQ would be required to use MQIS. In short, the best you can say is that generally MSMQ 1.0 uses MQIS and MSMQ 2.0 uses Active Directory to store settings and other data. It pays to know how your system is set up before you make any assumptions about data storage or other MSMQ features for the matter.

So, which storage methodology is better? For the most part, you really won't notice any difference. The real issue is one of efficiency and convenience. Active Directory is more efficient for a number of reasons (some of which we'll discuss in the sections that follow). The two most important efficiency features, though, are the fact that you now have a centralized database to use and the reduced cost of gaining access to the MSMQ configuration data that you need because of the way that Active Directory replicates itself.

TIP: The client can trust the data provided by MQIS because MQIS uses a secured RPC channel to transfer data. Essentially, the secured RPC channel ensures that the data is completely encoded so that no one can read it with a sniffer. We discussed RPC as part of DCOM in Chapter 4, so you may want to spend some time reading about DCOM if the features of RPC are new to you.

Now that you have a better idea of how MQIS and Active Directory fit into the picture, let's look at some specifics. The following sections are going to help you understand the MSMQ configuration database (no matter which form it takes). We'll begin by talking about the database elements and how much hard drive space you can expect a particular database configuration to consume. Next, we'll cover the issue of hosting. We'll talk about enterprise solutions and how the configuration data for one MSMQ setup gets propagated to other servers on the network. The final section will talk about MSMQ 1.0 and MSMQ 2.0 differences when it comes to storing configuration data. Even though these two MSMQ versions can work together, there are some very real problems you need to consider when working with a mixed environment setup.

Database Installation Requirements and Sizing

The MSMQ configuration database (either MQIS or Active Directory) is the central repository of configuration data for MSMQ. As previously mentioned, you'll never find any message data stored in this database. The sole intent of the configuration database is to store configuration information. So, what kinds of data will you see in this database? There are four essential types of entries, including sites, users, machines, and queues. In short, the entire MSMQ configuration relies on these four elements, one of which would be stored in Active Directory anyway (the user settings).

MSMQ requires a fairly limited amount of information for a small setup. Theoretically, an MSMQ configuration database could grow to an enormous size, depending on the needs of your organization. A corporation with satellite offices in many cities and countries could literally require hundreds of site entries, not to mention machines, users, and queues (which are the most numerous of any database entry even on small systems). However, even a small database requires some amount of room to begin with. You can predict the starting size of an MSMQ database using the following list as a guideline:

- ▼ Site   4.5KB
- ■ Machine   2.5KB
- ■ Queue   1.25KB
- ▲ User   2.5 KB

Using these four numbers, you can figure out the minimum space that you'll need for the MSMQ configuration database. For example, if you have a network with a PEC, a PSC, 2 BSCs, and 10 workstations with one user and 10 queues each, the minimum amount of space for the MSMQ configuration database would be (2 sites * 4.5) + (14 machines * 2.5) + (140 queues * 1.25) + (10 users * 2.5) = 244KB. As you can see, the calculation isn't difficult, and it pays to plan ahead if you plan on having a relatively large MSMQ setup.

Hosting

A component technology doesn't exist in a vacuum, it requires the participation of computers on the network to succeed. MSMQ is hosted on three types of machines: Primary

Enterprise Controllers (PECs), Primary Site Controllers (PSCs), and Backup Site Controller (BSCs). The following list provides a description of each machine type:

▼ **PEC**   Manages the MSMQ state information, including any database entries, for the entire enterprise. This is the main machine in your MSMQ setup and usually appears at the corporate site. This is also the PSC for the site at which it appears.

■ **PSC**   Manages all of the MSMQ state information for a particular site. These are the machines that you'll use for administering the MSMQ setup. Any change you make to one PSC is replicated on all other PSCs through MQIS or Active Directory. The PSC is responsible for updating any BSCs attached to its site.

▲ **BSC**   Provides load balancing for MSMQ sites with heavy message loads. While there can be only one PEC or PSC per site, you can have multiple BSCs. Each BSC will handle part of the overall message-processing load. In addition, the BSC is used for backup and recovery purposes. If a PEC or PSC goes down, then the BSC can be used to restore the current MSMQ state to a new machine.

Now that you have a little better idea of what these three computer types are, let's look at them in action. Figure 5-6 shows what a company setup might look like. Notice

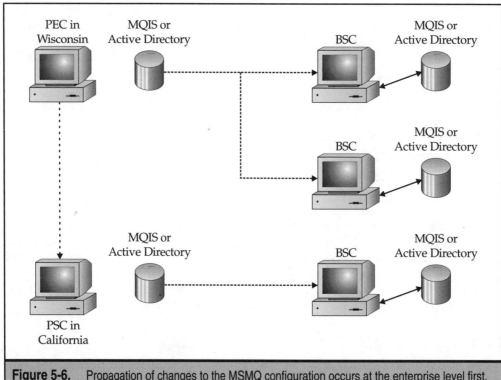

Figure 5-6.   Propagation of changes to the MSMQ configuration occurs at the enterprise level first, then at the site level

that corporate headquarters in Wisconsin includes a PEC and two BSCs, while the satellite office in California has a PSC and a single BSC.

It's important to understand how any changes you make to configuration information you make at one location will get propagated to other machines. Any changes that get made to the MSMQ configuration will first get stored on the local computer in the MQIS (MSMQ 1.0) or within Active Directory (MSMQ 2.0). The change will then get sent to any PEC or PSCs on the network, as indicated by the dashed line. The change will then be stored on that machine's MQIS or Active Directory. The individual PEC or PSCs will then update the BSCs for their site, as indicated by the dotted lines. Again, the database gets updated for backup purposes on the BSC machine.

MSMQ 1.0 versus MSMQ 2.0

One of the biggest differences from an MQIS perspective between MSMQ version 1.0 and 2.0 is that the 2.0 version doesn't require MQIS. MSMQ version 2.0 uses Active Directory to hold all of the required entries. Using Active Directory is a lot more efficient from a disk usage perspective and it also ensures that an administrator can access the MSMQ data from a centralized location. All of the reasons that developers are excited about Active Directory for general Windows 2000 administration apply to MSMQ as well.

TIP: From a cost perspective, MSMQ 2.0 is less expensive to run than MSMQ 1.0. The reason is simple, you no longer need SQL Server to contain the MSMQ database—this information is stored for you by Active Directory. In short, you need to purchase one less product when working with MSMQ 2.0, which could translate into big savings for your company.

So, why do I even mention MQIS in this book? There are two important reasons. The most important reason is that MSMQ 2.0 supports mixed environments. What this means is that you could have an environment that contains MSMQ 1.0 and MSMQ 2.0 machines and it would work just fine. However, to make the mixture work, MSMQ 2.0 still has to support MQIS on an as-needed basis. The database held by MSMQ 2.0 is replicated to the MSMQ 1.0 environment, which means that you'll actually have two data stores to worry about.

MSMQ 1.0 requires that you register a certificate for each PEC, PSC, and BSC on your network so that they can gain access to MQIS. However, since MSMQ relies on Active Directory to store the MSMQ settings, you don't need to register a separate certificate—the controllers already have access to Active Directory, so no additional access requirements are needed. In addition to reducing the number of certificates that the server must manage, using Active Directory in place of MQIS enhances performance because the server does less work when it comes to security. Yet Active Directory maintains a more secure environment than MQIS because of the new security features that Windows 2000 provides.

Working with Active Directory, rather than MQIS, will help in the performance department in another way. Any MQIS access incurs an immediate round-trip RPC penalty and increases network traffic. Since Active Directory is replicated throughout the network, all MSMQ configuration data accesses are actually local. You'll always see this penalty occur when using the MQOpenQueue() function to open the message queue. However, there are other times when you might not expect an MQIS access to occur. For example, both authentication and encryption can incur additional performance penalties by requiring an MQIS lookup.

PERFORMANCE ISSUES

There are lots of things to consider when it comes to MSMQ performance. The two obvious divisions to consider are those items that affect MSMQ itself and those that affect the application interacting with MSMQ in the form of MSMQ limitations. Performance penalties will affect the ultimate usefulness of your application and the ability of your network administrator to convince users to access the application while on the road. Unlike other kinds of applications, the delays suffered by slow network connections and other ills of both the Internet and disconnected applications will affect the overall performance of your application. In short, you need to gain every ounce of performance possible because there are a lot of factors outside of your control.

The following sections are going to look at two essential kinds of MSMQ performance problems: internal MSMQ performance problems and programming limitations that hinder application performance. While many of you will tend to focus on one set of problems or the other, it's important that you do your best to work around both types of performance problems.

MSMQ Internal Performance Problems

Even within MSMQ itself, there are a number of performance problems to consider. For example, the message delivery mode will affect performance. Some messages can be handled in memory alone when transferred from one server to another. Other messages require special handling. The following list looks at the various message delivery modes and what performance penalties they incur:

▼ **Express**   This delivery mode incurs the lowest performance penalty because all message transfers are handled within memory. However, this delivery mode is also quite risky because messages can be lost if a server fails. Since there isn't any record of where the message was when the failure occurred, there also isn't any way to determine if the receiving queue got a copy of the message. In short, there's a chance that more than one copy of the same message could be sent, even if no failure occurs.

■ **Recoverable**   A recoverable message incurs a little overhead because the message is written to disk before getting sent to the next server. Depending on the server load, the performance penalty can be almost negligible when using this delivery mode. Using the recoverable delivery mode also means that the message can be recovered after a system failure occurs. Unfortunately, because the message's progress across the network isn't tracked, the receiving queue actually has a higher chance of receiving multiple copies of the same message.

TIP: Recoverable delivery mode messages are optimized for multiple senders, usually multiple applications or threads that send messages from the same machine. The disk writes used to implement the recoverable delivery mode are batched, which reduces the performance penalty by allowing more simultaneous writes to disk. In fact, the use of batched writes and multiple threads for the receiving application can actually increase performance from 2 to 30 times (depending on server load, type and size of messages, and other types of environmental factors). Unfortunately, only MSMQ 2.0 users will see this performance enhancement—it's not available when using MSMQ 1.0.

▲ **Transactional** There are a lot of penalties for using this delivery method, even though it's the most secure method for transferring a message. Not only is the message written to disk at every server, but each server is also required to generate transaction log information, complete the current transaction, and create a new transaction for transferring the message to the next server in line. In short, this is the slowest but most secure way of moving a message across the network and should be reserved for those special situations when the receiving application can accept one and only one copy of any given message.

NOTE: These three bullets assume that you're performing what will be the most common type of message transfer, from one machine to another. You can also create applications that transfer data between local queues. Data transfer in this case will be nearly instantaneous no matter which delivery mode you use. Of course, the need for a recoverable transaction should remain high on your programming list when working with local queues, but the need for a transactional delivery mode is questionable in this case.

One of the ways to get around at least part of the performance penalty for using recoverable and transactional delivery modes is to ensure that the receiving application is ready at the time the message is sent. If the receiving application is ready to process data, then the server at the receiving end of the message trail won't write the message to disk (at least, not immediately). The message will be sent to the receiving application immediately and save that small fraction of processing time.

Express messages (and in some very rare cases recoverable and transactional mode messages) are stored in memory. It would seem that this would be the fastest way to deal with any type of MSMQ message. However, there's another hidden trap that you need to be aware of when dealing with messages. A single server might not be able to handle the messages as they arrive, which means that the messages will accumulate. Unfortunately, at some point the server will run out of physical memory and start paging the messages to disk. The end result of paging memory to disk is that you'll incur the same performance penalty as you would for a recoverable message, without any of the benefits. Ensuring that messages don't accumulate on the server will prevent the paging process from starting. Actually keeping express delivery mode messages in memory is essential if you want to reap the benefits that this delivery mode provides.

As previously mentioned, your disk setup can make a big difference in MSMQ performance as a whole. Dividing the three different types of disk activity that we talked about in the "Types of Disk Access" section of the chapter will help you gain some performance (up to twice the normal performance in some cases). Using high-end disk drives that include hardware drive striping can add another performance boost to your system (as much as 10 times the performance according to some sources).

One obvious performance hit is the size of the messages you create. Fortunately, there are several ways to reduce the size of the messages you send without seriously impacting the user's ability to work with the application or overall security. The following list provides you with some ideas on how to accomplish this task:

▼ **Use default settings**   Most MSMQ properties have default settings that are designed to optimize performance (occasionally at the expense of security). Using these default settings means that you don't have to send a custom property and decreases the overall size of the message.

■ **Reduce message size**   Make sure that the data you're sending to the server is actually required to process a request. There might be ways to reduce the size of the message without reducing the content that it provides. For example, the computer doesn't care if a message is well formatted—you could reduce message size without affecting content by removing the formatting information (unless someone will need to read the message with formatting intact later).

■ **Use one message instead of two**   Each message incurs special handling time. There are situations when it might be tempting to use multiple messages as a programming convenience. For example, when creating an order, you could create one message for the order header and additional messages for each item. A more efficient way to handle this situation from an MSMQ perspective would be to send a single message for the entire order.

■ **Support all delivery modes**   When writing an MSMQ component, ensure that it supports all of the delivery modes that MSMQ supports. That way, the sender isn't forced to use a delivery mode that exceeds the requirements for a given situation. Remember that an express delivery mode message won't incur the performance penalties that a transactional delivery mode message will.

▲ **Support Multiple Threads**   If the MSMQ component that you write can only handle one request at a time, it could become the major performance block in an application. A component that can handle multiple threads will allow the server to handle messages at the full capacity of the hardware and ensure that you're using server resources efficiently.

Processing Limitations that Affect Application Performance

MSMQ won't fix every programming problem you might have with your application today and, because of the way it's designed, it actually introduces a few new limitations that you need to be aware of. In short, MSMQ is another tool for your toolbox, but it shouldn't be viewed as the only tool. What Microsoft is attempting to do is create an environment where more than one tool may meet a particular need, and you need to consider the pros and cons of each tool before you use it. The following list will help you understand MSMQ limitations:

▼ **One-way message transport**   In previous chapters, we've looked at components that required one or more inputs, then produced some type of output. However, when you're working with MSMQ you can create components only with inputs and no outputs. The reason for this one-way transfer of information is easy to understand: the client and server may not be available at the same time. As a result, the server may not have a client to send a response to.

■ **HRESULT value limited**   Because the client may be sending a message to the server in disconnected mode, you can't expect the same kind of HRESULT that you've gotten in the past. When using MSMQ, an S_OK return may indicate that the data was received by the local queue instead of telling you that the transaction succeeded as a whole. This means that you have to limit your assumptions when designing the application.

■ **No synchronous result**   MSMQ provides asynchronous data transfer through messages. This means you can't expect instantaneous results from it. For example, the user may query the database for recent customer orders. If you store that information on the user's local hard drive, then you can expect to get a response even in disconnected mode. On the other hand, if the information only appears on the server, then you'll need to provide the user with some type of informational feedback that allows them to retrieve the information they need. In short, there are some situations when a connection is required. The best you can do is to download a subset of the company's database to the user's machine—those records that you think the user is most likely to need while in disconnected mode. This means that MSMQ applications require some level of intelligent download capability based on the user's schedule.

■ **Complete messages only**   Since the requestor may be unavailable when the server begins processing a request, the messages you send to the server's message queue have to contain complete information. For example, if you want to enter a new order into the fulfillment database, then all of the data required for that order have to appear within a single message. Unfortunately (despite assurances to the contrary), this may require some recoding on your part to get an application ready for MSMQ use.

▲ **Data by Value, Not by Reference**   C programmers as a whole are used to using pointers for everything. That won't work with MSMQ. You must send data by value, not by reference. The reason's fairly obvious when you think about it. A lack of direct connectivity means that the reference is worthless. Only discrete values will provide the information that the server requires.

As you can see, most of the limitations of MSMQ are based on the same thing that makes this technology so attractive in the first place. When you create a disconnected application, you have to assume certain things about the client and the server, like the inability of the server and client to talk with each other. This means that you'll have to think about the kinds of information both the client and server will require well in advance of the first trial on the road.

You can partially overcome the problems of disconnected applications by creating two different component message queues: one on the client and another on the server. Since message flow is a one-way process, you'll need two separate sets of components (or dual-purpose components) to implement this idea. Figure 5-7 shows one way that you could use this methodology to help support a user's need for customer information on the road.

As shown in Figure 5-7, this method does require an independent client with its own queue. In addition, both the client and the server will require a component to manage input to the queue. The client could have a listener component that allows the server to send it messages that respond to client requests. Likewise, the server will need a listener component to respond to client input. (The client to server message route appears as solid lines, while the server to client route appears in dashed lines.)

Obviously, you still won't get anything close to real-time response using this method, but it'll allow for smarter download of user requested data. For example, a user could place a list of names for the next day's sales meetings in a client-side queue. When a

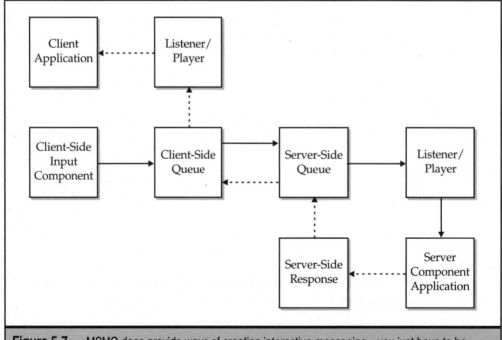

Figure 5-7. MSMQ does provide ways of creating interactive messaging—you just have to be creative in your approach

connection to the server gets created, the client-side queue would get transferred to the server. The server, in turn, could create a list of local client database entries based on the meeting list and download it to its local queue. The listener on the client would receive these new database entries and update the client's local database in the background as the user completes other tasks. In short, the user would always have access to the next day's client records from the company database, even though those records would normally require a direct connection. This is an example of smart application downloads. The one-way message connection can be overcome by using multiple components designed to provide a variety of services on both the client and server.

So, at this point you're probably thinking that you may not be able to use MSMQ because of your application's need to receive a response for every transaction. Actually, there are a lot of situations when the client machine doesn't require a response. For example, when a salesperson inputs orders, they really don't need any response from the server. In most cases, the salesperson will simply assume that the order made it to the server. If an update on order status is required, the salesperson could always issue a status request that will get answered during a later connection. As an alternative, the server could always assume that it needed to download active order status information and provide it during the user's regular connection time. In short, there are a lot of times when you simply don't need an instantaneous response to server input—an update the next day will work just as well.

There are going to be times when you absolutely have to have some kind of response to a request. For example, what if an exception occurs during order processing? The salesperson may have forgotten to include the customer ID on an order. In this case, there's another method that MSMQ provides for dealing with the situation. You can pass a reference to a response object on the client machine as part of your request. The messages are still passed one way and you still need two separate components to achieve two-way data transfer. In this case, however, the response is sent automatically. Obviously, you'll want to limit this kind of processing so that the connection between the client and server isn't overwhelmed during intermittent user contacts.

CHAPTER 6

Understanding the Application Types

COM has changed dramatically over the years. It used to be that COM provided access to two very different kinds of applications, and the uses for these applications were very easy to understand. However, as Microsoft has developed COM, the number and types of COM applications have increased. This diversification started with ActiveX. The two most common ActiveX technologies are ActiveX components and Active Document applications. However, many of us have also worked with Active Accessibility, Active Channel, Active Desktop, Active Input, Active Link, Active Script, and Active Server. (While there are many Active technologies today, Microsoft has stepped back from making ActiveX a synonym for COM—which has only confused the issue still further.) The list goes on, but you get the idea—COM isn't limited to a single kind of application anymore—it appears within every aspect of Windows programming today.

While the proliferation of COM on the desktop isn't news anymore, Microsoft's component technology upgrade is. COM+ is extending the uses for COM from the desktop and local network to the entire enterprise, including the Internet. Since COM+ provides a lot more in the way of application support, it's important to understand these new application types and the enhancements to current applications. Of course, this also means looking at the new or updated technologies that have been incorporated into COM to create COM+. The most important of these updated technologies include Microsoft Message Queue (MSMQ), Microsoft Transaction Server (MTS), and Distributed Component Object Model (DCOM). Some of the newer technologies include Active Directory (yet another one of those "Active" technologies that Microsoft has introduced along the way). There are also some technologies that fall into the same old thing, different name category. For example, Queued Components is nothing more than the extended part of MSMQ. Microsoft isn't introducing an actual new technology in this case; they're adding a new name to an extension of an existing technology.

NOTE: We've already discussed two of Microsoft's updated technologies at great length. For an in-depth discussion of MTS, look at Chapter 4. We discussed MSMQ in Chapter 5. It's important to realize that these technologies existed as separate products in the past. All that Microsoft has done is package these products as part of COM+ and added some COM-specific functionality to them. For example, MSMQ was originally designed to handle messages; it can now handle objects as well. Make sure you take the time to read about the differences between the original versions of MSMQ and MTS and their COM+ siblings. Understanding why these additions work as they do is very important in the context of this chapter.

This chapter is going to look at the various kinds of applications that you can create using COM+ in a variety of ways. In the first section we'll look at the pieces that make up a COM+ application. Next, we'll look at programming issues that you need to worry about, like performance, scalability, security, and availability. The next five sections contain the essence of COM application development today in the form of application types that you can create with relative ease using existing programming tools and special SDKs. In the next section, we'll look at a new Windows 2000 feature that works along with disconnected applications to ensure that the user has everything they need while working offline: the in-memory database. Finally, the last two sections of the chapter are going to look at two stand-alone technologies that will affect your COM+ application development: MSMQ and MTS. While one could argue that these two technologies have already been subsumed into COM+, the fact that they're managed separately, can be accessed separately from an application, and can even be installed separately tells an entirely different story.

UNDERSTANDING COM+ APPLICATION DIFFERENCES

COM applications execute mainly on the desktop. DCOM can extend the range of COM somewhat by allowing you to also execute part of the application on another machine. However, the fact remains that COM and DCOM essentially begin with the desktop, extend partly onto the LAN, and don't explore much farther than that. A company today doesn't stop with the LAN; it stops with the world. (Perhaps tomorrow, even the world will seem too small to hold applications that execute on a galactic level, but I'm getting ahead of myself.)

One of the main reasons that Microsoft has created COM+ is to extend COM onto the enterprise WAN and the Internet. In other words, COM+ is partly about extended functionality and partly about extended range. There's a reason that you want to use COM+ besides the new additions to the technology that Microsoft has provided like MTS and MSMQ integration. That reason is range—you can now create applications that aren't tied to the desktop or LAN. The fact is that enterprise-level applications no longer execute just on the LAN. Partner companies want to access your data, which means providing them with secure access to your company's database through a virtual private network (VPN). That same connection allows employees on the road to gain access to the corporate network while on the road. Today we finally have the resources to execute applications no matter where we are—one of those solutions is COM+.

COM applications are divided into two categories: in-process server and out-of-process server. Components use a combination of interfaces containing methods, properties, and events to work with the applications they support. At its very lowest level, COM+ provides essentially the same structure as COM. You'll still use methods to access component functionality. The component's behavior is still modified through the use of methods that change property values. Finally, a component still responds to user or other application stimulus through the use of events that your application can, in turn, react to. In short, COM+ isn't new—it's an extension of existing technology.

The easiest way to define COM+ is as a mixture of COM with MTS, MSMQ, and DCOM, and the addition of a few new components to make the transition complete. In short, COM+ is a technology that makes it possible for the developer to support enterprise-level applications without the limitations of previous COM efforts like DCOM. As a result, COM+ supports all of the same elements that COM provides.

I won't discuss these COM-specific elements in this section of the chapter. What I really want to look at are the differences between COM and COM+. What makes a COM+ application special? How is a COM+ application unique when compared to a COM application? These are important questions to answer because you need to know what new elements COM+ brings to the programmer's table.

> **NOTE:**   Some purists will tell you that COM+ is a true superset of COM and they're correct. COM+ does offer everything that COM has to offer, plus the ability to work seamlessly at an enterprise level. This section of the chapter takes some liberties with the usual definition of COM+ in order to explore what makes COM+ unique. It's usually a good idea when you're learning about a new technology to see how it differs from what you already know, then examine those differences in detail. So, it's important to read this section from the perspective of what makes COM+ unique, rather than this is a definition of COM+ as a whole.

Real versus Perceived Computing Power

I recently read an article by someone who noted that while the processing power of our machines has increased, the actual computing power has remained the same. At first this idea seemed ludicrous because processing power has indeed increased at an astronomical rate, which would make it appear that computing power has also increased. However, after reading some more and looking at recent postings in various newsgroups, it becomes apparent that computing power has remained relatively unchanged since the middle to the end of the 1980s. The reason is simple: The user interface has grown to consume nearly all of the new processing cycles available to do work in modern computers.

The user interface in applications today is smarter and more able to help the user get work done, but the power of the business logic behind that application remains essentially unchanged. In fact, after reviewing my notes for several Microsoft seminars, I noted that there was a common theme throughout all of these conferences. The idea that you can use a new user interface technology without changing the code for your business logic is a common one. Over the last 10–15 years, our focus has been on making applications more automatic and to reduce user error. Consider for a moment many of the user interface features that we take for granted like spelling checkers that check a document's spelling in the background while we type in the foreground. Spreadsheets and other common applications include wizards and automation galore—essentially reducing the user's need to think to the task at hand.

Is there anything wrong with improving the user interface at the expense of the business logic used to actually perform work? Theoretically, no—improving the user interface makes users more efficient, reducing business costs for both training and per transaction processing time. The point is that there are a lot of processing cycles used to create user interfaces today—processing cycles that could be used for business logic instead. COM+ signals more than the emergence of new technologies—it gives the developer the potential to decide when a user is needed and when one isn't.

Getting the user out of the data processing loop wherever possible will allow you to use more efficiently the new features that COM+ provides. There's a real-world example of enhanced data processing at your local supermarket. Stores use the UPC code and scanners today because users were just too slow at entering the data by hand. Computers can process the data much faster if user participation is reduced to a bare minimum. E-commerce takes this a step further by eliminating the salesperson altogether and allowing the shopper to foot the bill for getting those items at the counter entered into the cash register. In short, retail has already found a way to get the user out of the loop.

This brings us to the point of this whole discussion. There's a disparity in processing power used for actual business needs today versus the user interface. Let's look at some user interface versus business processing numbers (in general). In the mid 1980s, about 50 percent of the 8MHz processing power of a computer was used for the user interface. Using a 266MHz processor as an example and assuming that we're still using the same 4MHz for processing business logic, about 98.5 percent of the processor is engaged in working for the user or the operating system—a mere 1.5 percent is engaged in performing real business processing. Consider what you could do to productivity in your company if you could eliminate part or all of a user's participation in certain processing tasks. COM+ provides you with the tools you need to make advanced business processing without any user participation a reality—all you need to do is implement the required solutions.

Server-Based Components

COM was originally designed to operate at the desktop as a method for creating applications with prebuilt code in packages called components. This technology got extended to the network through DCOM; but still, you're essentially talking about a client view of component computing with DCOM. COM+ applications are all out-of-process servers, if that term really means the same thing it did with COM when it comes to working with COM+.

As you saw in Chapters 4 and 5, the methods that an application can use to access the server once you get MTS and MSMQ into the picture are nearly limitless. Not only do you have the direct connection capabilities that technologies like DCOM have to offer through the use of RPCs, but now you also have messaging capabilities of various sorts that are available through MSMQ. For example, unlike DCOM where you can't be absolutely certain that the data is going to get where you sent it and in one piece, adding MSMQ and DCOM together in COM+ allows you to make that assumption. The data you send from the client to the server will get to its destination, and vice versa. In short, the idea of what a server actually constitutes has changed. Yes, the component that your application will access still resides in a separate process (on a separate machine in most cases), but the interaction with that component will now vary according to the way that the application has been programmed.

COM+ Benefits

COM+ also makes changes in both COM terminology and purpose. COM is used to create what Microsoft calls *client components*. A client component is one that interacts with a single client at a time—like the pushbuttons and other objects used to create Windows applications. Yes, you can create server components with COM that a client can access through DCOM, but the effect is only slightly related to what COM+ components are designed to provide.

COM+ is used to create server components exclusively. For the most part, these server components will offer an application client some type of service—most generally the service will be offered in such a way that business rules you set up remain intact. These components differ from COM server components in a multitude of ways, but the three most important differences include location, scalability, and reliability.

The location element of COM+ is the server. By placing your business logic on the server, rather than as part of the application on the client machine, you reduce the amount of network traffic required to complete any given transaction. In addition, the business logic is now secure on the server, rather than open for casual viewing on the client. This means that security for your business as a whole improves. COM+ represents one of the few cases where improving security also means an improvement in overall server, network, and client efficiency. (Obviously, this assumes that you've written a COM+ component that's designed to make the best use of COM+ features—any technology can be inefficient in the wrong hands.)

Placing the component on the server also means that your component is now more scalable. The client doesn't need to know where the component is executing, simply that the component exists on the network somewhere. This means that you can have the same component running on multiple servers. Your application can scale to meet current user demands. Of course, this element of the COM+ picture won't really be complete until Microsoft makes Component Load Balancing (CLB), which should be by the time you read this.

The ability to make your component secure, ensure that data reaches its destination, and run on more that one server at a time all add up to reliability. The client won't ever experience downtime if you have multiple servers since the other servers in a cluster can pick up the additional load if one server goes down. In short, COM+ adds a reliability factor that COM simply couldn't provide.

Attributes, Context, and State

The combination of COM and MTS means that your components now have three new features and one additional level of access. Working with COM alone, you only have access to the component as a whole, the component class, and the individual interfaces that the component contains. These three levels of access work fine for components on the desktop because you can individually configure each component—these three levels of access won't work in many enterprise situations because they limit what you can do with the component externally with regard to configuration. This limited flexibility means, for example, that you can't set security at anything other than the component level when working with COM. COM+, on the other hand, allows you to access components at the method level. COM+ gives you finer control over the way things work inside the component without adding a lot of additional code or having to recompile the component later.

Along with this new level of access, a COM+ component incorporates the idea of state, context, and attributes. Attributes tell the server how you want to run the component or configure it in some way. For example, there's an attribute that tells the server that your component needs to run in a transaction and another that tells the server to use synchronization. Configuration options might include a list of people who are allowed to use the component.

Context is a combination of the attributes assigned to the component and the information obtained about the client machine through the client request (the client machine information could include the method that the client has used to make a connection to the server). If you'll remember from our conversation of role-based security in Chapter 3, context is especially important for understanding who's accessing your component and in what way. Context is used for more than just security; you could also use it to affect the way the component reacts to a LAN user versus one that's accessing the component through the Internet. In fact, the same user may receive different treatment depending on where they access the component. In short, context provides a safe environment for your component to execute in. The component knows everything that it needs to know about its environment in order to execute safely and efficiently.

The idea of context extends to components as well. If the current object requires the services of another component, then it can make the request of the server where that component is located. The server creates an instance of that component to create a new object that the initial object can use. The context for the new object is created from a combination of the new object's attributes and the information passed about the requesting object—nothing really changes in the way that the context is generated.

MTS has been referred to as a stateless environment, and it is from a traditional COM perspective. However, there still is state information involved with COM+. A component must be able to maintain state information in some way. The big difference with COM+ is where the state information is stored. You can store the state information about a COM+ component in any of these ways:

▼ Client managed

■ Per object

■ Shared transient state

▲ Persistent state

The type of state maintenance option used by a component is very important. For example, you can't use a per-object state management scheme for transactional components because the state can't be maintained across transaction boundaries. The reason for this limitation is that you don't want the various components in a transaction to see each other. A transaction needs to provide a very clear delineation between boundaries so that when an error occurs, MTS can roll back the transaction with relative ease and you won't have to worry about unexpected results that may occur when the transaction boundaries are "fuzzy" rather than clean. Data leaks between transactions are one sure way to completely ruin any chance you have of a complete recovery from a data error.

At this point, you may be thinking that per-object state management is completely incorrect for COM+. That's not quite the case. You can maintain state information on a per-object basis using member variables when working with Visual C++ classes. The difference between COM and COM+ is that you can't assume the state information within those member variables will be maintained across transaction boundaries—in fact, you should assume that any member variable supported state information will change between transaction boundaries. In short, if the lifetime of the object is less than the lifetime of the transaction, then maintaining state information within member variables will normally work fine. The only time you run into trouble is if an object will persist longer than the transaction—in this case, you have to find some other means of storing state information to avoid the data leaks that could prevent MTS from working as intended.

One of the ways to avoid the problems presented by per-object state management is to use client-managed states. In this scenario, you maintain the state information with the client instead of with the component. When Windows 2000 creates a new object for the client to use, the state information is passed along with the other client information to form the context for the object to work in. Obviously, the effect of using a client-managed state is the same as a per-object state mechanism; the only thing that changes is where the state information is maintained.

Sometimes you need to maintain object state information across transaction boundaries, but for some reason the cost of moving that state information from the client to the server is too high. In another scenario, you may want to maintain the same object state information for multiple clients. In either case, the solution is to use a shared transient state. This is actually a service provided by Windows 2000 in the form of the Shared Property Manager. The Shared Property Manager will use an area of the server's hard drive to store the object state information that gets collected as the transaction progresses. The state information is stored under a particular key—just like the keys used by database managers. The client or object will pass this key to the Shared Property Manager to request the state information for that particular object.

There are times when existing solutions can be used to answer questions posed by new technologies. The most flexible and scalable method to store state information is in a persistent store, like a database. Using a database is more flexible than any other method of storing state information because you have total control over how the state information gets stored and in what format it appears. By using a centralized database, you move the object state information off of one server and make it available to multiple servers. This means that objects that need to use the same state information will have access to that information no matter which server they run on. This is where the scalability factor comes into play—state information can be maintained in a central store and used by multiple servers just as easily as it can be used by one server.

Four Levels of Component Change

In the following sections, we're going to look at what I consider the four new or updated elements of a COM+ application: application, component, interface, and method. You should recognize these elements as things you'd discuss about a COM component. We'll discuss them in light of the issues of location, scalability, and reliability. In addition, we'll look at how the idea of state, context, and attributes affects these four elements. The goal of these four topic discussions is to help you understand how COM+ differs from COM; these sections aren't designed to help you understand how either COM or COM+ work.

Application

Microsoft has gone to great lengths to ensure that the applications you wrote yesterday will continue to work with COM+. In fact, using modified registry entries, you could theoretically rewrite your client-side-only application to maintain components on the server. The main advantages to this approach are listed below:

▼ **Security** Placing the components on the server will make them more secure. You can better control security on the server. Obviously, keeping components secure has the advantage of protecting your business logic, which normally includes sensitive information about the way you conduct business and perform certain tasks (like estimating the cost of services). However, one overlooked security advantage is that the final data remains off of the network. If someone were to monitor your network, the best they could hope to get is the raw, unprocessed data. In short, keeping components on the server, rather than the client, is a business imperative if you want to maintain maximum security.

■ **Application efficiency** There are certain disadvantages to running your application exclusively on the client. If you look at the processing power of your network as a single element, then working with individual components for each client is a waste of total processing power. It's more efficient to run the nonuser interface elements (the components) on the server, where object pooling and other new Windows 2000 features can optimize object resource usage.

■ **Execution speed** From a user perspective, a well-written application should execute quickly and not force the user to wait. Keeping an entire application on the client means that the client is responsible for all processing. This is fine if the client is a state-of-the-art machine, but most of the data entry personnel in a corporation won't have state-of-the-art machines. In this case, offloading certain business processing tasks to another machine may actually make the application run faster from the user perspective. What they'll see is the time required to process a request to the server, which takes a lot less time than local processing of the data, in most cases.

■ **Application reliability** We've already talked a great deal about how COM+ makes component-based application strategies more reliable. Rewriting an existing application to use these COM+ features will increase overall reliability in this case as well.

- ■ **Reduced network traffic**   Most applications today are written in such a way that they need to make a multitude of requests to the server, especially if that application is performing any form of database processing. Consider the simple act of looking up a user name in the server database. An application that uses all local components will need to get a connection to the database, gain access to the required recordset, determine if the user exists, get one or more records that match the search criteria, and finally select the single record that matches the user's choice. In short, it takes a minimum of five round-trips to perform a username search using conventional methods. Using the COM+ approach allows you to reduce the number of round-trips to three: make the search request, choose a user out of the records that matches the search criteria, and get the single record that the user has chosen to use for this particular transaction.

- ■ **Scalability**   As previously mentioned, placing the component on the server will allow you to scale your application to meet the needs of more users as your company grows. The user doesn't need to know (or even care) about which server will respond to their request, which means that COM+ can choose the least-loaded server dynamically. Of course, we'll have to wait until Microsoft releases CLB (or whatever they call it) before this particular advantage becomes a reality.

- ▲ **Maintainability**   This is the best part of the whole picture from both a network administrator and a developer perspective. It's much easier to update one component on a server than it is to install multiple components on individual user machines. Making an application easy to maintain means that it's more likely that updates will get made in a timely manner and reduce both help desk support requirements and administrator frustration.

Designing applications from the ground up to use COM+ will only enhance the advantages listed in this section. However, there's more for an application designer to look forward to from the application level. You'll need to design an application to use COM+ from the ground up to create an application that will work in disconnected mode. Likewise, the high-reliability application that allows you to use transactions to ensure data reliability will require a from-the-ground-up design approach.

Component

Making applications more reliable, faster, and more efficient are all fine goals for a developer to achieve, but they don't really do much for the developer personally. The application-level improvements that COM+ provides are all network administrator, management, or user related—the developer doesn't get much out of them. There are, however, vast improvements to component programming capabilities that the developer will get from COM+. I'll describe these improvements in detail as the book progresses, but the following list gives you some idea of how COM+ will improve things from a developer perspective:

▼ Queued Components (QC)

■ Loosely coupled events

▲ In-Memory Database (IMDB)

NOTE: Even though Windows 2000 won't ship with In-Memory Database (IMDB) capability, Microsoft plans to release a product with similar capabilities after the initial Windows 2000. Consider IMDB a place-holder for a technology that Microsoft will release in the future. Essentially, this new technology will allow you to create static databases that reside in memory instead of on disk. Keeping the database in memory will greatly improve both server efficiency and application response times. Obviously, developers will need to use this new capability with care—you'll use this for small databases that get used a lot like the names of states—not for standard databases with a lot of changeable data in them.

▼ Transactional Shared Property Manager (TSPM)

■ Object pooling

▲ Component Load Balancing (CLB)

NOTE: Component Load Balancing (CLB) is another technology that won't release with Windows 2000, but this one should be available by the time you read this book. Microsoft is already beta testing CLB, so you should see it released as a separate product. CLB is an essential COM+ technology, so you really do need to add it to whatever server setup you create. This is the part of COM+ that will allow you to run components on one or more servers and assign users to servers dynamically based on some criterion such as the current level of server load or the user's priority level. Obviously, Microsoft may choose to expand the role of CLB or change its feature set by the time you read this, so make sure you read any Microsoft-supplied documentation to get all of the CLB details.

In addition to all of these new programming features, existing technologies, like MTS, contain a lot of new features that the developer will be able to use to create components that are reliable, scale well, and still require a modicum of time to build. Theoretically, the amount of time required to create most components should decrease by 20 to 30 percent. This assumes that you're currently adding things like security by hand. (See the "Role-Based Security" section of Chapter 3 for details on how role-based security will affect your application programming strategy.)

At this point, you may be worried that writing COM+ components will require a to-tally different programming methodology. You'll be surprised to find that the component creation and access methodologies are still the same. Client applications will still need to ask the server to create an instance of the component in the form of an object. All access to the component still relies on methods that are bundled into interfaces. You'll still use IUnknown to query the component and find out what services it has to offer. All of these elements are still the same. What will change is the internal coding of the component itself, which is invisible to everyone in the outside world. As far as anyone outside of the developer is concerned, everything will remain the same as before.

To say there's no cost to using COM+ at all would be less than accurate. There are certain things that you won't be able to do anymore. For example, you can't reliably use the Microsoft Foundation Classes (MFC) Component Wizard to create COM+ components. Microsoft has concentrated all of their efforts on the Active Template Library (ATL) method of creating components. This means that developers who chose the simplicity of MFC over the flexibility of ATL will now need to learn ATL and the complexities that it involves. Fortunately, you can add MFC support to an ATL component, which means you don't have to create everything from scratch.

You'll also require new tools to work with COM+. Visual C++ currently requires installation of Service Pack 3 to provide debugging services under Windows 2000. In addition to the Visual C++ update, you'll need to install the Windows 2000 Platform SDK to access new COM+ features, and may require other SDK support as well. For example, you'll more than likely need a special SDK to access the CLB features of COM+ that will get released in a separate package. In short, don't expect to use COM+ without some additional setup on your development machine. The new COM+ components require support that Microsoft didn't include with Visual C++ 6.0. Hopefully, you won't need all of this additional support when the next update of Visual C++ arrives on the scene.

The fact that Microsoft chose to release Windows 2000 without either CLB or IMDB in place will likely mean that you'll face some additional complexity in creating COM+ components that rely on these features. Unfortunately, my crystal ball doesn't see that far in the future and I have no idea what additional complexity you'll face. Let's just say that it's usually better to get fully integrated packages when it comes to something as low level as the components that your application is based on.

Interface

From a coding perspective, working with interfaces in COM+ is the same today as it was with COM. However, there are some differences in the way that interfaces are handled that will more than likely affect the way that you actually code the interface. Figure 6-1 shows how a COM+ component looks in Component Services, the MMC snap-in used to configure various types of components under Windows 2000.

Notice that you no longer have to guess about which interfaces a component supports—they're listed as part of the Component Services display. Windows 2000 provides you with a lot more information about the components that are installed on the machine. You get a hierarchical display of each component, the interfaces it provides (at least those that are unique to that component), and the methods provided by that interface.

Windows 2000 allows you to configure interfaces as well. Remember that these interface attributes affect the component's context. You can change the operation of a compo-

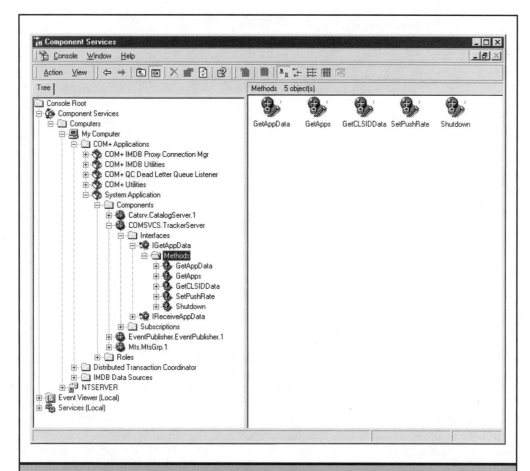

Figure 6-1. Component Services allows you to configure both interfaces and methods

nent using external attributes rather than internal coding. Normally, interfaces will provide access to at least three attributes: the general component information (including a description), whether the component is queued, and what level of role-based security the interface provides. Here's what a standard Interface Properties dialog box looks like.

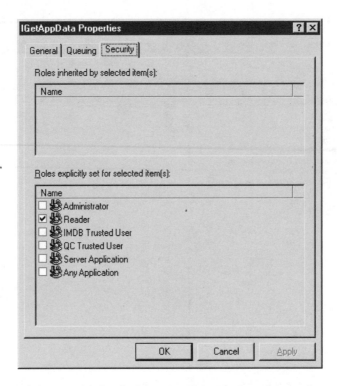

In this particular case, we're looking at the role-based security options for the IGetAppData interface. Notice that you can change access to just this interface by checking or unchecking one of the role-based security options. The fact that you can expose various attributes for the administrator to change means that while the method of accessing an interface is the same (so you don't have to change your client code), the options for coding the component itself have changed. You can now add a much greater level of flexibility to component coding, which means that the component will be able to better do its job.

Method

This is one of the most important changes for the developer and administrator alike. In the past, a developer had to contend with working with the component as a whole. Yes, you could access the individual interfaces, but even performing this task required specialized programming. Of course, doing anything other than calling the various interface methods using the pointer you obtained was completely out of the question. COM+ has changed all of this. Now you can modify the method attributes using the Component Services MMC snap-in shown in Figure 6-1.

Methods normally offer only two tabs of configuration information. The General tab will allow you to assign a description to the method. In addition, there's a checkbox that allows you to deactivate the object when the method call returns. The second tab, Security, allows access to role-based security, as shown here.

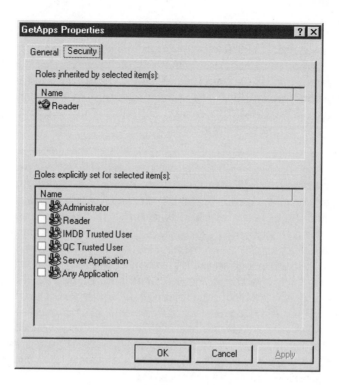

There's an important change to note in this particular illustration. The administrator had set the role-based security to allow the Reader role to access the interface associated with this method. Notice that the Reader role is shown as inherited at the method level. You can't revoke the privileges the Reader role has—any access granted at a higher level will automatically flow down to a lower level. If you wanted to grant access to only some of the methods of the IGetAppData interface to the Reader role, you would have had to grant that access at the method level instead of the interface level. This is an important role-based security issue to remember as you provide configuration instructions for the network administrator.

UNDERSTANDING THE PROGRAMMING ISSUES

Every time you change the method used to create applications for your company, there are programming issues to consider. For example, you need to consider whether a saving in development time is worth a change in how the user works with an application. In some cases, you'll need to consider this change because no matter what you do, the difference in the new technology will be apparent to the end user. Many COM+ components (application pieces) won't affect the user's perception of the application—others, like MSMQ, most definitely will. As part of the transition process from COM to COM+, you need to consider whether the user interaction change is positive or not.

There are hidden developer and company costs to consider as well. For example, the cost of updating to Windows 2000 has ranged from $500.00 per machine to a whopping $1,700.00 in recent trade press articles. No matter which way you look at it, an upgrade to Windows 2000 is required if you want to use COM+. These upgrade costs will most definitely affect how you write applications in the near future. In some cases, you may have to make a component Windows 2000–ready, but not actually use some component features until the entire company is upgraded.

WEB LINK: If you work in a large company, then it's quite possible that you're working with not one but several component technologies. COM may be only one of several solutions that you need to deal with on a daily basis. The only problem is that getting the different component technologies to talk to each other has been difficult, if not impossible, until recently. Many companies are looking at eXtensible Markup Language (XML) to solve their compatibility woes. You can find out more about XML in general at the World Wide Web Consortium (W3C) Web site at http://www.w3.org/. XML only provides a standardized method for marking documents up. There still has to be something to define what the content of the document signifies. That's where Microsoft's Simple Object Access Protocol (SOAP) comes into play. SOAP provides the means for exchanging data between COM and foreign component technologies like Common Object Request Broker Architecture (CORBA) using XML as an intermediary. Microsoft plans to release an update to Visual Studio next year that will allow a developer to access SOAP directly. You can find out more about the Microsoft view of SOAP at http://www.msdn.microsoft.com/workshop/xml/general/soaptemplate.asp. If you want to see the publicly available specification for SOAP in request for comment format, look at http://www.iepg.org/docset/ids/draft-box-http-soap-00.txt.

It doesn't take very long to realize that COM+ isn't going to be the free upgrade that Microsoft might want you to believe it is. COM+ will come with many very pleasant surprises in the form of reduced development time, increased user productivity, and enhanced application efficiency and reliability. However, those pleasant surprises will come with prices tags attached for the company, the developer, and the user. The following sections will make you better aware of some of the programming considerations when working with COM+. We'll look at the question of, "How much does it cost?" in detail.

Performance

There isn't any doubt about it; COM+ has the potential for increasing overall application efficiency through various means like object pooling. However, performance isn't just a matter of measuring how much time it takes for the user to complete a task or how long it takes the programmer to develop an application. Performance measurements can take a wide variety of other directions as well.

Consider for a moment how much each transaction costs. When you write an application using COM+ versus COM, will you see a reduction in the cost of each transaction on the server? The answer to this question is mixed. Yes, in the long term you'll see a reduction in the cost of each transaction as long as the application you develop uses COM+ features correctly and as long as Microsoft introduces the full range of features it's promised for COM+.

In the short term, however, the cost per transaction will go up for quite a few reasons. For one thing, it's going to take longer for you to develop the application because of the rather steep COM+ learning curve. There will also be increased equipment costs. A machine with 64MB of RAM just won't make it anymore. All of the object pooling, message queuing, transaction processing, and enhanced security features of COM+ cost both processing cycles and lots of memory. Even Microsoft has concerns about memory usage and is making an effort to help train developers on the efficient use of memory in a COM+ environment. Users are going to have to be retrained, if for no other reason than that the wealth of procedures they used for data entry in the past will now be reduced to one.

Getting enough network bandwidth is a constant problem for most companies. It seems like only a few months ago when megabit networks were all the rage—today, a gigabit network might be considered too slow. Voice, video, and various forms of multimedia have all taken their toll on the efficient use of network bandwidth. This is one area where COM+ shines. You can create server-side components that can greatly reduce the amount of traffic on a network. In some of my test cases, I've reduced traffic by as much as 70 percent—a vast reduction in anyone's book. However, this advantage also means that you need to develop with COM+ exclusively and that you have to build a suite of components that are designed to communicate with the client as little as possible to get the job done. (We'll look at a typical database example in Chapter 7, so you'll see what's involved for a typical enterprise application.)

Performance is one of the "no-win" scenarios for the developer. Whenever performance increases in one area, there's an associated cost in another. So, one of the first programming issues you'll need to consider with COM+ is how much it'll cost to implement this new technology. The gains you'll see can be large, but the costs are equally appalling. The question you need to ask is whether a full COM+ implementation is worth the costs involved. In many cases, performance concerns will dictate a phased approach to COM+ implementation; something that is not only feasible, but advocated in part by Microsoft.

Security

Security is one area where the combination of Windows 2000 and COM+ represents the very best that Microsoft has to offer today. When working with Windows 2000, you have access to new security technologies like Kerberos and Public Key Infrastructure (PKI). COM+ adds role-based security into the picture. (Chapter 3 has a full discussion of role-based security.)

All of these security options can add a confusion factor in addition to enhancing your ability to protect company data. For example, you may need to consider whether to upgrade current applications that rely on the Windows NT Challenge/Response security methodology, which in turn relies on Windows NT LAN Manager (NTLM) security. In many cases, the old security methods work fine for LAN-based applications, but in the world of the Internet you really need something more. The upgrade decision should be based on where you intend to run the application.

While it's relatively easy to secure your network from intrusion, there are other programming considerations when it comes to security. There are actually four levels of security that you need to consider for the typical COM+ application written for today's market. The following list outlines all four:

▼ **Server**   The server, as previously stated, is the easiest part of the application to secure. All you really need to do is right-click most objects in Windows 2000, choose whether you want to share the resource or not, then assign users to that resource. This is the part of the equation that few network administrators have trouble understanding.

■ **Network**   Creating a secure communication path is an important programming consideration. Some developers may think that Windows 2000 provides some new and more efficient method of security in the network itself, but at the very bottom of everything are Distributed Component Object Model (DCOM) and the remote procedure call (RPC) protocol. Neither of these network components are secure—you must perform some level of network configuration and add programming elements to the component to ensure that the network itself is secure. You'll always want to secure the lines of communication for a wide area network (WAN) or Internet application.

■ **Component**   The component you create is going to rely on some sort of data transfer to take place in order to communicate with the client. Securing the network makes it difficult for someone to intercept messages but does nothing for the data itself. Normally, you'll want to add some form of data encryption for both the data and the associated public key when designing an Internet application. This may also be an important consideration for WANs that are implemented using new Internet-based technologies like virtual private networks (VPNs).

▲ **User**   Any security plan you create has to include user security. The user represents the biggest chink in your security armor, and any security measures you take without the user in mind are a waste of time. Needless to say, this part of the security plan has to include a combination of physical and application security. You'll want to do things like verify the user's identity using the information contained on the domain controller if the data managed by the application you create is sensitive. Obviously, any level of user-level security will also include training, but that's an issue that's outside the scope of this book.

COM+ APPLICATION TYPES

Unlike previous renditions of COM, COM+ supports the idea of a true application type. An application type, in this case, isn't the same as the application types you think about on a client machine. For example, there are no database or spreadsheet application types when talking about COM+. Here's a list of the four COM+ application types:

▼ Library

■ Server

■ Proxy

▲ Preinstalled

WEB LINK: Microsoft has slowly built up some additional aids to help developers create fully integrated Distributed interNetwork Architecture (DNA) applications. As part of this effort, they've set up the Microsoft Visual Studio Interoperability Studio where you can learn about new products and download add-ons that will make the development process easier. For the most part, this site brings together all of the links to other Microsoft Web sites that you'd normally need to collect yourself. There are case studies (customer examples), tools, and other interoperability resources to be had on this Web site. You can find this Web site at http://msdn.microsoft.com/vstudio/centers/interop/default.asp.

Part of the reason for this new direction is that COM+ handles each kind of application differently. For example, the security for a library application is handled differently than the security for a server application. When working with a library application, the object executes in the client process and the client's security context is used for the object. On the other hand, server application executes out-of-process. The security context is derived using a combination of the component attributes and the client information supplied as part of the component request.

The following sections will help you better understand how the four types differ. It's important to know about the various COM+ application types because you'll need to know what type of application you want to develop.

Server Applications

The server application is an out-of-process server. It executes in its own process and creates its own context. You can access all of the COM+ services using a server application, and the full resources of the host machine are at your disposal (within the scope of the security settings at least).

You'll create the server application more often than any other COM+ application type because this is the most versatile form of application. Obviously, this is the kind of application that will execute on the server and produce the least amount of network traffic (if you optimize it that way).

Library Applications

A library application represents one of the newest ways to integrate components in an application. The library application executes in the client process. What this means is that while the library application file physically resides on the server and must be requested of the server, it actually executes on the client machine. The client downloads a library application from the server and uses it locally.

Because of the way that a library application is executed, there are some restrictions on the way you can work with it and the COM+ services that you can access. These restrictions make sense when you think about the client orientation of the library application. Here's a list of the restrictions:

▼   No remote access support

■   Can't use CLB

▲   Can't use Queued Components

Library applications can use role-based security. However, the level of access for a library application is limited by the client application's access. In other words, you can't create a component that will provide the client application with more access than it would normally get with its standard security settings. This limitation makes it impossible for a rogue component to damage the system or users to pry in areas of the server that they have no right seeing.

So, what are some of the advantages of library applications compared to standard client-side components? You get most of the same advantages that you would for a COM+ application but from a client-side perspective. For example, you'll still make component updates at the server, not the client machine. Access to the component is still secured by the server, not at the client. In fact, the client won't actually see a copy of the component on disk—it resides at the server and gets loaded into the client's memory. In short, using library applications allows you to get the best benefits of client-side components without many of the problems that client-side components pose.

Proxy Applications

When working with DCOM, you had to either use the DCOMCnfg utility to configure the client machine to access the remote application, or find some method to add the required registry entries through a remote application. Not only was this a difficult and error-prone process, but it required some amount of administrator time for each new client and each new version of the component. In short, the old methodology was time-consuming and almost unsafe from an application perspective.

COM+ provides the proxy application type. This isn't a component, but a proxy for a component that's registered on the server. The proxy application runs on the client machine and automatically adds information into the registry about the real component that resides on the server. This component information includes class identification (CLSIDs), program identification (ProgIDs), the remote server name (RemoteServerName), and marshalling information. This combination of entries will allow the client to access the component on the server without any additional intervention on the part of the administrator or developer. In short, Microsoft has automated what could otherwise be a time-consuming and error-prone task in COM+.

Preinstalled Applications

COM+ comes with a group of preinstalled applications. Some developers may think that these applications are for COM+ use only—many Windows services in the past have worked exactly this way. The opposite is true with COM+; you're now encouraged to use these preinstalled components to make your own programming job easier.

You'll find all of the COM+ applications in the COM+ Applications folder of the Component Services MMC snap-in. The number of applications you see partly depends on which optional services you install. For example, there are components related to Queued Components within this folder. Here's a list of the potential COM+ Applications folder entries:

▼ COM+ QC Dead Letter Queue Listener

■ COM+ Utilities

■ IIS In-Process Applications

■ IIS Out-Of-Process Pooled Applications

■ IIS System Applications

■ IIS Utilities

■ System Application

▲ Visual Studio APE Package

Notice that I've added one entry that isn't Windows 2000–specific. The Visual Studio APE (Application Performance Explorer) Package will only get installed when you have Visual Studio installed on the host computer. (Obviously, you'll also need to install this component as part of the Visual Studio installation.) You'll find that the COM+ Applications folder of the Component Service MMC snap-in can contain a wide variety of components that you may not have dealt with in the past. The whole purpose of placing components in this location is to make them more accessible to you. You'll find that using the Component Service MMC snap-in will give you a new appreciation of how COM as a whole works and provides flexibility that you've never had before.

OFFLINE APPLICATION CONSIDERATIONS

Offline or disconnected applications offer new opportunities to service the needs of users on the road. Using offline communication means that a user no longer needs a connection to the company to create orders or perform other tasks that might not require a direct connection, except to actually upload data to the company. We discussed many of these issues throughout Chapter 5.

There are other places where an offline application might be useful that we didn't discuss in Chapter 5. From a pure reliability perspective, every application could be considered an offline application. Using offline application construction techniques would allow every user to continue working even if the local server stopped working for whatever reason. Of course, whether this is a practical way to build applications or not depends on how much you're willing to pay in terms of system performance to get the reliability that an offline application provides.

The two main points to consider are that an offline application always presents the same user interface, even when a connection to the server doesn't exist. As a counterpoint, offline applications do reduce the efficiency of your application because every communication is packaged as a message. In addition, you need a machine that's able to act as an independent client, which will increase the hardware requirements for running the application. In short, offline applications aren't for everyone.

There are always compromise situations to consider as well. For example, you may not want to configure clients that have a direct connection to the server (within the same building or group of buildings) as independent clients because the likelihood of a severed connection is relatively low. If you use multiple servers, then the likelihood of a single server crash causing downtime is so low as to make the cost of lost efficiency too high. However, you might consider configuring satellite offices as independent clients—especially if the distance to the satellite office is such that a large number of potential problems could cause the connection to the server to get severed, even if no fault exists with company equipment. Using this approach would allow you to get the maximum benefit from offline applications and still preserve a maximum amount of application efficiency.

Even with this dual application setup approach, however, there are problems. For one thing, now you have to write essentially two versions of the same application. The first wouldn't use message queuing, while the second would. The point of this whole exercise is that there aren't any magic bullets in COM+, especially when it comes to working with new features like MSMQ and MTS. What you need to do is find the solution that will work best for your company's current setup. In some cases, this might mean taking the risk that the user won't be able to work because the connection with the company is down.

Laptop Improvements Make Disconnected Applications Possible

There are several laptop and notebook computer innovations that are making disconnected applications not only more desirable, but an essential tool for certain application classes. The first innovation making disconnected local applications a reality is continued improvements in power consumption and battery life. In the past, many users would rely on desktop machines, despite the fact that such machines were inconvenient for mobile needs, because desktop machines didn't incur any penalties with regard to uptime.

Data entry applications are unlikely to consume the full 10-Mbps bandwidth of even low-end Ethernet—at least, not at the individual machine level. Intel and other companies are currently finishing the Bluetooth specification, which would allow wireless network connections using 2.45GHz radio technology at a 1-Mbps data transfer rate. This means that someone like a network administrator could move from area to area in the company and never worry about switching computers. Moving from one building to the next would mean that any applications that the administrator relies on would have to operate in disconnected mode while the administrator works outside of the building. As soon as the administrator enters the next building, any data updates would take place in the background and the application would again operate in connected mode. The connectionless nature of Bluetooth makes this all possible because the user no longer needs to worry about making a physical connection to the system.

OK, so now you have an application that works even without a network connection and a user who doesn't need to worry about making a physical connection to the network. With such a high level of automation, there might be concerns about security. That's where the last new technology we'll discuss comes into play. Intel is also working on a new technology called Preboot Authentication Service (PAS). This technology would allow a laptop/notebook computer to verify a user's identity before it even booted the operating system. Verification would take place through various types of nonpassword technologies like a thumbprint reader. Other companies, like Veridicom, Inc., are taking a similar approach. The Veridicom BIOS eXtension (VBX) development kit includes a BIOS upgrade, security software, and a special fingerprint reader that will allow the laptop/notebook computer to verify a user's identity before the operating system boots. In sum, the technology for making disconnected applications a part of every enterprise scenario, not just for users on the road, is quickly becoming a reality.

WORKING WITH MTS AND MSMQ ALONE

Throughout this chapter we've looked at what you can do with COM+ that you couldn't do with COM alone. The changes in the Microsoft component strategy for Windows 2000 are very important. It won't take long for most developers to realize that the benefits of using COM+ far outweigh the problems of learning how to use it in the first place. (Given the current state of the Microsoft tools like Visual C++, the lack of documentation, and the problems with feature consolidation, the learning curve for the average developer will loom large indeed.)

What many developers won't realize is that MTS and MSMQ are still separate entities, even though it may appear that they're now consolidated with the rest of COM+. You can still write applications that use these products and the old applications you created in the past will continue to work as they did before. When writing new applications, you have access to all of the new MTS and MSMQ features we've described throughout the chapter. What this means to you, as a developer, is that you can create more robust MTS and MSMQ features and still not use the new component technology.

Another consideration for most developers is that Windows NT 4 didn't come with either MTS or MSMQ support installed. You had to install a service pack to get the required support, so the developer couldn't be absolutely certain that the target machine would have either MTS or MSMQ installed. Both of these products come as part of the default Windows 2000 package, which means you don't have to make any assumptions about the target machine. You can always depend on Windows 2000 to have the required support (or at least be able to tell the administrator to install the support using the standard Windows 2000 disks).

COM+ also forces you to make a decision about how both MTS and MSMQ are accessed within your application. You now have a choice between using a COM access method or accessing the MTS and MSMQ APIs directly. What difference does this decision make? Think of it as a choice between flexibility and development speed. You can add MSMQ functionality to a component very quickly using COM+. In addition, you don't have to learn a new way of doing things, so the learning curve is very small. However, this development speed comes at a cost because the Microsoft programmers have chosen a generic message structure for you when you use the COM+ approach. Fortunately, the generic message approach works fine, in most cases, and you don't need to worry about this issue. However, there are times when an application is expecting a specific message format. In this case, you'd need to use the MSMQ API directly because that's the only way you can choose a specific message format. In short, when working with COM+, you need to decide in advance what features you need and what you're willing to give up in order to gain development speed.

In the final analysis, Microsoft hasn't given you just one new tool in the form of COM+. They've given you multiple tools that can perform a wide variety of new tasks. As a Windows 2000 developer, you can't afford to look just at the surface of the application support that this product provides. You must look at the underlying technology as well. Windows 2000 offers more to the application developer now than just about any other version of Windows has in the past.

CHAPTER 7

A Transaction Driven Application

Data integrity and security are probably the two most important issues for information technology (IT) managers today. The concept of moving data from one place to another is relatively simple to understand. Implementing a solution that guarantees that each piece of data a user generates will arrive safely at its destination is quite a different story. There are many natural (like lightning) and human-related (like crackers) influences that can alter or even destroy the data before it reaches its destination.

We've talked about transactions from a theoretical perspective in several chapters of this book, so I won't cover the theoretical view again in this chapter. Make sure you check out the data transaction information in both Chapters 4 and 5 before you read this one. These two chapters give you the background needed to actually use MTS and MSMQ within a transaction-driven application.

This chapter will concentrate on a practical example of a transaction-driven application that consists of a client-side application, a client-side component, a server-side business object component, and a server-side database object component. These latter two components will appear in a single MTS component file. We'll create an application that uses MTS to ensure that the data created by the user arrives at its destination safely. In this case, we'll look at how MTS can interact with a SQL Server database using a simple order entry system. However, the principles that you'll learn in this chapter apply equally well to other kinds of transaction-driven applications as well. This simple scenario is the first step on the path to creating much more complex applications.

NOTE: Microsoft's documentation for Windows 2000 may lead you to believe that you can use an underpowered system and still make Windows 2000 run. I tested the example in this chapter on a 300MHz Pentium machine with 128MB RAM and 8GB free hard drive space. The results were terrible. I could literally watch the various screen elements draw one line at a time. While Microsoft will most likely fix some of the performance problems that I'm experiencing by the time you read this, you'll still need a system that can deliver a better than average level of performance to make this example work. My current server setup is a dual-processor 450MHz Pentium III with 512MB RAM and 16GB free hard drive space. My workstation is a single-processor 450MHz Pentium II with 512MB RAM and 8GB free hard drive space. Make sure that the system you use to test this example will provide adequate performance; otherwise, you'll spend lots of time watching the display draw one line at a time.

I've included two special sections in this chapter that address problems that you may run into when working with this example. The first section shows you how to install SQL Server 6.5 Developer Edition. Since SQL Server 6.5 is the product that comes with Visual Studio, I felt it was important to provide you with a way to work with an example using that product. Given the limitations of SQL Server 6.5 and the difficulty installing it, I would encourage you to upgrade to SQL Server 7.0 (or SQL Server 7.5 if it's available when you read this). Microsoft even provides a free SQL Server 7.0 Developer Edition. You can read more about this new addition to your Visual Studio Enterprise Edition product in the "Advantages of the Windows 2000 Developer's Readiness Kit" sidebar in this chapter.

The second addition is designed to address a problem that anyone working with SQL Server will experience—the lack of remote diagnostic aids. Yes, there are some aids available, but they really won't address all of your needs. This second section shows you how to use the Visual C++ Database Project to build a very simple diagnostic and query aid. You'll find that this aid becomes indispensable as the complexity of your applications increases. The ability to work with your database from the same IDE that you're using to create the application is a very big benefit of creating this simple project.

NOTE: This chapter assumes that you're using a two-computer setup with Windows 2000 Professional installed on one and Windows 2000 Server installed on the other. I used Visual Studio 6.0 Enterprise Edition with Service Pack 3 installed for this example. The development workstation also has the Windows 2000 Platform SDK and the COM+ SDK installed. (Microsoft may have combined the features of both SDKs into a single SDK by the time you read this.) You'll need the services of these SDKs in order to compile the application code. The example also assumes that you're using the SQL Server 6.5 Developer Edition because this is the product that comes with Visual Studio 6.0 Enterprise Edition. Using other database products will very likely require changes to the source code that are left as an exercise for the reader.

It's time to talk about the example program in this chapter. The remaining seven sections in this chapter correspond to the seven planning steps that you'll normally use when designing a simple database application that relies on Visual C++, COM+, and a DBMS like SQL Server. In the first section, we'll define the application, which includes creating the order entry database. Once the application is defined, we'll create the two server-side components you need to implement the transactional portion of the application. The first component will contain the business logic required to make the application work, while the second series of components allow you to interact with various elements of the database. You need both component types to create a COM+ application—there really isn't an easy way to combine both functions into one component.

That covers the server side of things; now let's look at the client. We'll begin by creating a client-side component. This component won't do very much other than provide communication between the server-side components and the application. However, the client-side component is where you'll normally add MSMQ functionality, if desired. In the next section, we'll create the application that will interact with the MTS component and associated database. The component is installed on the server, while the application appears on the user's workstation.

At this point, we have the server and client elements for our application. There are some administrative details we need to deal with next. MTS uses the Component Services MMC snap-in for configuration and logging purposes. You need to know how to use this snap-in before you can install a component on the server. Finally, we'll test the entire application. You'll be able to see all of the elements that we've created work together in order to ensure the data that the client creates is the same data that appears in the database.

WEB LINK: While you may be able to work with the examples in this chapter without applying Service Pack 5a to SQL Server, you'll definitely want to apply the service pack to avoid potential problems. Unfortunately, the service pack is no longer available from Microsoft's main SQL Server Web site—you need to download it from the Microsoft Support Downloads site at http://support.microsoft.com/support/downloads/LNP220.asp. There are two patches: one for the Alpha processor and another for the Intel platform.

INSTALLING SQL SERVER 6.5 DEVELOPER EDITION

The first step for this example, or any other "first database project" you work on, is to install SQL Server. It may seem a bit odd that I would add an installation procedure to the beginning of this chapter, but there are some problems using SQL Server versions 6.5 and 7.0 (all editions) with Windows 2000. The biggest problem affects both versions—the Distributed Transaction Coordinator (DTC) in Windows 2000 is incompatible with both versions of SQL Server. Unfortunately, the installation programs for both products fail to recognize the DTC for Windows 2000 is newer than the one provided with SQL Server and install the old DTC over the new Windows 2000 DTC. The result is that your Windows 2000 installation will be momentarily damaged until you fix the problem with the DTC. The damaged DTC affects a lot of different services, including all component services and Microsoft Message Queuing (MSMQ), which you'll recognize as two of the main topics for this book.

A second DTC-related problem affects SQL Server 6.5 Developer edition. You'll find that the Back Office portion of the Visual Studio 6.0 Enterprise Edition installation fails for no apparent reason. The only message you'll get is that the SQL Server and associated debugger installations failed. However, running the installation programs manually will show you that the problem is that the DTC can't be stopped automatically by the setup program. Once you get to this point, you can start figuring out why the whole SQL Server installation process is flawed in the extreme. With this in mind, the following procedure will help you get around the problems with the current SQL Server installation.

WARNING: Microsoft doesn't sanction this procedure. I've provided this procedure as a means to get around problems with the SQL Server 6.5 Developer Edition installation. This procedure has only been tested on a single server and probably won't work with server clusters. Only use this procedure on a test machine, as you may lose data on a production machine. There are no guarantees provided or implied with this procedure—you assume all risk for using it. This procedure assumes that you have a good understanding of how to remove and install software when working with Windows.

1. Open the Services MMC snap-in found in the Administrative Tools folder of the Control Panel.

2. Right-click the Distributed Transaction Coordinator service, then choose Properties from the context menu. Click the Dependencies tab and you'll see a list of dependent services like the one shown in the bottom list here.

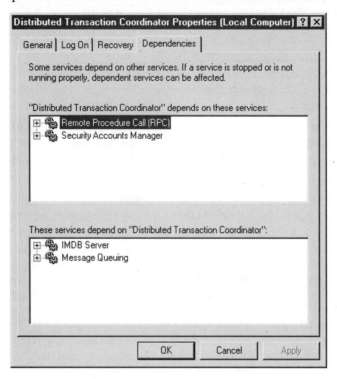

3. Make a list of each item in the dependency list, then click Cancel to close the Distributed Transaction Coordinator Properties dialog box.

4. Right-click each service entry listed in the Distributed Transaction Coordinator service dependency list, then choose Stop from the context menu. This step allows you to manually stop the dependent services so that you can stop the DTC itself. Make sure you record the name of each service that you stop manually because you'll need to restart these services manually later. In some cases, rebooting Windows 2000 Server won't be enough to restart the service for you; Windows 2000 will assume that you wanted the service to remain stopped for a reason since you stopped it manually.

5. Right-click the Distributed Transaction Coordinator service, then choose Stop from the context menu. The SQL Server 6.5 installation process will fail unless you manually stop the DTC. This is the problem that caused the installation to fail in the first place.

6. Place Visual Studio 6.0 Enterprise Edition, CD 2 in your CD-ROM drive. Double-click the Setup icon in the \SQL\I386 folder on the Visual Studio 6 CD to manually start the SQL Server 6.5 Developer Edition installation. Follow the installation steps as you normally would. These installation steps don't look like the ones that you'd follow for Visual Studio Back Office installation, but the questions are the same. Make sure that you answer each question just as you would for the standard installation process. When asked for the Product ID number, use the CD Key on the back of your CD holder. Once you have SQL Server installed; you'll want to install the SQL Server Debugger as well—which requires a separate manual installation.

7. Double-click the Setup icon in the \SQDBG_SS folder on the Visual Studio 6.0 Enterprise Edition CD to install the SQL Server Debugger. Just follow the installation steps as you normally would. You'll need to provide the CD Key again when asked.

WEB LINK: As part of this installation process, you need to install two service packs. The first service pack is part of Visual Studio (Service Pack 3 at the time of this writing). You'll find it at http://msdn.microsoft.com/vstudio/. The second service pack is SQL Server 6.5 specific (Service Pack 5a at the time of this writing). You'll find it at http://support.microsoft.com/support/downloads/LNP220.asp. It's very important to install both service packs before you reinstall the DTC. Otherwise, the service pack updates will damage the DTC again and you'll need to reinstall the DTC again.

8. Install Visual Studio Service Pack 3. It's really important that you install Service Pack 3 because you'll run into Windows 2000–related application development problems otherwise. At this point, you'll need to reboot. After the reboot, you'll notice that the Distributed Transaction Coordinator service no longer appears in the Services MMC snap-in. That's because SQL Server has replaced the Windows 2000 DTC with its own version. Make absolutely certain that SQL Server is working at this point. Open the various utilities and try creating a database. If something doesn't work, repair it now, because you won't be able to repair it later.

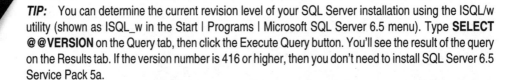

TIP: You can determine the current revision level of your SQL Server installation using the ISQL/w utility (shown as ISQL_w in the Start | Programs | Microsoft SQL Server 6.5 menu). Type **SELECT @@VERSION** on the Query tab, then click the Execute Query button. You'll see the result of the query on the Results tab. If the version number is 416 or higher, then you don't need to install SQL Server 6.5 Service Pack 5a.

9. Install SQL Server 6.5 Service Pack 5a, if necessary. There are a lot of SQL Server bugs repaired by this service pack and all application examples in this book assume that you have this service pack in place. Even though the SQL Server 6.5 Service Pack 5a Setup program doesn't ask you to reboot the server, you'll get better results if you do.

10. Use the Start | Run command to display the Run dialog box. Type **DTCSETUP** in the Run field, then click OK. Running this program should restore Windows 2000 DTC. You'll see a success or failure message box at the end of the installation process. Even though the DTCSETUP program doesn't ask you to reboot the server, you'll get better results if you do.

11. Check the Services MMC snap-in. You should see the Distributed Transaction Coordinator service listed again. If you don't see the Distributed Transaction Coordinator service, perform an upgrade installation of Windows 2000. Performing an upgrade installation may be time-consuming, but it will ensure that you retain your current operating system settings while restoring any damaged files.

12. Ensure that the Distributed Transaction Coordinator service is started. In most cases, Windows 2000 will automatically start it for you.

13. Open the SQL Service Manager found in Start | Programs | Microsoft SQL Server 6.5. Check all three services using the Services drop-down list box. All three should be started. If they aren't started, then try starting them manually.

14. Try working with the sample database you created earlier to ensure that SQL Server is actually working. Make sure you test the ability to administrate SQL Server as well by creating phantom users, then deleting them. You may want to try creating a very simple database as part of your test procedure.

15. Restart the services that you manually stopped earlier. It's especially important to restart the Message Queuing service. If Message Queuing won't start, then uninstall Message Queuing and reinstall it. Performing an uninstall, then a reinstall, will replace any missing files. At this point, you should have full SQL Server access and full Windows 2000 Server functionality. Of course, there are always extra steps you need to take to make this final, and this procedure is no exception. If stop at this point, you'll find that SQL Server will work, but that you won't be able to access it correctly from Visual C++. We need to do one more thing to complete the setup procedure.

16. Start the ISQL/w utility on the server (you'll find it in the Start | Programs | Microsoft SQL Server 6.5 folder).

17. Use the File | Open command to display the Open File dialog box.

18. Locate the \MSSQL\INSTALL folder.

19. Open the INSTCAT.SQL script, then click Execute Query on the toolbar. The script will run for quite some time. The Execute Query button will turn green again once the script has finished. This is your indicator that Visual C++ will now be able to access SQL Server normally through the various wizards.

20. Close the ISQL/w utility.

Advantages of the Windows 2000 Developer's Readiness Kit

The Windows 2000 Developer's Readiness Kit is a must have for all Visual C++ 6.0 developers. You'll find this product at http://msdn.microsoft.com/vstudio/order. It's actually a four-CD set that Microsoft has relabeled as the Visual Studio 6.0 Plus Pack. At the time of this writing, the Visual Studio 6.0 Plus Pack will continue to be free for the price of shipping and handling (less than $10.00 for U.S. residents in most cases).

CD1 is the Developer's Readiness Kit that includes some training and white papers, COM+ resources, and the Visual Studio Installer (the new one for Windows 2000).

CD2 contains the Microsoft Data Engine (MSDE) for Visual Studio 6.0. However, the MSDE is the 1.0 version, which means you should probably consider it more of a beta than a finished product. This CD also contains a Developer Edition of SQL Server 7.0, which you should probably consider using in place of SQL Server 6.5 in new projects.

CD3 is Microsoft Windows NT 4.0 Service Pack 4, which is kind of a surprise considering that SP6 (or maybe even higher) is already available. Unless you have Windows NT servers to update, this CD won't do you much good. Since we're concentrating on Windows 2000 in this book, I won't provide any additional information about this particular CD.

CD4 is more developer training. However, this training focuses on MSDE and SQL Server 7.0. The main focus of this training appears to be upsizing current SQL Server 6.5 applications to SQL Server 7.0 and using the MSDE.

CREATING A SQL SERVER REMOTE DEVELOPMENT AND DIAGNOSTIC AID

One of the problems you're going to face when working with complex applications of the type we'll cover in this chapter is remote debugging. Microsoft does provide a few tools that allow you to debug the application on the server from your desk, but for the most part you have to figure out innovative methods of debugging the application yourself. Unfortunately, the do-it-yourself category includes one very important element of this example: SQL Server.

Fortunately, there's a way to create a remote debugging tool that you can use with your SQL Server projects and it works with the Visual C++ IDE. What this means is that you don't have to spend a lot of time switching between tools to get any work done. A single tool will allow you to write code and check on SQL Server.

So, what is this "magic bullet" of remote SQL Server access? It's a Visual C++ project that I haven't seen a lot of people use. The reason they don't use it is because the project won't really allow you to do anything with an application. However, as we'll see a few moments, it does work wonders as a remote access tool. The first thing you'll need to do to make this work is create a new Visual C++ project. The following steps show you how.

NOTE: You must have the rights required to access the database that you want to work with. In many cases, you'll need ownership rights to make the example work properly because user rights aren't sufficient to make changes to the database schema. Make sure you take care of any security requirements before you begin this procedure.

1. Use the File | New command to display the New dialog box. You'll see a list of projects on the Projects tab, including the Database Project shown highlighted here.

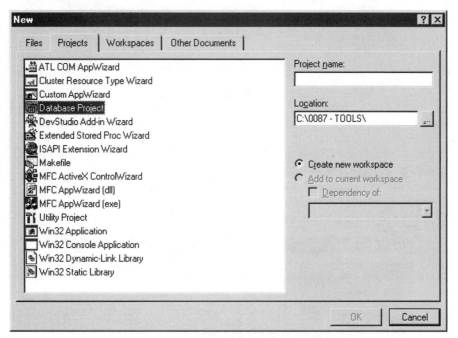

2. Highlight the Database Project option, then type a name in the Project Name field. (The example uses the name of DataSource.)

3. Click OK. Visual C++ will create a new project, then display the Select Data Source dialog box shown here. As part of the application creation process, we have to tell Visual C++ what data source to use. Essentially, a data source is the name and other access information for the database that you want to work with.

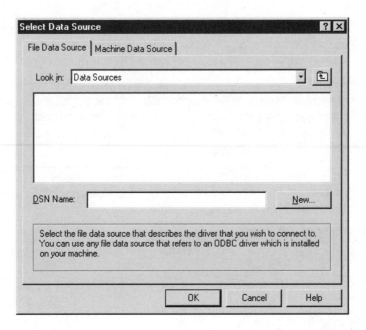

4. Click New. You'll see a Create New Data Source dialog box like the one shown here. This dialog box allows you to choose from one of ODBC drivers installed on your machine. These drivers contain all of the logic required to access the database and allow you to interact with it. Note that not every driver is created the same or requires the same information as input. We'll be looking at the SQL Server 6.5 driver in this chapter, so the screen shots you see may vary from the ones shown here if you use a different driver.

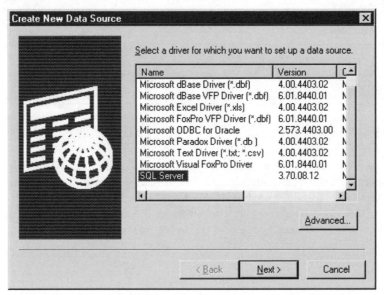

5. Highlight the ODBC driver that you want to use. The example uses SQL Server as an ODBC driver.

6. Click Next. You'll be asked to provide a name for the data source. The example uses OrderEntryAccess, but you could use any name you like.

7. Type a data source name, then click Next. You'll see a summary dialog box that tells which ODBC driver you're using, the type of data source you're creating, and the name of the data source.

8. Click Finish. At this point, what you see in the way of dialog boxes will vary by ODBC driver, even within the same database product line. I'll still assume that we're working with SQL Server, so you'll see a Create a New Data Source to SQL Server dialog box like the one shown here.

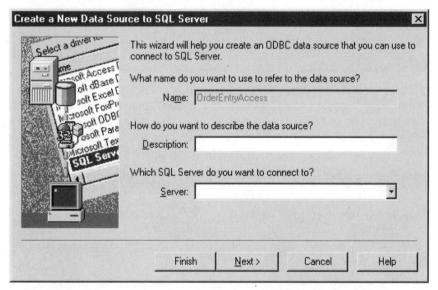

9. Type a description for the data source in the Description field. The example uses, "A data source for accessing the OrderEntry database."

10. Choose a server from the Server drop-down list box. Notice that you can choose a remote server or use the local server, which is the machine that you're logged into at the time.

11. Click Next. You'll be asked to choose an authentication method as shown here. The method you use will be determined by the method the network administrator used to set up the remote server and the database. In most cases, you should be able to use the Windows NT authentication method.

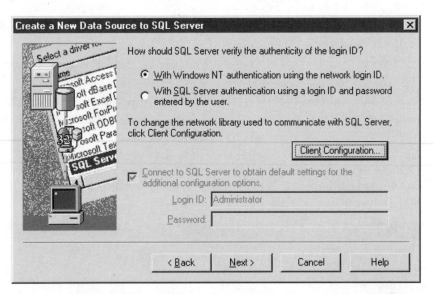

12. Choose an authentication method. Type a username and password, if necessary. Click Next. You'll see a dialog box that asks how you want to access the database, like the one shown here. Lots of the entries on this dialog box are application and database specific. However, there's one entry that you must change if you want to work with something other than the Master database for SQL Server.

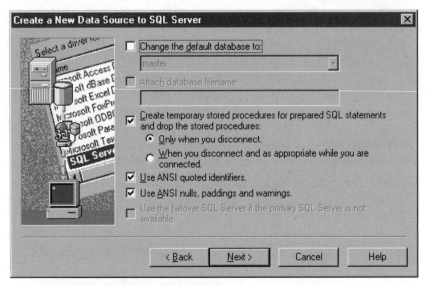

13. Check the "Change the Default Database to" option, then choose the database you want to work with from the drop-down list box. The example will use the OrderEntry database. (We'll create this database later in the chapter. You'll find instructions for creating the tables in the "Creating the Database and Associated Tables" section of the chapter.)

14. Click Next. You'll see a list of display and logging options like the ones shown here. In most cases, the settings will work fine. The log options are accessible through the Data Sources (ODBC) applet in the Administrative Tools folder of the Control Panel, so you don't need to activate logging now unless you plan to use it all of the time.

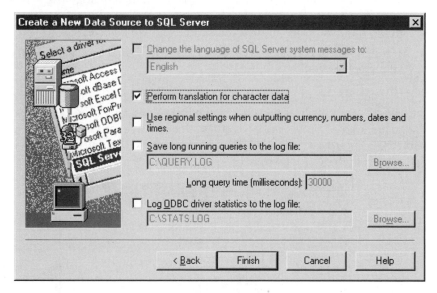

15. Click Finish. You'll see an ODBC Microsoft SQL Server Setup dialog box similar to the one shown here.

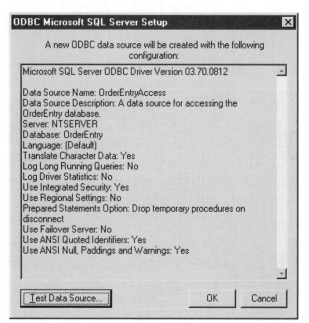

16. Click Test Data Source. If you've configured everything correctly, you'll see a success message. Otherwise, you'll need to click Cancel and recheck your settings. You must get a good connection test before you continue with the rest of this procedure.

17. Click OK two times to clear the various data source dialog boxes. You'll return to the Select Data Source dialog box where you'll see a new data source. This should have the name of the data source that we just created.

18. Highlight the new data source, then click OK. Visual C++ will finish creating the project for you.

At this point, you may be wondering what purpose this project serves. There isn't even any way to compile it. If you choose the Data View tab of the Workspace window, you'll see a hierarchical view of your database that looks surprisingly similar to the one in Microsoft SQL Enterprise Manager. The main difference, of course, is that you're only seeing a single database as shown here.

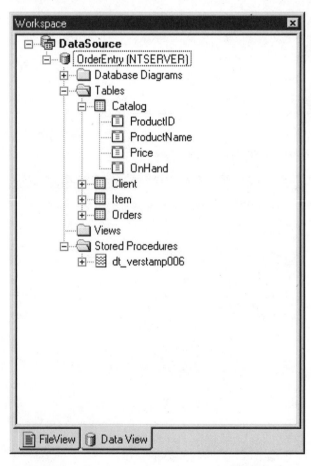

To make this project do something for us, we've got to create a query. Use the Insert |
New Database Item command to display the Insert Database Item dialog box shown here.

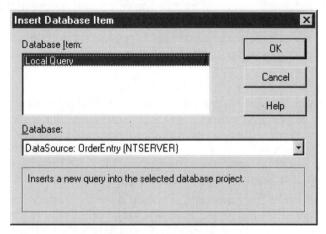

Choose Local Query from the list of database items, then click OK. At this point, you'll
see a new query window composed of four panes as follows:

▼ **Diagram**   Contains a diagram of the database query that you're creating. You
can save this diagram for future use. The diagram will show links between the
various tables of the database, which makes it easier to understand how one
table relates to another in the query you're creating.

■ **Grid**   Contains a list of the columns that you're using from each table. The
grid allows you to define how each column is used for sorting. You can also
limit the number of records retrieved by using Boolean expressions.

■ **SQL**   Displays the SQL statement created by a combination of entries in the
Diagram and Grid windows. You can also use this window for manually
entering SQL statements, which will turn out to be a very handy feature.

▲ **Results**   Displays the results of the query in the SQL window. You must press
the Run button to display the results of a query.

By now, it should be obvious that you can do a lot of database modeling with this display, in addition to creating new queries for use in your applications. Those are the intended uses for this particular kind of project. However, there's another purpose that you
can use this type of project for that isn't documented very well by Microsoft.

WARNING: This is an undocumented way to use the Database Project. Since this isn't a documented
way to use Visual C++, you may find that it doesn't work as anticipated with certain database products or
that your access to other products is severely limited. The only way to know what you can do with this technique is to actually try it on your workstation using a test database. Remember that stored procedures can
alter the contents and schema of a database, so you'll never want to use this technique on an operational
production database unless you actually know what will happen through personal experience.

SQL Server provides a wealth of stored procedures. Remember that I said you could type anything you wanted in the SQL pane, which means that you can type the name of a stored procedure in lieu of a standard query. You can try this out with the example database by typing **sp_who**, then clicking Run. You'll see a Visual C++ error message stating that it can't parse the SQL statement that you've typed in. Click OK to bypass this message. What you should see in the Results pane is a list of the users currently logged on to SQL Server.

There are a lot of stored procedures that could come in handy while working on your application. For example, if you want to see a list of the special stored procedures for your database, type **sp_stored_procedures** in the SQL pane, then click Run. You'll see a complete list of the stored procedures for the database, rather than the partial list that Visual C++ provides by default.

Some of these stored procedures require arguments in addition to the actual call. For example, the sp_dboption stored procedure falls into this category. If you call this stored procedure without adding an argument, then you'd see the options for the Master database, not the database that you're currently working with. If you wanted to find out the options set for the OrderEntry database, you'd need to type "**sp_dboption OrderEntry**", then click the Run button. Of course, there are a lot more stored procedures that require arguments than not. This is one of the reasons you want to try this out on a test database first. Make sure you keep notes on the order in which arguments are accepted and what type of arguments SQL Server is looking for.

As you can see, the Database Project can be a powerful tool. However, since it's use as a remote access tool is completely undocumented, you'll need to spend time learning how to use it. It's also important to keep this new tool in your arsenal in mind as you create new stored procedures for your database. You could use stored procedures to perform all kinds of programming-specific queries that would never get used in an application. In short, the Database Project is also completely flexible to your needs—a real plus in a world that's short on remote debugging tools.

DEFINING THE APPLICATION

As with any application, the first thing we'll need to do for this example is to define what we want the application to do. Normally, you'd do this as part of a complex specification document. We've all had to create design documents in the past, so I won't belabor the point of the importance of design documentation to creating a fully functional application in a minimum amount of time with the fewest number of bugs.

Before moving on to the application definition, however, let's talk about application definition requirements in a COM+ world for a few moments. (This will be an ongoing process, so if you don't see what you want here, we'll probably cover it in later chapters.) Since COM+ allows an application to work across multiple machines and even networks, the need to create a detailed picture of what you expect to provide as input to an application and expect to get as output is even more important than before. Unlike many applications, a COM+ application specification should also include the servers on which various parts of the application will execute so that you can take the purpose of a specific machine into account when designing the components that will run on that machine. Part of the description for this example is to place specific parts of the application on a particular machine. This principle holds true whether you use two machines, as we do in this example, or hundreds of machines, which is what happens in large corporate applications.

In Microsoft's *n*-tier approach to application design specified by the Distributed interNetwork Architecture (DNA), there are multiple servers involved in servicing the needs of a particular application, as shown in Figure 7-1. Each of these servers has a distinct purpose. For example, one server might be responsible for ensuring that user input is correctly formatted before adding it to the database.

Even if your application is made up of multiple components that reside on multiple servers, you can still ease the complexity of defining the application specification by tak-

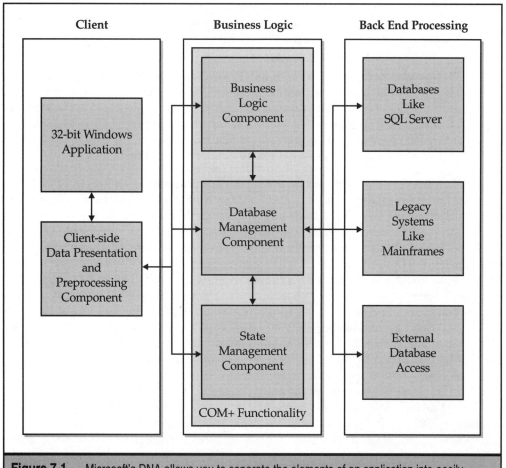

Figure 7-1.   Microsoft's DNA allows you to separate the elements of an application into easily managed modules

ing a DNA view of the application first. For practical purposes, what you're really looking at in Figure 7-1 is an extension of the common three-tier approach listed here:

▼ **Client** Contains all of the user and client-side processing. This is the tier that formats data for output to the user and checks user input for errors (in as much as possible). You can also use this tier for data preprocessing and to anticipate user data requests in an effort to reduce network traffic.

■ **Business logic** Allows the client application to interact with the server in a way defined by the business rules for your business. For example, this is the tier that determines whether the user has sufficient rights to access the requested data and what elements of the data record that the user is allowed to see. This is also the tier that requests data from any back-end processors and sends formatted data from the user to the database. Business logic can include a number of other things as well. For example, a single record may require input from multiple users, so this tier could alert users to the presence of new records that require their attention. I call this type of component a *state management component* because it helps keep the various parts of your application in sync.

▲ **Back-end processing** Provides database access and the input/output of complete data. This is the tier that manages the data for you, but doesn't format it for use. Every business runs on data, which is normally stored in the form of data records on a high-speed server. However, the contents of a single data record may actually come from several sources. In short, the efficient storage of data doesn't always necessarily match efficient use of the data by an end user.

The fact that you can't depend on seeing the application as a single entity anymore makes it imperative that you understand how the application works from a design perspective. Even using just two machines, as we'll do for this example, makes it much more difficult to see the application in action than in the days when everything resided on one desktop. As a result, monolithic applications don't work anymore. Modularity has taken on a new level of importance, which will become apparent as the chapter progresses. The main reason you'd use any component programming approach like COM+ is to ensure that you can move pieces of an application around without requiring any change to the application code. COM+ is all about application flexibility and the ability to write applications that don't depend on the ability to see the application as a whole. In fact, that's one of the main things that this example will demonstrate. The ability to place a component—which is part of a whole application, yet an independent part of that application—on a server and expect that an application will be able to access and use it is an important tenet of component programming.

The following sections of this chapter will help you explore the definition for our example application. We'll look at two main application components: the tasks that the application will perform and the database used to store application data. The tasks define what the user will do with the data stored in the database, while the database design defines how the user will access the data.

An Application Task Overview

As previously mentioned, the application we'll create in this example is a very simple order entry system. In this case, there are several sets of tasks that a user could perform, only a subset of which will actually appear in the example. The following list summarizes the types of tasks that a simple order entry system normally performs from the user perspective: (There are obviously other tasks going on in the background.)

▼ Add new orders

■ Edit an order

■ Remove an order

■ View the status of an order

■ Print completed order forms

■ Browse a list of orders

■ Add new customers

■ Edit customer information

■ Remove a customer

▲ Perform various types of database maintenance

Defining what tasks you want the application to perform is only the first step. Now we have to divide each of those tasks into three elements as defined by the DNA description that I presented earlier. For example, the task of adding a new order could be divided into the following three elements:

▼ **Client** For this particular task, you'd need to display a form containing a series of fields for each field in the database. You'd need to check with the business logic tier to determine which fields the user is allowed to see. In addition, there might be special considerations like list box entries that the user isn't allowed to use and you wouldn't need to display as a result. Once the form is filled out, this client tier would check the results of the input before sending the data off to the business logic tier. This code would perform generic checks like the ranges of numbers or, perhaps, matching ZIP code to city and state. This is the only part of the application that will execute on the client machine for this example.

■ **Business logic** There are a variety of things that you'd need to perform at this tier, depending on the size of your business. Our example will only use this tier to interface with the database management system (DBMS). However, a larger example might send a message to the company's inventory control system and check for product availability. As part of the order entry process, the business logic might assign a status or availability code to the order. The inventory control system would ask the shipping department to send the part if it's available, or ask manufacturing to create the part if the warehouse is currently out of stock. In short, creating the order sets off a chain of events that your business logic would need to track to ensure that the order gets fulfilled.

▲ **Back-end processing**   Our example will use SQL Server for the DBMS, but the same idea will work with other products. The back-end processing element could even be a mainframe. The point is that the back-end processing element normally manages the data required to make your business work. Many people think of data as something that humans consume, but it's also needed by your applications. For example, the user may never see some of the status codes assigned to each order in the database, but those codes will be used by the various application components to make decisions automatically. It's important to understand that the back-end processing element refers to all data, no matter what form it takes or where it resides.

An Overview of the Database

Our example application is relatively straightforward in this case, but the database management part of the equation requires some additional explanation. The task list in the previous section makes it clear that a single table database won't do the job of storing the data we need to manage. We'll need a set of four tables for the example order entry application, at a minimum. Anyone working on database applications for any length of time knows that there are few, if any, database applications that can work with just one table and still provide efficient data access. Table 7-1 provides a name for each table in the database and defines its purpose.

NOTE: I'm taking a couple of shortcuts here that you wouldn't normally take with an order entry system. For example, the Client table would normally get divided into several related tables to ensure that you have enough flexibility for future needs. A client may have several addresses, or you might need to accommodate several contacts for a single company. In this case, I'm using what amounts to a flat-file database for the client information. I've made every attempt to ensure that the shortcuts I've taken with the database design won't affect the real-world perspective that I'm trying to maintain throughout the example.

An In-Depth View of the Individual Tables

Now that you have a better idea of what the four tables will be used for, let's talk about the fields in each table. Remember that the purpose of this example is to create a simple order entry system of the type that a small company would use, but that could be expanded for a larger company's needs. In addition, we'll spend quite a bit of time looking at how various components can use MTS to ensure that the data gets from one end of the application to the other. The actual mechanics of the database are secondary in this example to the mechanics of the MTS-enabled components.

Name	Description
Client	Contains a list of the clients and their contact information. Obviously, this is a simplistic view, but it will work for a small order entry system. Larger order entry systems would contain additional information like the client's current credit rating and pointers to past purchases. It might even include a hierarchy of contacts within the client company.
Catalog	You need to know what you're selling before you sell it. This example will use a small static table to list the items for sale. In a larger order entry system, the catalog might be updated by the inventory control system to show only the items that meet a specific set of criteria, such as being in stock at the time of the order.
Orders	This table contains the one-time order information like a pointer to the client asking for the material and a method of payment. A more complex order entry system might include status information for the order. In even larger systems, the order might be archived after fulfillment so that your company could track client buying habits.
Items	A list of the items that the client has ordered from the catalog, along with the quantity of each item ordered. This lowest-level table is about the same in any order entry system. The bottom line is that no matter how complex the rest of the order entry system is, the whole process ends up listing items that you can supply to the customer and an indication of the client's need for those items.

Table 7-1.   A List of Tables for Our Order Entry System

The client database is nothing more than a simple contact database with some order entry information thrown in for good measure. Table 7-2 provides a description of the Client table and the fields that it contains.

NOTE: The Nulls column of Table 7-2 contains two values. If you check the Nulls column in the table definition, it means that Nulls are allowed in that field. You'd only allow Null values if the data in that field isn't absolutely essential to the operation of the database application. For example, not everyone has a middle name, so that information isn't crucial. On the other hand, the "Not checked" value indicates that the user has to enter a value for that field. This is especially important for key values, but it is also important for field values that could affect the business logic of your application.

Column Name	Datatype	Size	Nulls	Default
CustomerID	Char	5	Not checked	
FirstName	Char	40	Not checked	
MiddleInitial	Char	1	Checked	
LastName	Char	40	Not checked	
Title	Char	40	Checked	"Owner"
Company	Char	40	Checked	
Address1	Char	50	Not checked	
Address2	Char	50	Checked	
City	Char	50	Not checked	
State	Char	2	Not checked	"WI"
ZIP	Char	10	Not checked	
Country	Char	40	Checked	"United States"
Telephone1	Char	13	Checked	
Telephone2	Char	13	Checked	
LastContact	DateTime	8 (This value is automatically entered and you can't change it.)	Not checked	

Table 7-2.   Client Table Schema

TIP: SQL Server 7.0 and above supports the ANSI NULL instead of the NULL value supported by previous versions. What this means to you as a developer is that you'll need to pay close attention to the upgrade information for SQL Server should you decide to move this SQL Server 6.5 project to that platform. You may also need to modify your code, so be sure you take all potential changes into consideration.

Notice that I use a Char type for the CustomerID field. You'll find that all of the ID fields in this example use the Char type, even though many developers use an Int type in real-world databases. There are several reasons for this choice. The most important is flexibility. An Int field is limited to numbers alone. I could use a combination of numbers and letters for the ID fields should the need arise. The Char type is also less ambiguous than using Int. Depending on which version of Visual C++ you use, the value of an Int varies. Add to this mix the use of Visual Basic or other languages to access the component, and you have the potential for a real mess.

Of course, no design decision comes for free. There are some disadvantages to using the Char type as well. The most important problem is search time. It takes longer to search a Char type field than an Int type. To gain the flexibility that a Char field provides, you have to give up some speed. The Char type also requires more space on disk than the Int type. Obviously, in today's world of huge hard drive arrays, the disk space concern is less important.

The Catalog table shown in Table 7-3 is another area where we're going to cheat a little for this example. In this case, it's not the format of the table that will differ from a standard database, but the content of that table. We'll use a very simple static table, in this case, to reduce the complexity of the application. Normally, you'd need some method for users to add or subtract catalog entries, and to then be able to track which catalog items are actually available for sale at any given time. Depending on the kind of database you're setting up, the catalog may consist of items that are only sold during certain times of the year—like heavy coats near the end of summer, through fall, and during part of the winter. Our example application won't consider many of these complexities, but you'll need to consider them as part of a production application.

The Orders table shown in Table 7-4 merely tracks which order numbers belong to a particular client. Notice that it doesn't repeat the information found in the Client table because this information already appears in that table. However, the Client table only contains the information of the person placing the order, not the receiver of the order. In many cases, the shipping address will be different than the address of the client contact, so we need to provide an additional set of fields for this purpose. You could automatically set both sets of fields the same to save data entry time when the addresses match. Fields missing from this table include normal business requirements, like method of payment and the date agreed upon for delivery. These fields aren't all that important in the context of this example, but you'd need to include them with a production system.

The final table for this database is the Item table, with the columns shown in Table 7-5. This table contains a list of the items ordered by the client. Notice that the Price field gets repeated from the Catalog table. The order entry database needs to reflect the price of a product at the time that the order was completed, not the current price of the product. Obviously, there are going to be times when you need to repeat information within a database for historical purposes, even though this practice is normally frowned upon.

Now that we have all of the tables defined, it's time to look at how they'll interact. Figure 7-2 shows how the primary keys and foreign keys of the various tables will allow the order entry system to work. We'll create indexes for each of these primary keys in the sec-

Column Name	Datatype	Size	Nulls	Default
ProductID	Char	5	Not checked	
ProductName	Char	50	Not checked	
Price	Money	N/A	Not checked	
OnHand	Int	N/A	Checked	0

Table 7-3.   Catalog Table Schema

Column Name	Datatype	Size	Nulls	Default
OrderID	Char	5	Not checked	
CustomerID	Char	5	Not checked	
FirstName	Char	40	Not checked	
MiddleInitial	Char	1	Checked	
LastName	Char	40	Not checked	
Title	Char	40	Checked	"Owner"
Company	Char	40	Checked	
Address1	Char	50	Not checked	
Address2	Char	50	Checked	
City	Char	50	Not checked	
State	Char	2	Not checked	"WI"
ZIP	Char	10	Not checked	
Telephone1	Char	13	Checked	
Telephone2	Char	13	Checked	

Table 7-4. Orders Table Schema

tion that follows. For now, all you need to know is that the tables are designed to interact with each other. While we won't use all of the interactions for the example program, a model like the one in Figure 7-2 is very important when working with any database project because it helps to keep the various data interactions in view. Large databases with lots of tables can quickly become so complex that you really can't see what the data is doing without a model of this type.

Column Name	Datatype	Size	Nulls	Default
ItemID	Char	5	Not checked	
OrderID	Char	5	Not checked	
ProductID	Char	5	Not checked	
Quantity	Int	N/A	Not checked	1
Price	Money	N/A	Not checked	

Table 7-5. Item Table Schema

All of the relationships in Figure 7-2 are one too many. For example, one client can have many orders and each order can have many items within it. As you can see, this is a fairly standard database setup—there isn't anything too unusual to consider from a data handling perspective if you've worked with database applications in the past.

Creating the Database and Associated Tables

It's time to create the database and associated tables. In this section I'll help you define the database itself, create a database structure, assign security, and finally, create the required database indexes. We've already looked at the design of the database and associated tables in the previous sections, so I won't be covering that issue again. In fact, in some places, the procedures in this section have been shortened with the idea that creating these tables will be a repetitive process where only the schema changes.

Once you've finished creating a database in SQL Server (step one of the process we'll look at in this chapter), you need to design the elements within it (the remaining three steps that I talked about in the previous paragraph). There are actually four steps in the design process (at least for this simple example). First, we'll need to create all of the tables used to store data. Next, we need to create the fields within those tables that the user will need to store the various kinds of order entry data. Third, we'll need to assign permissions to access the database. Without these permissions, no one will be able to access the database and enter data into it (except the system administrator, of course). Finally, we'll provide some indexes to order the data for display.

Now that you have some idea of what we're going to do, let's look at the process in more detail. The following sections of the chapter will help you create the OrderEntry database, define the various tables it contains, add security to those tables, and finally, create indexes that will be used to interact with the tables.

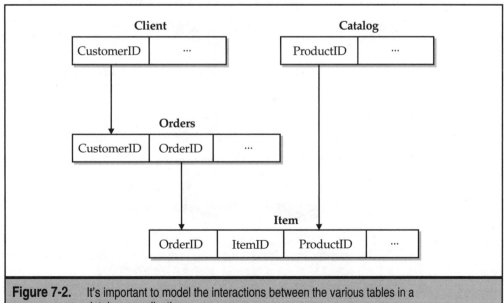

Figure 7-2.   It's important to model the interactions between the various tables in a database application

Defining the OrderEntry Database

As previously mentioned, the first thing we need to do before any database design can take place is to create the database itself. The following procedure assumes that you have the Enterprise Edition of Visual Studio, with SQL Server Developer Edition installed. I'll also assume that you've set up any security required to access both the database server and the SQL Server installation.

NOTE: Your screen may or may not match the screen shots shown in this section of the chapter. I used a Windows 2000 Server and the version of SQL Server 6.5 Developer Edition that comes with the Visual Studio package for this example. If you're using a different version of Windows or a different configuration of SQL Server, your screen will most likely look different than mine. In addition, this chapter assumes that you've created a clean test installation of SQL Server on your server. Finally, the test application will always access the database over a network, which is what you'll need to do to check central file access.

1. Open SQL Enterprise Manager. You'll see a Microsoft SQL Enterprise Manager window like the one shown in Figure 7-3. This is where you'll perform all management functions with SQL Server, including designing databases for use by clients. Notice that the figure shows both the Database Devices and the Databases folders open. We'll use these two folders as the example progresses. The first thing we need to do is create a database device.

2. Right-click the Database Devices folder, then choose New Device from the context menu. You'll see the New Database Device dialog box shown here. A database device is the physical file used to hold the database. The database has everything needed to store your data, including both tables and procedures. We'll look at the contents of our test database later in the procedure.

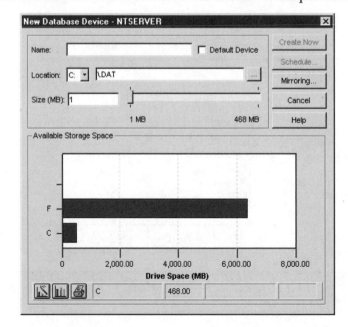

Figure 7-3.   Microsoft SQL Enterprise Manager allows you to design and manage databases on your database server

3. Type a database device name in the Name field. I used Orders for the purposes of this example.

4. Type the initial size of the database file in the Size (MB) field. I used 15 for this example since our test data won't be very large. Obviously, a production database will be much larger, and you'll need to provide additional space for growth while keeping the available space on your server in mind.

5. Click Create Now. SQL Server will create the database device that you requested. It'll display a success message once the database device is available for use. (If you don't see a success message, you'll need to stop the procedure now and check your SQL Server installation. Also, make sure that you actually have the space required to hold your database on the server.)

6. Click OK. You should see a new database device named Orders appear in the Database Devices folder. Now it's time to add the database itself.

7. Right-click the Databases folder, then select the New Database option on the context menu. You'll see the New Database dialog box shown here. Notice that it contains a list of all the database devices that SQL Server currently has installed.

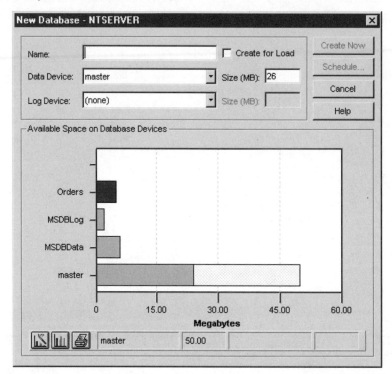

8. Type the name of your database in the Name field. I used OrderEntry for the sample application.

9. Choose the Orders database device in the Database Device field.

10. Click Create Now. You'll see the OrderEntry database added to the Databases folder.

Adding Tables to the OrderEntry Database

At this point, we're ready to start designing the database. Let's begin by adding tables to our database as shown in the following procedure.

NOTE: The system administrator account (sa) can access every part of SQL Server, including any new databases you create.

1. Open the OrderEntry database hierarchy and you'll see two folders, one of which is Objects.

2. Right-click on the Objects folder and choose New Table from the context menu. You'll see a Manage Tables dialog box like the one shown here.

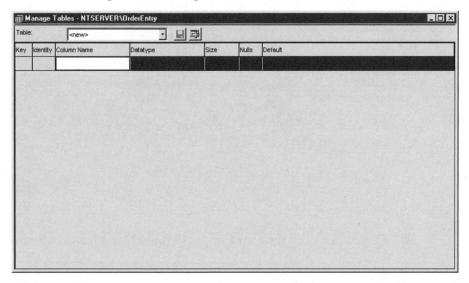

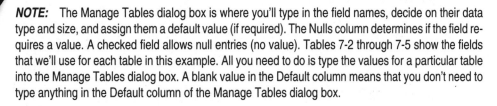

NOTE: The Manage Tables dialog box is where you'll type in the field names, decide on their data type and size, and assign them a default value (if required). The Nulls column determines if the field requires a value. A checked field allows null entries (no value). Tables 7-2 through 7-5 show the fields that we'll use for each table in this example. All you need to do is type the values for a particular table into the Manage Tables dialog box. A blank value in the Default column means that you don't need to type anything in the Default column of the Manage Tables dialog box.

3. Type the field entries for one of the tables listed in Tables 7-2 through 7-5. Don't type all of the tables at once—just work on one table's worth of field entries, then proceed to the next step.

4. Click Advanced Features and you'll see the Manage Tables dialog box change as shown here. We need to add a primary key (the unique ID key for this table) and foreign keys (those obtained from other tables). Figure 7-2 shows the relationships between the various tables. For example, the Orders table has one primary key (OrderID) and one foreign key (CustomerID). There's one exception to this particular scenario. The Item table has two primary keys: ItemID and OrderID. As we'll see later, it takes the combination of these two fields to define a unique table entry, so you need to use both as the primary key.

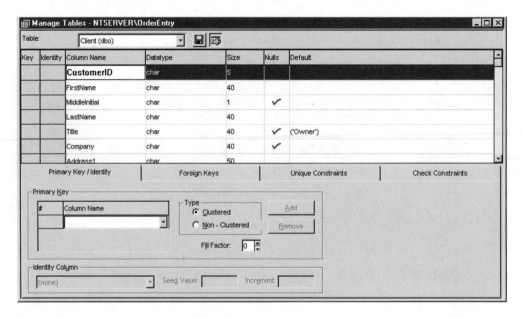

5. Select the primary key field name in the Column Name field, then click Add.

NOTE: There aren't any foreign keys for either the Client or Catalog tables, so you can skip Step 6 when working with these tables.

6. Click Foreign Keys. You'll see a list of available foreign keys in the Key Columns list. Match the name of the foreign key in the current database with the one in the referenced table. For example, when working with the Orders table, you'll choose the CustomerID entry in the Key Columns list and choose CustomerID from the Foreign Key Columns list. Click Add.

7. Click the Save Table button when you finish entering the information into the Manage Tables dialog box. You'll see a Specify Table Name dialog box like the one shown here.

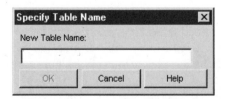

8. Type the name of the table that you're working on in the New Table Name field, then click OK. For example, when working on the Client table, you'd type **Client** in this field. Click the Close box to close the Manage Tables dialog box.

9. Repeat Steps 2–5 for each of the tables listed in Tables 7-2 through 7-5. When you finish creating the tables, the Objects/Tables folder should contain the entries shown in Figure 7-4. This figure also shows the other entries we've made to date in the clean SQL Server setup.

TIP: If you want more control over the initial appearance of your table, click the Additional Features button in the Manage Tables dialog box. You'll be able to set up the primary key, one or more foreign keys, any unique constraints, and a set of rules for checking those unique constraints. There are other ways that you can set things like the primary and foreign keys, but the Additional Features button allows you to set everything from one place.

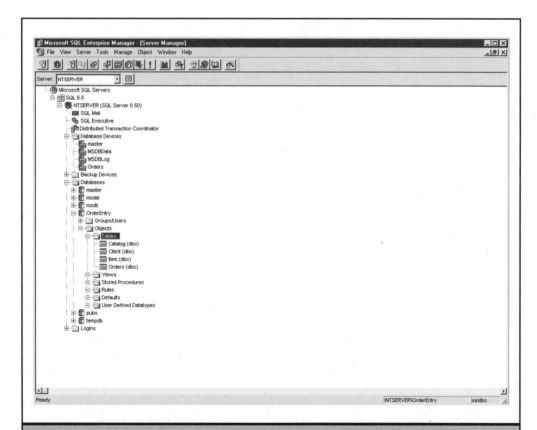

Figure 7-4. Our completed list of tables for the OrderEntry database includes all of the entries from Tables 7-2 through 7-5

OrderEntry Database Security Concerns

There are two tasks left to perform before we can start creating a connection to our database. The first task is to set the security for our database. To do that, we'll need to make changes to the Group/Users folder in the OrderEntry database (see Figure 7-4). Right-click Groups/Users, then choose New Group from the context menu. You'll see a Manage Groups dialog box like the one shown here.

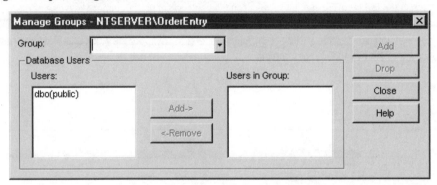

TIP: It's important to remember that there are many levels of security used by a COM+ application to ensure that your data remains secure. Adding security to the database is just one part of a much larger overall picture. You'll also want to read about the security provided by Windows 2000 and COM+ in the "Role-Based Security" section of Chapter 3 as part of understanding the security measures in place for the example application. The easiest way to look at security under Windows 2000 is that every object, no matter what type of object it is, has some type of security attached to it. Even though different types of objects may employ a variety of security methodologies, all are protected to some extent. Of course, it's equally important to realize that no security scheme is perfect. Monitoring your security measures is always essential because crackers are notorious for finding holes in supposedly perfect security measures.

Type **Administrators** in the Group field, then click Add (you may not need to click Add—SQL Server may move the users automatically when you finish typing **Administrators**). You'll see Administrators added to the Groups/Users hierarchy. Type **Users** in the Group field, then click Add. You'll see Users added to the Groups/Users hierarchy. Notice that we've set up three groups for the example table: Public, Administrators, and Users. The public at large only needs to view the contents of the database. We really don't want them to change anything, so they only get the Select permission, which allows them to view the records. Users need to be able to view and modify the records. They also need to add new records and delete old ones, so users as a group get the Select, Insert, Update, and Delete permissions. Finally, the Administrator group requires full access to the table, so they get all of the available permissions. You'll need to be careful handing out this privilege since anyone in the Administrator group will have full access to everything the table has to offer.

Since the database owner (dbo) is the one who owns the databases for our example, we need to give this object administrator privileges. Right-click the dbo object, then choose Edit from the context menu. You'll see a Manage Users dialog box like the one shown here.

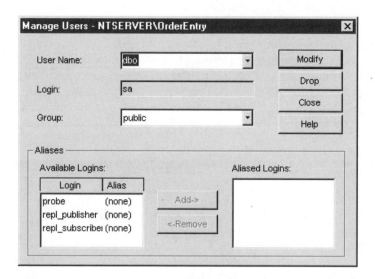

Choose Administrators in the Group field, then click Modify. You'll see the dbo object move from the Public group folder to the Administrators group folder. Obviously, you can also add users to the various group folders and perform other security management tasks. For the moment, we'll move on to other setup issues.

Now that we have some groups and users set up, it's time to assign various permissions to the tables. Right-click the Client table object shown in Figure 7-4, then choose Permissions from the context menu. You'll see an Object Permissions dialog box like the one shown here.

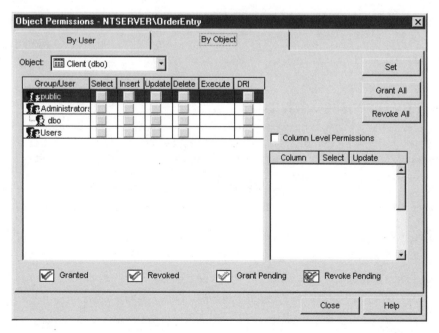

The Object Permissions dialog box allows you to determine who gets what level of access to a particular table. It's important to give each user only the level of access they actually require to prevent damage to your database and its contents. When you finish setting security for the Contacts table, click Set to make the changes permanent, then Close to close the Object Permissions dialog box. This is how I set the permissions for all of the tables in this example (note that the dbo automatically inherits the permissions granted to the Administrators group).

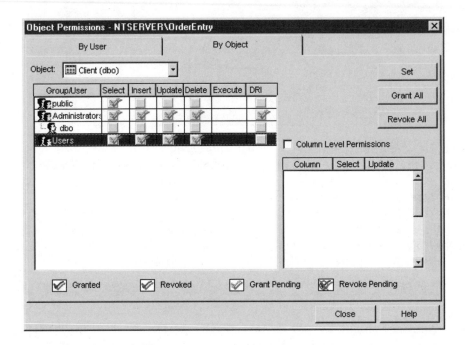

OrderEntry Database Backup Concerns

This chapter is showing you how to create a simple order entry database. If you lose the data, it's not going to be that big of a loss. However, the data in your production system is another issue. The data in a production system is worth more than the total cost of all of the systems that it runs on in most cases. Consider the time required to re-enter the data if a system crash destroys the database, not to mention the business lost while the reentry process takes place. Of course, this assumes that you have a hard copy of the data to work with.

Regular data backups aren't an optional part of your application. You should plan to make daily backups at a minimum, or even more often if the database or the amount of data entered each day is large. The reason is simple: It takes a lot less time to create a backup of your data than it does to re-create it later.

SQL Server provides a couple of different methods for backing up your data. The best method, at least from an administrator perspective, is to stop the three services associated with SQL Server and then back up the entire MSSQL directory (unless your data is stored somewhere else). This ensures that you'll get all of the data backed up and can restore the data later with minimum effort. Of course, this solution won't work in a lot of cases. For one thing, stopping the three SQL Server services makes the databases that it manages inaccessible. If your company runs 24 hours a day, then you won't be able to shut these services down.

There's another way to create a backup of your database—directly, while the services are still running. Look again at Figure 7-3 and you'll see a folder named Backup Devices. As with other SQL Server operations, you need to create a backup device before you can perform the backup process. Don't confuse these backup devices with an actual piece of hardware like a tape drive. SQL Server will allow you to back up your data to a directory on the hard drive or to a physical piece of hardware. The default device provided with SQL Server will send the backup to the \MSSQL\BACKUP folder. Creating a new backup device is easy. Just right-click the Backup Devices folder, and then choose New Backup Device from the context menu. You'll see a New Backup Device dialog box like the one shown here.

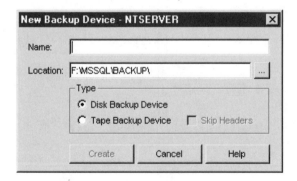

Notice that this dialog box allows you to choose between a disk backup device and a tape backup device. All you need to do is enter the name of a new backup device, then supply a device location. Type the name of backup device—I'll use MyBackup for this chapter, but you can use any name you want. Placing the backup in the \MSSQL\BACKUP folder will work just fine.

WARNING: SQL Server installs a default backup device called diskdump. This device sends the backup you create to the system's NULL device. You can't retrieve dumps sent to the NULL device, and this device won't create a file on your server drive. In short, you can't use the diskdump device to create a backup of your SQL Server database.

Once you have a backup device, creating the backup is easy. Right-click the database you want to back up, and then choose Backup/Restore from the context menu. You'll see a Database Backup/Restore dialog box like the one shown here.

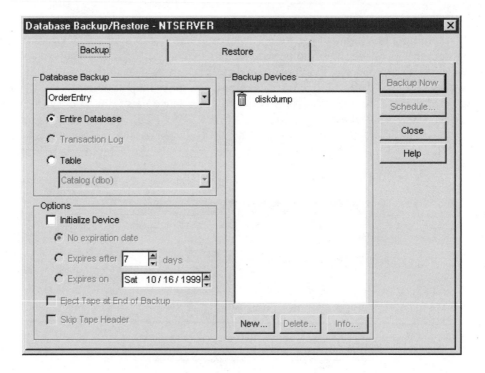

TIP: If you haven't initialized the backup device, click the Initialize Device option, then choose an expiration date for the backup. SQL Server will automatically initialize the device for you before it begins the backup process. As part of the initialization process, you'll see a Backup Volume Label dialog box that contains the name of the backup device and the associated volume name. In most cases, you can simply click OK at this dialog box to accept the default volume name.

Notice that there isn't any way to select all of the databases for backup; you'll have to back them up one at a time. Select the database that you want to back up from the Database Backup drop-down list box, highlight one of the devices in the Backup Devices list, then click Backup Now if you want to perform the backup immediately. Clicking Schedule will allow you to schedule the database for an immediate, one-time, or recurring backup as shown here.

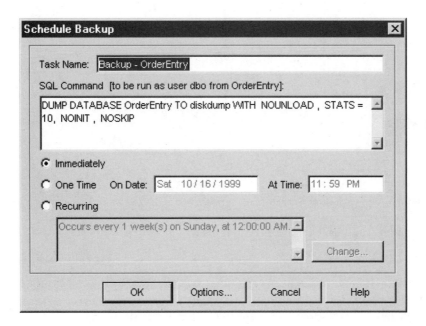

All you need to do to complete the offline backup part of this process is to back up the data in the backup device file. The backup device file has a DAT extension and the same name as the backup device that you created. You'll find this device file in the directory that you chose for the backup.

Creating the OrderEntry Database Indexes

Our final task is to set up the required indexes for our table. An index allows the user to see the table in sorted order. All you need to do is right-click the Client table entry, then choose Indexes to open the Manage Indexes dialog box shown here.

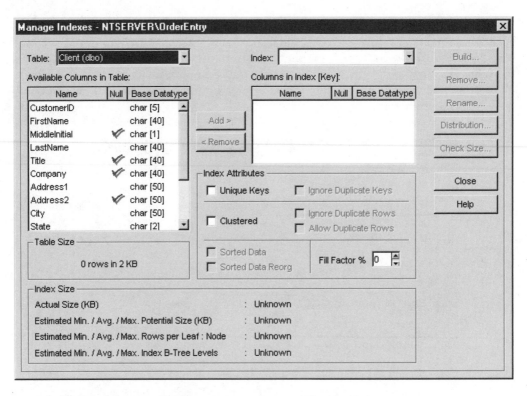

We'll create two indexes for our Client table—the number that you actually need to set in a given circumstance depends on how many ways you need to see the data ordered. Type **LastName** in the Index field. Highlight the LastName entry in the Available Columns in Table list, then click Add. Do the same thing for the FirstName entry. Click the Build button. You'll see an Index Build dialog box that asks if you want to build the index now or wait until later. Click Execute Now. SQL Server will pause for a few moments, then take you back to the Manage Indexes dialog box. You've just created the first index.

TIP: As part of the process of creating primary keys for the tables, SQL Server will automatically generate one index for you. This index is for the primary key. For example, when you look at the Client table, there will already be a predefined index for the CustomerID field.

The second index is built using the same technique. Type **ZIPCode** in the Index field. Choose the ZIP, LastName, and FirstName fields (in that order) from the Available Columns in Table list. Click Build, then Execute Now to create the index. The second index is ready to go. Click Close to close the Manage Indexes dialog box. At this point, the database is ready for use with our example, even though there are other tasks you'd perform to make it ready for use in a production environment.

The N-tier View of the Project

At this point, we've taken a detailed look at the database and the various requirements for manipulating it. We really haven't look at what's required to create the application for this example. By now you should realize that even the simplest COM+ application is going to be an order of magnitude more complex than other applications you've created in the past. This means that you need to consider whether COM+ is really the solution you need. If your goal is to create a simple application for working with data on a LAN, you'll probably be better off using one of these older approaches. In many cases, especially when using the new OLE DB features on Visual C++, the work required to create a simple LAN-based application is almost trivial.

The application in this chapter looks like a lot of work, and it is. However, it won't take long to realize that our sample application has many advantages over the simple applications of the past. Most notably, you'll see that accessing the data from any location is possible because of the arrangement of components servicing the application. The data is also more secure and access more reliable. In short, all of the preparation time and coding will pay dividends that you can't easily equate to the work required to produce an old technology application. The COM+ application we'll produce in this chapter really is a new kind of application that needs to be judged on its own merits.

As you saw in Figure 7-1, Microsoft is serious about making applications both scalable and easier to maintain. We're going to take an *n*-tier approach to application development in this chapter that's very similar to what you saw in Figure 7-1. In fact, the application overview shown in Figure 7-5 should look very familiar by now. No, you won't be required to run multiple servers to test this application—you could theoretically test it on a single machine. However, to get the full benefit out of the example and to really test the resulting code, you need to test the application on two machines as shown in the diagram.

TIP: There are some situations when you may want to start out with one development machine, then move to two machines as development progresses. A single-machine approach will allow you to test the application logic without any chance of outside interference from errant network connections and the like. In addition, a single-machine approach tends to hide some communication-related problems; allowing you to get the business logic in place for further testing. You must eventually test your application on a minimum of two machines because COM+ tends to hide some coding errors on a single-machine setup. For example, there was an error in the CoCreateInstanceEx() call in my original example that didn't show up with a single-machine setup. The problem only appeared when I moved to a two-machine (client and server) setup. In short, you can start developing your application on one machine to make things easy, but plan on using two machines for later development when working with COM+.

As you can see, the test application, MTSTest, and the client-side component will exist as separate files. MTSTest will use CoCreateInstance() to create a local copy of the client-side component. The COrderRequest class methods will use CoCreateInstanceEx() to

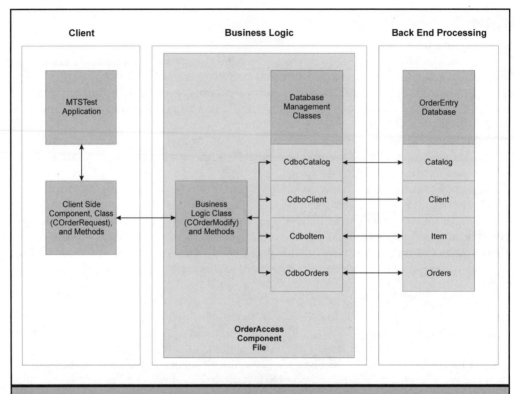

Figure 7-5.   The sample application for this chapter uses the *n*-tier development approach

create a server-side copy of the server-side component, OrderAccess. Within the OrderAccess file are the five classes we'll use to implement business and database objects. COrderModify, which is the business object, will contain all of the methods required for the client to gain access to the data within the database. There's one database object class for each of the tables within the database. You'll see later in the chapter why we need this many classes. We would, in fact, need one class for every type of query required by the application and business logic. In other words, if you want to execute a stored procedure, you need a separate class to perform that task.

CREATING THE SERVER-SIDE COMPONENTS

Defining and building the database was only the first part of the data management process. Now it's time to build a series of object classes that applications will use to access the database that we've created. There's only one business object class. Each kind of database access will require a separate class—in this case, we'll create four, but the number of classes you need in an enterprise-level application will depend on the kinds of queries you want to create. This set of object classes will use transactions to ensure that each database entry gets made at least once, but only one time. Of course, the business object class will be responsible for implementing your company's business policies, while the database object classes will need to take care of all of the normal database requirements like adding and deleting records.

The following sections divide the process of creating our example component in three main sections. The first section will look at what you need to do to create the component shell. We'll create and implement the business object first, then the database objects (you'll see that the database objects are trivial to add once we get to that point in the chapter). We'll be creating an Active Template Library (ATL) component in this case, because there aren't any user interface or cross-language compatibility requirements to worry about. In addition, ATL will provide better flexibility during the coding process. Finally, there really isn't any way to use MFC in this particular case—Microsoft has essentially relegated MFC to creating application components like pushbuttons.

The second section will show you how to add code to make the component work. In most cases, we won't be looking at every detail that you'd normally need to consider for a production component. The whole purpose of this component is to show you how you'd create an ATL-based MTS component in general. Our goal is to see what you'd need to do to create a component that will use MTS effectively to ensure that the data you work with remains intact.

The third and final section will take a very quick look at what you need to install the component on the server as an application. We aren't going to take a full tour of the Component Services MMC snap-in at this time—we'll just talk about the mechanics of using it for this example. Look at the "Working with the Component Services MMC Snap-In" section of the chapter for more detailed information about this particular utility. You'll want to know all about the Component Services MMC snap-in before you begin your first production project.

Creating the Component Shell

Let's create the component shell for this example. One of the benefits of using ATL is that you can create lightweight components that don't rely on a lot of outside resources. The disadvantage to using ATL is that the IDE and associated wizards do very little of the work for you. This means that it takes longer to create even a simple shell for an ATL component. Advantages and disadvantages aside, you can divide the component shell creation process into four parts: creating the project, inserting an object, adding properties, and adding methods (other components will have additional features, but this is all we'll need for this example).

Starting the Project

The first thing we'll need to do is create a new project. Unlike an MFC control, however, creating a project isn't sufficient for creating an ATL-based control in general—it only creates a shell that will eventually hold a class object like the business and database objects we'll create in this chapter. The ability to finely hone the content of an ATL-based control is one of the biggest advantages that supporters for this type of control talk about. When talking about COM+ server-side controls, ATL is your only choice if you want to use Visual C++ as a development language. The following procedure will get you started creating the component shell (the procedure assumes that you have Visual C++ 6 started):

1. Use the File | New command to display the New dialog box shown here.

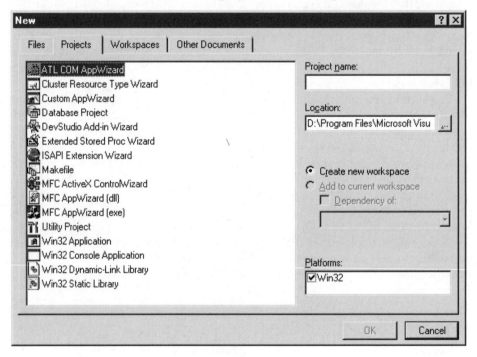

2. Choose the Projects tab of the New dialog box and highlight the ATL COM AppWizard icon.

3. Type **OrderAccess** in the Project Name field, then click OK. You'll see the ATL COM AppWizard - Step 1 of 1 dialog box shown here (see the "Understanding the ATL COM AppWizard - Step 1 of 1 Options" sidebar for details on this dialog box).

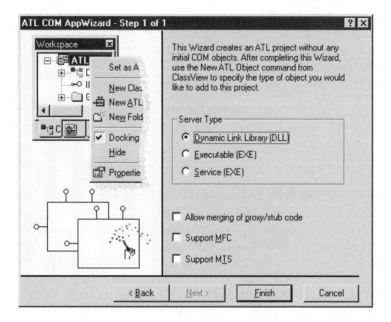

4. Choose a Server Type option. The example uses the Dynamic Link Library (DLL) option.

5. Check any of the support options. The example uses the "Allow merging of proxy/stub code," Support MFC, and Support MTS options. The example code assumes that you have MFC support enabled, so make sure you check all three options.

6. Click Finish. You'll see the New Project Information dialog box shown here.

TIP: One of the things you should notice is that the New Project Information dialog box mentions nothing about either the MFC or MTS support added to this project. This is one time when this final check doesn't help you check your settings, making it more important to double-check them before you start coding your project.

   7. Click OK. The ATL COM AppWizard will create the new project for you.

Understanding the ATL COM AppWizard - Step 1 of 1 Options

The first ATL COM AppWizard dialog box that you see looks deceptively simple, yet it affects your entire project in ways that make one project type totally incompatible with other project types. Notice that there are three kinds of projects that you can choose from: Dynamic Link Library (DLL), Executable (EXE), and Service (EXE). Since an MTS component is an in-process server (just like the ActiveX components you use to build applications), we'll use the DLL option. If we had been creating an out-of-process server or a Windows 2000 service, then we would have chosen one of the EXE options.

There are also three configuration options to choose from. The "Allow merging of proxy/stub code" option allows you to create a single DLL that contains everything needed for the component in a single file. Normally, the component's proxy/stub code appears in a separate DLL to allow that part of the component to reside on the user's machine. We'd usually check this option simply because it offers a certain level of convenience in keeping all parts of the component in one place. While this option is absolutely necessary for an ActiveX control, it isn't absolutely essential for an MTS component.

The Support MFC option allows you to use MFC calls in your component. This would defeat the purpose of using the ATL method of component design for an ActiveX control, but is a matter of personal taste when working with an MTS component. The main reason to avoid using MFC with an ActiveX control is that you can't be sure what version of the MFC support files are installed on the user machine and therefore can't control file dependency errors very easily. When working with an MTS component, you have absolute control over the server configuration, so using MFC within the component isn't as likely to cause problems and can speed up the development process greatly.

Finally, the Support MTS option allows you to use Microsoft Transaction Server with your ActiveX control. Needless to say, since we're creating an MTS component, we absolutely have to check this option. This is one option that you normally wouldn't check for an ActiveX control because ActiveX controls execute on the client side. Only server-side control projects would ever require this feature, and only if you were creating a component that's designed to interact with MTS in some way.

Inserting the Business ATL Object

At this point, we have a server shell. If you look at the methods provided, you'll find everything needed to create the IUnknown interface, register or unregister the component, perform a few housekeeping chores, and nothing more. That's one of the benefits of using ATL instead of a strict MFC approach. You get to decide exactly what your control contains and what functionality it provides. Nothing is done for you.

However, now we have to make our shell into an MTS component because that functionality doesn't exist in the current setup. Fortunately, making this shell into an MTS component isn't hard. All we really need to do is add the appropriate ATL object and some code to make the control functional. The following procedure will show you how to add one type of ATL object to the code. There are many more options than the one we'll look at here, but at least this example will get you started.

1. Use the Insert | New ATL Object command to display the ATL Object Wizard dialog box shown here. One look at the number of available categories should tell you that ATL is extremely flexible.

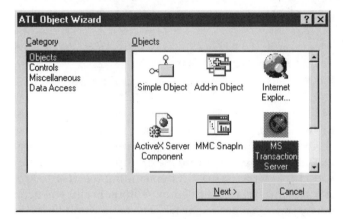

2. Choose the Objects category. Notice that this category includes a wealth of non-ActiveX control types. For example, you'd choose this category if you wanted to create an MMC SnapIn or an Internet Explorer object. In short, this category is designed to allow you to create a multitude of service-oriented components.

TIP: If you want to create an ActiveX component, then choose the Controls category, where you'll find a fairly extensive list of ActiveX control types. These types include Full (you can use it everywhere), Lite (a control with limited functionality), Composite (contains more than one full control), and HTML (a special control used on Web pages). There are also combinations of these basic control types, such as Lite Composite. None of the ActiveX component types would provide enough functionality when working with MTS, so none of them are the right choice in this case. The Database category would allow you to create an OLE DB provider or consumer, which would provide low-level access to the database as a whole. We'll be working with the OLE DB Consumer object type later in the chapter.

3. Highlight an object icon. The example uses an MTS Transaction Server Component since this is the type that's most capable of working with MTS to ensure that our database transactions remain secure.

4. Click Next. You'll see the ATL Object Wizard Properties dialog box shown here. This is where we'll define the various properties for our ActiveX control.

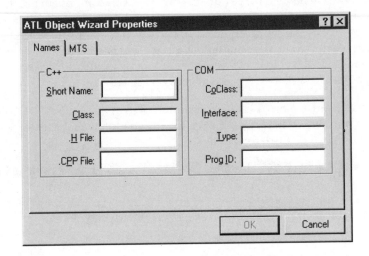

5. Fill out the various pages of the ATL Object Wizard Properties dialog box to meet the needs of your particular component. Table 7-6 shows the settings you'll need to use to create the example MTS component. I explain the MTS specific settings in the "Understanding the MTS Settings" sidebar. Note that many properties get filled out automatically when you type in one property value on a particular tab. The table won't include these automatic entries since Visual C++ makes them for you, and you should assume that the automatic entries are correct unless the table tells you otherwise. While you can change the automatic entries, using them as is tends to make the code easier to read and your control work with less debugging later.

6. Click OK. The ATL Object Wizard will create the required class and interface for you.

Tab	Property	Value
Names	Short Name	OrderModify
MTS	Interface	Dual
	Support IObjectControl	Checked
	Can Be Pooled	Checked

Table 7-6.   On/Off Button ATL Object Property Values

Understanding the MTS Settings

MTS components support both the Dual and Custom interface options. In most cases, you want to use the Dual interface option so that your component works with languages that use either the Visual C++ or Visual Basic method for working with interfaces. The only time you need to use a custom interface is if the language you're trying to support doesn't follow the standard methodology for working with interfaces. Note that using a custom interface can also provide faster component access since you have complete access over the interface and the component won't be hampered by generic code designed to work with a variety of component types.

The IObjectControl interface is optional, but very useful if you want to implement object pooling in your object. (You also need this interface to implement the Activate() and Deactivate() methods.) Normally, a component gets used by a client, then immediately discarded. Object pooling allows MTS to cache the resource that the object represents for a period of time in the hope that another client will need it. The delay allows MTS to use processor cycles more efficiently, improving overall system performance when an object is called upon at a fairly high rate. In most cases, you only want to implement IObjectControl for objects that clients call upon often since the delay does impose a memory penalty.

The Can Be Pooled option allows you to set the component to allow the use of object pooling. Checking this option is essential if you want to give the network administrator the option of using object pooling. You'll only need to check this option when a component has a very high probability of getting reused almost immediately. This is a particularly handy option for database components since they'll get used on a continuous basis and object pooling represents a major performance enhancement.

Adding Some Business Object Methods

At this point, we have a program shell, but no methods (at least none related to the task at hand) within the object. In the "An Application Task Overview" section of the chapter, we discussed several tasks that an application of this type might perform. For the purposes of this example, we'll allow the user to add, edit, and remove orders, and add, edit, and remove customers. To do this, we'll need 13 methods: GetCatalogItem(), AddOrder(), GetOrder(), EditOrder(), RemoveOrder(), AddItem(), GetItem(), EditItem(),RemoveItem(), AddCustomer(), GetCustomer(), EditCustomer(), and RemoveCustomer(). Obviously, this isn't a full-fledged implementation of the application, but it should provide enough information for you to create MTS components that perform this type of work. The following steps help you add the required methods to the OrderModify object.

TIP: Visual C++ is still a low-level development language that offers developers little protection from themselves. For example, you can add properties to a component designed for server use. Unfortunately, adding properties to a server-based component will make the component nonfunctional. Sure, it'll compile, but you won't be able to access it. Of course, adding properties where they really aren't needed raises another question: "Why add them in the first place?" For this reason, you need to carefully consider what you add to the components you build and how. Features that may not seem important at the outset can become decidedly important once the project is underway. Likewise, you may add a feature now that will prove less than useful later.

1. Right-click the IOrderModify interface, then choose Add Method from the context menu. You'll see an Add Method to Interface dialog box like the one shown here. This is where you'll add the definitions for a new method.

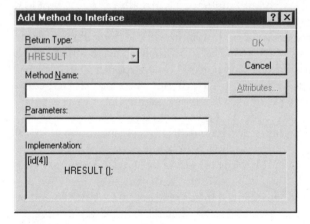

2. Type one of the Method Name and Parameters field entries from Table 7-7 into the Add Method to Interface dialog box.

Method Name	Parameters
GetCatalogItem	[in, out] BSTR *pbstrProductID, [in] BSTR bstrDirection, [out] BSTR *pbstrProductName, [out] CURRENCY *pcurrPrice, [out] int *piOnHand
AddOrder	[in] BSTR *pbstrOrderID, [in] BSTR *pbstrCustomerID, [in] BSTR *pbstrFirstName, [in] BSTR *pbstrMiddleInitial, [in] BSTR *pbstrLastName, [in] BSTR *pbstrTitle, [in] BSTR *pbstrCompany, [in] BSTR *pbstrAddress1, [in] BSTR *pbstrAddress2, [in] BSTR *pbstrCity, [in] BSTR *pbstrState, [in] BSTR *pbstrZIP, [in] BSTR *pbstrTelephone1, [in] BSTR *pbstrTelephone2
GetOrder	[in, out] BSTR *pbstrOrderID, [in] BSTR bstrDirection, [out] BSTR *pbstrCustomerID, [out] BSTR *pbstrFirstName, [out] BSTR *pbstrMiddleInitial, [out] BSTR *pbstrLastName, [out] BSTR *pbstrTitle, [out] BSTR *pbstrCompany, [out] BSTR *pbstrAddress1, [out] BSTR *pbstrAddress2, [out] BSTR *pbstrCity, [out] BSTR *pbstrState, [out] BSTR *pbstrZIP, [out] BSTR *pbstrTelephone1, [out] BSTR *pbstrTelephone2
EditOrder	[in] BSTR *pbstrOrderID, [in] BSTR *pbstrCustomerID, [in] BSTR *pbstrFirstName, [in] BSTR *pbstrMiddleInitial, [in] BSTR *pbstrLastName, [in] BSTR *pbstrTitle, [in] BSTR *pbstrCompany, [in] BSTR *pbstrAddress1, [in] BSTR *pbstrAddress2, [in] BSTR *pbstrCity, [in] BSTR *pbstrState, [in] BSTR *pbstrZIP, [in] BSTR *pbstrTelephone1, [in] BSTR *pbstrTelephone2
RemoveOrder	[in] BSTR bstrOrderID
AddItem	[in] BSTR *pbstrItemID, [in] CURRENCY *pcurrPrice, [in] BSTR *pbstrProductID, [in] long *plQuantity, [in] BSTR *pbstrOrderID
GetItem	[in, out] BSTR *pbstrItemID, [in] BSTR bstrDirection, [out] CURRENCY *pcurrPrice, [out] BSTR *pbstrProductID, [out] long *plQuantity, [in, out] BSTR *pbstrOrderID
EditItem	[in] BSTR *pbstrItemID, [in] CURRENCY *pcurrPrice, [in] BSTR *pbstrProductID, [in] long *plQuantity, [in] BSTR *pbstrOrderID

Table 7-7.   Method Names and Parameters for the IOrderModify Interface

Method Name	Parameters
RemoveItem	[in] BSTR bstrItemID, [in] BSTR bstrOrderID
AddCustomer	[in] BSTR *pbstrCustomerID, [in] BSTR *pbstrFirstName, [in] BSTR *pbstrMiddleInitial, [in] BSTR *pbstrLastName, [in] BSTR *pbstrTitle, [in] BSTR *pbstrCompany, [in] BSTR *pbstrAddress1, [in] BSTR *pbstrAddress2, [in] BSTR *pbstrCity, [in] BSTR *pbstrState, [in] BSTR *pbstrZIP, [in] BSTR *pbstrCountry, [in] BSTR *pbstrLastContact, [in] BSTR *pbstrTelephone1, [in] BSTR *pbstrTelephone2
GetCustomer	[in, out] BSTR *pbstrCustomerID, [in] BSTR bstrDirection, [out] BSTR *pbstrFirstName, [out] BSTR *pbstrMiddleInitial, [out] BSTR *pbstrLastName, [out] BSTR *pbstrTitle, [out] BSTR *pbstrCompany, [out] BSTR *pbstrAddress1, [out] BSTR *pbstrAddress2, [out] BSTR *pbstrCity, [out] BSTR *pbstrState, [out] BSTR *pbstrZIP, [out] BSTR *pbstrCountry, [out] BSTR *pbstrLastContact, [out] BSTR *pbstrTelephone1, [out] BSTR *pbstrTelephone2
EditCustomer	[in] BSTR *pbstrCustomerID, [in] BSTR *pbstrFirstName, [in] BSTR *pbstrMiddleInitial, [in] BSTR *pbstrLastName, [in] BSTR *pbstrTitle, [in] BSTR *pbstrCompany, [in] BSTR *pbstrAddress1, [in] BSTR *pbstrAddress2, [in] BSTR *pbstrCity, [in] BSTR *pbstrState, [in] BSTR *pbstrZIP, [in] BSTR *pbstrCountry, [in] BSTR *pbstrLastContact, [in] BSTR *pbstrTelephone1, [in] BSTR *pbstrTelephone2
RemoveCustomer	[in] BSTR bstrCustomerID

Table 7-7.   Method Names and Parameters for the IOrderModify Interface *(continued)*

3. Click OK. Visual C++ will create the requested method for you.

4. Repeat Steps 1 through 3 for all of the methods we require for this example. You should end up with the 13 methods shown in Table 7-7.

Inserting the Database ATL Objects

Our business object, COrderModify, is set up at this point. We'll add code to the various methods in the next section. It's time to create the various database objects required to implement this example. It's important to remember that there will be one database class for every kind of access we want to the database.

Visual C++ will actually create two classes for you. The first is the database class, and it'll have a name of Cdbo<Table Name> for table access. We'll be accessing each table in the sample database. This example won't show you how to work with views and stored procedures, but the principle is the same. The second database class is the accessor class. While your component requires this class to access the table, we won't actually work with it in this example—and I don't see any reason to interact with it when working on production applications either. For the most part, this is an automatically created class that you won't need to modify.

Now that you have some idea of what will happen when we create these classes, let's create them. The following procedure will show you how to add the required database objects to the OrderAccess component. These objects will appear as separate interfaces—they just appear in the same file as the business object.

1. Use the Insert | New ATL Object command to display the ATL Object Wizard dialog box.

2. Choose the Data Access category. You'll see two database objects like the ones shown here. The first database object type allows you to create a database provider—the server that allows a client to access the server. In most cases, you won't need to use this option unless you're interacting with a custom database. The second object type, Consumer, is the one that we'll use in this case. It allows you to use an existing database through a database provider.

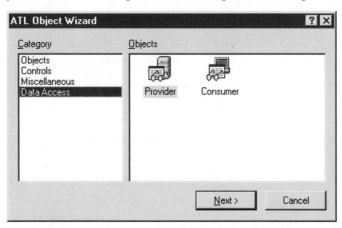

3. Highlight the Consumer object. This is the object that will allow us to access the OrderEntry database.

4. Click Next. You'll see the ATL Object Wizard Properties dialog box shown here. This is where we'll define the various properties for our ActiveX control.

Note that you really can't fill out much of the information in this dialog box. We'll need to define a data source first.

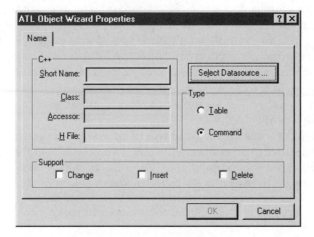

5. Choose the Table option (since we want to access a table), and then click Select Datasource. You'll see the Provider tab of the Data Link Properties dialog box shown here. This is where you'll select the method of accessing the database. The most flexible option for this example is the Microsoft OLE DB Provider for SQL Server. The provider you choose for a production application depends on the application requirements and the DBMS you choose.

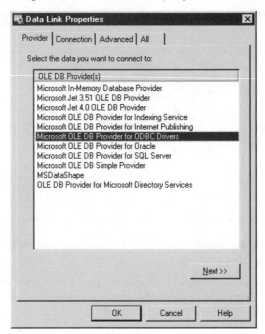

6. Highlight Microsoft OLE DB Provider for SQL Server, and then click Next. You'll see the Connection tab of the Data Link Properties dialog box shown here. This is where we'll select the server and data source used for this example.

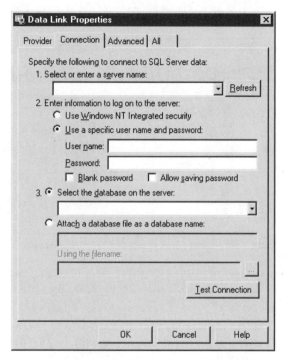

7. Choose a server from the "Select or enter a server name" drop-down list box. Note that if you don't see a server in this list box, you can click Refresh to gain access to a list of servers. If you don't see the server listed, stop now. You must fix the connection problem with your server before you can proceed. Simply typing the server name won't be sufficient to gain access to it later.

8. Choose a security option. In most cases, the "Use Windows NT Integrated security" option will work fine. If you have set security on the database in such a way that the application will need a specific username and password, make sure you enter this information in the fields provided and choose the "Use a specific user name and password" option.

9. Choose OrderEntry in the Select the database on the server drop-down list box. If you don't see the OrderEntry table listed, stop. You must be able to see the table at this point for the example to work. Make sure that you've selected the correct server, entered the correct username and password information, and that you have rights to the OrderEntry database on the server.

10. Click Test Connection. You'll see a test connection succeeded message if the connection information is correct. The connection must pass this test before you can proceed. If you can't get the connection to pass, make sure you installed SQL Server properly and installed all of the required patches. Make sure you run the InstCat script as well—we covered this as part of the SQL Server installation procedure.

11. Click OK twice. You'll see the Select Database Table dialog box shown here.

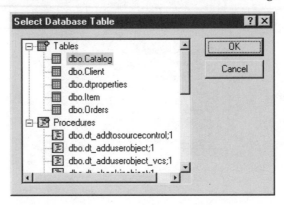

12. Highlight one of the four tables for this example. You'll need to perform this procedure four times, once each for the Catalog, Client, Item, and Orders tables.

13. Click OK. The Select Database Table dialog box will go away and you'll see the ATL Object Wizard Properties dialog box again. Notice that Visual C++ has filled in the names of the class and associated files for you. Normally, you'll want to keep these default names to make it easier to identify the database classes. At this point, we need to decide what level of access we want to provide to the tables.

14. Check the Change, Insert, and Delete options. This will allow us full access to the tables. When working with a production system, you need to choose levels of support that reflect the activities that the user will actually perform with the database.

15. Click OK. Visual C++ will create two new classes for you as previously described.

16. Perform Steps 1 through 15 for all four tables in our database.

Adding the Component Code

We talked about the 13 methods that make up this example in the previous section of the chapter. Each of those methods is designed to allow the application to access the OrderEntry database in a specific way. Of course, the end result of this access is to either move data from the user's machine to the database, or from the database to the user's machine. This simple action requires quite a bit of code; but for the most part, the actions that the code performs are the same no matter which table you deal with.

This section of the chapter is going to look at a single sample of the component code. I'll discuss any noteworthy departures from this code that you'll find in the other 12 component methods. You'll find the complete code for all 13 methods as part of the source for this book. For now, let's take a look at the example. Listing 7-1 shows what you can expect to see when working with this type of component—at least in general.

```
STDMETHODIMP COrderModify::GetCatalogItem(BSTR *pbstrProductID,
                                          BSTR bstrDirection,
                                          BSTR *pbstrProductName,
                                          CURRENCY *pcurrPrice,
                                          int *piOnHand)
{
    IObjectContext    *pInstanceContext;  // Object context
    HRESULT           hr;                 // Operation result.
    CdboCatalog       dboCatalog;         // Catalog Database
    CString           oSProductID;        // Product ID Search Value
    CString           oDProductID;        // Product ID Database Value
    CString           oOldValue;          // End of File Comparison
    CString           oFirstID;           // Beginning of File Comparison
    CString           oPrevValue;         // Previous Product ID Value
    CString           oDirection;         // Converted Direction Value

    AFX_MANAGE_STATE(AfxGetStaticModuleState())

    // Get an object context.  The object context is used for
    // transactions.
    pInstanceContext = NULL;
    hr = GetObjectContext(&pInstanceContext);

    // If the object context retrieval fails, find out why.
```

```
    if (FAILED(hr))
    {
        if (hr == E_INVALIDARG)
            AfxMessageBox(""Invalid Instance Context Variable"");

        if (hr == E_UNEXPECTED)
            AfxMessageBox(""An Unexpected Error Occurred"");

        if (hr == CONTEXT_E_NOCONTEXT)
            AfxMessageBox(""No Context Associated with Object"");

        AfxMessageBox(""Object Context Not Obtained"");
        return hr;
    }

    // Open the Catalog table.
    hr = dboCatalog.Open();

    // If the Catalog table opening fails, report an error.
    if (FAILED(hr))
    {
        AfxMessageBox(""Table Open Failed"");
        return hr;
    }

    // Move to the first record in the table and record its ID.
    hr = dboCatalog.MoveFirst();
    oFirstID = dboCatalog.m_ProductID;
    oFirstID.Remove('' '');

    // Tell Visual C++ that we''ll be converting BSTR values.
    USES_CONVERSION;

    // Convert the direction value.
    oDirection = OLE2T(bstrDirection);
    oDirection.Remove('' '');

    // The user wants to refresh the current record.
    if (oDirection == ""Refresh"")
    {
```

```
    // Convert the search and database values into CStrings
    // for easier comparison, then remove the excess spaces.
    oSProductID = OLE2T(*pbstrProductID);
    oSProductID.Remove('' '');
    oDProductID = dboCatalog.m_ProductID;
    oDProductID.Remove('' '');

    // Keep comparing the two strings until we find the
    // search value in the database or we come to the end
    // of the records.
    while (oDProductID != oSProductID)
    {
        // Save the current database value for later comparison.
        oOldValue = oDProductID;

        // If the current record isn''t the one we''re looking
        // for, then move to the next record.
        dboCatalog.MoveNext();

        // Perform the required string conversion.
        oDProductID = dboCatalog.m_ProductID;
        oDProductID.Remove('' '');

        // See if we''re at the end of the file.
        if (oOldValue == oDProductID)
        {
            // End the search.
            break;
        }
    }
}

// The user wants to go to the next record.
if (oDirection == ""Next"")
{

    // Convert the search and database values into CStrings
    // for easier comparison, then remove the excess spaces.
    oSProductID = OLE2T(*pbstrProductID);
    oSProductID.Remove('' '');
```

```
oDProductID = dboCatalog.m_ProductID;
oDProductID.Remove('' '');

// Keep comparing the two strings until we find the
// search value in the database or we come to the end
// of the records.
while (oDProductID != oSProductID)
{
    // Save the current database value for later comparison.
    oOldValue = oDProductID;

    // If the current record isn''t the one we''re looking
    // for, then move to the next record.
    dboCatalog.MoveNext();

    // Perform the required string conversion.
    oDProductID = dboCatalog.m_ProductID;
    oDProductID.Remove('' '');

    // See if we''re at the end of the file.
    if (oOldValue == oDProductID)
    {
        // End the search.
        break;
    }
}

// Move one more record if possible.
if (oOldValue != oDProductID)
    dboCatalog.MoveNext();
}

// The user wants to go to the next record.
if (oDirection == ""Previous"")
{

    // Convert the search and database values into CStrings
    // for easier comparison, then remove the excess spaces.
    oSProductID = OLE2T(*pbstrProductID);
    oSProductID.Remove('' '');
```

```
oDProductID = dboCatalog.m_ProductID;
oDProductID.Remove('' '');
oPrevValue = oFirstID;

// Keep comparing the two strings until we find the
// search value in the database or we come to the end
// of the records.
while (oDProductID != oSProductID)
{
    // Save the previous record value, but only if we''re not
    // at the end of the table.
    if (oOldValue != oDProductID)
        oPrevValue = oDProductID;

    // Save the current database value for later comparison.
    oOldValue = oDProductID;

    // If the current record isn''t the one we''re looking
    // for, then move to the next record.
    dboCatalog.MoveNext();

    // Perform the required string conversion.
    oDProductID = dboCatalog.m_ProductID;
    oDProductID.Remove('' '');

    // See if we''re at the end of the file.
    if (oOldValue == oDProductID)
    {
        // End the search.
        break;
    }
}


// Move to the previous record if possible.
if (oFirstID != oPrevValue)
{
    // Move to the first record.
    dboCatalog.MoveFirst();

    // Perform the required string conversion.
```

```
        oDProductID = dboCatalog.m_ProductID;
        oDProductID.Remove('' '');

        // Beginning from the start of the table, look for the
        // previous record value.
        while (oDProductID != oPrevValue)
        {
            // If the current record isn''t the one we''re looking
            // for, then move to the next record.
            dboCatalog.MoveNext();

            // Perform the required string conversion.
            oDProductID = dboCatalog.m_ProductID;
            oDProductID.Remove('' '');

        }
    }

    // Otherwise, ensure that we''re at the first record.
    else
        dboCatalog.MoveFirst();
}

// Place the current database record values into the variables.
*pbstrProductName = T2BSTR(dboCatalog.m_ProductName);
*pcurrPrice = dboCatalog.m_Price;
*piOnHand = dboCatalog.m_OnHand;
*pbstrProductID = T2BSTR(dboCatalog.m_ProductID);

// Close the database connection.
dboCatalog.Close();

// Complete the transaction.
pInstanceContext->SetComplete();

// Release the object context.
pInstanceContext->Release();
pInstanceContext = NULL;

// Tell the client that everything went OK.
return S_OK;
}
```

The first thing we do in each method is obtain the current object context. Remember that one of the reasons we want to use MTS in the first place is to increase data integrity and application reliability through the use of transactions. The act of getting the object context allows us to vote on the outcome of the transaction. In addition to voting on the transaction, you can detect whether the application is currently in a transaction, determine whether the caller is in a specific role, determine whether security is enabled, and either enable or disable a commit. You can read more about how MTS works in Chapter 4.

Once we've obtained an object context, it's time to open the table (or perform some other query). In this case, we're looking at the Catalog table. If the table opening fails, the current component code outputs a simple message box. There's a problem with this approach that you need to know about, however. Normally, you'd just return the error code (contained in hr) to the client. You don't want a message box to pop up on the server because there won't be anyone working at the server to close it. I'm using message boxes in this example to make it easier to diagnose and troubleshoot problems with the code. You can follow this route as well, but you need to remove all message box code from the component before you install it on a production system.

The next step is to move to the first record in the table. If you don't do this, then queries on the table will fail. Opening the table doesn't necessarily make any data available. The component code must establish a pointer into the table at a known position before you can operate on the table in any way.

At this point, we're ready to do something with the table itself. This means working with the BSTR variables passed into the method by the client. Converting the BSTR values into a CString that you can work with in Visual C++ requires that you add the USES_CONVERSION macro to the code. The conversion from BSTR to CString is relatively easy—all you need to use is the OLE2T function. Note that the resulting string will contain both leading and ending spaces. You can use the Remove method of the CString class to get rid of these spaces as long as the string contains just one word, as will be the case with both bstrDirection and pbstrProductID. If the string in question is made up of multiple words, then you'll need to take a multistep approach when removing the leading and trailing spaces.

Remember that there are three possible directions (or commands) associated with the GetCatalogItem() method: Refresh (stay at the current record), Next, and Previous. The code takes care of the Refresh command first. Notice that the first thing we do is place the pbstrProductID value in a CString to make it easier to work with. The TCHAR m_ProductID value from the ProductID field of the Catalog table is likewise converted. Now, we perform a loop operation. The current value of the ProductID field of the Catalog table is compared to the ProductID value passed by the user. When these two values compare, we've found the record that the user is looking for and can stop the search. Otherwise, the table pointer is advanced to the next record and the new ProductID field value converted to a CString. There's always a possibility that the user will pass a nonexistent value to the component, so the last bit of code checks for the end of the table. If we reach the end of the table before finding the search record, then the user passed a nonexistent value and the component will leave the record pointer at the last record in the table. You could perform a lot of other tasks at this point, like sending an error value back to the user rather than a record—I've chosen this approach to keep the example simple.

The Next bstrDirection value works much like Refresh did. We still search through the table from the beginning until we find the record currently pointed to by pbstrProductID. In this case, however, we perform one additional step. If we aren't already at the end of the table, then the code will move the record pointer one more time. The resulting return values to the client will make it appear that we've moved to the next record of the table. Since the Product ID file of the user's display will also get updated, pressing Next multiple times will result in continued movement through the table until we reach the end of the table.

The Previous bstrDirection value works similar to the other two values, but we need to perform some extra work in this case. The "Dealing with SQL Server Movement Limitations" sidebar explains some of the problems of trying to move the record pointer back one record when working with SQL Server. The short story is that even though there's a Prev() method provided with the dboCatalog object, SQL Server prevents us from working with it. This means that the code has to perform extra processing in order to find which record is previous to the one that the user is currently looking at. So, we have to pass through the table the first time looking for that previous record. Once we find it, we can use it as the new Product ID field value. A second search from the beginning of the table will place the record pointer at this value. Obviously, the code still needs to look for the end of the table. In this case, however, we also need to look for the beginning of the table. Remember, the record pointer must not move before the beginning of the table—it must point to an actual record. In this case, the code simply moves to the first record if the new ProductID matches the first ProductID in the table.

At this point, we've found the record that the user requested. Placing the record's field values into the variable pointers passed by the client is relatively easy. TCHAR values are easily converted into BSTR values using the T2BSTR() function. The other field values are directly transferred from the table to the client without any conversion. Once the data is transferred, we close the table to minimize the risk of damage.

The transaction has completed successfully, so we vote to complete it using the SetComplete() method of the object context. If the transaction had failed, then we would have voted to abort the transaction using the SetAbort() method. Once the voting is complete, there's no need to retain the object context, so the pointer is released and set to NULL. Finally, the method returns and the client receives the specified record.

Now that you know how the method works in general, let's look at some departures from this standard code. The first of these departures is in the code that deals with the Client table. That table includes a LastContact field. When we create the database and accessor classes for the Client table, you'll see that the LastContact field is shown as a DBTIMESTAMP data type. In fact, the DBTIMESTAMP data type is actually a structure that contains the various time elements as numbers. As a result, we can easily convert the DBTIMESTAMP data type (which won't travel very well to other languages) to a BSTR. The following code shows an example of this conversion that's used in the GetCustomer() method (note that some code isn't shown for the sake of clarity):

```
// Convert the LastContact field to a string.
itoa(dboClient.m_LastContact.day, oDay.GetBuffer(2), 10);
oDay.ReleaseBuffer(-1);
itoa(dboClient.m_LastContact.month, oMonth.GetBuffer(2), 10);
oMonth.ReleaseBuffer(-1);
itoa(dboClient.m_LastContact.year, oYear.GetBuffer(4), 10);
oYear.ReleaseBuffer(-1);
oDate = oDay + ""/"" + oMonth + ""/"" + oYear;

// Place the current database record values into the variables.
*pbstrLastContact = T2BSTR(oDate);
```

As you can see, we treat the m_LastContact member variable as we would any other data structure. You'll find that the process of reversing this conversion is just as easy. While Visual C++ may provide a conversion route that performs this task more automatically, you'll find that going this route gives you more precise results when it comes to entries in the Client table. For example, the automated conversion routines normally add a time in—using midnight if no time is provided as part of the call. Obviously, this kind of extraneous information only adds to the size of the database without offering the user anything more in the way of data. That's why there are times when a manual conversion, like the one shown here, is actually better than using the built-in functions.

The Item table requires some special handling as well. Remember that a unique item is identified by a combination of an ItemID and an OrderID field entry. For example, item 1 of order 1 is different than item 1 of order 2. As a result, we'll need to look at two input criteria for this particular data access item. The code is essentially the same as before. The only thing that has changed is the concepts behind the code. It's no longer sufficient to use one criterion to look something up—we need to look at two elements. Obviously, this is only the component-side consideration—the client-side part of the equation is even more complex since we'll have to retrieve data from multiple tables to fill out an item-related form.

Dealing with SQL Server Movement Limitations

The accessor class that Visual C++ creates for you includes methods for moving to the next and previous database records. Unfortunately, SQL Server only supports forward movement—you can't go to the previous record with any ease. SQL Server was originally designed as a transaction-oriented relational DBMS. Batch processing normally references records in a forward direction only, not in a backward direction. As a result, this feature was left out of SQL Server, which means that this product doesn't work as well as it could in today's GUI environment.

There are a few ways to get around this problem. The first is to use the approach shown in Listing 7-1. You use variables to track the current and previous record positions within the table. The problem with this method is that you end up looking through the table twice every time someone clicks the Previous button. While this isn't a problem for small tables, it would become a serious problem when working with a large table—the user might have to wait relatively long periods of time when clicking the Previous button near the end of the table.

Another method is to use cursors (or bookmarks) to keep track of your current position within the database itself. Using cursors is far more complex than the method shown in Listing 7-1, but is also much more efficient since you only have to search the table once to find what you need. This is the method you should rely on for large tables.

Obviously, the most efficient methodology for implementing a Previous button is to refrain from implementing a previous method on the server at all. You could implement a Previous button on the client by tracking the previous record locally and simply performing a search for that value. However, there's a downside to this method as well. If you implement all of the database manipulation logic on the server, you can be sure that the application will act in a particular way all of the time. Leaving part of the processing to the client means that you have to implement this strategy on every client you build and that the technique used will vary from client to client.

Hopefully, Microsoft will eventually fix this problem. The best place to implement a previous method is within the DBMS itself. The developer shouldn't be responsible for handling something that's in the realm of the DBMS. For now, however, we'll still be responsible for implementing a previous method when and where it's needed. The technique you use to implement it depends on the size of the table you need to manage and the complexity of the application environment.

Registering and Installing the Component on the Server

At this point, we have a component that can be used to access and modify the SQL Server database created earlier in the chapter. However, that component still isn't very useful. We need to place it on the server, register it, and finally, allow the user to access it by installing it on the server.

NOTE: Visual C++ will tell you that you need to register the MTS component on the server using the MTXREREG utility. This utility isn't used with Windows 2000—it isn't even included with the package. The MTXREREG utility was included as part of the Windows NT 4 Option Pack and the instructions in the Visual C++ IDE reflect usage instructions for that older package.

We'll use the Component Services MMC snap-in to register and install the OrderAccess component (which includes the COrderModify class). You'll find Component Services in the Administrative Tools folder, found in the Control Panel. Figure 7-6 shows what the Component Services MMC snap-in looks like. For those of you who have used MTS Explorer in the past, the snap-in version should look about the same except for a few changes in nomenclature.

TIP: Microsoft has provided some tools that you need to know about as part of the Windows 2000 Platform SDK. Some of these tools are installed for you as part of the Windows 2000 Platform SDK installation process. Depending on the options you choose, you'll find a folder containing the tools in your Start | Programs menu. Other tools aren't installed automatically. For example, the MTXStop utility is provided in the \Platform SDK\Samples\COM\Tools\MTXStop folder. Make sure you look in the various sample application directories that ship with the Windows 2000 Platform SDK to ensure that you have full access to all of the tools that this product provides. Since MTXStop doesn't ship with Windows 2000, you must install it from the Windows 2000 Platform SDK.

Creating the COM+ Application

The first thing we need to do is create a new application for our component. The following procedure shows you how to add a new application to Component Services (this is a different process than you may have used for other component types):

1. Move the component to a convenient directory on the server. I normally use a central repository for my custom components, but you can use any management scheme you like, including creating special folders for each

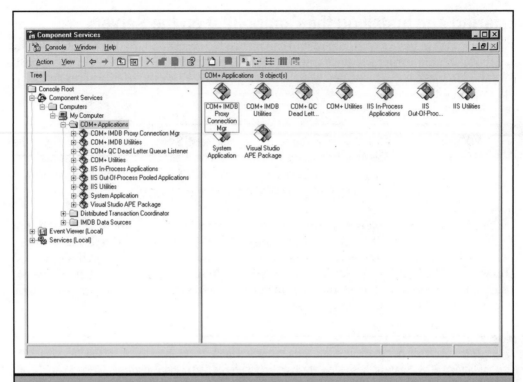

Figure 7-6.   The Component Services MMC snap-in is where you'll work with MTS components

project you work with. Now we need to register the component with the server.

2. Open the Component Service MMC snap-in, if you haven't done so already.

3. Highlight the COM+ Applications entry, then select the Action | New | Application command from the toolbar. You'll see a Welcome to the COM Application Install Wizard dialog box.

4. Click Next. You'll see an Install or Create a New Application dialog box like the one shown here. The "Install pre-built application(s)" option is specifically designed to allow you to install third-party applications. These applications

come with an installation file with an MSI extension that contains all of the particulars about the application. Since we're developing our own application, we'll need to use the "Create an empty application" option.

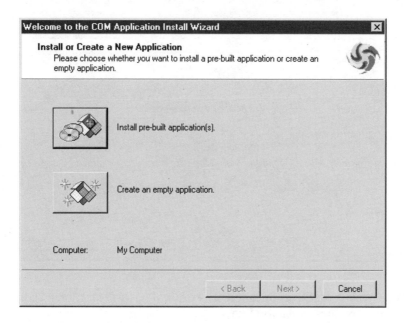

5. Click "Create an empty application." You'll see the Create Empty Application dialog box like the one shown here. This dialog box allows you to enter a name for your application. It also asks you to decide between a library and a server application type. In most cases, you'll choose the "Server application" option because it allows the components you create to execute in a separate process. Library applications execute within the creator's process, which means that an errant component can cause the entire application to fail. In addition, library applications don't support load balancing, remote access, or queued components. Library applications do, however, execute faster because there are fewer process boundaries to cross. We discussed the issue of library versus server applications in the "COM+ Application Types" section of Chapter 6. Be sure to read about all four types of application that COM+ supports before you begin creating new components that support this technology.

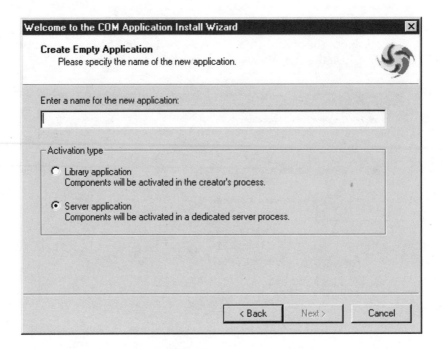

6. Type a name for the application. The example uses OrderEntry Database, but you can use any name you like.

7. Choose between the "Server application" and "Library application" options. The example application uses the "Server application" option because it allows more complete testing of the component and better protection during debugging.

8. Click Next. You'll see a Set Application Identity dialog box like the one shown here. This dialog box allows you to choose the identity of the person used to run the component. You'll normally choose the "Interactive user" option because it allows you to test for role-based security using the identity of the person logged in to the server. The second option, "This user," allows you to set the component up to run as a specific person. It's handy for those situations when you know another server, rather than a user, will always call the component. Using this setting is convenient because the component will always allow the same level of access no matter which person is logged in to the machine.

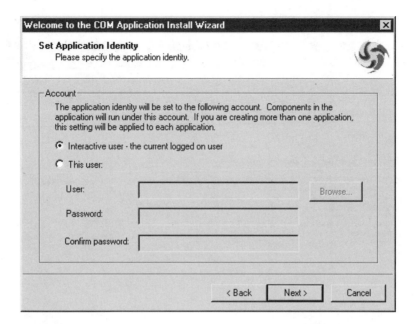

9. Choose the "Interactive user" option, then click Next. You'll see a final COM Application Wizard dialog box.

10. Click Finish. The new application will appear in the list of applications in the COM+ Applications folder, as shown in Figure 7-7. Notice that Windows 2000 automatically creates a directory structure that you can use for working with the component. We'll use this directory structure in the steps that follow to fully configure the COM+ application for use.

Adding Components to a COM+ Application

The application that we've just defined acts as a container for our component. In fact, you could place multiple components within this directory structure—the whole idea is to keep the various applications on the server separate, not necessarily to restrict how you add new components to the server. At the moment, we still don't have the component created in the previous section installed in Component Services. The following steps will allow you to install the component, even if it isn't registered on the current machine:

1. Open the Order Entry Database application and you'll see two folders, Components and Roles, as shown in Figure 7-8. (You must highlight the

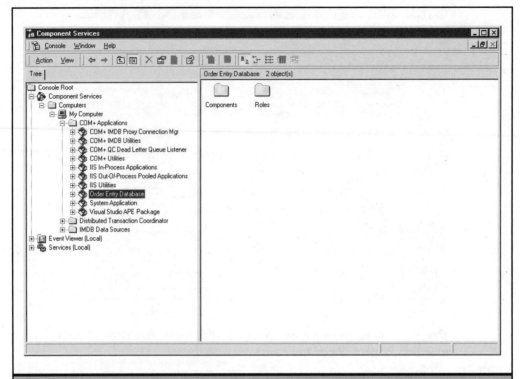

Figure 7-7. Windows 2000 automatically creates the directory structure required to fully configure your COM+ application

Components folder as shown in Figure 7-8 to add new components to the application.) The Components folder will hold any components you want to install for the application. The Roles folder allows you to create security roles that you can later assign to the application, an individual component, or a method within the component.

2. Highlight the Components folder, then use the Action I New I Component command to display the COM Component Install Wizard dialog box.

3. Click Next. You'll see the Import or Install a Component dialog box like the one shown here. The "Install new component(s)" option allows you to install components that you've placed on the server, but haven't

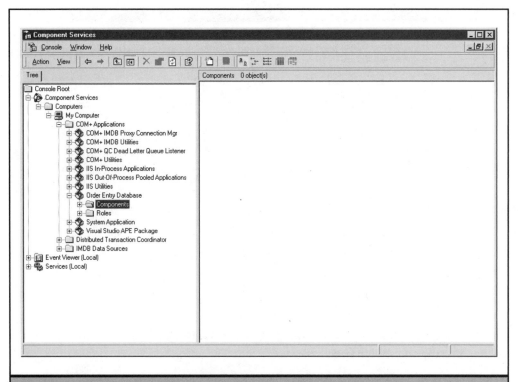

Figure 7-8. All COM+ Applications contain two folders like the ones shown here

registered yet. This is the option that you'll use when your development platform and the server are on two different machines. The "Import component(s) that are already registered" option allows you to add components that have already been registered on the server. This is the option you'll choose for updates (when the GUID is exactly the same for the new component as it was for the old one) or when the component has been registered for some other reason. For example, you may be using your development machine as the test server. We'll look at the installing a new component first. If you're importing a registered component, then proceed with Step 8.

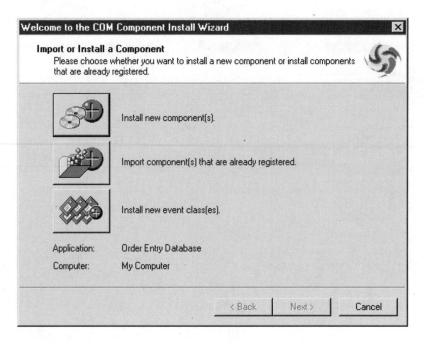

4. Click "Install new component(s)." You'll see a "Select files to install" dialog box like the one shown here.

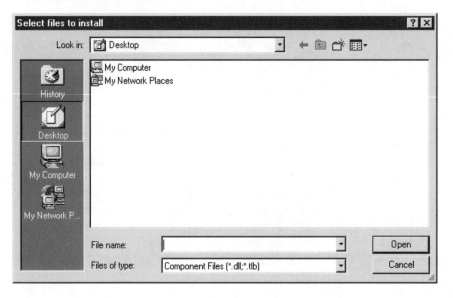

5. Find the component file that you want to install. The example uses OrderAccess.DLL. Highlight the file, then click Open to complete the selection process. You'll see an "Install new components" dialog box similar to the one shown here. Note that the figure shows what you should see when working with the example program. The example contains both components and a type library—you'll need both for COM+ applications. If you create a separate set of component and type library files, then you'll need to add both files to the list to get a complete installation. Clicking the Add button at this point would allow you to add another file to the list (along with any components that the file contains). Our component is also shown as a COM+ component type and the wizard has found interfaces within the component (the wizard won't tell you which interfaces have been found at this point—hopefully, it found the ones you wanted to expose). You need to check all of these items as part of the component setup.

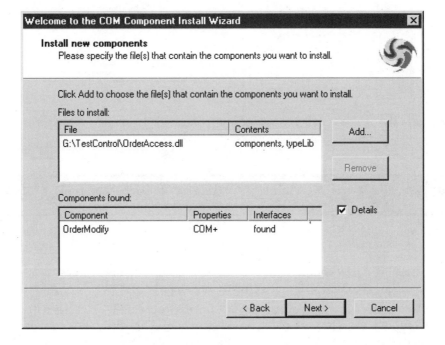

6. Click Next. You'll see a final COM Component Install Wizard dialog box.

7. Click Finish to complete the "Install new component(s)" installation process. You'll see the new components added to the right pane of the Component Services window, as shown in Figure 7-9. At this point, we're finished

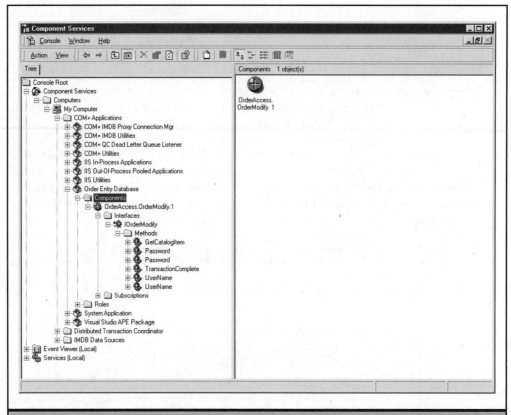

Figure 7-9. The Component Services window will contain the new components you've installed once you complete the COM Component Install Wizard

installing a new component. The remaining steps in this procedure are for installing a component that's already registered.

8. Click "Import component(s) that are already registered." You'll see the Choose Components to Import dialog box shown here. This dialog box contains a list of all of the components that are installed and registered for use on the server. If you don't see your components in this list, then you need to click the Back button and proceed with Step 4 to install the component and register it (the registration process happens automatically).

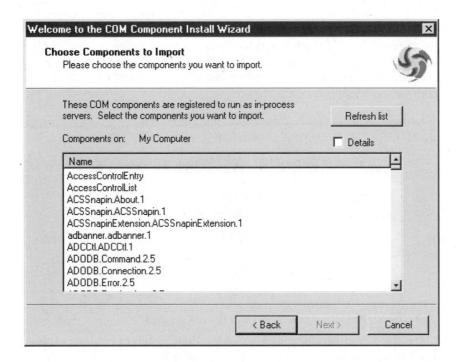

9. Locate the OrderAccess.OrderModify.1 component in the list and highlight it (you'd depress the CTRL key to select a second component).

10. Click Next. You'll see a final COM Component Install Wizard dialog.

11. Click Finish to complete the Install new component(s) installation process. You'll see the new components added to the right pane of the Component Services window as shown in Figure 7-9.

Adding Security to a COM+ Application

Now we have a COM+ application and an associated component installed within the Component Services snap-in. However, the component isn't completely operational yet because we haven't installed any security for it. Theoretically, we could get by without adding any security, but role-based security is one of the new features of COM+ that promises to make life a lot easier for the network administrator and developer alike.

To add role-based security to the component, you'll need to create at least one (preferably two) roles. We'll call the first role Administrator so that someone logged in as this role will be able to access all of the methods within the OrderAccess component. The second role can be any other value, but for this example we'll use User. The User role will be able to access any of the nonconfiguration methods within the component. In other words, the user will be able to do things like look up a part in the catalog, but they won't be able to modify the contents of the catalog. (Obviously, you don't want to give the user the ability to modify the company's product line.) The following procedure will get you started adding a role to the application:

1. Highlight the Roles folder, then use the Action | New | Role command to display the Role dialog box shown here.

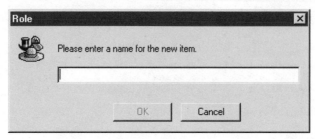

2. Type a name for the role, then click OK. For the example, we'll use Administrator for one role and User for the second.

3. Open the Administrator (or User) folder, then highlight the Users folder. Use the Action | New | User command to display the Select Users or Groups dialog box shown here. This is where you'll choose the users that can access components using the Administrator role.

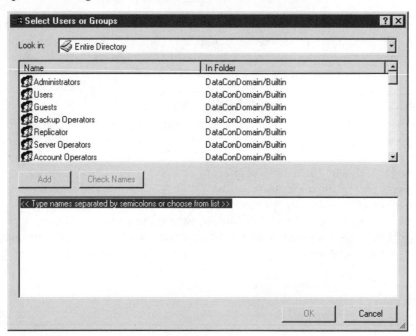

4. Highlight the Administrators entry, then click Add. You'll see the Administrator added to the list of users.

5. Click OK. Administrator will get added to the Users folder in the Component Services window.

6. Repeat Steps 1–5 for the User role. However, in this case, use either your own name or a test username instead of Administrator for the Users folder. Figure 7-10 shows a typical example of the security setup for this example. Obviously, any production components you create will have a more complex security setup that allows users to access the components you create in specific roles.

I've chosen not to implement any form of security within the OrderAccess component because that would defeat the purpose of using the highly configurable role-based security option. If I had implemented security within the component, then any change to the company structure might also mean a change to the code within the component. In most cases, you don't want to add security to your component anymore—you'll want to add using the Component Services snap-in.

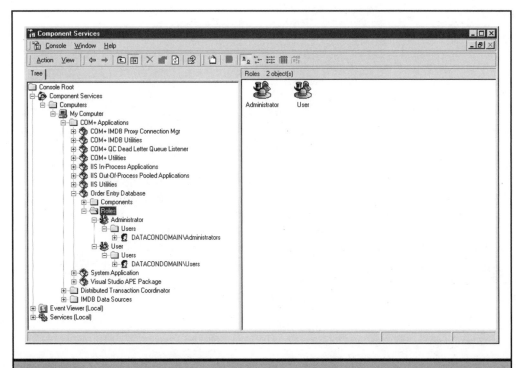

Figure 7-10. Role-based security allows you to define the access a user gets to the methods within a component based on the role that user performs

With this change in methodology in mind, let's see what you'd need to do to add security to the OrderAccess component. Right-click the OrderAccess.OrderModify.1 component and choose Properties from the context menu. You'll see an OrderAccess.OrderModify.1 Properties dialog box like the one shown here.

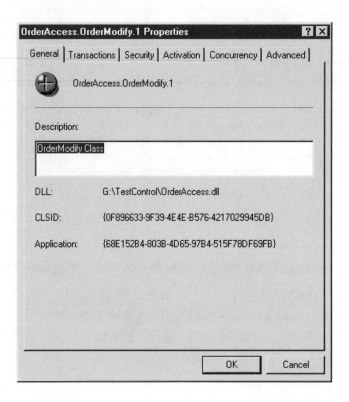

As you can see, the OrderAccess.OrderModify.1 Properties dialog box allows you to configure a relatively wide range of component options, including whether the component supports transactions. There are also options for allowing the component to engage in object pooling (normally a good idea with database components) and concurrency. Click the Security tab and you'll see the Security tab of the OrderAccess.OrderModify.1 Properties dialog box, like the one shown here. Notice that both of the roles we've created are available for use with this component.

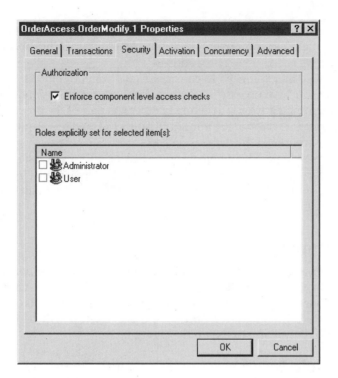

As soon as we added roles to the application, Component Services assumed that we wanted to use security and enabled it for us. The way that the Security tab of the OrderAccess.OrderModify.1 Properties dialog box is set, no one can access the component right now. What you'll need to do is check the roles that you want to access the component. For the purposes of this example, check both Administrator and User so that anyone can access the OrderAccess component. You can also adjust security at the application and method level by opening the Security tab for either object level.

CREATING THE CLIENT-SIDE COMPONENT

Everything on our server is ready to go. If you had a client-side component and a test application built, you could access the database right now. This section is going to help you with the first of the two remaining requirements, building the client-side component. The client-side component isn't going to be very complex in this case. All it's designed to do is create a communication path between the client and the server. Later, you could add a variety of things to the client component, including MSMQ capability and the ability to redirect client requests based on registry entries.

There's one issue that you need to consider as part of your COM+ application development strategy. You have no way of knowing how your application is going to work at this point, and there isn't any way to debug it either. As part of the process of building the client-side component and testing it, you should build a small test application. This application should test just one of the database objects that we created earlier and test just one part of your business logic. The whole purpose behind this test application is to remove some of the complexity of testing your COM+ application as a whole. In addition to creating the client-side component, we'll create a small application that will test your ability to access the Catalog table.

Creating the Component Shell

Just like the server-side component, we'll begin the client-side component by creating a component shell. This section will help you perform all of the setups required to make the client-side component work. We'll follow the same basic steps that we used when creating the server-side component—obviously, the exact setup will be different, and we won't need to install the component on the server later.

Starting the Project

The first thing we'll need to do is create a new project. Even though the project creation process will be similar to what we did for the server, there are differences in the options you'll need to select. The following procedure will get you started creating the component shell (the procedure assumes that you have Visual C++ 6 started):

1. Use the File | New command to display the New dialog box.

2. Choose the Projects tab of the New dialog box and highlight the ATL COM AppWizard icon.

3. Type **OrderClient** in the Project Name field, then click OK. You'll see the ATL COM AppWizard - Step 1 of 1 dialog box (see the "Understanding the ATL COM AppWizard - Step 1 of 1 Options" sidebar for details on this dialog box).

4. Choose the Dynamic Link Library (DLL) server option.

5. Check the "Allow merging of proxy/stub code" and Support MFC options. (Don't check the Support MTS option or the component will compile with errors and may not work as anticipated.) The example code assumes that you have MFC support enabled.

6. Click Finish. You'll see the New Project Information dialog box.

7. Click OK. The ATL COM AppWizard will create the new project for you.

Inserting the Client ATL Object

At this point, we have a client component shell. We'll need to add an ATL object to handle the client-side processing needs. As with the server-side business object, there's only one client object. However, this object will contain one method for each of the access requirements that we talked about in Table 7-7. Interestingly enough, the client component will use the same criteria for defining the method calls.

1. Use the Insert | New ATL Object command to display the ATL Object Wizard dialog box. Unlike the previous object classes we created, the client component doesn't really need any special features. It won't operate with databases or work with MTS. In fact, since we're not using this object within the client as a visible application feature like a pushbutton, we really don't need to use the ActiveX component features either. This particular component is just a simple object—something small that allows us to communicate with the server component.

2. Choose the Objects category.

3. Highlight the Simple Object icon.

4. Click Next. You'll see the ATL Object Wizard Properties dialog box. The Names tab will look much like the other ATL objects in the past. Of special interest in this case is the Attributes tab, which looks like the one shown here. Notice that Visual C++ gives you quite a bit of control over the attributes of even a simple object.

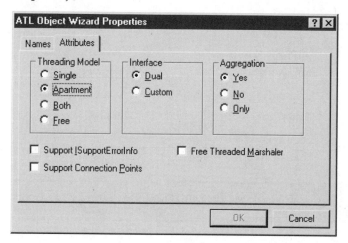

5. Fill out the various pages of the ATL Object Wizard Properties dialog box to meet the needs of your particular component. Table 7-8 shows the settings you'll need to use to create the example client-side component. Since this is a simple component, we won't need aggregation, which is a useful feature if you want to make complex components using simple ones. Normally, you'd want to support the ISupportErrorInfo interface. However, given the kind of application we're working with, you can't depend on getting any error information from the server, so adding this interface isn't necessary. The same holds true for connection points. The server won't be able to fire events, so we don't need to support connection points here either.

NOTE: Many properties get filled out automatically when you type in one property value on a particular tab. The table won't include these automatic entries and you should assume that the automatic entries are correct unless the table tells you otherwise. While you can change the automatic entries, using them as is tends to make the code easier to read and your control work with less debugging later.

6. Click OK. The ATL Object Wizard will create the required class and interface for you.

Adding Some Client Component Methods

The methods for our client component are set up exactly the same as the server-side component. You won't need to add any additional methods since the client-side component is for communication purposes only. Refer to the "Adding Some Business Object Methods" section of the chapter for instructions on adding the client component methods. Make sure you actually add these methods before you proceed with the chapter.

Tab	Property	Value
Names	Short Name	OrderRequest
Attributes	Threading Model	Apartment
	Interface	Dual
	Aggregation	No
	Free Threaded Marshaller	Checked

Table 7-8. On/Off Button ATL Object Property Values

Adding the Component Code

The client component code is very simple when compared to what happens on the server. In this particular case, the exact same thing happens in every client component method—only the variables change to match the data being passed by the user to the server. This section will look at the GetCatalogItem() method. You'll find the source for the other 12 methods associated with this component in the book's source code. Listing 7-2 shows what the GetCatalogItem() method looks like.

```
STDMETHODIMP COrderRequest::GetCatalogItem(BSTR *pbstrProductID,
                                           BSTR bstrDirection,
                                           BSTR *pbstrProductName,
                                           CURRENCY *pcurrPrice,
                                           int *piOnHand)
{
    IOrderModify*    m_pDoTest;    // Interface Pointer
    HRESULT          hr;           // Query Result.
    MULTI_QI         mqi;          // Interface we want to query.
    COSERVERINFO     pSInfo;       // Server information.

    AFX_MANAGE_STATE(AfxGetStaticModuleState())

    // Initialize the interface pointer.
    m_pDoTest = NULL;

    // Initialize the COM environment.
    CoInitialize(NULL);

    // Initialize the server information.
    pSInfo.pwszName = L""\\\\NTServer"";
    pSInfo.pAuthInfo = NULL;

    // Initialize the result structure.
    mqi.pIID = &IID_IOrderModify;
    mqi.pItf = NULL;
    mqi.hr = 0;

    // Create an instance of the object.
    hr = CoCreateInstanceEx(CLSID_OrderModify,
                            NULL,
                            CLSCTX_ALL,
                            &pSInfo,
                            1,
                            &mqi);
```

```
    // If the creation failed, exit.
    if (FAILED(hr))
    {
        // The class isn''t registered.
        if (hr == REGDB_E_CLASSNOTREG)
            AfxMessageBox(""The class isn''t registered on the server."");

        // One or more of the arguments was invalid.
        if (hr == E_INVALIDARG)
            AfxMessageBox(""One or more of the arguments were invalid."");

        // None of the requested interfaces are available.
        if (hr == E_NOINTERFACE)
            AfxMessageBox(""None of the interfaces are available."");

        // Only some of the requests succeeded.
        if (hr == CO_S_NOTALLINTERFACES)
            AfxMessageBox(""Some of the interfaces aren''t available."");

        // Display the general failure message and exit.
        AfxMessageBox(""Object Creation Failed"");
        return hr;
    }

    // Check the result of the individual interface query.
    hr = mqi.hr;
    if (FAILED(hr))
        {
        AfxMessageBox(""Couldn''t retrieve the interface pointer."");
        return hr;
        }

    // Store the interface pointer in our local variable.
    m_pDoTest = (IOrderModify*)mqi.pItf;

    // Get the catalog information.
    hr = m_pDoTest->GetCatalogItem(pbstrProductID,
                                   bstrDirection,
                                   pbstrProductName,
                                   pcurrPrice,
                                   piOnHand);
    if (FAILED(hr))
        AfxMessageBox(""Catalog Request Transfer Failed"");


    // Uninitialize the COM environment.
```

```
CoUninitialize();

// Tell the requesting application that every worked OK.
return S_OK;
}
```

The client component is by far the easiest code in this example to understand, but the most error-prone code to implement. This is the component that will take the information generated by the client and pass it to the server-side component. There usually aren't any problems transferring the data—the problems normally occur when creating the connection in the first place. As a result, when you write your client-side component, you need to add extra error-handling code in the connection area of the application. Listing 7-2 shows the bare minimum that you should implement, and it usually pays to add more.

The first thing we do in the example code is initialize the interface pointer and the COM environment. There aren't any weird considerations here—all you need to do is ensure that you actually perform this step in your code.

Since we're going to use CoCreateInstanceEx() in this component (because it allows us to access components on another server), we'll have to set up two data structures as well. The first data structure contains the path name for the server. In this case, I'm using a Universal Naming Convention (UNC) format. There's a wealth of other formats you can use, including some that work with the Internet (like IP addresses). The second element of this data structure is another structure containing server authentication information.

NOTE: You must change the UNC format server name in Listing 7-2 to match the name of your server. Unless your server happens to have the same name as mine, the example code won't work on other machines. There are other ways to handle the server name problem, including the use of automatically downloaded registry entries. However, any method you use will require an initial server entry name somewhere. I chose this method of designating the server name because it represents the easiest method of allowing you to modify the example code to match your server setup.

CAUTION: Using an authentication structure within a client component should be the option of last resort. In most cases, you're going to set this structure to NULL since you'll want to use the user's credentials for verification on the server. The only time you'd create an authentication structure is if you wanted the client application to access the server using something other than the user credentials. Using an authentication structure allows you to log in to the server using credentials that may exceed those of the user. In short, you're overriding the beneficial features of the Windows 2000 built-in security mechanism to ensure that the user will have the required access. It's usually better to ask the network administrator to give the user the required rights, rather than short circuit Windows 2000 built-in security in this way. That way, the administrator will be aware of threats to the network, rather than having a surprise that got hard-coded into an application.

The second data structure is what Microsoft refers to as an array of result structures. There's an important piece of information that Microsoft doesn't provide when working with the result structure, but it is inferred by their example code. Notice the method I use to set this structure up in Listing 7-2. Since there's only one interface required for the example, I set the structure up as shown. If I were requesting more than one interface, then the variable would be handled as an array, not as a single element as shown. Failing to use the correct strategy when working with the result structure will cause an ambiguous error when working with the CoCreateInstanceEx() function. Make sure you check for this problem when debugging an errant client-side component. The error message you get back isn't very helpful in this case, and the bug is very easy to overlook (since the code looks like it should work just fine).

It's time to use the CoCreateInstanceEx() function to access the remote server. Notice that the function requires input similar to CoCreateInstance(). You still need to provide the ClassID of the class that you want to access. In addition, you can provide the interface pointer of a container component if you want to use aggregation. Always set this second argument to NULL to ensure that the call will succeed. You'll also need to provide the execution context (CLSCTX_ALL is the best choice in most cases, since the server name is specified as part of the COSERVERINFO data structure). The COSERVERINFO data structure comes next. Finally, you need to provide a number indicating the number of interfaces in the MULTI_QI (results) data structure that follows as the final argument.

NOTE: DCOM doesn't currently support any form of aggregation. Unfortunately, except for a small note, Microsoft doesn't really point this fact out. Visual C++ will allow you to compile and register a component that relies on DCOM aggregation without producing any error. In fact, the only clue you get that there's a problem is when you use the component. It will produce a variety of error messages, none of which have anything to do with the cause of the problem. What this means to you as a programmer is that the second CoCreateInstanceEx() argument should always be NULL. If you want to use aggregation locally, then using CoCreateInstance() is less error prone. In short, aggregation and CoCreateInstanceEx() don't go together now and probably won't in the near future.

I can't emphasize enough that you need good error trapping for this call. All you need to do is compare the number of standard error messages provided for CoCreateInstance() to those for CoCreateInstanceEx() to see what I mean. The code in Listing 7-2 shows the bare minimum that you should implement. Using a try...except is an even better idea. In short, CoCreateInstanceEx() is going to be a common source of problems, so you should consider looking here first when your application begins to experience unexplainable connection errors with the server.

CoCreateInstanceEx() also requires some additional postcall processing that you don't have to perform when working with CoCreateInstance(). The first thing you need to do is check the failure status of each of the interfaces you requested. There are situations when the CoCreateInstanceEx() call can return some, but not all, of the requested interfaces. As a result, you need to check each interface result separately using the hr value in the result data structure for that interface.

If you do obtain an interface pointer, then it's going to be of the pvoid variety, which can't be used directly by your component. You need to typecast the resulting interface pointer to match the pointer that your application is expecting or the interface pointer will appear to be inaccessible.

At this point, we have an interface pointer to a component on a remote server. All we need to do to finish the transaction is to pass the information to the server component, then uninitialize the COM environment. You still have to check for a failure after you pass the data to the server because the connection between the client and server can get severed before you have a chance to pass the data. In short, you can't assume that the server is going to be there at any given time because it appears on a remote machine. Uninitializing the COM environment ensures that memory gets released and the COM unloads any DLLs that you loaded. However, in this case, the act of uninitializing the COM environment becomes even more important because you need to free the RPC connection (DCOM link).

Creating a Simple Catalog Test Application

As previously mentioned, you really need to test the various database connections separately. The reason is simple: The lack of debugging tools in Visual C++ added to the complexity of even a simple COM+ application make component testing a must. Yes, we'll create a full-fledged application later in the chapter (in the "Creating a Test Application" section); but for now, let's look at an example of a very simple test application that retrieves just one catalog item.

NOTE: While this section talks about the work done to test the Catalog table access, it's very important that you test access to all tables (or other query types) individually. You'll find example applications in the sample source code for testing access to all four tables using the same technique shown here. The Catalog table was selected for demonstration purposes. The other table samples were eliminated due to space considerations.

Creating the Dialog Program Shell

We'll begin, as usual, by creating the program shell. There isn't any reason to make this application complex—in fact, simplicity is a real plus in this case. With this in mind, we'll use a simple dialog-based application that allows us to move between Catalog table records. The program won't allow use to change anything about the table—just view its contents. The following procedure will get you started (I'll assume that you've already started Visual C++):

1. Use the File | New command to display the New dialog box.

2. Choose the MFC AppWizard (exe) project and type **CatalogTest** in the Project name field.

3. Click OK and you'll see the MFC AppWizard - Step 1 dialog box shown here.

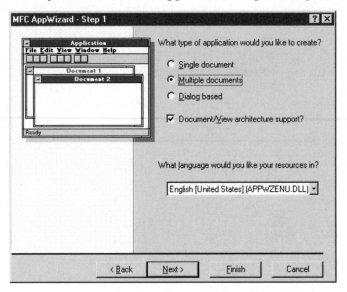

4. Choose the "Dialog based" option, and then click Next. You'll see the MFC AppWizard - Step 2 of 4 dialog box shown here. Let's keep this example simple by removing any unnecessary features like the About Box.

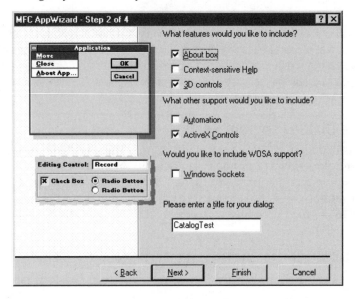

5. Uncheck the About box option. Type **Catalog Table Test** in the "Please enter a title for your dialog" field.

6. Click Finish. You'll see a New Project Information dialog box like the one shown here.

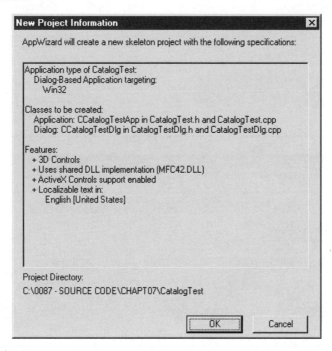

7. Click OK. Visual C++ will create the new project for you. It should also display a dialog box for you to work with.

Designing the Catalog Test Application Dialog Box

There are several things we need to consider when designing the simple dialog box for our first application. If you look at Table 7-3, you'll see that the Catalog table contains four fields: ProductID, ProductName, Price, and OnHand. The ProductID field is the unique identifier for this table, so we'll need to use it to access the records within the table. Any other kind of request could generate multiple return values, which is something we really don't want to test for at the moment.

Just looking at a single record isn't going to be very interesting either. What we really need is a way to look at the current, next, and previous records. The current record can be defined in two different ways. We could say that the current record is the one that the application has provided by default. This means that we'd start at the beginning of the data-

base and use the Next and Previous buttons to move from record to record. While this
will test sequential record access, it won't help much with random access—a far more
common event with database management. As a result, we need a second method of defining the current record through user input of a particular record number.

With these criteria in mind, we'll need three pushbuttons: Refresh (current record),
Next, and Previous. We'll also need four edit boxes to display the current record data.
Figure 7-11 shows dialog box layout for this example. Table 7-9 contains the various edit
box and pushbutton settings.

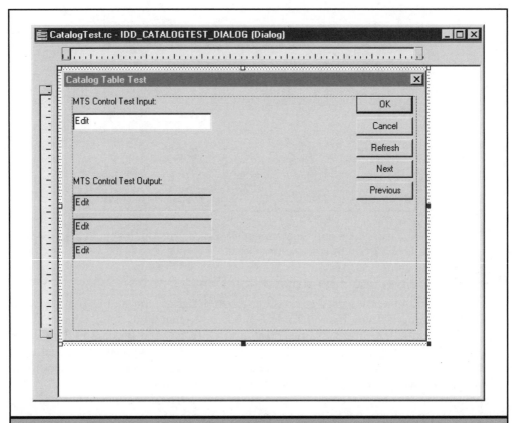

Figure 7-11.   This is the dialog box layout we'll use for the Catalog table test application

ID	Setting	Value
IDC_PRODUCTID	Tab stop	Checked
	Number	Checked
IDC_PRODUCTNAME	Tab stop	Not checked
	Read only	Checked
IDC_PRICE	Tab stop	Not checked
	Read only	Checked
IDC_ONHAND	Tab stop	Not checked
	Read only	Checked
IDC_REFRESH	Caption	Refresh
IDC_NEXT	Caption	Next
IDC_PREVIOUS	Caption	Previous

Table 7-9. Catalog Table Test Dialog Box Control Settings

Creating Member Variables for the Catalog Test Application

Now that all of the controls are in place, we need to provide a means to access them from the application. One of the first things we'll need to do is provide some method to access the contents of the four edit boxes. The following procedure will help you assign member variables to the four edit boxes.

1. CTRL-double-click the IDC_PRODUCTID edit box. You'll see an Add Member Variable dialog box like the one shown here.

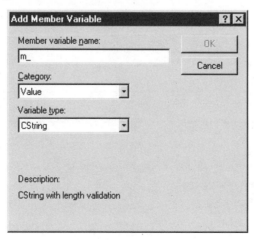

2. Type **m_productID** in the "Member variable name" field.

3. Choose Control in the Category field.

4. Verify that the "Variable type" field is set to CEdit and not CString.

5. Click OK.

6. Perform Steps 1 through 5 for the other three edit boxes. Use member variable names of **m_productName** for the IDC_PRODUCTNAME, **m_price** for the IDC_PRICE, and **m_onHand** for the IDC_ONHAND edit box controls.

7. Use the View | ClassWizard command to display the MFC ClassWizard dialog box. Click the Member Variables tab. Your dialog box should look similar to the one shown here.

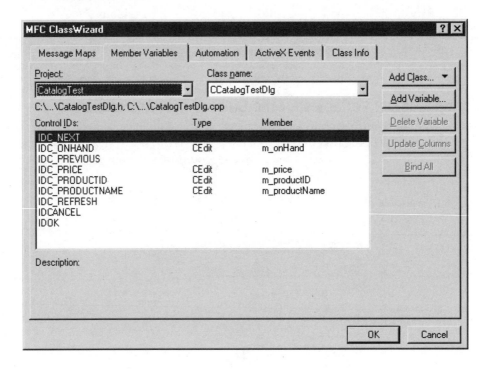

Creating Event Handlers for the Catalog Test Application

We'll also need to provide event handlers for the three pushbuttons that will control our progress through the database. The following procedure will allow you to create the three event handlers that we need:

1. Right-click the IDC_REFRESH button, then choose Events from the context menu. You'll see the "New Windows Message and Event Handlers for class CCatalogTestDlg" dialog box shown here.

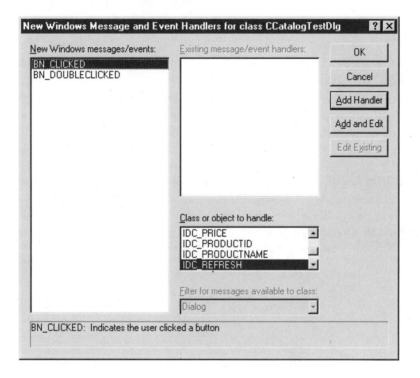

2. Highlight BN_CLICKED in the "New Windows messages/events" list box.
3. Click Add Handler (or Add and Edit if this is the last button) to add an event handler to the application. You'll see an Add Member Function dialog box like

the one shown here. You'll normally use the default name for the function since there isn't a good reason to change it.

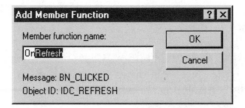

4. Click OK. BN_CLICKED will move to the "Existing message/event handler" list box.

5. Choose the next button in the "Class or object to handle" list (IDC_NEXT or IDC_PREVIOUS).

6. Perform Steps 2–5 for the remaining buttons. Remember to click Add and Edit, rather than Add Handler for the last button. Visual C++ will take you directly to the event-handler functions so that you can add code to them.

Adding Some Code to the Next, Previous, and Refresh Buttons

It's time to add some code to the example program. Listing 7-3 shows a representative example of the code you'll need to implement the Next, Previous, and Refresh buttons. I didn't include all three methods in the chapter since they work in a similar way. (You'll find the code for all three buttons in the source code for the book.)

```
void CCatalogTestDlg::OnRefresh()
{
    CString         oProductID;          // Text from edit box on dialog.
    BSTR            bstrProductID;        // Converted product ID.
    CString         oProductName;         // Converted product name.
    BSTR            bstrProductName;      // Product name from database.
    int             iOnHand;              // Number of items on hand.
    CString         oOnHand;              // Converted number of items on hand.
    CURRENCY        currPrice;            // Product cost.
    BSTR            bstrPrice;            // BSTR for price conversion.
    CString         oPrice;               // Converted price.
    IOrderRequest*  m_pDoTest;            // IOrderRequest Interface Pointer
    HRESULT         hr;                   // Result of Operations
    CString         oDirection;           // Direction of Database Travel

    // Convert the first input value to a BSTR.
    m_productID.GetWindowText(oProductID);
    bstrProductID = oProductID.AllocSysString();
```

```
// Initialize the interface pointer.
m_pDoTest = NULL;

// Initialize the COM environment.
CoInitialize(NULL);

// Create an instance of the object.
hr = CoCreateInstance(CLSID_OrderRequest,
                      NULL,
                      CLSCTX_ALL,
                      IID_IOrderRequest,
                      (void**)&m_pDoTest);

// If the creation failed, exit.
if (FAILED(hr))
{
    // Make sure the class was registered.
    if (hr == REGDB_E_CLASSNOTREG)
        AfxMessageBox(""DoTest Class Not Registered"");

    // Make sure we can aggregate the class.
    if (hr == CLASS_E_NOAGGREGATION)
        AfxMessageBox(""Class Can''t be Aggregated"");

    // Display the general failure message and exit.
    AfxMessageBox(""Object Creation Failed"");
    return;
}

// Refresh the current record information.
oDirection = ""Refresh"";
hr = m_pDoTest->GetCatalogItem(&bstrProductID,
                               oDirection.AllocSysString(),
                               &bstrProductName,
                               &currPrice,
                               &iOnHand);
if (FAILED(hr))
    AfxMessageBox(""Catalog Check Failed"");

// Display the Product Name output value.
oProductName = bstrProductName;
m_productName.SetWindowText(oProductName);

// Display the Price output value.
VarBstrFromCy(currPrice,
              0,
              LOCALE_NOUSEROVERRIDE,
              &bstrPrice);
```

```
oPrice = bstrPrice;
m_price.SetWindowText(oPrice);

// Display the On Hand output value.
itoa(iOnHand, oOnHand.GetBuffer(10), 10);
oOnHand.ReleaseBuffer(-1);
m_onHand.SetWindowText(oOnHand);

// Update the Product ID value.
oProductID = bstrProductID;
m_productID.SetWindowText(oProductID);

// Uninitialize the COM environment.
CoUninitialize();
}
```

The client application is responsible for providing a ProductID value to the server. The full-fledged application we'll create a bit later in the chapter will do this through a list box. The sample application only displays one record at a time, so we'll use the edit control for this information. The first thing we need to do then is get the user-entered value from the edit control and convert it into a BSTR that the server control will understand.

Once we have the ProductID that we want to look up, it's time to initialize an interface pointer variable, initialize the COM environment, and obtain a pointer to the client-side component interface. These are the same three steps that you'd perform to gain access to any component on the local machine. Notice that these three steps include error trapping. The code checks to see if the HRESULT value (hr) equals anything other than S_OK, then tries to provide detailed error information (when available). You'll also need to provide two additional code entries to gain access to the client-side component. The first appears in the CatalogTestDlg.CPP file as:

```
// Include support for the IOrderAccess Interface.
#include ""..\OrderClient\OrderClient.H""
```

This header file provides interface information like the methods that the interface supports and the arguments you must provide to use them. The compiler uses this information to verify that you've accessed the interface correctly within the application. The second entry appears in the CatalogTestDlg.H file as:

```
// Include support for the IOrderAccess Interface.
#include ""../OrderClient/OrderClient_i.c""
```

This second entry contains a list of all the globally unique identifiers (GUIDs) for the component that you want to access. These GUIDs correspond to entries in the registry where their component has registered itself. Your application will use these GUIDs to access the component and instantiate an object that your application can use to eventually gain access to the database.

The last thing we need to do before we access the component is to decide on an action to perform with the table. In this case, we'll refresh the data for the ProductID value that the user has entered at the dialog box. The component also supports getting the next and the previous records. In normal processing, you'll find that getting the current or the next record is usually sufficient for most operations. The only time you really need to worry about a previous record method is when you're building a GUI front end for an application as we're doing here. Even though you won't normally use the previous record method, it usually pays to add one to the component at the outset, rather than wait until you actually need this functionality in a future application.

The only OrderRequest component method we're testing in this sample application is the GetCatalogItem() method. Notice that the ProductID, like the rest of the values, is passed as a pointer, not as a value. It might not seem like a good idea to pass yet another pointer, but it's important in this case for several reasons. The most important reason is that the user may enter a nonexistent value. Passing a pointer means that the application can update the application to show the ProductID that matches the rest of the returned data. The various components in this application have been designed in such a way that they always return a record, even if the record doesn't match the user's search criteria. Obviously, there are a number of component failures that could occur, so we need to check on them after the call returns.

The last four sections of code in the method convert the data we receive from the components into something that Visual C++ can use. Since COM uses different data types than Visual C++ does, some of these conversions can get troublesome. The easiest conversion is BSTR to CString. All you need to do is copy the BSTR into a CString. This, by the way, is one of the reasons you want to have MFC support enabled. Without MFC support, you'd need to do a lot more work to convert that BSTR.

You'll remember that the currPrice variable is of type CURRENCY, which isn't a native Visual C++ data type. In this case, we don't have a convenient method to convert CURRENCY to something that Visual C++ can understand. You need to use the VarBstrFromCy() method to convert the CURRENCY value into a BSTR first. The BSTR is relatively easy to convert into a CString after that. Visual C++ does provide access to a wealth of API functions found in OLEAUT32.DLL. You'll want to learn about these functions because they become very important when working with DBMS in Visual C++.

The iOnHand conversion is a very common one that you could use for things other than COM. All you need to do is use a CString with the C itoa() function. Since this function is looking for an LPTSTR and not a CString, you'll need to use the GetBuffer() method and provide a length value for the buffer size. Don't forget to release the buffer using the ReleaseBuffer() method after using something like the itoa() function. Otherwise, you'll get really strange results from the CString. Note that I used a value of -1 for the ReleaseBuffer() method. Using -1 tells the method that you want to trim the resulting string—a good idea if you want to keep excess spaces to a minimum.

The final bit of code in this example uninitializes the COM environment. You need to remember to perform this task whenever you work with COM. Otherwise, your application can, and will, produce memory leaks and other undesirable problems. I normally add this call as part of adding CoInitialize() at the beginning of my code. It's a good habit to get into that will save you a lot of grief looking for "nits" in your code later.

Performing the Test

We're finally ready to perform a test on the Catalog table. As previously stated, the reason for this simple test is that COM+ provides such a complex development environment and few debugging tools. We're using the divide and conquer method to reduce the complexity of finding bugs in our application. All you need to do is run the application, enter values in the upper edit box, and look for the appropriate results. Clicking Refresh should display the current record. The Next and Previous buttons will take you to the next and previous records in the table, respectively. Here's what your application should look like in operation.

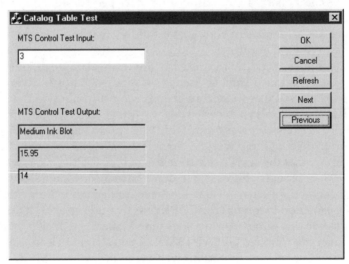

CREATING A TEST APPLICATION

We have a database and a component that we can use to access it. Now it's time to create an application that will provide the user interface portion of our example. The whole purpose of this application is to present the data in a way that the user can easily understand.

In addition, the application will provide some level of error trapping that will detect input errors before the information gets sent to the server. Once the data arrives at the server, the component we created earlier will take over. In short, the application doesn't really need to worry about interacting with the database.

There are a lot of different ways to present database information to the user, and the example in this section looks at just one method—the method that was most convenient for me to use for the example. In sum, this example is more designed to exercise the client-side and server-side components than it is to show you how to design user interfaces. Considering the complexity of this example, the chapter will only look at getting information from the server, not at actually manipulating it. You'll find additional functionality with the source code for this chapter.

The following sections will help you perform three tasks. First, we'll need to create an application shell. We'll use a very simple dialog-based application for this example. There are a lot of other ways that you could tackle the user interface portion of this example, but creating a dialog-based interface will likely prove the easiest method of doing so. Second, we'll create the user interface elements—the various objects that the user will need to interact with the database like fields. Finally, we'll add some application code to the example.

Once we have the application completed, we'll test it. This particular example won't test every facet of the components that we've created. However, you'll walk away with enough information to create enterprise-level COM+ applications of your own.

Creating the Application Shell

The first thing we need to do is create an application shell. I've chosen a multiple document interface (MDI) application for this example. In a real-world situation, you may find that a dialog-based or single-document interface (SDI) application will work better. Using MDI allows us to concentrate on one view of the data at a time—something that should reduce user confusion for real-world applications as well. The following procedure will help get you started in creating the test application:

1. Use the File | New command to display the New dialog box.

2. Choose the MFC AppWizard (exe) project and type **AppTest** in the Project name field.

3. Click OK and you'll see the MFC AppWizard - Step 1 dialog box.

4. Choose the Multiple documents option and ensure the "Document/View architecture support?" option is checked.

5. Click Next three times. You'll see the MFC AppWizard - Step 4 of 6 dialog box shown here. In an effort to keep the application simple, we'll remove a few features that you may or may not choose to implement with your application.

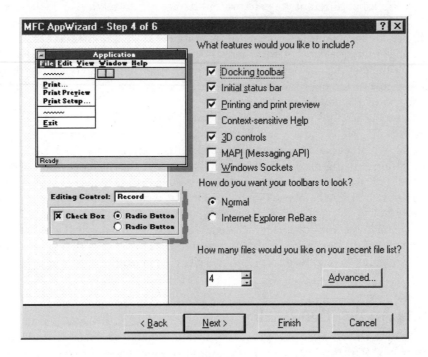

6. Uncheck the "Docking toolbar" and "Initial status bar" options. Set the "recent file list" option to 0 instead of 4. This is one option you'd probably set to 0 anyway since the user won't be opening random files with this application—the database entries will be chosen automatically. You could also remove the print support that's provided by default since you'll normally need to provide several custom print routines, but we'll leave it in place for this example.

7. Click Next twice. You'll see the MFC AppWizard - Step 6 of 6 dialog box shown here. We need to choose a view for our data. The default CView class leaves too much work for us to do. Using the CFormView class is a much better option since it allows us to create one or more forms that the user can select.

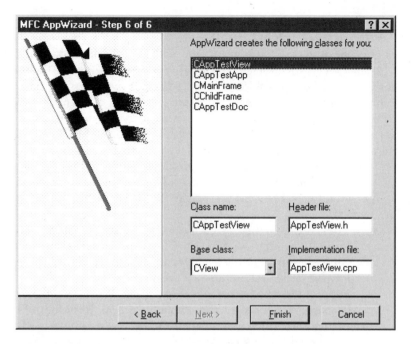

8. Choose CFormView in the "Base class" drop-down list box.

9. Click Finish. You'll see the New Project Information dialog box shown here.

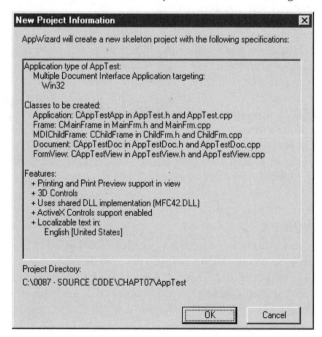

10. Click OK. Visual C++ will create the application shell for you.

Defining the User Interface

The number of types of views that you include with your application depends on the needs of the users. Obviously, efficiency is another concern. Allowing the user to enter and edit records as quickly as possible is always a design concern for any database application. In short, I've optimized the user interface options, the views for our example application, to exercise the components that we've built in increasing levels of complexity. The three views will allow you to see the components in action at three levels of activity.

The client view is the least intensive since all we need to do is display a single client at a time. We've already done this as part of the previous examples in the book, so adding this feature to the test application should be a snap. This part of the application uses a single component method by itself—it places the smallest load on the programming we've performed in the past.

The order view comes next. In this case, we're using two of the tables in the database together. Look at Figure 7-2 again to see how the Client and Orders tables relate. As you can see, this view will represent a middle level of component testing. We'll need to coordinate the output of two component methods to create the view.

The item list view provides the highest level of testing. It relies on the output of all four tables in our database. We'll need to coordinate the output from four of the component methods; and, depending on how you set up the view, you may have to perform some repetitive searches. In short, this is the view that best tests the components we've created.

Designing the Client Application View

Let's begin with the easiest of the three views, the client view. We'll use the default form for this view. You should see this form immediately after the application is created. Figure 7-12 shows what the form should look like. Table 7-10 provides a complete list of the controls on this form and tells you how to configure them. Note that you'll need to add member variables for each of the edit boxes and event handlers for each of the pushbuttons. Table 7-10 also contains the member variable or event handler name that you'll use for each of the controls. We talked about adding member variables in the "Creating Member Variables for the Catalog Test Application" section of the chapter. Adding event handlers is covered in the "Creating Event Handlers for the Catalog Test Application" section of the chapter.

Adding a New Form

We've used the default form that Visual C++ provides for the first view. To add a second view, we'll need to create another form. Adding the form is very easy. All we need to do is right-click the Dialog folder on the ResourceView tab of the Workspace windows, then choose Insert from the list. You'll see an Insert Resource dialog box like the one shown here.

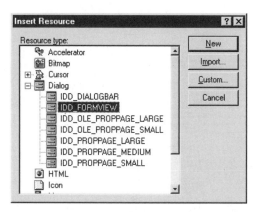

Figure 7-12.   The client view provides the minimum level of component testing

ID	Setting	Value	Member Variable or Event Handler Name
IDC_CUSTOMERID	Tab stop	Checked	m_customerID
	Number	Checked	
IDC_FIRSTNAME	Tab stop	Not checked	m_firstName
	Read only	Checked	
IDC_MIDDLEINITIAL	Tab stop	Not checked	m_middleInitial
	Read only	Checked	
IDC_LASTNAME	Tab stop	Not checked	m_lastName
	Read only	Checked	
IDC_TITLE	Tab stop	Not checked	m_title
	Read only	Checked	
IDC_COMPANY	Tab stop	Not checked	m_company
	Read only	Checked	
IDC_ADDRESS1	Tab stop	Not checked	m_address1
	Read only	Checked	
IDC_ADDRESS2	Tab stop	Not checked	m_address2
	Read only	Checked	
IDC_CITY	Tab stop	Not checked	m_city
	Read only	Checked	
IDC_STATE	Tab stop	Not checked	m_state
	Read only	Checked	
IDC_ZIP	Tab stop	Not checked	m_zip
	Read only	Checked	
IDC_COUNTRY	Tab stop	Not checked	m_country
	Read only	Checked	
IDC_TELEPHONE1	Tab stop	Not checked	m_telephone1
	Read only	Checked	
IDC_TELEPHONE2	Tab stop	Not checked	m_telephone2
	Read only	Checked	
IDC_LASTCONTACT	Tab stop	Not checked	m_lastContact

Table 7-10. Client View Control Settings

ID	Setting	Value	Member Variable or Event Handler Name
	Read only	Checked	
IDC_REFRESH	Caption	Refresh	OnRefresh()
IDC_NEXT	Caption	Next	OnNext()
IDC_PREVIOUS	Caption	Previous	OnPrevious()

Table 7-10. Client View Control Settings *(continued)*

Highlight the IDD_FORMVIEW dialog type, then click New. Visual C++ will add a new dialog box to your list of resources. We'll want to change the name of the form. To do that, right-click the dialog box and choose Properties from the context menu. You'll see a Dialog Properties dialog box. Change the name of the dialog box by changing the ID field on the General tab. The example will use IDD_ORDER_FORM for the order view and IDD_ITEM_FORM for the item list view.

Besides changing the name of the form, we need to add a class for it. CTRL-double-click the dialog box and you'll see an Adding a Class dialog box like the one shown here.

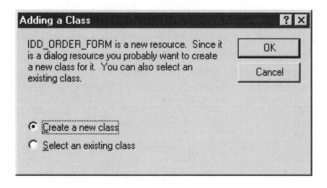

Since this is a new form, we'll need a new class for it. Ensure that the "Create a new class" option is selected, then click OK. You'll see a New Class dialog box like the one shown here.

New Class

Class information

Name:

File name:

Change...

Base class: CDialog

Dialog ID: IDD_ORDER_FORM

OK

Cancel

Automation

(•) None

( ) Automation

( ) Createable by type ID:

Type **COrderView** in the Name field for the order view and **CItemView** in the Name field for the item view. No matter what you name the new dialog box class, you must select CFormView in the "Base class" field. Otherwise, what you'll create is a standard dialog box, which isn't what we need for the example. Click OK to complete the process—Visual C++ will create the new class for you.

There are several additional features that we could add at this point. The features you add depend a great deal on how you want your application to look. At a minimum, we need to define a template string. This template string will define the title bar and other elements of the new document template. See the "Understanding Document Template Strings" sidebar for more information about document template strings. All that we really need to do to create the document template string for this example is to open the String Table resource shown in Figure 7-13. Notice that there's already one document template string in place—IDR_APPTESTYPE. You'll want to change this default string to look like this:

```
\nClient View\nClient View\n\n\nAppTest.Document\nAppTes Document
```

TIP: The other two resources commonly associated with views are an icon and a menu with the same ID as the template string. You can choose to add special versions of these items or copy existing versions.

ID	Value	Caption
IDR_MAINFRAME	128	AppTest
IDR_APPTESTYPE	129	\nAppTes\nAppTes\n\n\nAppTest.Document\nAppTes Document
AFX_IDS_APP_TITLE	57344	AppTest
AFX_IDS_IDLEMESSAGE	57345	Ready
ID_FILE_NEW	57600	Create a new document\nNew
ID_FILE_OPEN	57601	Open an existing document\nOpen
ID_FILE_CLOSE	57602	Close the active document\nClose
ID_FILE_SAVE	57603	Save the active document\nSave
ID_FILE_SAVE_AS	57604	Save the active document with a new name\nSave As
ID_FILE_PAGE_SETUP	57605	Change the printing options\nPage Setup
ID_FILE_PRINT_SETUP	57606	Change the printer and printing options\nPrint Setup
ID_FILE_PRINT	57607	Print the active document\nPrint
ID_FILE_PRINT_PREVIEW	57609	Display full pages\nPrint Preview
ID_FILE_MRU_FILE1	57616	Open this document
ID_FILE_MRU_FILE2	57617	Open this document
ID_FILE_MRU_FILE3	57618	Open this document
ID_FILE_MRU_FILE4	57619	Open this document
ID_FILE_MRU_FILE5	57620	Open this document
ID_FILE_MRU_FILE6	57621	Open this document
ID_FILE_MRU_FILE7	57622	Open this document
ID_FILE_MRU_FILE8	57623	Open this document
ID_FILE_MRU_FILE9	57624	Open this document
ID_FILE_MRU_FILE10	57625	Open this document
ID_FILE_MRU_FILE11	57626	Open this document
ID_FILE_MRU_FILE12	57627	Open this document
ID_FILE_MRU_FILE13	57628	Open this document
ID_FILE_MRU_FILE14	57629	Open this document
ID_FILE_MRU_FILE15	57630	Open this document
ID_FILE_MRU_FILE16	57631	Open this document
ID_EDIT_CLEAR	57632	Erase the selection\nErase
ID_EDIT_CLEAR_ALL	57633	Erase everything\nErase All
ID_EDIT_COPY	57634	Copy the selection and put it on the Clipboard\nCopy
ID_EDIT_CUT	57635	Cut the selection and put it on the Clipboard\nCut
ID_EDIT_FIND	57636	Find the specified text\nFind
ID_EDIT_PASTE	57637	Insert Clipboard contents\nPaste
ID_EDIT_REPEAT	57640	Repeat the last action\nRepeat
ID_EDIT_REPLACE	57641	Replace specific text with different text\nReplace
ID_EDIT_SELECT_ALL	57642	Select the entire document\nSelect All

Figure 7-13.   The String Table resource will hold the document template strings for the document views we create

We'll also need document template strings for the other two views. To add a string, right-click the String Table resource, then choose New String from the context menu. You'll see a String Properties dialog box like this one.

Understanding Document Template Strings

The template string resource is an important part of creating multiple views for any application. This is the one resource you should always include for any view since it defines what will appear in places like the File Open dialog box. Seven substrings are associated with the template string resource, as listed here:

▼ **Window Title (SDI Applications Only)**   Changes the value shown in the application's title bar when the user creates a new document.

■ **Document Name**   This is the default document name. The application will combine this name with a sheet number. For example, if you supply a value of MyDoc, then the first document the user creates will be MyDoc1. Untitled is the default value for this string.

■ **New File Document Name**   If your application supports multiple views that can create new files, then the application will display a dialog box asking the user what kind of document they want to create when using the File | New command. This string determines the document name that will appear in the New File dialog box. You normally need to use a descriptive rather than an exact name; in this case, like worksheet. If you don't supply a value for this substring, then the user won't be able to create new files with this view.

■ **Filter Name**   The filter string gets displayed in several common dialog boxes. It's usually a description document name along with the filter extension. For example, you might supply a value of "Text Files (*.txt)" for a text file filter name. If you don't supply a value for this substring, then the user won't be able to use the File | Open command to open a file of this type.

■ **Filter Extension**   This is the file extension associated with the template. For example, you might supply a value of *.txt for a text file template. If you don't supply a value for this substring, then the user won't be able to use the File | Open command to open a file of this type.

■ **File Type ID**   Use this substring to define the registry document type. In other words, this substring is used to create the key in the HKEY_CLASSES_ROOT hive of the registry. The user will never see this substring. However, if you don't supply this substring, then the user won't be able to open files of this type using applications like Windows Explorer. (They can still open the file from within the application itself.)

▲ **File Type Name**   This is the name of the document as you want it stored in the registry. Some applications use this value when displaying information about the file, so a descriptive name is always a plus. Make certain that you supply this value if you supply a file-type ID. Otherwise, the user may see a blank file type identification in some applications.

Type **IDR_ORDER_TYPE** for the order view or **IDR_ITEM_TYPE** for the item view. Type **"\nOrder View\nOrder View\n\n\nAppTest.Document\nAppTes Document"** for the order view or **"\nItem View\nItem View\n\n\nAppTest.Document\nAppTes Document"** for the item view in the Caption field. Click OK to add the new string.

Designing the Order Application View

It's time to look at the order view. Remember that we'll be looking at a combination of the customer view (for current address information) and the Orders table (for the shipping address and order ID). As a result, a lot of what you did for the previous view will work for this view as well. Use Table 7-10 for the customer information. Note that we don't include the last contact date as part of this form. Figure 7-14 shows the IDD_ORDER_FORM dialog box that we'll use for this view. Table 7-11 contains all of the new table entries we'll use for this example.

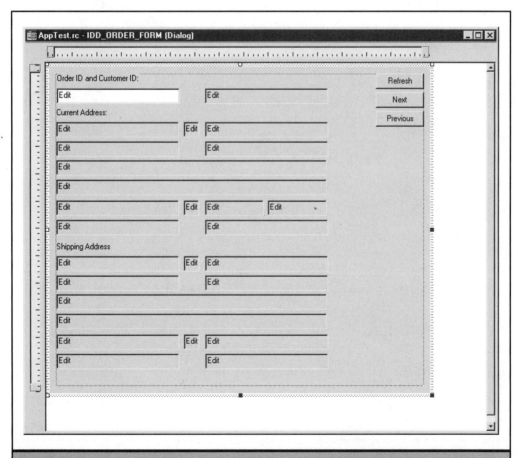

Figure 7-14. The order view allows us to see the Client and Orders tables interact

ID	Setting	Value	Member Variable or Event Handler Name
IDC_ORDERID	Tab stop	Checked	m_orderID
	Number	Checked	
IDC_FIRSTNAME2	Tab stop	Not checked	m_firstName2
	Read only	Checked	
IDC_MIDDLEINITIAL2	Tab stop	Not checked	m_middleInitial2
	Read only	Checked	
IDC_LASTNAME2	Tab stop	Not checked	m_lastName2
	Read only	Checked	
IDC_TITLE2	Tab stop	Not checked	m_title2
	Read only	Checked	
IDC_COMPANY2	Tab stop	Not checked	m_company2
	Read only	Checked	
IDC_ADDRESS3	Tab stop	Not checked	m_address3
	Read only	Checked	
IDC_ADDRESS4	Tab stop	Not checked	m_address4
	Read only	Checked	
IDC_CITY2	Tab stop	Not checked	m_city2
	Read only	Checked	
IDC_STATE2	Tab stop	Not checked	m_state2
	Read only	Checked	
IDC_ZIP2	Tab stop	Not checked	m_zip2
	Read only	Checked	
IDC_TELEPHONE3	Tab stop	Not checked	m_telephone3
	Read only	Checked	
IDC_TELEPHONE4	Tab stop	Not checked	m_telephone4
	Read only	Checked	
IDC_REFRESH2	Caption	Refresh	OnRefresh2()
IDC_NEXT2	Caption	Next	OnNext2()
IDC_PREVIOUS2	Caption	Previous	OnPrevious2()

Table 7-11.   Order View Specific Control Settings

Designing the Item List Application View

The last view we'll create for this application is the item list view. Most of the elements for this display will look familiar since we've used them in the previous two views. The important thing to consider is that we've gone from one, to two, and now to four tables represented in one view—the complete view of a single item of a customer's order. There's a point to this whole evolution. COM+ doesn't give you much in the way of debugging tools, so you must take the time to build applications slowly—as we've done in this chapter. Figure 7-15 shows the item list view dialog box form. Table 7-12 contains the settings for the new controls that we've added for this example. Make sure you look over Tables 7-10 and 7-11 as well.

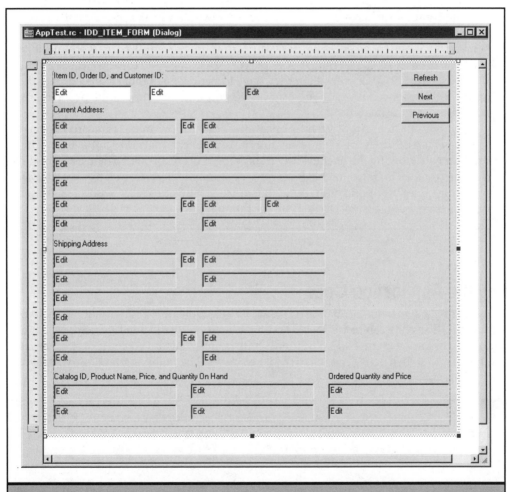

Figure 7-15. The item view shows all four tables in motion

Keystrokes, Another More Is Less Paradigm

Common wisdom is to reduce the number of keystrokes that a user has to make to enter data into the computer, especially when it comes to database applications. In the minds of most developers, fewer keystrokes translate into higher user productivity. However, this isn't always the case. There are times when allowing the user to use more keystrokes will produce higher productivity levels.

Let's look at the source of the currently accepted methodology first. In the early days of computers, data was entered using keypunch cards. It was likely that the operator didn't have a clue what the data meant or didn't care even if they did know. As a result, fewer keystrokes did result in higher productivity.

Today, however, the user does have an idea of what the data they're entering into the computer means. Forcing them to use fewer keystrokes can actually result in lost productivity because the user has to manually translate the data. Consider something as simple as entering the date. Using the current theory, it should take less time to enter 10/22/99 than it does to type 22 October 99. However, if the user is thinking about 22 October 99, then they have to perform a manual translation to the application-preferred format. The user has to pause to think about the problem, resulting in lost productivity.

The bottom line is that your application should allow maximum productivity whenever possible by providing an interface that feels natural to the user. This might mean allowing the user to enter data using more than one format. You should include routines to translate the data from the user-preferred format to the common format used by the application. A small feature like this probably won't take much of your time, but users will thank you for doing it.

Adding the Application Code

Now that we have some forms and a few menu selections to work with, it's time to add some code. The code can be divided into four functional areas: one for each of the views and a fourth for the menu code. The menu code is included as a separate section because it allows us to switch between each of the three views. The following sections will discuss each of the functional areas.

NOTE: Since each of these views builds on the information provided by the previous view, each area will discuss only the code that's unique to that section. You'll want to read through all four sections to build a complete version of the example. Skipping to the last section probably won't yield a working example.

ID	Setting	Value	Member Variable or Event-Handler Name
IDC_ITEMID	Tab stop	Checked	m_itemID
	Number	Checked	
IDC_PRODUCTID	Tab stop	Not checked	m_productID
	Read only	Checked	
IDC_PRODUCTNAME	Tab stop	Not checked	m_productName
	Read only	Checked	
IDC_ONHAND	Tab stop	Not checked	m_onHand
	Read only	Checked	
IDC_PRICE	Tab stop	Not checked	m_price
	Read only	Checked	
IDC_QUANTITY	Tab stop	Not checked	m_quantity
	Read only	Checked	
IDC_PRICE2	Tab stop	Not checked	m_price2
	Read only	Checked	

Table 7-12.   Item List View Specific Control Settings

Writing the Client View Code

The client view code begins much like the test application we created earlier in the chapter. The main difference is that this version is specific to the Client table. There are also a few tweaks in this code that make it more user friendly. We'll begin by adding the appropriate #include directives. The first one appears in the AppTest.H file as follows:

```
// Include support for the IOrderAccess Interface.
#include ""../OrderClient/OrderClient_i.c""
```

Notice that we're not placing this #include in the view file as we did in the past—we're placing it in the application-level file to ensure that all of the views can access the interface information. The second #include directive appears in the AppTestView.CPP file. Here's what it looks like:

```
// Include support for the IOrderAccess Interface.
#include ""..\OrderClient\OrderClient.H""
```

The main code for this example appears in Listing 7-4. It works very much the same as the catalog example we discussed in Listing 7-3, so I won't provide a detailed description this time. All that has changed is the table that we're using—the method used to obtain the information from the server-side component (through the client-side component) is very much the same. Listing 7-4 shows the OnRefresh() method. The OnNext() and OnPrevious() methods are written in precisely the same way. The only thing you need to change is the value of the oDirection string to either "Next" or "Previous."

```
void CAppTestView::OnRefresh()
{
    CString         oCustomerID;         // Text from edit box on dialog.
    BSTR            bstrCustomerID;      // Converted product ID.
    CString         oFirstName;          // First name text.
    BSTR            bstrFirstName;       // First name from server.
    CString         oMiddleInitial;      // Middle initial text.
    BSTR            bstrMiddleInitial;   // Middle initial from server.
    CString         oLastName;           // Last name text.
    BSTR            bstrLastName;        // Last name from server.
    CString         oTitle;              // Title text.
    BSTR            bstrTitle;           // Title from server.
    CString         oCompany;            // Company text.
    BSTR            bstrCompany;         // Company from server.
    CString         oAddress1;           // Address1 text.
    BSTR            bstrAddress1;        // Address1 from server.
    CString         oAddress2;           // Address2 text.
    BSTR            bstrAddress2;        // Address2 from server.
    CString         oCity;               // City text
    BSTR            bstrCity;            // City from server.
    CString         oState;              // State text
    BSTR            bstrState;           // State from server.
    CString         oZIP;                // ZIP Code
    BSTR            bstrZIP;             // ZIP Code from server
    CString         oCountry;            // Country text.
    BSTR            bstrCountry;         // Country from server.
    CString         oLastContact;        // LastContact date in text format.
    BSTR            bstrLastContact;     // LastContact from server.
    CString         oTelephone1;         // Telephone1 text.
    BSTR            bstrTelephone1;      // Telephone1 from server.
```

```
CString         oTelephone2;        // Telephone2 text.
BSTR            bstrTelephone2;     // Telephone2 from server.
IOrderRequest*  m_pDoTest;          // IOrderRequest Interface Pointer
HRESULT         hr;                 // Result of Operations
CString         oDirection;         // Direction of Database Travel

// Convert the first input value to a BSTR.
m_customerID.GetWindowText(oCustomerID);
bstrCustomerID = oCustomerID.AllocSysString();

// Initialize the interface pointer.
m_pDoTest = NULL;

// Initialize the COM environment.
CoInitialize(NULL);

// Create an instance of the object.
hr = CoCreateInstance(CLSID_OrderRequest,
                      NULL,
                      CLSCTX_ALL,
                      IID_IOrderRequest,
                      (void**)&m_pDoTest);

// If the creation failed, exit.
if (FAILED(hr))
{
    // Make sure the class was registered.
    if (hr == REGDB_E_CLASSNOTREG)
        AfxMessageBox(""DoTest Class Not Registered"");

    // Make sure we can aggregate the class.
    if (hr == CLASS_E_NOAGGREGATION)
        AfxMessageBox(""Class Can''t be Aggregated"");

    // Display the general failure message and exit.
    AfxMessageBox(""Object Creation Failed"");
    return;
}

// Refresh the current record information.
oDirection = ""Refresh"";
hr = m_pDoTest->GetCustomer(&bstrCustomerID,
                            oDirection.AllocSysString(),
                            &bstrFirstName,
                            &bstrMiddleInitial,
```

```
                                &bstrLastName,
                                &bstrTitle,
                                &bstrCompany,
                                &bstrAddress1,
                                &bstrAddress2,
                                &bstrCity,
                                &bstrState,
                                &bstrZIP,
                                &bstrCountry,
                                &bstrLastContact,
                                &bstrTelephone1,
                                &bstrTelephone2);
    if (FAILED(hr))
        AfxMessageBox(""Client Table Check Failed"");

    // Display the Customer ID output value.
    oCustomerID = bstrCustomerID;
    m_customerID.SetWindowText(oCustomerID);

    // Display the first name.
    oFirstName = bstrFirstName;
    m_firstName.SetWindowText(oFirstName);

    // Display the middle initial.
    oMiddleInitial = bstrMiddleInitial;
    m_middleInitial.SetWindowText(oMiddleInitial);

    // Display the last name.
    oLastName = bstrLastName;
    m_lastName.SetWindowText(oLastName);

    // Display the title.
    oTitle = bstrTitle;
    m_title.SetWindowText(oTitle);

    // Display the company name.
    oCompany = bstrCompany;
    m_company.SetWindowText(oCompany);

    // Display the first address line.
    oAddress1 = bstrAddress1;
    m_address1.SetWindowText(oAddress1);

    // Display the second address line.
    oAddress2 = bstrAddress2;
    m_address2.SetWindowText(oAddress2);
```

```
    // Display the city
    oCity = bstrCity;
    m_city.SetWindowText(oCity);

    // Display the state
    oState = bstrState;
    m_state.SetWindowText(oState);

    // Display the ZIP code
    oZIP = bstrZIP;
    m_zip.SetWindowText(oZIP);

    // Display the country name.
    oCountry = bstrCountry;
    m_country.SetWindowText(oCountry);

    // Display the date of last contact.
    oLastContact = bstrLastContact;
    m_lastContact.SetWindowText(oLastContact);

    // Display the primary telephone number.
    oTelephone1 = bstrTelephone1;
    m_telephone1.SetWindowText(oTelephone1);

    // Display the secondary telephone number.
    oTelephone2 = bstrTelephone2;
    m_telephone2.SetWindowText(oTelephone2);

    // Uninitialize the COM environment.
    CoUninitialize();
}
```

There's one last change we need to make. The OnInitialUpdate() method configures the form for initial display. Right now, the user will see a blank form because of the way that the form code is written. It might be nice to allow the user to see an initial record, so we'll need to modify the OnInitialUpdate() method. Listing 7-5 shows the changes you'll need to make in bold.

```
void CAppTestView::OnInitialUpdate()
{
    CFormView::OnInitialUpdate();
    GetParentFrame()->RecalcLayout();
    ResizeParentToFit();
```

```
// Initialize the display.
m_customerID.SetWindowText(_T(""1""));
OnRefresh();
}
```

As you can see, updating the form automatically is easy. All we need to do is place a customer number in the m_customerID member variable, then call the OnRefresh() method. The OnRefresh() method does what it normally does with a value that gets placed in the Customer ID field of the form.

Writing the Order View and Item List View Code

There aren't many surprises when it comes to the order view or item view code. As with the previous view, we need to include support for the IOrderAccess interface by adding an #include directive in the OrderForm.CPP file like this:

```
// Include support for the IOrderAccess Interface.
#include ""..\OrderClient\OrderClient.H""
```

We'll also want to add the OnInitialUpdate() code that we did in the previous example (with the appropriate changes for the order ID). However, you'll notice that the OnInitialUpdate() method isn't included with the default class. You can easily remedy this problem by adding the appropriate method using ClassWizard. Simply use the View | ClassWizard command to display the MFC ClassWizard dialog box. Choose COrderForm (or CItemForm) in the Class name and Object IDs fields. Highlight OnInitialUpdate in the Messages field, then click Add Function. Listing 7-6 shows the code that you'll need to add to the OnInitialUpdate() method for the order view in bold (note the additional line of code for resizing the parent window as necessary). Listing 7-7 shows the same code for the item list view.

```
void COrderForm::OnInitialUpdate()
{
    CFormView::OnInitialUpdate();
ResizeParentToFit();


    // Initialize the display.
m_orderID.SetWindowText(_T(""1""));
OnRefresh2();
}

void CItemForm::OnInitialUpdate()
{
```

```
        CFormView::OnInitialUpdate();
ResizeParentToFit();


    // Initialize the display.
m_itemID.SetWindowText(_T(""1""));
m_orderID.SetWindowText(_T(""1""));
OnRefresh3();
}
```

There's one little gotcha when working with this code that I should mention. Even though the order view is simply a combination of the code used for the order test earlier in the book and the client code in Listing 7-4, you do need to be aware of the oDirection value. When you make an initial query for the order information, the oDirection variable has to be set to the direction you want to go (refresh, next, or previous). However, when you get the client information, the record pointer is already set at the record we want to look at. All you need to do is refresh the information in the client data variables. In short, you only need to go to the next record once—not multiple times.

Making the Views Work

At this point, we have three views, but only one of them will get displayed—the client view. There isn't much magic involved in making all three views accessible. We've already done part of the work by creating the proper resources. All we need to do now is make the application aware of the additional views. The first thing we need to do is add two #include directives—one for each view, as shown here to the AppTest.CPP file:

```
// Include the order and item list views.
#include ""OrderForm.H""
#include ""ItemForm.H""
```

Now that we've got the proper #includes in place, all we need to do is add two additional templates to the InitInstance() method. Listing 7-8 shows these two additions in bold.

```
    // Register the application''s document templates.  Document templates
    //  serve as the connection between documents, frame windows and views.

    CMultiDocTemplate* pDocTemplate;
    pDocTemplate = new CMultiDocTemplate(
        IDR_APPTESTYPE,
        RUNTIME_CLASS(CAppTestDoc),
        RUNTIME_CLASS(CChildFrame), // custom MDI child frame
        RUNTIME_CLASS(CAppTestView));
    AddDocTemplate(pDocTemplate);
```

```
// Add the Order View
pDocTemplate = new CMultiDocTemplate(
IDR_ORDER_TYPE,
RUNTIME_CLASS(CAppTestDoc),
RUNTIME_CLASS(CChildFrame), // custom MDI child frame
RUNTIME_CLASS(COrderForm));
AddDocTemplate(pDocTemplate);

   // Add the Item View
pDocTemplate = new CMultiDocTemplate(
IDR_ITEM_TYPE,
RUNTIME_CLASS(CAppTestDoc),
RUNTIME_CLASS(CChildFrame), // custom MDI child frame
RUNTIME_CLASS(CItemForm));
AddDocTemplate(pDocTemplate);

   // create main MDI Frame window
   CMainFrame* pMainFrame = new CMainFrame;
   if (!pMainFrame->LoadFrame(IDR_MAINFRAME))
       return FALSE;
       m_pMainWnd = pMainFrame;
```

Notice that both additions are essentially the same. The first step is to create a new document object. This document object includes a resource entry. There's only one entry, so all three of the resources (form, menu, and icon) that you want to use must have the same ID. The document class comes next. Our application didn't do anything with the document class, so we could use the same one for all three views. However, if you wanted to do something special, like create one HTML document and another form document, you'd have to create a separate document class for each unique view. The frame class comes next. In most cases, you'll always use CChildFrame. Finally, you'll include the view class. This particular item has to be unique for each view that you want to include in the template. Once the template is defined, you add it to the list of available templates using the AddDocTemplate() method.

Testing the COM+ Application

It's finally time to take a look at all the work we've done. When you start your application, you'll see a dialog box like this one.

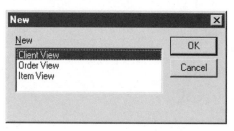

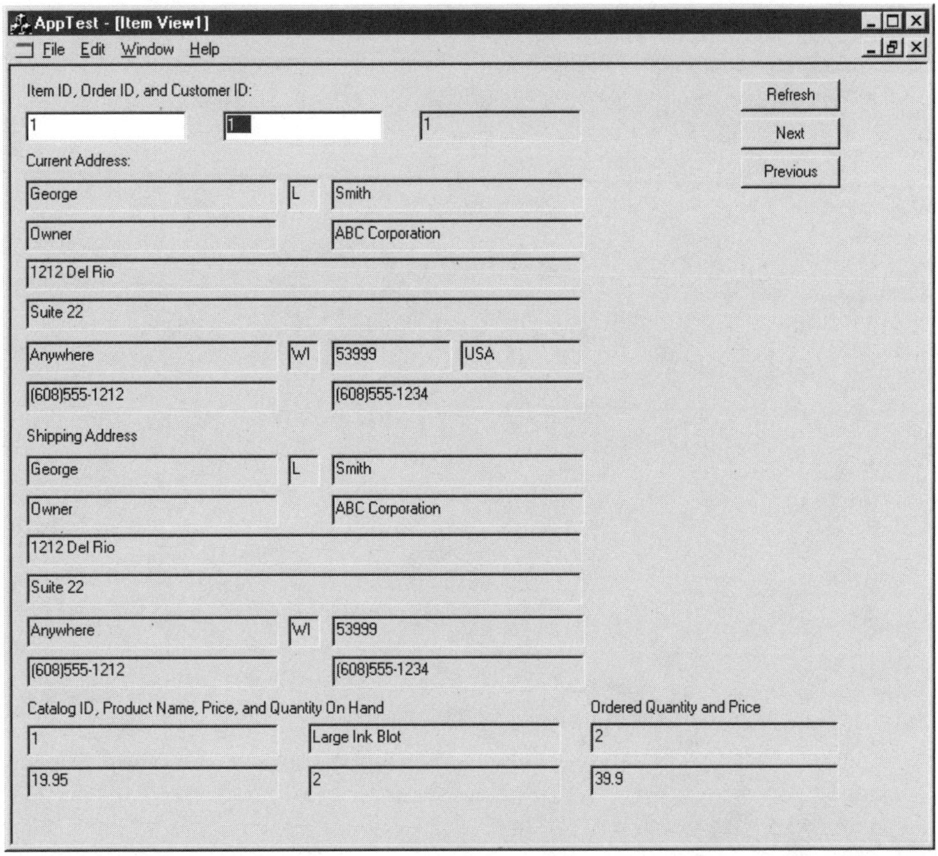

Figure 7-16. The completed application allows four tables to interact to provide the end user with a complete display of a single order item

This is the application asking which view you want to start with. Let's take a look at the most complex view the application has to offer. Figure 7-16 shows an example of what you'll see when you try the application out. Obviously, the exact field entries you see will depend on how you add test records to the tables.

CHAPTER 8

Dealing with Transaction Failure

T ransactions, no matter what their source or destination, don't always work as anticipated. If every transaction worked as you thought it would, then there wouldn't be
any need for something like Microsoft Transaction Server (MTS) in the first place. It's
because transactions fail that you need this component of COM+. The whole purpose of including MTS is to ensure the reliability of data transmission from one point to another. As
previously mentioned, MTS ensures that each transaction occurs once, but only once.

This chapter is about failure—at least the failure of MTS to transmit data from one
point to another. You can divide the topic of failure into two topics: the cause of failures
and the remedies to fix them. Knowing the source of a failure is important if you want to
prevent it from happening in the future. In addition, you must know the source of a failure before you can fix anything. Of course, having a remedy allows you to recover from
the failure without a large loss of time or resources. That's what the two sections of this
chapter are all about—finding the source of failures, then applying a remedy to overcome
the failure.

WEB LINK: Transaction failures aren't limited to programming problems, human error, and acts of nature. In some cases, the cause of failure is a problem with MTS, MSMQ, or some other Windows 2000
component. Fortunately, Microsoft makes it relatively easy to find out if there's some problem with their
products that you need to know about, as long as you have some idea of what question to ask. Check out
the Microsoft Knowledge Base Search Web site at http://support.microsoft.com/search/default.asp. This
page will help you find problems and, in many cases, solutions as well.

The sample code in Chapter 7 provides you with some good ideas on what kinds of
transaction failures can occur as a result of COM-, DCOM-, and COM+-related failures.
For example, the failure to create either the client-side or the server-side component can
cause a transaction to fail. Whenever an error like this occurs, the component will need to
vote to abort the transaction, causing the transaction to fail from secondary events. In
short, the transaction is at the top of the pyramid and all of the failure causes below it in
the application pyramid can cause ultimate failure of the transaction itself. Obviously,
failures that affect the transfer or integrity of the data are more likely to cause transaction
failure than those that affect the user or the server. In short, component creation failures
will always cause a transaction failure, but the inability of the application to display the
data delivered through components from the server is unlikely to cause the transaction itself to fail.

It's important to remember throughout this section that a failure scenario occurs because one or more of the components involved in a transaction voted to abort the transaction rather than allow it to complete. In other words, the failure indication occurs as part
of the transaction process; it's designed to work this way. You'll actually write the code
that votes to abort the transaction as part of the application building process, so you're
the one who's best able to figure out what when wrong when a failure occurs. We looked
at some very rudimentary transaction voting code in Chapter 7—we'll expand on that
code in this chapter.

When a transaction failure does occur, MTS will attempt to roll back the transaction and perform it again. Normally, one or two tries are all that MTS needs to complete the transaction successfully and allow the application to get on with the next job. It's when the transaction can't complete for some reason that you need to get involved. Detecting situations when the transaction won't ever complete is important because MTS will doggedly attempt to complete the transaction until the problem resolves itself, you step in to stop the transaction, or code within your application detects and fixes the problem. Obviously, this last choice is the best because it's automatic.

The first section covers the cause of failures. There are two modes in which programming failures can occur: connected and disconnected. Connected mode applications always have access to the server, while disconnected mode applications have intermittent server access required to perform updates. (In addition to programming errors, there are failures caused by natural occurrences like lightning and those of human source that we won't cover in detail in this chapter.) Establishing that a failure occurred at one time or the other is important because the cause of failure in each situation is different.

The second section is about recovering from a failure. Normally, MTS does a fairly good job of recovering from failure without administrator intervention as long as the components you create provide the right type of input. In short, from an administrator perspective, MTS is fairly automatic. From a developer perspective, MTS needs a lot of input, which means that you need to perform relatively intense error recovering within your application. We'll divide the topic of error recovery into three areas: determining the source of an error, understanding the error codes that MTS provides to you, and finally, adding error-handling code to your components.

TIP: If you've used previous versions of MTS, you know that there are some relatively distinct error codes for certain types of conditions. Microsoft has attempted to augment these error codes in Windows 2000, making it possible for you to provide better error handling within the application code.

FAILURE SCENARIOS

The ability to recognize and cope with application failure begins with good design and implementation. For example, in Chapter 7 we placed AfxMessageBox() calls within both the server-side and the client-side components. This is a troubleshooting aid, and you really won't want to leave those messages in place—especially on the server. The correct way to handle failure recognition is to pass unique error codes from the server, to the server-side component, through the client-side component, and, finally, to the client application. The client application can then display an error message stating the cause of the problem and where the problem occurred (at least in most cases).

Obviously, displaying informational dialog boxes won't do everything you need them to do, especially in the case of one component operating across multiple servers. A dialog box serves to alert the user to a problem and a potential source of that problem—nothing more. You need to couple the error message display with one or more event log entries.

These entries will help the network administrator find the precise server where the error occurred and obtain more information about the problem, in many cases. The event log should be the place where you put detailed error information to help the administrator. Placing this information in the error message itself normally serves to confuse the reader more than help the situation.

In short, failure recognition is a two-phase process from a messaging perspective. First, you need to make the user aware of the problem so that the user can contact the network administrator (or developer). The message should provide a cause of the problem in a way that the user can understand—rather than the ambiguous messages that many applications present today. The second phase occurs when the network administrator locates the appropriate event log entries on either the user's machine or the server (depending on where the error occurred). This two-phase approach will allow the user to help the administrator find the exact cause of a problem and greatly reduce the amount of time required to find and troubleshoot the problem.

Of course, there are many classes of problems and the error messages that your application produces should reflect those classes. We talked about one class of problem earlier—component failure. However, there are other classes of errors that you'll encounter when working with COM+.

The first problem that you may encounter when working with COM+ applications is how to maintain fault tolerance. By default, MTS places all of the components in a COM+ application in the same server process. So, in the example in Chapter 7, both the business object and the database object would be placed in the same server process by default. The problem with this approach is that a failure by one component affects all of the other components in the COM+ application. In short, a COM+ application may experience multiple transaction failures because one component experiences problems. This is an example of a design and implementation failure, versus a problem within an entire group of components. One component is allowed to create a domino effect within your application because of a flawed setup.

The obvious solution to this problem is to place all of the components in separate server processes (which would mean changing the example in Chapter 7 to use separate projects for business and database objects). That way, a failure of one component won't necessarily affect the operation of any other component. In short, this setup provides many benefits, especially during the debugging stage of your application, because you'll always be able to detect the component that actually failed rather than weed through a lot of components that might not have failed normally. Of course, no design and implementation solution is perfect. The problem with this approach is that the speed of the transactions slows because each transaction has to cross several process boundaries. In addition to reduced speed, server resources get wasted allocating additional memory and processor cycles to run each component separately.

WEB LINK: We're looking at a lot of programmer-specific issues in this chapter that apply to transaction-oriented COM+ applications. In other words, we're concentrating on a lot of the component issues that you'll run into when creating a total application solution, not the application as a whole. However, there are a lot of different ways in which an application can fail, some of which look suspiciously like a transaction failure. A plethora of "red herring" clues is one of the problems that developers face today because applications are becoming more complex and more difficult to troubleshoot. One of the ways that you can make sure your application won't fail when you move it to Windows 2000 is to ensure it meets or exceeds Microsoft's stringent Windows 2000 compatibility requirements. You can find out about these new requirements by looking at the Microsoft Windows 2000 Application Compatibility article at http://msdn. microsoft.com/isapi/msdnlib.idc?theURL=/library/techart/win2000appcomp.htm. This article helps you understand the most common causes of application compatibility problems in Windows 2000 and why these problems first appeared in Windows 2000. In short, it helps you to understand why applications that worked fine in the past are failing today.

It's important to understand that a COM+ application helps keep all of the components required for a particular transaction type together. Applications may require more than one type of transaction to get the job done. As a result, one of the more efficient ways to handle fault tolerance is to group associated components into separate processes along transaction lines. That way, a failed component affects only one of many possible transactions, allowing the application to partially succeed at least. This solution reduces the impact of using multiple processes on execution speed and incurs a minimal penalty on system resources as well. How would you implement this in the real world? For the example in Chapter 7, you would have created one business object and database object pair for each of the application actions that we discussed. A single application request would result in activation of one or more of these pairs, but each pair would be performing a completely separate part of the task—like requesting the current catalog record data. This solution optimizes the use of system resources and reduces the complexity of finding errors, with an obvious addition of development complexity. (As I mentioned earlier, there are few perfect solutions.)

We'll cover more of these design and implementation issues as the book progresses so that you can see the issues in context of where you'd actually require a solution. Once you get past these implementation issues, however, there are a lot of ways that an individual component can fail. For example, a communication failure or a message garbled by line noise can cause a variety of problems, including unreadable data. Human error also plays a part in failures that you need to be able to handle within the MTS component to ensure that the transaction still takes place as anticipated or that the user is asked to fix the problem. In many cases, even though these problems aren't the result of poor programming practice or even of the component itself, the component is still responsible for detecting and handling the failure. MTS depends on component input to determine the success or failure of the transaction. In addition, MTS depends on the component to assist in recognizing the cause of failure and provide some form of error handling.

> **TIP:** Some developers may be tempted to place range- and value-checking code for an application within the application itself. However, if you plan to access the same database from multiple applications, then it's very likely that there will be some overlap in the component-level functionality required for each of the applications. Obviously, you don't want to increase network traffic by having to ask the user to fix flawed input. The solution, then, is to place the range- and value-checking code within the client-side component. In this way, you can use the same input-checking code over several applications and reduce the amount of development time for each application as a whole.

You can divide the kinds of errors that will occur during a transaction into two categories: connected and disconnected. The following sections will explore the two categories and help you understand the various types of failure scenarios that your components will have to overcome.

Connected

A connected transaction is one where all of the parties are online at the same time. This is the traditional kind of application that we've all worked with in the past—you assume that the various connections are available and don't need to add extra error checking in case they're not available. In most cases, MSMQ doesn't get into the picture during a connected transaction because everything is processed in real time. The client generates a new invoice or other kinds of database input, which gets sent through the client-side component and the LAN directly to the business and database objects on the server. This object, in turn, sends the data to the object that interacts with the database. Finally, the data gets entered into the database for later processing and retrieval. In short, the connected scenario is very unlikely to fail given the way that MTS handles transactions on the server.

There aren't any fail-safe operations in the world of the Windows computer, however. As Windows gets more complex, the number of failure modes only increases. In short, you need to expect errors to occur, especially while COM+ is still in its infancy (which it will be for the foreseeable future). With this in mind, let's look at some of the failures that you'll potentially deal with as part of your COM+ applications. The following list provides you with an overview of some of the failure modes that a connected COM+ application could suffer. Obviously, this list isn't complete, but it should give you a very good idea of what to look for:

▼ **Failed network connection**   What happens if a client starts sending today's receipts and the network connection gets broken? You might find yourself with half an invoice on the server. Network connections can break for a number of reasons, many of them not under the user's control, so this represents one of the very real possibilities in a connected scenario. In most cases, MTS will automatically recover from this error. However, you can ensure that you detect those times when MTS failed to do the job by itself by performing things like range checks on the various fields of the record that you want to enter into the database. In addition, you can create record packages where an entire record is packaged with a header that includes a cyclic redundancy code (CRC) for the packaged data.

■ **Lack of permission**   Windows 2000 security is very complete. Role-based security makes it possible to protect components to a very high degree and makes it impossible for a user to do anything more than the network administrator thinks is necessary. However, Windows 2000 security is also very fragmented. A COM+ application exercises many parts of the server. It's possible to give the user permission in one area of the server, yet deprive them of the rights they need to complete an action in another part of the server. For example, giving the user the proper rights to all of the components in our application in Chapter 7 isn't enough—they also require rights to the various tables in SQL Server. Given our current application structure, the application could create both the client-side and server-side components and request the data. However, what happens when SQL Server denies the request? A production-level system needs to be able to handle this problem, which won't be apparent to the user due to all of the levels of abstraction between SQL Server and the application (any error messages will appear on the server—something we want to avoid).

■ **Component interactions**   As we saw in Chapter 7, the minimum number of components for any given COM+ application is three. You must have a client-side component, a business object, and a database object as a minimum to create most enterprise-level applications. In most cases, the problems of using COM+ don't warrant its use for less complex application types, so the three-component application minimum is very realistic. What this means to you as a developer is that the problem of component interactions is greatly increased over a standard application. This is one of the most common problems that I ran into during the development of the very simple application in Chapter 7. One component would work fine, but some interaction between it and the next component in line would cause the application as a whole to fail. Obviously, this problem will occur more during development than when the application is placed on a production system. However, even after development, expectations by one member of the development team with regard to input from a previous component might not be met. Coordination between the various components is extremely important with COM+ applications. You can find out more about this whole COM component issue by reading the "Getting the DLL Knowledge You Need" sidebar in this chapter.

■ **Unanticipated server loads**   It isn't all that unlikely that your application will run across multiple servers. In fact, Microsoft's lectures often depict a minimum of three machines for a COM+ application: client, business logic server, and database server. So, what happens if a client makes a request of the business logic server that the database server can't handle due to the current load? This isn't a situation that many COM developers currently face, but it's going to become very common with COM+ applications. In short, hardware limitations are going to become more of a problem as time passes. Your application and its associated components will need to deal with loading issues in addition to the issues that applications normally deal with. That's why the introduction and implementation of component load balancing (CLB) is so important. Unfortunately, CLB will be part of a separate product release rather than the core Windows 2000 release—you'll need to check for CLB support in addition to everything else that your application has to do.

■ **DLL interactions** COM+ doesn't exist in a vacuum. In fact, this version of COM relies on more operating system services than any previous version. That's why even small discrepancies in DLL support at the server end can make a big difference in application performance, which can include application failure. For example, we saw in Chapter 7 that older versions of SQL Server will overwrite your Distributed Transaction Coordinator (DTC), which can cause transaction failures in your COM+ applications. Fortunately, the client end of things is actually easier to deal with. The client-side component tends to smooth things out a bit and make it less likely that you'll experience DLL interactions on the client end. In short, COM+ is more sensitive to DLL issues on the server side of the application (where you have more control) and less sensitive on the client side of the application (where you have less control) than previous versions of COM. You can find out more about this whole DLL issue by reading the "Getting the DLL Knowledge You Need" section later in this chapter.

■ **Unacceptable user input** We've looked at this problem before, so this section will contain just a brief mention of the problem. You must perform range and value checks of data for a COM+ application. Remember that there are situations when the user won't get immediate feedback. This means that you have to check the data for accuracy on the client side whenever possible. In most cases, you'll perform this check within the client-side component.

■ **Resource allocation failures** This problem usually goes hand in hand with server load, but can happen at other times as well. A server-side component may need to allocate resources to create another object or to perform work itself. In some situations, the resources may not be available on the current server, even if the server has plenty of processing capability. Since you can't count on contacting the user and the administrator is unlikely to look at the server display, the application needs to determine whether it should wait for the resources to become available, pass the task to a component on another machine, or abort the transaction.

▲ **Unforeseen failures** There are some failures that fall into the unforeseen class. No matter how good you are at predicting the potential causes of application failure, the fact remains that you can't predict them all. A timing failure can occur at random intervals and there really isn't any way to predict when one will happen. The code governing many of the timed events in

Windows isn't even accessible from your application. Natural events like lightning storms are equally unpredictable. The key word here is flexibility. An application must be prepared to provide flexible error detection—the generic error-handling routine that allows the application to recover or fail gracefully when the unexpected happens (and it will).

TIP: If you really think your code is bulletproof, put it in the hands of several complete novices. It's almost guaranteed that someone will find some way to make your code fail. The fact of the matter is that the error-proof application is a myth and always will be. No matter how much time you spend debugging the application, it will fail. Always design your application, its error detection, and error remedies with this idea in mind. A well-designed application is as bug-free as you can make it, but it also contains the code required for the application to recover or fail gracefully when the inevitable happens.

Getting the DLL Knowledge You Need

The problem of DLL interactions is an ongoing issue. Windows is complex enough that a fix by Microsoft in one place normally results in a new problem somewhere else. Your best defense against DLL interaction is knowledge. Microsoft gives you the knowledge you need in order to avoid many kinds of DLL interaction issues in two ways: Knowledge Base articles and utility programs.

Using the Microsoft Knowledge Base is fairly easy. You'll find the Microsoft Knowledge Base at http://support.microsoft.com/servicedesks/msdn/search/default.htm. Figure 8-1 shows a typical example of what the Microsoft Knowledge Base Web site looks like. You can search this site by product, issue, or Knowledge Base article number (Microsoft's support staff will often provide these numbers as a way to find the article quickly). Make sure you take the time to check this site out in order to avoid problems related to Microsoft product upgrades.

Notice that the Microsoft Knowledge Base Web site shown in Figure 8-1 has a special feature that allows you to search the Knowledge Base for recent articles. The default setting allows you to search for new articles within the last seven days, but you're certainly not limited to that number. I use this feature once a week to view summaries of new issues that Microsoft has added to the Knowledge Base. This keeps me up-to-date on current issues without expending a lot of time in searches. Using this technique also makes me aware of articles that I may need to look up later on.

Microsoft also makes a wide assortment of utilities available that allow you to check the version numbers of the various components on your machine. (Unfortunately, they still don't make one utility that allows you to check everything on your machine at once.) For example, you'll find the Microsoft Data Access Components (MDAC) Component Checker at http://microsoft.com/data/download.htm. The MDAC Component Checker will allow you to check the current revision levels of MDAC components on your machine. You'll need the most current version of MDAC in order to make the examples in this book run, so this is a good utility to look at. When you first start the MDAC Component Checker, you'll see a Component Checker - Choose Analysis Type dialog box like the one shown here.

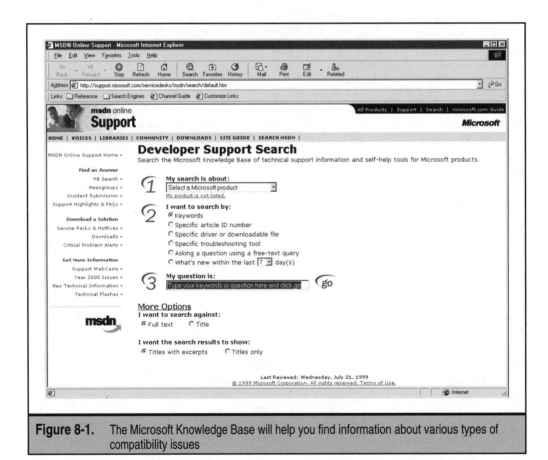

All you need to do is choose one of the three options. In most cases, you'll choose the first option if you want to check to see what your machine has to offer. The second option will allow you to analyze your system for a specific level of support. The third option sim-

Figure 8-1. The Microsoft Knowledge Base will help you find information about various types of compatibility issues

ply scans your machine for information without performing any type of analysis. In other words, the third option won't highlight any areas where your MDAC support is lacking.

Once you make a selection and click OK, MDAC will scan your system, perform any required analysis, and display the window shown in Figure 8-2. Figure 8-2 shows the results of the analysis in the Summary Report folder. In this case, the program didn't find any errors. If there had been errors, you would have seen a list of them in the Summary Report folder and the associated detail folders. There's one detail folder each for files, COM components, and registry entries.

The detail folders will tell you the current status of every file associated with MDAC, as well as provide detailed information about that file. Figure 8-3 shows an example of how the COM details would look for my installation. Not shown in this figure are details like the file description and version number. The entries in this detail view provide enough information to determine the exact state of the MDAC installation on the current machine.

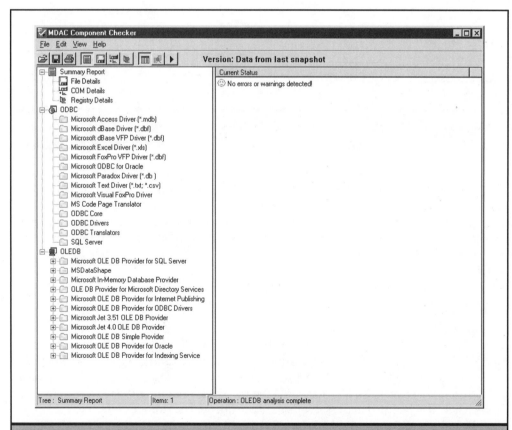

Figure 8-2. The MDAC Component Checker tells you a lot about your current system's database support status

Figure 8-3. Detail views are an essential part of determining the status of your setup

There are two additional areas in the MDAC Component Checker that we haven't talked about yet. The ODBC and OLE-DB folders provide you with information about these specific parts of database communication. This includes DLLs and associated registry entries. So, if you wanted to find out more about the SQL Server OLE-DB provider that we used in Chapter 7, you could use the MDAC Component Checker to do so with relative ease.

Disconnected

Disconnected applications usually begin with a client that's not physically connected to the server. For example, an employee on the road might work in disconnected mode. In this case, MSMQ does get involved with the transaction. The user adds a new invoice to the database that gets stored locally by MSMQ. As soon as a connection gets made from the client machine to the network, MSMQ forwards the message containing the new invoice to the server where it gets stored in the server's message queue. The storage of the message in two different queues can cause problems because the message is essentially open to corruption during this time. In addition, MSMQ can add its own failures to the mix, greatly increasing the chance for a failure. (Don't get the idea that you'll have constant failures—the chance of failure is still relatively low, even with all of the additional data movement taking place.)

The additional data handling that a disconnected application performs means that you must provide more error handling as well. There are more checks that you need to perform to ensure that data remains error free. Of course, both MSMQ and MTS help you with this process, but there are still things that you need to perform that apply specifically to your application. So, in the case of a disconnected application, you start out with the list of errors that we talked about for a connected application, and add those that relate to working with an application in disconnected mode.

NOTE: The problems listed in this section are in addition to those experienced by a connected application. In other words, a disconnected application faces special problems because of the disconnected nature of the data transfer. As a result, it's important to determine whether an application will run in disconnected, connected, or both modes early in the design process. An application running in disconnected mode requires additional protection, but disabling this additional error handling when the application runs in connected mode will result in higher throughput and better efficiency.

Unlike the connected scenario discussed in the previous section, you have to face the possibility of catastrophic failure when working with a disconnected application. A catastrophic failure is one in which the data generated by the user can't be saved under any circumstance. Here's a short list of catastrophic failure candidates:

▼ **Hard drive failure**   This is the most catastrophic of all failures and there isn't any way to protect against it except through regular system maintenance. Companies that regularly run diagnostics on their equipment and replace aging equipment will experience this particular problem less often. Creating backups of the data on the user's machine will help, too. Of course, creating a backup while the user is on the road is problematic at best. It seems as if there isn't any way for you as a developer to do much more than cross your fingers when it comes to this kind of failure. However, there are some steps that you could take, like ensuring you maintain application state information in a separate location such as a central database on the server. Updating state information every time the client makes contact will at least allow you to detect a failure in progress, potentially alert the user to the problem, and definitely make it easier to recover from the failure later.

■ **Errant data entry**   You may wonder why I didn't include this particular problem in the connected application area. After all, a user can make mistakes in entering data just as easily with a connected application as one that operates in disconnected mode. The reason is simple: a connected application can provide nearly instant feedback for this type of problem. The disconnected application may not obtain a connection to the network for days, perhaps even weeks. By that time, the user has forgotten why he or she has made an entry in a certain way. Remember that one of the reasons we're using COM+ is so the business logic for our application remains secure on the server—local machines provide too much opportunity for security breaches that could expose sensitive company methodologies. In many cases, detecting this kind of error is relatively easy, but the detection won't occur right away. You need to come up with a method that allows the user to make the right entries either immediately when the data is entered or as part of a remedial process handled as a separate procedure.

NOTE: Errant data entry occurs when the user has provided data in the right format and within the right range that still isn't correct for some reason. For example, when entering an order, the user could type a catalog number that's either for another product or not in use. Unlike unacceptable user input, the client-side component really can't do much with this kind of error because it requires a query to the database. This is a server-side issue where the database object handles the error as part of the response from the database management system (DBMS).

■ **Configuration errors**   Remember from Chapter 7 that our connected application required configuration at the server, not at the client. The server-side configuration includes creating an application for the component, adding role-based security, and deciding which users will fit in which roles. A disconnected application relies on an independent MSMQ client. This means there's client-side configuration in addition to the configuration that occurs on the server (we'll talk about these configuration issues more in Chapter 10). What this means is that the user now has access to a part of the application that requires some type of configuration. In short, you need to make sure that things like the MSMQ queues actually exist before you use them and that they're configured for use.

■ **Data overruns**   A laptop's hard drive gets used for a lot of different purposes—not just to hold the messages in the MSMQ queues. At some point, if a user remains disconnected for a long enough time, the laptop (or other remote machine) will begin running low on hard drive space. A disconnected application has to perform some level of monitoring for this condition and advise the user to make contact with the server as needed to upload pending messages.

■ **Client configuration**   A server is always under the control of the administrator. In addition, since the server affects the entire company, it normally has better resource management and tends to be more stable. A client, on the other hand, isn't always under the control of the administrator. A user may decide to install nonsupported applications that the administrator doesn't know about. In addition, there's a much greater possibility that the client will have a greater number of operating systems to deal with. In short, the client configuration tends to introduce random and unforeseen errors into the computing environment that may cause client-side data corruption in ways that couldn't occur with a connected application.

TIP: Ensuring you have appropriate security policies in place will reduce the number of client configuration problems the application will face. Since disconnected applications will currently run only on the relatively secure Windows 2000 platform, you can control things like the applications that the user installs. However, it won't be long before other versions of Windows will also support MSMQ, which means you could create disconnected applications for them. These other Windows platforms aren't as secure as Windows 2000, making them less appropriate for disconnected applications of the sort we're discussing in this book. As a result, you'll want to use Windows 2000 wherever possible to ensure maximum platform security and robustness, then add the appropriate security policies after installation is complete. You could also add checks to the application installation routine that would warn the administrator of any potential problems with installing your application on another Windows platform.

▲   **Additional complexity**   Application reliability is inversely proportional to the number of application components. As you add more components, an application can be expected to fail more often. This holds true for any class of application, not just a disconnected application. It does become part of the picture here because a disconnected application has queue management to consider. So, for two applications of the same functionality, the disconnected application will be less reliable than its connected counterpart.

ERROR-RECOVERY METHODS

Now that you have some idea of why and how errors occur, it's time to look at some of the ways that you can detect and recover from them. We'll also look at what you can do when recovery isn't possible. In some cases, the best you can hope to achieve is a graceful failure, rather than a complete collapse of the application.

The following sections take a look at error recovery. We'll begin with various methods of detecting errors. Your application has to be able to detect an error before you can do anything about it. The next section looks at various methods of interpreting error codes generated by various parts of an application. Error codes represent one of the best ways to pass information along to another part of an application that can actually do something about a pending error. Next, we look at what you can do to recover from the error. Finally, we'll look at things you can do to reduce the impact of a failure.

NOTE: This section of the chapter deals with theory of error detection and recovery. The "Writing Error Handling Code" section of the chapter will put the theory into practice. We'll modify the example from Chapter 7 to provide better error handling.

Detecting the Source of the Error

There are actually two phases to error detection. You need to determine which error has occurred and the source of that error. Windows relies on common error codes to indicate a failure, but since the error codes are the same for a given call, knowing that an application has returned a certain error code doesn't tell you where the error occurred. To give you a better idea of a real-world situation where this might occur, consider the programming example in Chapter 7. There are two places where we create components: at the client and at the server. If the component creation process fails, Windows will return an error code. Unfortunately, this error code has to flow all the way back to the client through the HRESULT before you'll see a message about it. So, while you know there's a component creation failure, you don't know whether that failure occurred on the client or the server.

Detecting a catastrophic error is the easy part of the problem. It usually isn't hard to determine that an application has an error. One of four things will happen:

▼   The application will terminate.

■   The application will receive an error message.

■   Windows will generate an error message.

▲   A user-detectable event will occur, like display corruption or a slowing of system performance.

Detecting noncatastrophic errors is only as easy as the error-detection code you add to the application. Range and error checks should be easy to handle. All you need to do is check the user input for specific values. Data entry errors are more subtle, and the level of detection possible depends on the kind of application you're working with.

Once you've detected the error, you need to identify a source. Microsoft gives you a variety of choices when it comes to detecting an error source. There are also some programming techniques you can use if none of these standard source-detection methods will work. The following paragraphs describe each of these source-detection methods and help you understand how they fit into the overall picture.

Using Event Logs

Event logs have been around for quite some time, so they represent one of the better known methods of providing application information to the administrator in a way that the administrator is already familiar with. There are actually three different event logs (Application, Security, and System) under Windows 2000 and you could create more if necessary. You'll find these logs in the Event Viewer shown here.

Type	Date	Time	Source	Category	Event	User	Computer
Information	12/4/1999	11:41:44 AM	MSDTC	CM	4156	N/A	MAIN
Information	12/4/1999	11:41:44 AM	MSDTC Client	CM	4156	N/A	MAIN
Information	12/4/1999	11:35:07 AM	MSMQ	Kernel	2060	N/A	MAIN

Normally, you'll use an Application event log entry. Each of these log entries provides a quick view of the event, including an event code and source of the event. You can double-click the event entry to see detailed information as shown here.

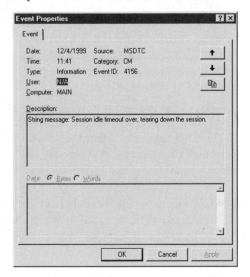

If you wanted to provide some additional information to the administrator, you'd do it with the Description field. The Data field (not used for the event shown here) will contain the data associated with the event. You could place the data that caused the error here, giving the administrator more clues as to why a transaction or message delivery failed.

EVENT LOG TYPES   Events are also registered by type. There are five different event types, three of which you can use for components and applications. (The Success Audit and Failure Audit event types are for security use only.) Here is a description of the three event types we'll talk about in this section.

Event Type	Description
Information	This is an event that your application can generate to tell the administrator about an application occurrence that didn't result in an error. For example, you could register an event when the component loads or unloads. If the component loads once or twice a day, the administrator might be interested to learn when it does load so that he or she can anticipate server loads. On the other hand, this isn't the kind of event that you'd want to generate if your component loads every few seconds.

Event Type	Description
Warning	A Warning event indicates that some type of minor problem has occurred, but nothing that would prevent the application from successfully completing its task. For example, you might include a Warning event if your application detects a low resource condition. The administrator would then be alerted to the fact that the server needs some type of optimization or that the hard drive needs to be cleared.
Error	This is the event that we're most concerned about in this chapter. An Error event occurs when the application has encountered a condition that prevents it from successfully completing its current task (if not fully, at least partially). You'll want to use this event as an alternative to displaying dialog boxes onscreen.

The event logs are physically stored in the \WINNT\system32\config folder of your hard drive in files with an EVT extension. Since more than one application can write to the event file at the same time, you'll never want to write to these files directly. What you'll use instead is a series of API functions specifically designed to work with the event logs.

EVENT LOG–SPECIFIC FUNCTIONS   Working with the event logs is similar to working with any file on the hard drive. You open the file for reading using the OpenEventLog() function or the one for writing using the RegisterEventSource() function. You can use the handle that these functions return to work with the event log. Likewise, when you get done reading or writing the event log, you close it using the CloseEventLog() or DeregisterEventSource() functions.

CAUTION: Neither of the event log opening functions returns a Windows kernel handle—these are special event log handles. Never use the CloseHandle() function to close the event log. Always use the appropriate event log–specific function.

Both the OpenEventLog() and RegisterEventSource() functions accept the Universal Naming Convention (UNC) name of the server you want to access as the first parameter. This means that you can use a single server to log all events, or place the event log entry on the current machine (the method I recommend). It also allows you to read entries off of any server on the network for which you have rights to the event log.

The second parameter for the RegisterEventSource() function is a source name, which is a custom entry in the registry. Figure 8-4 shows a typical log file registry entry. As you can see, an application entry normally consists of two entries, the location of the application on disk and the types of event log entries that the application supports. There are other registry entries that you can make—we'll cover these as part of the sample application that follows.

Notice that the registry entry we're looking at is for the Application log. There are other entries for the other two logs. If you wanted to make entries for any of the other

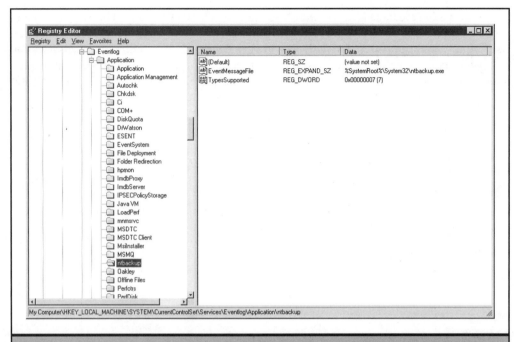

Figure 8-4. Using the event log for your application means making custom entries in the registry

logs, then you'd need to add registry entries for them as well. The OpenEventLog() function can take a custom source name of the same type as the second parameter, or you can provide the name of an event log that you want to look at.

Now that we have a handle to the event log, we can either read it or write an event report to it. I'm going to concentrate on the writing aspect of the event log because you'll seldom, if ever, need to read from the event log. You'll write to the event log using the ReportEvent() function. This function accepts input for all of the data that we talked about earlier, plus the handle to the event log.

WORKING WITH EVENT LOG MESSAGES Anyone who's worked with the Event Viewer knows that you can obtain some fairly useful help in the Description field of the Event Properties dialog box. Those messages are part of a special resource that you can't create within the Visual C++ IDE. Event logs use numbers to reference the category and event type. Using numbers allows the Event Viewer to create relatively small log files. In addition, the Event Viewer can translate the number stored in the log into a human-readable string by looking the value up in the application's EXE file or a special resource DLL.

Creating the message resource is relatively easy. All you need to do is create a text file and place some specially formatted entries in it (I'll explain these entries in a few moments).

You compile the message file with the Message Compiler (MC) utility. This utility will create an RC and a BIN file for you. The RC file contains a reference to the BIN file that you can use within your application. MC will also create a header (H) file with definitions that you can use to reference the messages from within your application. Listing 8-1 contains the source for this special message file. I placed the file in the EventCheck source directory and gave it the name of EventMsg.TXT.

```
MessageIDTypedef=WORD
MessageID=0x3000
SymbolicName=TEST_MESSAGE
Language=English
This is a test error message where you also said: %1
.

MessageIDTypedef=WORD
MessageID=0x1
SymbolicName=ON_INIT
Language=English
During Initialization
.

MessageIDTypedef=WORD
MessageID=0x2
SymbolicName=CREATE_COMPONENT
Language=English
Creating a Component
.

MessageIDTypedef=WORD
MessageID=0x3
SymbolicName=GET_DATA
Language=English
Getting Data
.

MessageIDTypedef=WORD
MessageID=0x4
SymbolicName=SEND_DATA
Language=English
Sending Data
.
```

NOTE: There's one special addition you need to make at the very end of Listing 8-1. You need to add one additional line feed after the last period. Otherwise, MC will report an error in your source file even though there isn't any.

As you can see, there are five entries in this file, all of which look pretty much the same. The MessageIDTypedef entry defines the type of the message ID, the numeric equivalent of the message. Next comes the MessageID. You can use any numbering scheme you'd like for the message type entries. There's one message type entry—the first one in the group. The message type entries would correspond to the error that occurred in your application (the error number and the message ID number don't need to match, however).

The remaining four entries are message categories. A message category would allow you to define where an error occurred in the application, sort the messages by type, or show which component experienced the error. In this case, you must number the first message category 1—the rest of the categories must follow sequentially. We'll see later why this distinction is important.

The SymbolicName entry comes next. This is the name that you'll use to reference the entry within your application. It's the same as assigning a #define to the MessageID.

The next three lines are taken as a group. The first line defines the language that the message in the next line applies to. A message type entry can also contain macro substitutions within the text. For example, the first message contains a %1 as part of the message. This value will be replaced with some additional text from within the application (we'll see how this works later). You can have multiple copies of this group of three entries—one for each of the languages you want to support.

At this point, you have a text file containing five groups of entries. Save the file and exit to a DOS command prompt. You'll compile the text file using the following command line:

```
MC EventMsg.TXT
```

NOTE: You won't find the MC utility in any of the Visual C++ entries in the Start menu. This utility is in the Visual C++ BIN directory and only works at the command line. In most cases, there should already be a path set up for the Visual C++ BIN directory at the DOS prompt for you, so accessing the MC utility at the DOS command prompt should be relatively easy.

A SIMPLE EVENT LOG EXAMPLE   The best way to demonstrate how the event log works is to create a very simple example that allows you to generate event log entries. Start by creating a simple dialog-based application using the MFC AppWizard. The example will use a project name of EventCheck. I've given the application a nice title of "Event Logging Example" (MFC AppWizard - Step 2 of 4 dialog box), but that's it. You'll see the usual blank dialog box at this point. We'll begin by adding some simple controls to it as shown in Figure 8-5. Table 8-1 contains a list of the controls and the setting changes you'll need to make for them. This table also contains a list of memory variables or event handlers for each control as appropriate.

The next thing we'll want to do is create the code that will make the entries in the registry for us. Our test application will support both message types (essentially error codes)

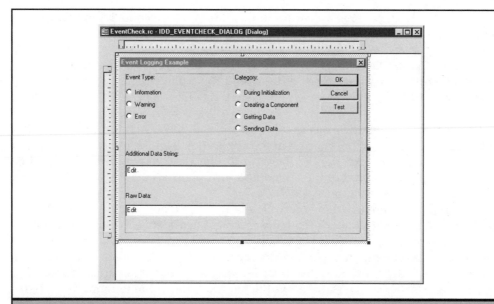

Figure 8-5. The Event Log Generation Check dialog box contains some simple controls for creating event log entries

and message categories (a method for grouping errors), so we'll need four registry entries. Listing 8-2 contains the code that you'll need to add to the InitInstance() method of the EventCheck.CPP file in bold (the listing doesn't show the entire method, but there's enough surrounding code so you'll know where to add this new code).

```
BOOL CEventCheckApp::InitInstance()
{
DWORD   dwResult;    // Result of registry key creation.
CString oData;       // Data stored in registry value.
char    cType[5] = {0x7, 0x0, 0x0, 0x0, 0x0};    // Types supported value.
char    cCategory[5] = {0x4, 0x0, 0x0, 0x0, 0x0};    //Categories supported.

    AfxEnableControlContainer();

    // Standard initialization
    // If you are not using these features and wish to reduce the size
    //  of your final executable, you should remove from the following
    //  the specific initialization routines you do not need.

#ifdef _AFXDLL
    Enable3dControls();            // Call this when using MFC in a shared DLL
#else
    Enable3dControlsStatic();      // Call this when linking to MFC statically
```

```
#endif

// Create or open the event logging registry key.
RegCreateKeyEx(
HKEY_LOCAL_MACHINE,
"SYSTEM\\CurrentControlSet\\Services\\Eventlog\\Application\\EventCheck",
0,
NULL,
REG_OPTION_NON_VOLATILE,
KEY_ALL_ACCESS,
NULL,
&m_hkey,
&dwResult);

    // Write the EventMessageFile string.
oData = AfxGetApp()->m_pszHelpFilePath;
oData.Replace(".HLP", ".EXE");
RegSetValueEx(
m_hkey,
"EventMessageFile",
0,
REG_SZ,
(BYTE *)oData.GetBuffer(_MAX_PATH),
_MAX_PATH + 1);
oData.ReleaseBuffer(-1);

    // Write the TypesSupported DWORD.
RegSetValueEx(
m_hkey,
"TypesSupported",
0,
REG_DWORD,
(BYTE *)cType,
4);

    // Write the CategoryMessageFile string.
RegSetValueEx(
m_hkey,
"CategoryMessageFile",
0,
REG_SZ,
(BYTE *)oData.GetBuffer(_MAX_PATH),
_MAX_PATH + 1);
oData.ReleaseBuffer(-1);

    // Write the CategoryCount DWORD.
RegSetValueEx(
m_hkey,
"CategoryCount",
```

```
0,
REG_DWORD,
(BYTE *)cCategory,
4);

    // Close the key now that we're done with it.
RegCloseKey(m_hkey);

    CEventCheckDlg dlg;
    m_pMainWnd = &dlg;
```

ID	Setting	Value	Member Variable or Event-Handler Name
IDC_INFORMATION	Tab stop	Checked	m_information (CButton)
	Group	Checked	
	Caption	Information	
IDC_WARNING	Tab stop	Checked	
	Caption	Warning	
IDC_ERROR	Tab stop	Checked	
	Caption	Error	
IDC_INITIALIZE	Tab stop	Checked	m_initialize (CButton)
	Group	Checked	
	Caption	During Initialization	
IDC_COMPONENT	Tab stop	Checked	
	Caption	Creating a Component	
IDC_GETDATA	Tab stop	Checked	
	Caption	Getting Data	
IDC_SENDDATA	Tab stop	Checked	
	Caption	Sending Data	
IDC_STRINGDATA	Tab stop	Checked	m_stringData (CEdit)
IDC_RAWDATA	Tab stop	Checked	m_rawData (CEdit)
IDC_TEST	Tab stop	Checked	OnTest()

Table 8-1.   Event Log Generation Check Dialog Box Control Settings

There are three main tasks that we need to perform to create the required registry entries. The first is to create or open the event-logging registry key. Figure 8-6 shows where the registry key will fit within the registry itself. The act of calling RegCreateKeyEx() gives us a handle to the open registry key. The next thing we'll do is create the four registry values associated with that key using the RegSetValueEx() function. If the registry value already exists, then the registry will be overwritten with the new value—rather than create another value entry of the same name. Finally, the application closes the registry using the RegCloseKey() function.

Let's look at the RegCreateKeyEx() function a little closer. You need a handle to an open key to use this function. Fortunately, there are predefined keys that you can use to access each of the registry hives. Since this entry exists in the HKEY_LOCAL_MACHINE hive, I used the predefined key for the function call. The next thing you need to provide is the full path (not including the hive) to the new registry key you want to create. If this key already exists, and you have the rights required to access it, Windows will simply open the existing key for you rather than create a new one. I've never used the next two arguments, and it's unlikely that you'll need to do so since the first one is reserved and the second one specifies the object type (class) of the key. The fifth argument tells Windows whether you want to create a volatile or nonvolatile key. A volatile key will be destroyed when the hive is unloaded. The next argument tells what level of access you want to the key. Since we're creating a new key, it's relatively safe to ask for complete access to it. The next argument allows you to define a specific level of access for this call, rather than use the calling thread's privileges. Finally, the last two arguments contain the new handle for the key and the results of the call. The call results are one of two values. Either Windows will create a new key or open an existing key.

TIP: Windows 2000 allows you to specify a new registry-key creation value of REG_OPTION_ BACKUP_RESTORE, which allows you to open the key for the purpose of backing it up or restoring it. When using this option, Windows 2000 will ignore the level of access desired argument (KEY_ALL_ ACCESS for this example). It'll open the registry key with the privileges needed for backup, restore, or both functions, depending on what privileges the calling thread has enabled.

Using the RegSetValueEx() function requires a little work because of the way that the function accepts arguments. There are two kinds of values we have to create. The first kind is a DWORD that defines the number or types of strings that our event log message resource (created in the "Working with Event Log Messages" section of the chapter) will support. The second kind is a pointer to the location of the file that holds the message strings. For this example, we'll use the application, but you could create a separate resource DLL if you wanted to. One of the problems with RegSetValueEx() is that it only accepts strings. This means we have to use a relatively convoluted method to get the DWORD values transferred to the registry, which is why we're using char arrays in this example. Getting the path to the application is equally convoluted. I used AfxGetApp() to obtain the path to the application's help file, then simply changed the extension from

HLP to EXE. Since this application doesn't have a help file, the m_pszHelpFilePath variable will always point to the EXE file location.

There are six arguments for the RegSetValueEx() function. The first is the handle to the open registry key that we obtained using RegCreateKeyEx(). The second argument contains the name of the registry value we want to set. If this registry value doesn't exist, then Windows will create it. The third argument is reserved, so I set it to 0. The fourth argument is the type of registry value we want to create. In this case, we'll create either a string or a DWORD. There are a variety of value types for different purposes. The last two arguments contain the data for the value entry and the length of that data.

Now that we have the required registry entries in place, it's time to look at the code for adding the event log entries. This code will appear in the OnTest() method that's associated with the Test button. You'll find it in the EventCheckDlg.CPP file. Listing 8-3 shows what this code will look like.

```cpp
void CEventCheckDlg::OnTest()
{
    HANDLE   m_hEvent;        // Handle to the current event.
    short    sType;           // Event type being entered.
    short    sCategory;       // Event category being entered.
    LPCSTR   lpcstrData;      // String data for the event description.
    CString  oStringData;     // String data temporary storage.
    LPCSTR   lpcstrRaw;       // Raw data for the event.
    CString  oRawData;        // Raw data temporary storage.
    DWORD    dwRawData;       // Raw data length.

    // Determine the current event type.
    switch (GetCheckedRadioButton(IDC_INFORMATION, IDC_ERROR))
    {
    case IDC_INFORMATION:
        sType = EVENTLOG_INFORMATION_TYPE;
        break;
    case IDC_WARNING:
        sType = EVENTLOG_WARNING_TYPE;
        break;
    case IDC_ERROR:
        sType = EVENTLOG_ERROR_TYPE;
        break;
    }

    // Determine the current event category.
    switch (GetCheckedRadioButton(IDC_INITIALIZE,IDC_SENDDATA))
    {
```

```
case IDC_INITIALIZE:
    sCategory = ON_INIT;
    break;
case IDC_COMPONENT:
    sCategory = CREATE_COMPONENT;
    break;
case IDC_GETDATA:
    sCategory = GET_DATA;
    break;
case IDC_SENDDATA:
    sCategory = SEND_DATA;
    break;
}

// Place the string data in a variable.
m_stringData.GetWindowText(oStringData);
lpcstrData = oStringData.GetBuffer(80);
oStringData.ReleaseBuffer(-1);

// Place the raw data in a variable and get its size.
m_rawData.GetWindowText(oRawData);
lpcstrRaw = oRawData.GetBuffer(80);
oStringData.ReleaseBuffer(-1);
dwRawData = oRawData.GetLength();

// Obtain an event handle so that we can register
// events.
m_hEvent = RegisterEventSource("Main", "EventCheck");
if (m_hEvent == NULL)
{
    AfxMessageBox("Failed to get the event handle.");
    return;
}

// Report and application event.
ReportEvent(
    m_hEvent,
    sType,
    sCategory,
    TEST_MESSAGE,
    NULL,
    1,
```

```
        dwRawData,
        &lpcstrData,
        (LPVOID)lpcstrRaw);


    // Close the event handle.
    DeregisterEventSource(m_hEvent);
}
```

The first part of the sample code converts the various dialog inputs into something we can use for the event log call. As previously mentioned, there are three types of event entries we can make: information, warning, and error. The first switch statement places the appropriate event type constant into the sType variable.

The next switch statement determines the event category. It looks like we're using Windows constants again; but, in this case, they come from the EventMsg.H file that we created using MC. The EventMsg.H file contains four event categories that correspond to the choices on the application's dialog box. One of these four entries gets placed in sCategory for later use.

Remember the %1 we placed in the test error message? The next bit of code retrieves the string that will replace the %1 in the event log. All we need, in this case, is the string placed in an LPCSTR variable. You'll see in a few moments that the normal CString object conversions won't work (at least not easily), in this case, so the extra conversion step is required.

The raw data for our event log entry is really a string. You can, however, include any binary data that you'd like in the raw data. The use of a string, in this case, is for convenience only. Using a string allows you to see how the raw data entry works a little better. Since we're working with binary data, we could have sent the CString to the event log, but we'll perform the conversion again to see the string easier. You also have to get the length (size) of the binary data.

We're finally ready to register an event with the event log. The first thing you need to do is obtain a handle to the event log using the RegisterEventSource() function. Remember that the handle you get is a kernel handle, so you need a special function to close it (as we'll see in a few moments). The only two things you need to get an event handle are the name of the computer that you want to create the event log on and the name of an event entry key in the registry. (We create this key during the InitInstance() method call.) As part of getting the handle, you must check for a NULL return value. If the call failed for some reason, you won't be able to proceed with the rest of the example.

NOTE: You'll need to change the name of the computer in the RegisterEventSource() call in Listing 8-3 unless your computer has the same name as mine. Change this value to the name of your workstation or server.

Once we have a handle to the event log, we can report an event using the ReportEvent() function. This function takes nine arguments, most of which you're familiar with. The first argument is the event log handle, followed by the message type and category constants. The next entry is an error code. We've only defined one constant, TEST_MESSAGE, for this example, so I've placed it in the function call directly. Normally, you'd pass a special number that corresponds to the HRESULT passed back by a function call. The next relevant argument is the number of strings that we'll pass—you can pass more than one. Each string has to have a unique substitution macro in the event message starting with %1. The next argument is the size of our raw data, which is the length of the raw data string in this case. Since we're dealing with binary data, the event log will add only the number of bytes that you tell it to add from the raw data argument. The last two arguments are the two strings we created for this example. Note that you have to pass the raw data as LPVOID. Again, this is because the raw data is treated as binary input.

The final bit of code in the OnTest() method is the DeregisterEventSource() function call. This call closes the event log handle. You must use the appropriate handle closing call when working with event logs.

At this point, the example is fully functional. However, there's one additional bit of code you should add to ensure that the example works as intended. Listing 8-4 contains code that you'll need to add to the InitDialog() method found in the EventCheckDlg.CPP file. All that this code does is initialize the dialog box controls to a known value. This helps ensure that a click of the Test button doesn't produce unexpected results. You don't have to add this code, but it's a good idea to do so.

```
    // Set the icon for this dialog.  The framework does this automatically
    //  when the application's main window is not a dialog
    SetIcon(m_hIcon, TRUE);          // Set big icon
    SetIcon(m_hIcon, FALSE);         // Set small icon

// Initialize the dialog box values.
m_information.SetCheck(1);
m_initialize.SetCheck(1);
m_stringData.SetWindowText("This is a test.");
m_rawData.SetWindowText("This is some raw data.");

    return TRUE;  // return TRUE  unless you set the focus to a control
```

The last thing we need to do in the EventCheckDlg.CPP file is add an #include for the EventMsg.H file. You can add this #include at the top of the file as shown here:

```
// Include the event messages.
#include "EventMsg.h"
```

We're not quite done with the example yet, but you'll want to compile it and test for errors. If you test the application at this point, and look in Event Viewer for the entry, you'll notice that the event log entry will have an error number, but not an error message associated with it. That's because we haven't included the error messages as a resource in the application. We need to make a special resource file entry that's compatible, but not supported by the Visual C++ IDE. With this in mind, you need to make this resource file entry after you've tested every other element of the application. Make sure you close the EventCheck project before you go any further in this section.

TIP: Visual C++ won't allow you to hand edit the RC2 (resource) file unless there's an error in the file—it automates the task of editing this file for you, which is normally a performance boost. The RC and RC2 files are merely text files. You can use any pure text editor, like Notepad, to edit them, as we'll do in this example. What will happen if you add the event-log message resource entry in the RC2 file, then try to edit the file using the Visual C++ IDE, is that the Visual C++ IDE will import the BIN file that contains the event messages. Once it does this, the imported BIN file will cause a compile error and you won't be able to open the RC2 file within the Visual C++ IDE anymore as a graphic file—all you'll see is the text that makes up the RC2 file. The example isn't broken. All you need to do is remove the imported BIN file and add the reference to it back in. The example will then compile as normal.

One of the files in your source code directory will be EventMsg.RC. This is the resource file that was automatically created for you by the MC utility. We'll need to open this file using a plain text editor like Notepad (which is a good choice since the file is small). There should be several lines of code in this file, including a reference to the EventMsg.BIN file that contains the event messages for the application. Here's what the EventMsg.RC file should look like:

```
LANGUAGE 0x9,0x1
1 11 MSG00001.bin
```

Copy the contents of the EventMsg.RC file to the Windows clipboard using the Edit | Copy command. Now, open the EventCheck.RC2 file using Notepad instead of the Visual C++ IDE. Go to the very end of this file, add a new line, then paste the contents of the clipboard using the Edit | Paste command. Save the EventCheck.RC2 file. Open the EventCheck project in the Visual C++ IDE again. Look at the ResourceView tab of the Workspace window. You should see a new resource entry like the one shown here if you successfully added the EventMsg.RC file contents to your project. Resist the urge to open any of the resources in your project—especially the new resource. Recompile your application—it's ready for final testing.

Start your application, choose some settings, and then click Test. The first place you'll want to check is the registry. Your application should have made the new entries shown in Figure 8-6. Notice that the new key is in the SYSTEM\CurrentControlSet\Services\EventLog\Application\ path. If you don't place the entry in the correct place, then you won't be able to use the event logging mechanism properly. Also look at how the valued are entered. Even though we sent four strings to the registry, two of the strings are now DWORD values.

Now that you've checked the registry, let's open a copy of the Event Viewer. Look in the Application event file and you should see an entry made by your application similar

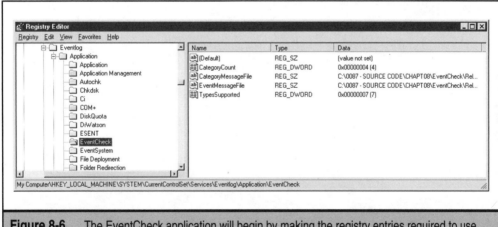

Figure 8-6. The EventCheck application will begin by making the registry entries required to use the event log

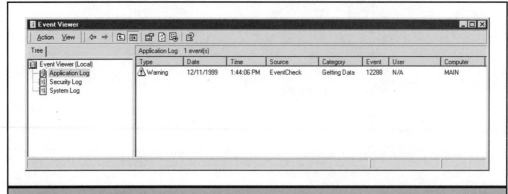

Figure 8-7.   The Event Viewer will allow you to see the new event log entry made by the application

to the one shown in Figure 8-7. In this case, I've used a Warning message type and a Getting Data category, along with some explanatory data.

Notice that the entry in Figure 8-7 includes the category that we assigned to the event log entry. If the registry entry in Figure 8-6 hadn't included the proper category resource pointer, this entry wouldn't have appeared in plain text, even if the messages are included within the application itself. You could sort on the Category column to group like entries together. Double-click on the event log entry, and you'll see an Event Properties dialog box similar to the one shown here.

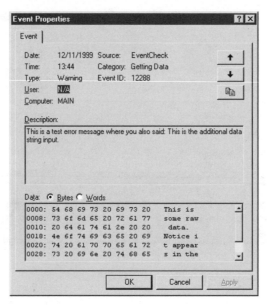

Notice that both the test message and the additional message we typed in the dialog box appear in the Description area of this dialog box. The raw data that we provided in the form of a string appears here as well. As you can see, creating event log entries is a bit convoluted, but it is certainly an effective way of dealing with errors in your server-side COM+ components.

There's one additional bit of user information I'd like to provide. Notice that the Event Properties dialog box includes three buttons in the right side. The first two buttons allow you to move to the previous and next entries. The third button allows the administrator to copy the contents of the dialog box to the clipboard. You can use these contents to paste the event log entries into some other application or include the contents as part of an email message. Listing 8-5 shows what the event log clipboard entry looks like.

```
Event Type:    Warning
Event Source:    EventCheck
Event Category:    Getting Data
Event ID:    12288
Date:        12/11/1999
Time:        1:44:06 PM
User:        N/A
Computer:    MAIN
Description:
This is a test error message where you also said: This is the additional data string input.
Data:
0000: 54 68 69 73 20 69 73 20    This is
0008: 73 6f 6d 65 20 72 61 77    some raw
0010: 20 64 61 74 61 2e 20 20     data.
0018: 4e 6f 74 69 63 65 20 69    Notice i
0020: 74 20 61 70 70 65 61 72    t appear
0028: 73 20 69 6e 20 74 68 65    s in the
0030: 20 72 61 77 20 64 61 74     raw dat
0038: 61 20 61 72 65 61 2e        a area.
```

Notice that this is the same data that appeared in the dialog box. The only difference is that you can now save it for some other purpose. In addition, you can view the raw data all in one area without having to scroll. This is an important consideration when there's a lot of raw data associated with a particular event log entry.

Using a Response Queue

Error handling is problematic for COM+ applications for a number of reasons. The very hardest problem to get around is the separation of the client and server. The physical separation between client and server makes it hard to report errors within a specific time frame, much less fix them in a timely fashion. Obviously, using multiple components on more than a few servers only compounds what is a serious problem for developers. Reporting an error to the user on a server in another building is probably going to elicit a less than helpful response. Even if the user has some idea of what to do, there's no guarantee that the remote administrator will be able to fix the problem quickly. Of course, there are other problems to consider, but we've covered most of them previously in the book.

While the event-logging system will work with COM+, you'd think that Microsoft would have come up with something better—especially for applications working in disconnected mode. Yes, an event log entry can be detailed and explicit about the source of an error, but you're still depending on the administrator to actually open the log and read it. The only disconnected-mode-specific technique that you can rely on besides the event- logging system is the MSMQ response queue that we've discussed in previous chapters.

MSMQ applications can only transfer data one way; there isn't a two-way communication process. So, when you make an order, the order goes to the server, but the server can't respond. A two-way communication channel would imply constant communication, which is counter to the purpose behind using MSMQ in the first place. If an application makes a query that requires a response, the response has to appear in a response queue. The response queue relies on a second set of components to create the one-way communication channel from the server to the client. A response only appears in the response queue if there's currently a connection between the client and the server; otherwise, the query is merely queued on the client machine to await a server connection.

NOTE: We won't be working on a response queue example in this chapter. Response queue programming techniques will appear in Chapter 10 as part of the MSMQ programming example. While this example will show the response queue being used to implement two-way data flow between the client and the server, you can use the same techniques for error handling—only the message has changed.

Response queues do provide one method of error handling for disconnected applications. However, you'll find that even the response queue technique is problematic. A user won't get notification of errors in a database entry until well after they make it. Obviously, this limits the ability of the user to respond to events that need immediate attention.

Think about this scenario for a second. An employee goes out on the road to visit Customer A and makes some new orders. At the end of week 1, the employee contacts the company, uploads the new orders, and downloads a new price list. The orders are placed in a server queue because of the load from other employees, who are also on the road. The company assumes that the orders will be processed over the weekend.

This employee now goes to Customer B and makes a whole bunch of new orders. At the end of week 2, the employee contacts the company, uploads the new orders, and downloads both a new price list and comments from the orders of week 1. The comments are loaded in a response queue, so depending on how the application is written, the employee may not even know they exist. Since it's the end of the week, the employee shuts down and goes out to party.

Now it's Monday of week 3. The employee only now notices that some of the orders from week 1 didn't get processed for some reason because the application checks the response queue and provides the employee with some type of notification. Do you really think that employee is going to remember why the orders were made the way they were? However, the employee dutifully fixes the orders the best that a remote setup will allow (remember, the application is operating in disconnected mode so the resources available at the company are unavailable). The fixed orders are queued on the client machine since the employee is on the road and operating in disconnected mode.

Friday of week 3, the employee uploads the fixed orders from week 1 and the new orders from Customer C. He or she also downloads a new price list and any new response queue items. By this time Customer A has received some, but not all, of the items ordered. More likely than not, the customer will call the company to ask for a status on the orders that haven't appeared in the order database yet because of errors made by the salesperson during week 1. It doesn't take much to see the confusion that follows as the customer gets two of each of the remaining items.

Can you see a recurring pattern for disaster here? While using a response queue and disconnected applications is better than things were in the past, there must be some better answer. Even if the employee checks in every day (which might be unreasonable in many cases), there are going to be unacceptable delays and a certain confusion factor that wouldn't exist with paper orders. (Paper orders imply human processing, where little oddities in the way an order is expressed wouldn't be a problem.)

It might be tempting for a developer to rely on response queues to the exclusion of everything else, but they really are a limited answer in some cases. You should use response queues when interaction with the employee on the road is absolutely essential and time isn't a factor. The following list provides some alternative solutions to the problems of working with response queues that might provide a more timely response (but more programming headaches as well):

▼ **Artificial intelligence (AI)**   Adding some type of AI into disconnected applications is one alternative that most companies haven't explored, but may offer solutions to current problems. (AI wasn't feasible in the past because it requires relatively large amounts of computing power.) Using a rule base would allow the component to fix many order entry problems the same way that a human counterpart would when working with paper orders. Still, it's not the best solution available because AI requires lots of computing power and an optimized rule base to do its job well. Even so, there's a limit to what you can expect from any form of automation.

■ **Email queries**   Email might be another alternative. The server component could send the email to the employee on the road. This email might contain a simple message stating that the employee needs to check in early to download response queue messages. Of course, this solution depends on the employee having email access, which might be easier to obtain than direct company access, but is still not feasible all of the time.

▲ **Event log entries**   The reason that an event log entry is so good is that now a human is involved in the loop and can contact the employee for the required information. In other words, the event log would allow a fix while the employee is still thinking about Customer A. However, there are two problems with this method. First, it assumes that the network administrator regularly checks the event log entries—which isn't an absolute. Second, it assumes that the network administrator is trained to react properly to the event log messages, which incurs other problems. In short, while an event log entry will alert the network administrator to problems with the server, they're not the best solution to data entry problems.

Working with Journal Messages

The Queued Components (QC) feature of Windows 2000 (which is based on MSMQ) allows you to perform certain types of automated error handling and reliability enhancement. A message is normally transmitted without being copied to the server's hard drive. This makes transmitting the message a lot faster, but incurs reliability problems. If the server loses power or experiences an error while transmitting a message, then the message will be lost. Since the client is unlikely to look for the lost message and may even be offline at the time of the error, there isn't any way for the system to recover from the error.

Journal messages represent one method of automated error handling for disconnected applications. Using a journal entry means giving up some performance because all of the messages are copied to the server's hard drive before being sent to the next server. In addition, the messages are transmitted as part of a transaction, which means that a lost message will be detected. We talked quite a bit about both of these issues previously in the book, so I won't talk about them again here. You can find out more about the theory behind the message transport itself in the "Understanding the Message Queue Types" section of Chapter 5. The "Parts of a Message" section of the same chapter will help you understand how a message is constructed to include journal support.

Dealing with the Dead Letter Queue

Automation for QC is like automation for anything else—it only performs the tasks that it's designed to do and then only within certain limits. When you create a QC application that supports transactions and journals and the application experiences errors, QC will continue trying to deliver the message. However, QC doesn't perform these retries continuously or at the same level of frequency as a new message.

There are six levels of private queues that QC creates for the purpose of message retries. A message that fails gets moved to the first level of the private queue so that it doesn't block other messages in the standard queue. After a certain time interval, QC will try the message again. If the message fails a certain number of retries, it gets moved to the next level of private queue, where it gets retried less often. Retries keep happening until the message has exhausted all six levels of private queues. At this point, the message gets moved to the dead letter queue. At this point, it's up to you to do something with the message; QC won't do anything more with it.

In most cases, you need to provide some type of QC listener specifically designed to handle the dead letter queue. It probably won't get called very often, but you still need to provide some support for the dead letter queue, just in case its services are needed. We talked quite a bit about the dead letter queue previously in the book, so I won't talk about the nonerror-handling issues again here. You can find out more about the theory behind the message transport itself in the "Understanding the Message Queue Types" section of Chapter 5.

So, how do you handle a message that appears in the dead letter queue? One of the first methods you could try is to create an event log entry. The reason I keep mentioning the event log as a method for handling various kinds of COM+ application errors is that the network administrator can access it from a remote location and is likely to look there for other problems with the server. However, the network administrator won't look at the event log every day, so there are probably other methods you can use to alert the network administrator to the problem if time is critical.

Email is probably the fastest way to send a message to the network administrator, but now you have to add some more custom code to your dead letter queue listener to support remote messages. Delivering an email message is a lot more complicated than making an event log entry because now you have to deal with the vagaries of online communication. I'd recommend this approach only if time is very critical.

It turns out that there may be a very simple, very configurable solution to the problem of what to do with those dead letter messages. You can simply move the errant message to one of the private queues, then set an alert for it in the Performance Logs and Alerts. This method might not be quite as fast or as direct as the email approach, but it requires a lot less programming on your part and is almost certain to elicit a fast response. Let's take a closer look at this approach.

Begin by opening the Computer Management MMC snap-in. Figure 8-8 shows one view of this snap-in. Notice that I've opened the Performance Logs and Alerts folder to show you the Alerts folder it contains. We'll work with this folder in a few moments. Also highlighted in Figure 8-8 is the Private Queues folder. Notice that there are four private queues that we can choose from to hold the errant message.

OK, you've got a QC listener that's looking for messages in the dead letter queue for your application. The only thing it knows how to do is to move that message to the \private$\notify_queue$ queue. How do we notify the network administrator about the errant message? The following procedure will show you how to set up an alert that will notify the network administrator about the errant message without any extra coding on your part:

1. Right-click Alerts in the Performance Logs and Alerts folder, then choose New Alert Settings from the context menu. You'll see a New Alert Settings dialog box like the one shown here.

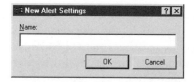

2. Type in a descriptive name for the alert, then click OK. You'll see a Properties dialog box for the alert similar to the one shown here. At a minimum, you need to define a counter for an alert. It's the counter that's the secret in this case. We'll also want to set up some additional alert features for this particular alert use.

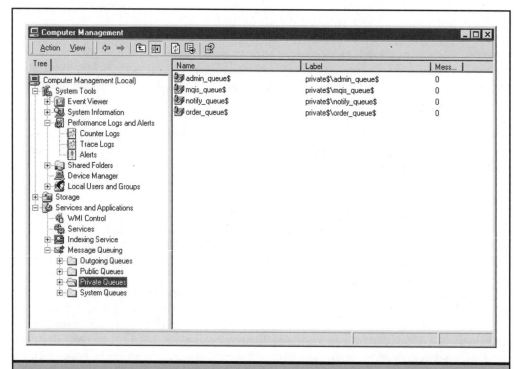

Figure 8-8. The Computer Management MMC snap-in, not Component Services, is the place to look for a solution to your dead letter queue message problems

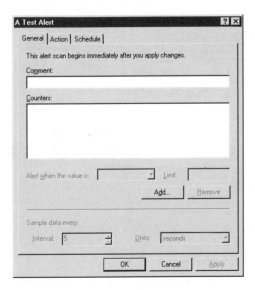

3. Click the Add button on the General tab. You'll see a Select Counters dialog box like the one shown here.

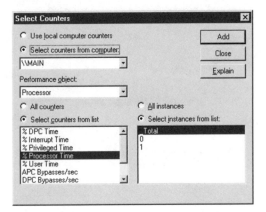

4. Choose MSMQ Queue in the "Performance object" drop-down list box. We're choosing this particular counter so that we can monitor the contents of the queue and alert the network administrator to any errant messages. At this point, you should see the \private$\notify_queue$ queue as one of the entries in the "Select instances from list" list box, as shown here.

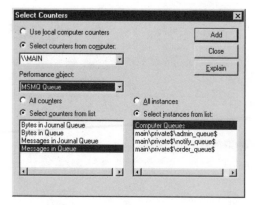

5. Choose the \private$\notify_queue$ entry, then click Add. Click Close to close the Select Counters dialog box. At this point, some of the other entries on the General tab will get enabled.

6. Choose Over in the "Alert when the value is" field and 1 in the Limit field. This will tell the alert to do something when there's a message in the \private$\ notify_queue$ queue. Your dialog should look similar to the one shown here.

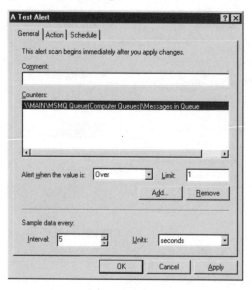

7. Click the Action tab. This is where we'll choose what the alert will do when there's a message in the queue. The two actions that we're interested in are: "Log an entry in the application event log" and "Send a network message to." Notice that you have to add a name to the network message entry. I've included my own name, in this case, but you'd normally include the name of a

group of administrators or the single administrator responsible for this server. The Action tab should look similar to the one shown here.

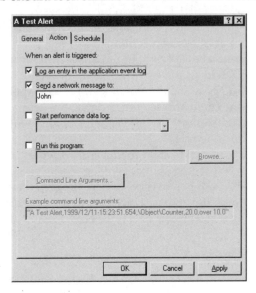

8. Click OK to complete the alert.

Programming Techniques

In most cases, the methods that we've talked about in the previous sections will help you identify the source of an error. In many cases, they'll also provide additional information about the error that will help you in troubleshooting the problem. However, there are a very few situations where the HRESULT value is all that you're going to get from the application, which makes detecting the precise source of an error difficult, to say the least.

NOTE: The technique in this section will only work for COM+ applications that don't use QC. Remember that QC applications deal with one-way data transfer—they don't return any kind of result. Since this technique relies on working with the HRESULT value, there isn't any way to use it effectively with QC applications.

One of the methods that I've used in this case involves adding a constant value to the HRESULT. Each error source uses a different constant and the constants are large enough to prevent error code overlap (where two different error codes could have the same number depending on what error source they're attached to). For example, if there are 20 possible error codes, you might use a constant interval of 100. This particular method works well where several different application modules use the same call and detecting the exact source of an error becomes difficult as a result.

Error detection becomes a two-part process. First, you detect the source of the error by checking the HRESULT value against the constants for the application. Second, you subtract the constant from the HRESULT to obtain the actual error code value. This two-part process is relatively straightforward to code and results in much finer resolution of application errors to specific areas of the application.

There are, however, several disadvantages to this technique. For one thing, the client application has to be written in such a way that it can detect both the error codes and the source constant. If you add a new component (with a correspondingly new constant), you also have to rewrite the client application to detect the new constant. In addition, the use of special error codes will reduce the appeal of the component to other programmers, reducing the possibility of code reuse.

Another possibility is to generate an event log entry, then try to fix the problem locally to prevent user confusion. We talked about event logs earlier, so I won't cover them again here. This technique works well in situations where the error is very minor and you can be assured that the administrator will actually look at the event log. Microsoft currently uses this method to track various types of service errors.

Interpreting Error Codes

There's a problem with the set of HRESULT codes that you get back from a call to a function—they're very generic. Consider the errors that you get back from a call to CoCreateInstanceEx(). This call will return errors that tell you whether the component is registered on the server, if one or more of the arguments is invalid, or whether the interfaces you requested are available. What happens, however, if the network administrator makes a setting change that prevents the component from initializing properly? In most cases, you're going to get some type of generic error that won't tell you anything about the problem. A developer could spend hours trying to figure out which component generated the error, much less the configuration problem that caused it. We've already dealt with the problem of locating a source as part of the "Programming Techniques" section of this chapter, but that still won't help you much in the configuration department.

Unfortunately, you're now in the unenviable position of attempting to interpret an error code that the operating system won't really help you with. A robust application will require equally robust error handling, but implementing the required level of error handling can be very difficult, to say the least. There are a few different approaches you could take to resolve this issue, all of which are complex.

The first approach would be to place the CoCreateInstanceEx() function call within a try...catch structure. The client-side component could use RPC to communicate with the server in the event of an initialization failure. You could use standard calls to query the current settings of the component and determine whether the component is properly registered. However, this approach assumes that the client-side component has a connection to the server and that the user has the proper rights to perform this kind of task. While you could get around the security issue by using impersonation, the other problem can't be resolved. Both of these assumptions make this approach useless for QC applications.

Another approach would be to create a diagnostic component on the server. You could send a simple message to the diagnostic component for additional information. This approach has several advantages over the try...catch method. For one thing, you could theoretically use it with a QC application. This approach also has fewer security problems and will reduce network traffic. The problem with this approach is that the diagnostic component has to be very robust, which means writing a lot of code. In addition, you now have yet another component to create, and reliability becomes an issue as well.

Dealing with Error Overload

Hopefully, you'll write the perfect application and application-specific errors will be minimal or even nonexistent. Like it or not, however, you'll have to deal with errors. The complex nature of COM+ applications makes it very unlikely that your application will be unscathed by the wealth of user and environmental conditions that can cause data errors and component corruption. In fact, the larger your application, the more you can count on handling errors. With this in mind, there's another problem that you have to deal with when working with COM+ error reporting of any kind. The network administrator could literally get overloaded with error information—it's like information overload, only more stressful.

We talked about one method of dealing with this problem in the "Using Event Logs" section of the chapter—sorting the entries to help detect message patterns. However, in this case you're limited to two sorting criteria: three levels of error message type and any number of levels of error message category. These two sorting criteria do go a long way toward helping the network administrator deal with application errors, but they won't be enough on large enterprise-level applications. An administrator could still end up with a lot of messages that look really critical, but aren't.

The best way to deal with this situation is to write an event log entry parsing component that will parse the error entries and alert the administrator to the most devastating and critical errors through a network broadcast message. You obviously want to restrict this methodology to the most critical of errors—those that have to be fixed right now and not later. A major component failure or an excessive number of dead letter queue messages are two examples of the kinds of errors that you'd want to parse.

An event log entry parsing component would have to look at four different criteria to work properly. The first task is to look at the error message type (information, warning, or error) and weigh the probability of the event containing critical information accordingly. The second task is to add a second weighing factor by looking at the event entry category. A category called component initialization failure is likely to be more critical than a category of data send error.

Once you have these two weighing factors in place, you need to perform a keyword search on both the description and the raw data. A computer can't make a judgment call about the severity of an event in the same way that a human can. The best you can hope to achieve is to sort out the event log entries that contain certain keywords in sufficient quantity to warrant concern. Once you have a list of critical words and the weighing factor of the event log entry, you can use a rule base to determine whether the message is important enough to alert the network administrator immediately.

At this point, you're asking yourself if it's worth all the work required to implement such a complex background task on a server that's almost certainly overloaded. There are several problems to consider. Just how complex is your application, and how many people do you have to service it? Many companies are downsizing today, and network administrator time is becoming ever more valuable. The development time for complex event log entry parsing will be paid back in reduced network administrator management time if the application you're dealing with is complex enough to generate a large number of errors.

In short, this is an add-on that you'll need to consider after the application is in place and running for some period of time. The amount of parsing you perform will be directly proportional to the number of messages that the network administrator has to handle. There are no easy answers here; but, then, that's why you're being paid the big dollars.

Staging a Recovery

So far, we've talked about detecting and reporting errors to the network administrator. We've also covered a few automated techniques for dealing with errors. The problem is that errors don't always fit into nice neat categories and some automated error-handling techniques won't work with every error of a particular class. A major concern, then, is giving your application the very best opportunity to recover from an error. External techniques like automated error handling and network administrator intervention are fine, but getting the application to help itself is even better.

WEB LINK: You aren't alone when it comes to diagnosing complex problems with COM+. Microsoft provides a wealth of Web sites and newsgroups that we've already talked about in the book. However, if you need more individualized attention and want to contribute to the future of COM+, try the Microsoft DCOM discussion list group at DCOM@DISCUSS.MIRCROSOFT.COM. This discussion list group tends to discuss rather esoteric subjects, so your chances of getting general help here are rather slim. However, if you're working on a complex project where head-scratching time is exceeding development time, then this discussion list group may be the answer you're looking for. Remember that you can also gain access to various MSMQ resources, including information about error handling, at http://www.microsoft.com/ntserver/appservice/exec/overview/MSMQ_Overview.asp. This Web site specializes in overview information about MSMQ as a whole, but the resources are especially interesting—it's where you'll find new tools as Microsoft develops them, along with other Web sites that provide useful information. Another good Web site to check out is the Microsoft Message Queuing Services (MSMQ) Tips Web site at http://msdn.microsoft.com/isapi/msdnlib.idc?theURL=/library/backgrnd/html/msmqtips.htm. This Web site is in a commonly asked questions format and provides a lot of answers about things that can commonly go wrong with an application.

The number one tool at your disposal when it comes to handling errors internally is the try...catch structure. This structure allows you to try an operation. If the operation fails, then the catch portion of the structure provides an opportunity for you to either provide robust error handling or, hopefully, fix the error.

In another part of the chapter I discussed the problem of the HRESULT values returned by a call to another component. For example, CoCreateInstanceEx() is extremely limited in the number of codes that get returned. In some cases, you'll get an unknown error that may defy easy explanation or handling.

You can provide some additional recovery options by exploiting the contents of the WinError.H file and by knowing how error messages are structured. The WinError.H file contains a list of Windows error codes broken down by their component parts. For the purposes of this discussion, each HRESULT is a 32-bit value that contains the information shown in Table 8-2.

As you can see, there are shades of meaning to the HRESULT that you can break down and use to determine what course of action your application needs to take. Yes, there are going to be times when you just can't handle the error, but at least this process gives your application a better chance of recovering from the error, or at least allowing the administrator to do so more quickly.

TIP: A trip through the WinError.H file can prove to be very enlightening. This file shows you HRESULT values at their most basic level. However, it's also interesting to check out error values provided by other header files. These error values can tell you a lot about the kinds of things that Microsoft expects to go wrong with a generic application. You can use the combination of generic error information and HRESULT values to create your own error values (make sure you set the Customer Code Flag) for application-specific errors.

It's not too difficult to figure out that if Microsoft provides a specific format for HRESULT values, then there will be a way to manipulate the values as well. There are, in fact, a series of macros you can use to work with the HRESULT values returned by various Windows and COM calls. The following list provides an overview of some of the more important macros that you can use to decipher HRESULT values:

▼ **HRESULT_CODE**   Returns the error code portion of the HRESULT.

■ **HRESULT_FACILITY**   Returns the facility (error source) portion of the HRESULT.

■ **HRESULT_SEVERITY**   Returns the severity level of the HRESULT.

▲ **MAKE_HRESULT**   Allows you to create an HRESULT value that consists of an error code, an error source (facility), and a severity level.

Bits	Purpose	Description
0–15	Facility status code	This is the actual error code. It defines what the facility's current status is and could indicate what you need to do to fix it. This is the most unique part of the HRESULT and would require extensive programming to provide a complete solution.
16–27	Facility code	Defines where the error occurred. For example, a facility code of 3 indicates that the error happened in system storage and a facility code of 14 tells you that the error happened in MSMQ. Knowing the facility code can help you determine if the problem is easily fixed by your application, or if you'll have to pass it along to some other part of Windows.
28	Reserved	N/A
29	Customer Code Flag	A flag that indicates this status code is customer defined. It's normally set for custom error codes. You won't normally need to worry about this value when breaking an HRESULT down for analysis.
30–31	Severity	Defines how severe the error is. There are four severity levels: Success, Informational, Warning, and Error. The severity level can help you determine just how concerned you need to be about the error. For example, you can always ignore a Success message. Informational messages can normally be ignored as well, but you may want to create an event log entry. Warning messages will require some type of handling, but they can normally wait until the network administrator has time to work with the error if your application can't handle it immediately. You should always try to fix Error messages if possible or alert the administrator immediately for severe problems when you can't.

Table 8-2. HRESULT Bit Values

As you can see, there isn't any easy way to set the customer flag using macros, so you'll need to do this manually after you create the HRESULT. There are also three error-detecting macros that are commonly used: SUCCEEDED, FAILED, and IS_ERROR. We've used the first two quite a bit in this book, and they're commonly used in other codes. The IS_ERROR macro is interesting because it allows you to differentiate between error returns and those of either an informational or warning nature. You could use this macro to test for calls that completely failed so that you could hand them off to the operating system immediately.

NOTE: There are also macros for handling SCODEs (status codes). According to recent Microsoft literature, the SCODE is becoming obsolete. You should avoid using SCODEs wherever possible in your code. When working in the 32-bit environment, the SCODE and HRESULT values are normally equal anyway.

CHAPTER 9

Sending Messages
and COM Objects

Microsoft Message Queue (MSMQ), now referred to as Queued Components, is a very powerful part of COM+ because it provides the means for transferring data from one point to another on the network. As with many other elements of COM+, MSMQ does extend existing technology. In this case, it extends DCOM in two ways. First, MSMQ allows you to send both messages and objects. Second, MSMQ allows you to work in both connected and disconnected modes. That's what this chapter is all about. We're going to take a more detailed look at the MSMQ component of COM+ from a functional perspective.

NOTE: At the time of this writing, it isn't certain which term Microsoft will use for the MSMQ element of COM+. While Queued Components does appear within the user interface in several places, most of the MSMQ documentation still refers to this element as MSMQ. For the sake of clarity, I'll use MSMQ to refer to the messaging component of COM+ throughout the chapter. However, be aware that the term Microsoft uses for this term at the time Windows 2000 is released may change.

The first section of this chapter looks at the communication scenario. I'll answer the question, "What must take place to ensure proper application communication?" from the programmer's perspective. We'll take a detailed look at three essential elements of the communication scenario: message type, the data transfer sequence, and the types of queues you can use to store messages. It's important to understand that these three separate elements are combined in different ways using various configurations to achieve certain communication results. A fourth section will provide you with a quick overview of the two APIs at your disposal for working with MSMQ at a low level—you'll find that each API has specific advantages. The goal of this section, then, is to understand what tools you have at your fingertips to obtain specific programming goals.

In the second section of the chapter, we'll create and install a listener/player application that you could use as the basis for writing a service or specialty component. All that the listener portion of the component does is wait in the background for a message to appear in the queues that it services. Once a message does appear in the queue, the player component reads the contents of the message and passes them along to the component that will perform the actual data processing. The combination of recorder, player, and listener form the difference between an MSMQ application and one that's created for normal use. You can see this relationship of components in Figure 9-1. The components that we'll create in this chapter are highlighted for emphasis. Notice that we're concentrating on the needs of an independent, rather than a dependent, client in this case—the principles are the same in both situations.

NOTE: We'll create the recorder component for our example as part of the client application in the third section of the chapter. Remember from Chapter 5 that the recorder component creates a message for the client and places it in a local queue. MSMQ then reads the message created by the client and places it in a queue on the server. Likewise, the second section of the chapter will show you how to create the listener/player portion of the application. Remember from Chapter 5 that the listener removes the message from the server side queue, while the player sends the instructions in the message body to the server side component. In this chapter, we'll combine all three functions (listener, player, and server side processing) into a single server side application.

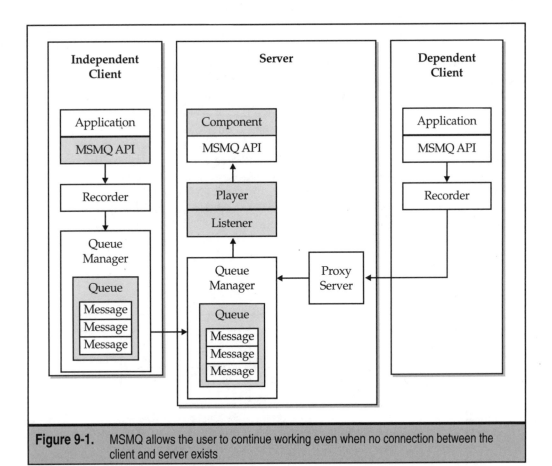

Figure 9-1.   MSMQ allows the user to continue working even when no connection between the client and server exists

At this point, we have the communication link for the application, but no user interface. The third section of the chapter will show you how to create a client application that relies on the messaging services provided by MSMQ. These services will allow the application to operate in such a way that a real-time connection with the server isn't required. Obviously, this means that the client will need to send data only—you can't use it to look data up unless the client is willing to wait until the server gets around to performing the lookup. When the server is required to provide a response, an application can't use the same path to transfer the server response. A second path, including a response queue on the client, is required to make the round trip. A message data transfer is one-way—you can't return anything. Figure 9-2 shows an example of a response queue setup.

The fourth section of the chapter will look at some MSMQ administrative issues. Like everything else in Windows 2000, MSMQ relies on an MMC snap-in for administrative purposes. We'll look at what you need to do to maintain MSMQ and check the queues for problem messages. Obviously, some of these administrative requirements will normally fall on the shoulders of the network administrator, but it's important for the developer to know how to perform them as well.

The final section of the chapter will look at the testing process for the application. As with any COM+ application, an application that relies on queued components operates in a complex environment. This means that you'll need to spend extra time testing the application and provide robust error handling.

Note that this chapter is showing you how to work with the raw MSMQ capabilities that Windows 2000 provides. In Chapter 10, we'll look at the Queued Components portion of the picture. Queued Components are based on MSMQ. What they do is abstract the low-level details of MSMQ so that all you need to worry about is the business logic in your application. Comparing the two chapters will give you a better idea of the trade-offs of using one technology over the other. For the most part, you'll find that using MSMQ directly requires a great deal more coding, but also provides a lot more flexibility. On the other hand, using Queued Components greatly reduces development time and the amount of time required to debug an application.

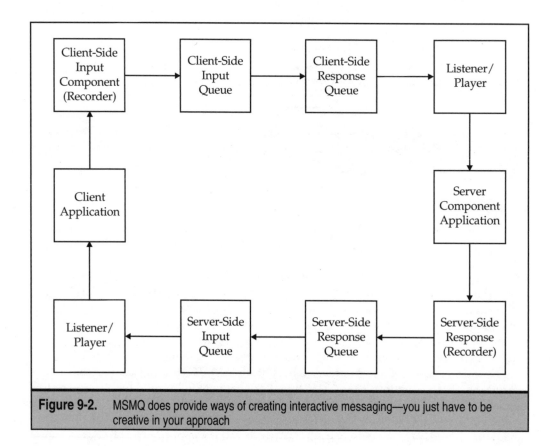

Figure 9-2.   MSMQ does provide ways of creating interactive messaging—you just have to be creative in your approach

Gaining Access to the Administrative Tools

Microsoft didn't pack all of the MMC snap-ins supported by Windows 2000 Server on the Windows 2000 Professional CD. However, you can still get a copy of these snap-ins installed on the workstation to allow for remote management of server resources. All you need to do is find the ADMINPAK.MSI file in the i386 folder of the Windows 2000 Server CD, then install it on your workstation. The icon for the new Microsoft Installation (MSI) database file looks like the one shown here.

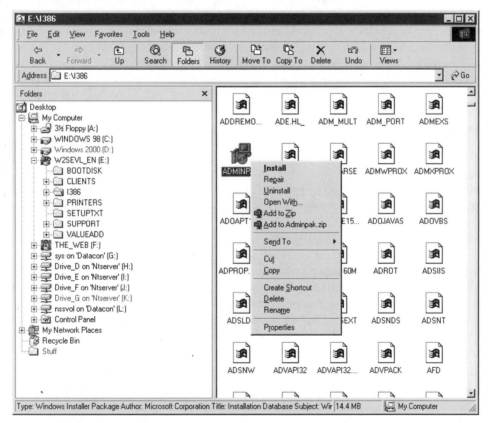

The ADMINPAK.MSI file contains instructions for installing all of the administrative tools that you get as a default on the server. Installation is easy: all you need to do is right-click the icon and then choose Install from the context menu. You can use these tools to remotely administer server-specific services as well as add functionality you may not have on your local computer. Obviously, you want to be very selective about installing these tools since they do allow users to perform administrative functions (the server is still protected—so you don't actually need to worry about the tools creating a security breach).

AN OVERVIEW OF THE COMMUNICATION SCENARIO

Getting data from one point to another is the basic goal of any messaging API like MSMQ. However, there are certain costs to using a messaging API because it's designed for an entirely new class of application. The most important thing to understand is that MSMQ and its sibling, Queued Components, aren't designed to replace real-time connection technologies like DCOM. MSMQ is designed to allow you to write applications that use server resources efficiently and allow the user to work offline when response time isn't critical.

In fact, it's not all that unlikely that you'll write one or more mixed-mode applications for your company. One part of the application, like stock checks, may require dedicated access to the server. Order entry, on the other hand, isn't something that needs to be taken care of immediately. This part of the application would work just as well in an offline mode as it does with a direct server connection. You may even create special versions of the application for those users who spend a lot of time on the road. A laptop may have access to a subset of the catalog right on the hard drive. The "offline" catalog would allow a user to take orders while on the road, but wouldn't allow the user to do things like check current order status or inventory levels until they established a connection with the company.

MSMQ is a dedicated one-way transfer mechanism between the client and server, as we'll see throughout the chapter. The ability to provide a response queue means that a user can get verification of message transfers and handling, but at the server's leisure. Response queues aren't for immediate user gratification—they're simply sanity checks in those situations when a user must know what's going on with the messages created by the application.

The following sections are going to look at this whole issue of communication in more detail. You need to understand what MSMQ offers in the way of tools for establishing and maintaining communications when working with a distributed application. This begins with an understanding that you have two different APIs at your disposal. We'll talk about this in the first section. The remaining three sections will look at the communication needs of the applications that we'll create in this chapter. However, they'll also offer you a broad view of application communication for MSMQ as a whole.

Two APIs

Microsoft actually provides two different APIs for working with MSMQ. The first is the familiar C function call method that we've all relied on since day one. The second is a series of ActiveX controls contained in the MQOA.DLL file that you'll find in the Windows 2000 System32 folder. These ActiveX controls encapsulate all of the functionality found in the first API, but in an easier-to-use form. If you need to work with other languages, like Visual Basic, then the ActiveX controls are really your only choice. The function call method only works when you're going to be using C alone for your development efforts.

NOTE: We'll use the ActiveX control method of accessing MSMQ in this chapter. While using C-style function calls does provide the programmer with better access to some MSMQ features, using the ActiveX controls is much easier and faster in most cases. In fact, unless you have extreme programming needs, the ActiveX control approach will most likely help insulate your application from the vagaries of change that MSMQ will go through as it matures.

Let's take a quick look at the function call API that many developers will use for C-only development. Table 9-1 provides a list of these function calls and provides a brief description of their purpose.

Function Name	Category	Description
MQFreeMemory	Message	Frees the memory used to transfer certain types of data. The memory must be allocated by MSMQ before you can free it using this function.
MQGetOverlappedResult	Message	Retrieves the error or success code for the current message. This code is part of an overlapped structure used to retrieve the message asynchronously. You should only call this function after the event is signaled or you get a completion port notification.
MQReceiveMessage	Message	Allows the application to look at messages in the queue. Peeking a message allows the application to see the message contents without actually removing the message from the queue. On the other hand, receiving a message means that it will get removed from the queue. This function supports a time-out value that can be set to INFINITE in order to allow an application to wait until a message appears in the queue. The function also supports the use of cursors to move around the queue in a random fashion.
MQSendMessage	Message	Places a message in the specified queue. The content of the message is determined by a message properties data structure. This function will allow you to send messages normally, or within an MSMQ or MTS transaction.

Table 9-1.   An Overview of MSMQ Functions

Function Name	Category	Description
MQGetMachineProperties	Miscellaneous	Returns the capabilities of the machine containing the Queue Manager. This may not be the local computer in the case of a dependent client. The Queue Manager properties data structure contains the list of capabilities returned by this call.
MQGetPrivate-ComputerInformation	Miscellaneous	Returns the capabilities of the specified machine without referring to Directory Services. The information is returned in a private properties data structure.
MQCloseQueue	Queue	Closes the specified queue and frees the resources used to manage it. This function doesn't remove any existing messages from the queue.
MQCreateQueue	Queue	Allows the application to create a new public or private queue. Public queues are registered with the directory service, enabling other computers to locate the queue and use it if necessary. Private queues are registered only on the local machine and won't get registered for public use.
MQDeleteQueue	Queue	Removes the specified queue. Public queue registrations are removed from the directory service, while private queues are removed from the local registry. You can't remove private, connector, dead letter, or journal queues located on a remote computer.

Table 9-1. An Overview of MSMQ Functions *(continued)*

Function Name	Category	Description
MQGetQueueProperties	Queue	Returns the requested properties for a specific queue. The message queue properties data structure contains the returned information and determines which property values are requested.
MQHandleToFormatName	Queue	Creates a format name based on a queue's handle. MSMQ doesn't normally store the format names—they're created using this call. You'll need format names when working with the MQOpenQueue, MQGetQueueProperties, MQSetQueueProperties, MQGetQueueSecurity, and MQSetQueueSecurity functions.
MQInstanceToFormatName	Queue	Creates a format name based on a queue's instance information. MSMQ doesn't normally store the format names—they're created using this call. You'll need format names when working with the MQOpenQueue, MQGetQueueProperties, MQSetQueueProperties, MQGetQueueSecurity, and MQSetQueueSecurity functions.
MQOpenQueue	Queue	Opens a queue for reading or writing of messages. There are essentially three levels of open: peek, receive, and send. You can't open a journal queue for sending messages.

Table 9-1. An Overview of MSMQ Functions *(continued)*

Function Name	Category	Description
MQPathNameTo-FormatName	Queue	Creates a format name based on a queue's path name. MSMQ doesn't normally store the format names—they're created using this call. You'll need format names when working with the MQOpenQueue, MQGetQueueProperties, MQSetQueueProperties, MQGetQueueSecurity, and MQSetQueueSecurity functions. This function only works with public and local private queues.
MQSetQueueProperties	Queue	Sets the requested properties for a specific queue. The message queue properties data structure contains the new property information and determines which property values are set.
MQCloseCursor	Queue cursor	Closes the cursor and allows MSMQ to recover the associated resources. A cursor points to a specific location within the message queue—it allows your application to track which messages are serviced. MSMQ automatically closes any open cursors when it closes the queue, but it's a good idea to perform this task as a separate step.
MQCreateCursor	Queue cursor	Creates a new cursor for the specified queue. A cursor can help the application maintain a pointer to a location within the queue, which will allow the application to track which messages require processing.

Table 9-1. An Overview of MSMQ Functions *(continued)*

Function Name	Category	Description
MQLocateBegin	Queue search	Allows the application to find the first public queue fitting the specified search criteria. You'll use the MQLocateNext function to retrieve the search results. This function won't work with private queues since these queues don't appear in Directory Services. This function will allow you to restrict the number of queues returned by the search using a special restriction parameter.
MQLocateEnd	Queue search	Ends a public queue search and releases the resources used by the search results.
MQLocateNext	Queue search	Obtains the public queue information originally located by the MQLocateBegin call.
MQFreeSecurityContext	Security	Frees the memory used to create a security context using the MQGetSecurityContext call. A security context is used by MSMQ to verify the sender and content of a message.
MQGetQueueSecurity	Security	Returns the security descriptor for the specified queue. The security descriptor originally gets set during queue creation. MSMQ will allow you to modify the settings for creating, deleting, and opening the queue for the purpose of sending or receiving messages. You can also change the settings for getting and setting queue properties and the queue security descriptor. MSMQ won't allow you to change the security descriptor of a journal, dead letter, or foreign queue.

Table 9-1.   An Overview of MSMQ Functions *(continued)*

Function Name	Category	Description
MQGetSecurityContext	Security	Returns the security context information required to attach a certificate to a message prior to transmission. You must free the memory used by this function call using the MQFreeSecurityContext function. If your application needs to attach more than one certificate to a message, you'll need to call this function once for each certificate.
MQRegisterCertificate	Security	Registers an internal or external certificate with Directory Services.
MQSetQueueSecurity	Security	Sets the security descriptor for the specified queue. The security descriptor originally gets set during queue creation. MSMQ will allow you to modify the settings for creating, deleting, and opening the queue for the purpose of sending or receiving messages. You can also change the settings for getting and setting queue properties and the queue security descriptor. MSMQ won't allow you to change the security descriptor of a journal, dead letter, or foreign queue.
MQBeginTransaction	Transaction	Creates an internal (rather than an MTS) transaction that an MSMQ application can use to ensure the integrity of a message transfer.

Table 9-1. An Overview of MSMQ Functions *(continued)*

As you can see from Table 9-1, there are functions for just about every purpose. The ActiveX controls work somewhat differently than the functions do. We've already examined the basics of the ActiveX controls in Chapter 5. You can see a list of these ActiveX controls in Table 5-2. We'll take a closer look at how these controls work as the chapter progresses. For the most part, there aren't any surprises. The MSMQ ActiveX controls do require a bit of extra work to use, but you'll find that they behave just like any other controls that you've used in the past.

Defining the Message Type

Messages come in a variety of sizes and shapes. The two human-readable forms of identification for the message are the message body and the message label. Besides these two human-readable forms of information, the message type is also determined by a number of message properties, including the transactional state, message priority, message privilege level, and the kind of message that gets created.

The example code is going to allow you to set a number of the message parameters and see how they affect the display of the message. For example, the priority setting will determine the message's position within the list. It also determines when the listener/playback component will process the message.

The point is that any application you develop that will use MSMQ in a raw form is going to require some flexibility with regard to message handling. You'll want to define the types of messages that your application will process and you'll need to include a certain level of flexibility when it comes to message transmission alternatives. For example, you may find that it's not always possible to include full message encryption when an employee is overseas.

One of the message properties that your application will never use, but will be part of any application that uses a response queue, is the MsgClass property. This property is one of the criteria by which you can sort messages within the message queue. The default setting for messages sent out by your application is MQMSG_CLASS_NORMAL. This setting appears as "Normal" in the Class field of the Queue Messages folder.

In addition to the normal messages that your application will send, there are a variety of specialty messages that the Queue Manager, operating system, or server component will send to the client as well. For example, there are two positive acknowledgement messages: MQMSG_CLASS_ACK_REACH_QUEUE and MQMSG_CLASS_ACK_RECEIVE. The first is used by the Queue Manager to indicate that the message arrived safely at its destination, while the second is used to indicate that the receiving application picked the message up. Neither of these positive acknowledgments indicates that the receiving application did anything at all with the message, nor do they tell you whether the receiving application was able to use the content of the message. In short, you know that the message got to its destination, but it's up to the receiving application to acknowledge the message and there isn't any requirement for the receiving application to perform this step. MSMQ is definitely designed as an application strategy where absolute certainty isn't a requirement—at least not certainty in a way that the client can verify. (Obviously, the use of transactions mitigates some of the concerns you might have about data security and lack of corruption.)

In addition to positive acknowledgements, there's a wealth of negative acknowledgements, many of which help you understand the reasons for message transmission failure. For example, a message failure may occur when the message is encrypted incorrectly or the user doesn't have the required rights to the message queue. There are other negative acknowledgments that occur when a message isn't formatted correctly or if one of the message fields requires a different value. We've already covered the various message fields in Table 5-1 of Chapter 5, so we won't talk about them again here. However, it's important to understand how the content of these various fields can change the way that a message is received by MSMQ.

Using response messages also incurs some additional baggage in the original message. You need to provide a message queue object as part of the ResponseQueueInfo parameter of the message. This response queue must appear on the client machine as a separate queue. You have to use a separate queue in order to prevent confusion for the receiving application. Otherwise, the receiving application won't know whether a message is an original created by the client or one of the responses generated by any number of components along the way.

The example application isn't going to go to the extreme of providing any form of acknowledgment to the client. The first application will generate the messages and assume that the second application will pick them up and do something with them. This configuration represents the normal way that MSMQ applications operate and makes the requirements for putting the message together minimal.

Understanding the Data Transfer Sequence

Figure 9-1 shows a typical data transfer sequence for an MSMQ application. The example application will use a similar sequence. As with most MSMQ applications, the client will generate a message and place it in the queue. MSMQ will take care of the requirement to move the message from the client queue to the server queue. Finally, a second application (instead of a service or component) will pick messages up from the server queue.

Normally, you'd assume that the server component is running all of the time and that the message will be taken care of immediately after it gets placed in the server's queue. In this case, however the server application might not be running. The point is that you can stop the server-side processing in order to see what a queue message looks like. If the application were running all of the time, the entire process would be too short for you to see the message generated by the client in the first place.

Creating the Required Queues

There are quite a few ways to create the queues required by an application. If you want absolute control over the queue creation process, you can create the queues manually using the Computer Management MMC snap-in. All you need to do is right-click the folder

where you want to place the queue (usually the Public Queues folder), and choose New |
Public Queue from the context menu. You'll see a Queue Name dialog box similar to the
one shown here.

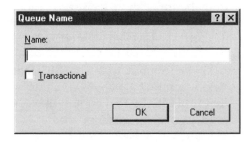

At this point, you need to type a queue name. If you want all message transfers to take
place within a transaction, you'll also need to check the Transactional check box. Message
transfers normally occur within an MSMQ transaction, and checking the Transactional
option allows you to gain further benefits by using MTS as the transaction coordinator.

Once you create the new queue, you need to perform any required setting changes for
the queue. Right-click the new queue, then choose Properties from the context menu.
You'll see a queue Properties dialog box like the one shown here.

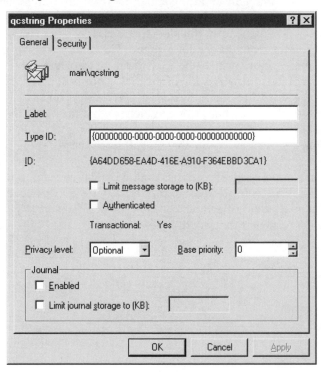

The "Limit message storage to (KB)" field of the General tab reduces the chance that a single application will upload one or more huge messages that will devour the drive space on your server. You can set this field to a value that's a little larger than the biggest message you expect to see from the application. If an application does attempt to upload a really large message, the problem will get detected immediately and the application will be able to handle at least this particular problem immediately (assuming you set up all of the queues the same way).

You'll use the Authenticated check box to tell MSMQ that you want all messages checked to ensure that the person sending it really is who they say they are. This is one of several security features built into MSMQ that should make it tougher for crackers to break into your system using fake messages. However, the Authenticated option won't prevent tampered messages from getting added to the queue. To ensure that the content of the message remains private, you'll need to set the Privacy level to Body as a minimum (you can set this value higher for MSMQ 2.0 using message field options).

Every message has a priority assigned to it. The higher the priority number, the lower the message is on the list of messages to get processed. The Base priority setting determines what default priority setting will get used for the queue. Interestingly enough, even though MSMQ defaults to a priority level of 3 for messages, the queue will default to a priority level of 0. The default level of 3 makes a lot more sense since you'll have some messages that require immediate handling and others that can wait for later processing.

Journals are a way of recording what messages get transferred from the current machine. In most cases, MSMQ simply transfers the message to the receiving machine and then deletes the message from the sender's queue. The sender ends up without any kind of backup of the message because of the way message transfers are handled. Checking the Enabled option of the Journal section of the dialog box will tell MSMQ to keep a copy of the message in the journal folder of the queue. Obviously, you don't want these journal messages to consume the entire hard drive, which is what they'll do for an active system that transfers a lot of messages. As a result, you should also check the "Limit journal storage to (KB)" option and set it to a value that will allow the application to store a few day's worth of journal entries.

The Security tab of the queue Properties dialog box allows you to set security for the queue itself. This security is in addition to the security for the application, the messages that MSMQ transfers from one machine to another, and other security settings for the receiving machine. Here's what the Security tab looks like.

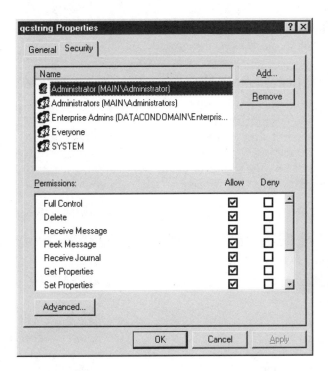

As you can see, this is a typical security setup for Windows 2000. You can use the Add and Remove buttons to add or remove groups or individual users. Notice that the list of permissions are those that you'd associate with message handling. Clicking Advanced will display a list of detailed security settings that you can use to control the precise way that an individual or group interacts with the queue.

CREATING A LISTENER/PLAYER APPLICATION

There are a number of ways to create a listener/player application when working with MSMQ. I chose the application approach for this chapter since it allows us to do some things that a service or component wouldn't allow. For one thing, using the application approach allows us to suspend processing as needed to see the message in the queue and determine how it's put together.

This example relies on a dialog-based application. We're going to create the application shell in the first section that follows. Once the application shell is put together, we'll create a dialog form to display the information received from the message queue. Finally, we'll add some code to make everything work.

Creating the Listener/Player Shell

The listener/player application's main responsibility is to pick up messages from the queue, decipher their content, then display that content onscreen. With this in mind, we can display a somewhat simple dialog-based application to handle the processing requirements. The application won't need any test pushbuttons or things of that nature because the user won't be interacting with the application, except to view the results of message transfers. The following procedure will help you create the test application:

1. Use the File | New command to display the New dialog box shown here.

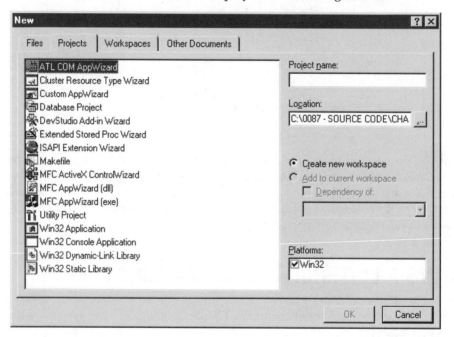

2. Highlight the MFC AppWizard (exe) option, type **MSMQMon** in the Project Name field, then click OK. You'll see the MFC AppWizard - Step 1 dialog box shown here.

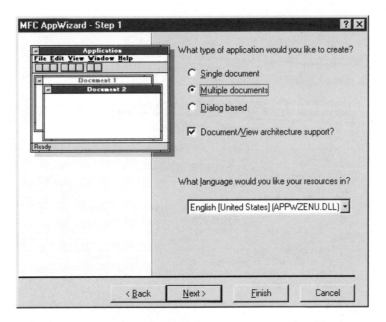

3. Choose the Dialog Based option, then click Next. You'll see the MFC
    AppWizard - Step 2 of 4 dialog box shown here. This is where you choose
    application appearance options like the title bar text and whether the
    application will include an About Box.

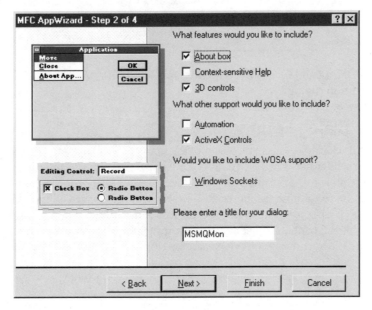

4. Uncheck the About Box option. Type **MSMQ Monitor** in the "Please enter a title for your dialog" field.

5. Click Finish. You'll see a New Project Information dialog box like the one shown here.

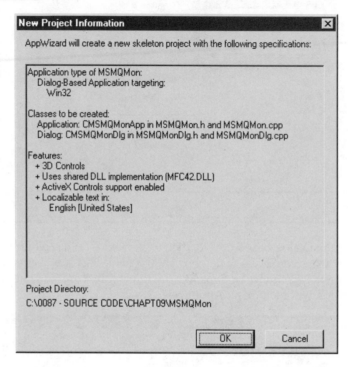

6. Click OK. Visual C++ will create the application for you and display the initial application dialog box.

Designing the Dialog Form

The form for this example will display four of the many MSMQ message fields. These are the four fields that will either change with every message or are under the direct control of the sending program for this example. The fields you use in a real-world example will depend on the application requirements. Figure 9-3 shows what the form will look like. Notice that there aren't any user configurable controls on this form—they're all used for display purposes only. Table 9-2 contains a list of control settings for this example. This table also contains a list of memory variables or event handlers for each control as appropriate.

Adding Playback Code

It's time to add some code to the monitoring program. In this case, we're going to modify the way that an existing function, OnInitDialog(), works. The program will run, but

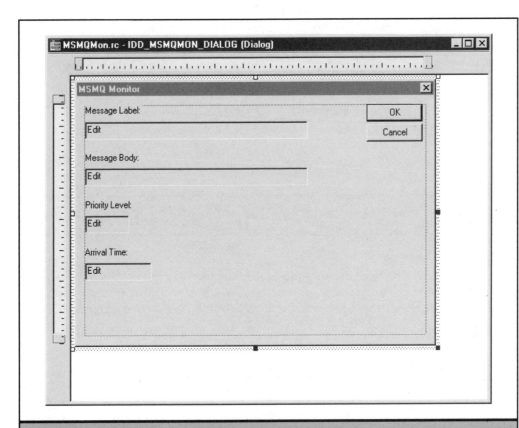

Figure 9-3. The example uses a simple test form

ID	Setting	Value	Member Variable or Event-Handler Name
IDC_MSG_LABEL	Size	200 × 14	m_msgLabel (CEdit)
	Tab stop	Unchecked	
	Read-only	Checked	
IDC_MSG_BODY	Size	200 × 14	m_msgBody (CEdit)
	Tab stop	Unchecked	
	Read-only	Checked	
IDC_PRIORITY	Size	40 × 14	m_priority (CEdit)

Table 9-2. Queued Component Test Application Control Settings

ID	Setting	Value	Member Variable or Event-Handler Name
	Tab stop	Unchecked	
	Read-only	Checked	
IDC_ARRIVAL_TIME	Size	80 × 14	m_arrivalTime (CEdit)
	Tab stop	Unchecked	
	Read-only	Checked	

Table 9-2.   Queued Component Test Application Control Settings *(continued)*

won't display anything until there's a message in the message queue. Once the program detects a message in the message queue, the dialog box will display the information within the message. Listing 9-1 shows the changes you'll need to make in bold.

```
BOOL CMSMQMonDlg::OnInitDialog()
{
CString oError;      // Error data.
CString oText;       // Message text elements.

    CDialog::OnInitDialog();

    // Set the icon for this dialog.  The framework does this automatically
    // when the application's main window is not a dialog
    SetIcon(m_hIcon, TRUE);          // Set big icon
    SetIcon(m_hIcon, FALSE);         // Set small icon

// Initialize the COM environment.
CoInitialize(NULL);

    try
{
// Always create the Queue Information and Queue
// structures within the try...catch block.
IMSMQQueueInfoPtr    qInfo("MSMQ.MSMQQueueInfo");
IMSMQQueuePtr        qObject;
IMSMQMessagePtr      qMessage("MSMQ.MSMQMessage");

        // Begin by filling out the queue structure.
qInfo->PathName = ".\\TestQueue";
qInfo->Label = "Test Queue";
```

```
        // Create the queue if necessary.
try
{
qInfo->Create();
}
catch (_com_error comerr)
{
// Check the return value.
HRESULT hr = comerr.Error();

        // No problem if the queue already exists; otherwise,
// throw an error.
if (hr != MQ_ERROR_QUEUE_EXISTS)
{
throw comerr;
}
}

        // Open the queue for use.
qObject = qInfo->Open(MQ_RECEIVE_ACCESS, MQ_DENY_NONE);

        // Wait an infinite amount of time to receive any messages.
qMessage = qObject->Receive();


        // Create dialog content from the message.
m_msgLabel.SetWindowText(qMessage->Label);

        oText = _bstr_t(qMessage->Body).copy();
m_msgBody.SetWindowText(oText);

        itoa(qMessage->Priority, oText.GetBuffer(2), 10);
oText.ReleaseBuffer(-1);
m_priority.SetWindowText(oText);

        oText = _bstr_t(qMessage->ArrivedTime).copy();
m_arrivalTime.SetWindowText(oText);

        // Close the queue once we're finished.
qObject->Close();

    }

    // Display the error information.
catch (_com_error comerr)
{
HRESULT hr = comerr.Error();
ltoa(hr, oError.GetBuffer(20), 10);
```

```
oError.ReleaseBuffer(-1);
AfxMessageBox("unexpected error: " + oError);
}

    // Uninitialize the COM environment.
CoUninitialize();

    return TRUE;  // return TRUE  unless you set the focus to a control
}
```

As you can see, this application performs quite a few tasks getting and displaying a message from MSMQ. The first thing we need to do is initialize the COM environment. If you were creating a component, rather than an application, you'd need to set the component up as a multithreaded apartment to provide adequate processing capability. However, for the purposes of this example, the default settings will work just fine.

The next thing you'll notice is that the code begins execution within a try...catch block. The reason is simple: there isn't any guarantee that you'll find a message in the message queue to process. There are also other problems the application could experience. It's essential to set up this type of structure whenever you work with MSMQ.

One of the first things we need to do is create the three objects used to work with queues: a queue information object, the queue itself, and a message. All three of these objects are created within the try...catch block since there isn't any guarantee the host machine will provide access to the required ActiveX controls.

Accessing the queue comes next. Part of this process is to create the queue information object, then check to make sure the queue actually exists using the Create() method. If the queue already exists, then there isn't a problem. Otherwise, we need to throw an error message based on the error message returned by MSMQ. The final step is to open the queue and place a pointer to it in the qObject object.

Receiving a message comes next. The Receive() method can be set to wait a specified time before returning, or you can simply allow it to wait until there's a message in the queue to process as we've done here. When the Receive() method does return, the code places the resulting message in the qMessage object. Note that using the Receive() method also removes the message from the queue.

Now that we have a message to work with, it's time to look at some of the techniques you'll need to interact with the message fields. As you can see from the code, the message label is fairly straightforward—it's always text. This is the same information that appears as the message title within the message queue. All we need to do is place the label in a CString and display it in the dialog box.

Microsoft couldn't assume very much about some parts of the message. For example, the message body could contain text, but it could just as easily contain numeric values or another object. As a result, Microsoft uses a variant data type for the message body. The fact that there are few guarantees about certain types of data means that you'll have to perform some unusual data-handling tasks when you work with the message data. We'll use a special operator on the message body, _bstr_t, which encapsulates the BSTR data type. You'll use the copy() method of the _bstr_t object to actually retrieve the BSTR value from the message body.

The Priority message property is a simple long integer. Since the priority value ranges from 0 to 7, we can use the itoa() function to convert it from a number to a string. The one caveat here is that you need to release the CString buffer on oText before you use it for any other operation. Using a value of -1 removes all of the dead space within the variable.

Working with the ArrivedTime message property presents some interesting challenges. The Microsoft documentation lists this property as a data variant data type. Unfortunately, the value appears to be incompatible with the CTime class. This means you have to convert it to a string first, then construct a new CTime object using the string, rather than convert the value directly. Since we really didn't need to manipulate the individual time values, the sample code doesn't show the CTime value. However, it does show how to perform the string conversion using the same _bstr_t object that we used previously for the message body.

The final step of actual message processing is to close the queue. Make absolutely certain you perform this step or MSMQ will assume that the queue is open. As of this writing, it doesn't appear that MSMQ will detect when an application leaves the queue open, which means that MSMQ won't automatically close the connection. As a result of the open queue, your application could create a resource leak that will eventually cause system performance and stability problems. Fortunately, Windows 2000 should eventually detect the loss of an errant component and close the associated resources.

We're finally back to the catch part of the original try...catch structure. You'd normally place some type of retry code in this section of the application or make an event log entry as we did in Chapter 8. For the purposes of this example, I simply converted the error number to a string, then displayed a message box showing what error occurred.

The final step is to uninitialize the COM environment. Using CoUninitialize() is important for all of the usual reasons in this case. It releases resources that were locked by the thread and unloads any unneeded DLLs. However, in this case, it also severs any connections between the client and server for the purpose of processing messages. Given that a connection uses resources on both the client and server, it's very important to release them before the application exits.

At this point, the code for this example is essentially complete. We'll also need to import the MSMQ ActiveX controls for this example. These controls are found in the MQOA.DLL file in the System32 folder. The following addition to the MSMQMonDlg.CPP file will allow your application to use the MSMQ ActiveX controls:

```
// Required for message queue ActiveX support.
#import "mqoa.dll" no_namespace
```

Using the #import Directive

The #import directive comes in handy when you have an ActiveX control that contains a type library (or a type library by itself). You can use the #import directive with DLL (or derivatives like the OCX), EXE, TLB, and ODL files. In the example in this chapter, we're using the #import directive to add the ActiveX controls found in the MQOA.DLL file to the application.

There are quite a few attributes that you can use with the #import directive. In the case of this example, we're using the no_namespace attribute to prevent the namespace information for the MQOA.DLL file from appearing in the application's IDL file. (The application doesn't require an IDL file and there isn't any point in generating an IDL file as a result of importing the MQOA.DLL file.)

Using the #import directive always results in the addition of two files to your application source, both of which have the same name as the imported file or type library. The first is called the primary header. It contains seven different data sections that all work together to define the interface to the ActiveX controls as shown here. (The primary header elements must appear in the order shown.)

1. A file heading that consists of boilerplate information. The heading normally contains an #include statement for COMDEF.H and a list of any macros used within the header.

2. Forward references and typedefs, including data structures.

3. Smart pointer declarations of the methods within the type library. This is the main section of the header file and tells the application which methods the type library contains. Using these smart pointer declarations eliminates the need to use IUnknown interface methods to learn about and then use the other interfaces within the type library. It also eliminates the needs to call CoCreateInstance() for each new object.

4. Various typeinfo declarations. This section includes class definitions and other items that expose the individual typeinfo items.

5. GUID definitions similar to those that are normally generated by MIDL. This includes interface names in the form CLSID_CoClass and IID_Interface. This is an optional header section, but it's normally included.

6. An #include statement for the secondary header. This file has the same name as the ActiveX control or type library file, with a TLI file extension.

7. A file footer that consists of boilerplate information. In most cases, this section consists of a single statement, #pragma pack(pop).

The secondary header contains the actual method declarations. Looking through this file can be very instructional because you can learn more about how the type library functions. In addition, you can often find hidden methods using this technique. Finally, a lot of the Microsoft documentation is geared toward Visual Basic users. Browsing this file can help you create Visual C++ specific implementations of Visual Basic routines that are found in the Microsoft documentation.

CREATING A TEST APPLICATION

The listener/player application is ready to go. All you need to do is start it and the application will sit in the background waiting for a message to appear in the message queue. Of course, we still don't have an application to send messages to the queue. That's what we'll do in this section of the chapter—create an application capable of sending new messages to the message queue.

We'll use the same three-step approach in this section of the chapter that we used in the previous section to build the example application. The first section will create the application shell. Next, we'll add some controls to the application's dialog form. Finally, we'll add code to make the controls functional.

Creating the Test Application Shell

The test application's main responsibility is to generate messages for the queue. With this in mind, we can display a somewhat simple dialog-based application to handle the processing requirements. The following procedure will help you create the test application:

1. Use the File | New command to display the New dialog box.

2. Highlight the MFC AppWizard (exe) option, type **MSMQTest** in the Project Name field, then click OK. You'll see the MFC AppWizard - Step 1 dialog box.

3. Choose the Dialog Based option, then click Next. You'll see the MFC AppWizard - Step 2 of 4 dialog box shown here. This is where you choose application appearance options like the title bar text and whether the application will include an About Box.

4. Uncheck the About Box option. Type **MSMQ Test Application** in the "Please enter a title for your dialog" field.

5. Click Finish. You'll see a New Project Information dialog box like the one shown here.

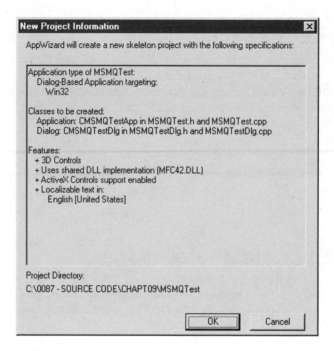

6. Click OK. Visual C++ will create the application for you and display the initial application dialog.

Designing the Test Application Dialog Form

The form for this example will provide input for three of the many MSMQ message fields. These are the three fields that you'll normally change no matter what kind of application you create. The fields you use in a real-world example will depend on the application requirements. For example, our test application doesn't do anything with any of the encryption or transactional fields of the message. Figure 9-4 shows what the form will look like. As anticipated, there are two edit boxes for changing the message values, a combo box for changing the message priority, and a Test pushbutton that will allow us to actually send the message to the queue. Table 9-3 contains a list of control settings for this

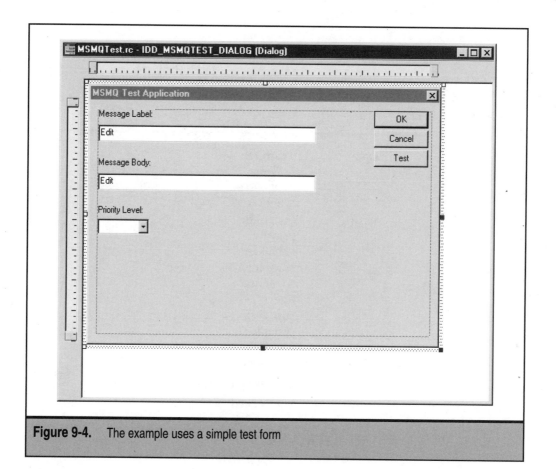

Figure 9-4.   The example uses a simple test form

example. This table also contains a list of memory variables or event handlers for each control, as appropriate.

The combo box may require a little special tweaking to get it to work properly. Normally, the drop-down displays a scroll bar unless you resize the drop-down area. To do this, click on the combo box's down arrow and you'll see a drop-down appear like the one shown in Figure 9-5. Just drag the bottom of this drop-down to match the size of the text you want to display.

ID	Setting	Value	Member Variable or Event-Handler Name
IDC_MSG_LABEL	Size	200 × 14	m_msgLabel (CEdit)
IDC_MSG_BODY	Size	200 ×14	m_msgBody (CEdit)
IDC_PRIORITY	Size	48 × 12	m_priority (CComboBox)
	Data	0 through 7, Press CTRL-RETURN between each of the priority values to place it on a separate line. Make sure you provide only values 0 through 7.	
	Sort	Unchecked	
	Vertical scroll	Unchecked	
	Drop-down list box size	48 × 115	
IDC_TEST	Caption	Text	OnTest()

Table 9-3. Queued Component Test Application Control Settings

Adding the Test Code

It's time to add some code to our test application. Listing 9-2 shows the code that you'll need to add to the OnTest() method to make it functional. Even though some of the code

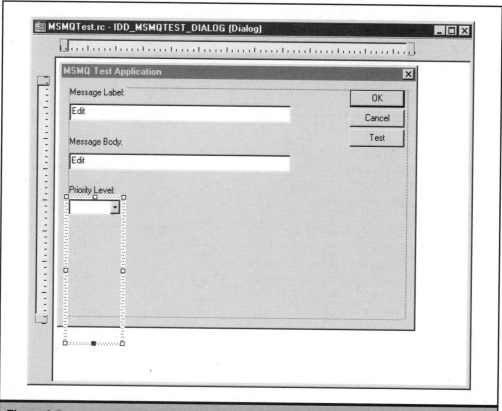

Figure 9-5.   The drop-down list box may require a little extra sizing

looks similar to the code we used for receiving messages, be very careful in entering this code since there are some distinct differences between sending and receiving messages.

```
void CMSMQTestDlg::OnTest()
{
    CString oError; // Error data.
    CString oText;  // Message text elements.

    // Initialize the COM environment.
    CoInitialize(NULL);

    try
    {
        // Always create the Queue Information and Queue
```

```
    // structures within the try...catch block.
    IMSMQQueueInfoPtr    qInfo("MSMQ.MSMQQueueInfo");
    IMSMQQueuePtr        qObject;
    IMSMQMessagePtr      qMessage("MSMQ.MSMQMessage");

    // Begin by filling out the queue structure.
    qInfo->PathName = ".\\TestQueue";
    qInfo->Label = "Test Queue";

    // Create the queue if necessary.
    try
    {
        qInfo->Create();
    }
    catch (_com_error comerr)
    {
        // Check the return value.
        HRESULT hr = comerr.Error();

        // No problem if the queue already exists; otherwise,
        // throw an error.
        if (hr != MQ_ERROR_QUEUE_EXISTS)
        {
            throw comerr;
        }
    }

    // Open the queue for use.
    qObject = qInfo->Open(MQ_SEND_ACCESS, MQ_DENY_NONE);

    // Format and send the message.

    m_msgBody.GetWindowText(oText.GetBuffer(80), 80);
    oText.ReleaseBuffer(-1);
    qMessage->Body = oText.GetBuffer(80);

    m_msgLabel.GetWindowText(oText.GetBuffer(80), 80);
    oText.ReleaseBuffer(-1);
    qMessage->Label = oText.GetBuffer(80);

    m_priority.GetWindowText(oText);
    qMessage->Priority = atoi(oText.GetBuffer(2));
    oText.ReleaseBuffer(-1);
```

```
    qMessage->SenderIdType = MQMSG_SENDERID_TYPE_SID;

    qMessage->Send(qObject);

    // Close the queue once we're finished.
    qObject->Close();

  }

  // Display the error information.
  catch (_com_error comerr)
  {
    HRESULT hr = comerr.Error();
    ltoa(hr, oError.GetBuffer(20), 10);
    oError.ReleaseBuffer(-1);
    AfxMessageBox("unexpected error: ");
  }

  // Uninitialize the COM environment.
  CoUninitialize();
}
```

The first part of this code is about the same as the message reception code shown in Listing 9-1. The code begins by initializing the COM environment. It then proceeds to create the required variables and open the queue. Again, you must be sure to create the MSMQ-specific objects within the try...catch structure since there are more than a few possible problems that your application could encounter.

One of the first differences that you'll notice is that we don't need to do anything with the queue object once the queue is open and ready to receive messages. Receiving messages requires direct interaction with the queue, while sending messages is part of the message object's functionality. Notice that we also open the queue for sending rather than receiving messages. In most cases, there isn't a good reason to open the message queue for simultaneous sending and receiving—an application usually performs just one of the two tasks.

Once the queue is open, the code can begin filling out the message. At a minimum, you should provide a message body and label as shown in the example. Since we know that the message body will contain a string, there isn't any additional code for working with the message body in this case. However, the message body can contain a wealth of other data types, so it's important to realize that the same code could place an integer, date, or other information within the message body, along with certain types of persistable objects.

Two special entries for this example are the setting of the priority and the addition of a sender identification type. The priority value is an integer between 0 and 7 (inclusive). A value of 0 gives the message the highest possible priority, while a value of 7 is the lowest possible priority. We'll see in a few moments that the priority is an important part of the message-processing mechanism, and you really need to set it for every message.

There are two different sender identification types you can use with a message. MQMSG_SENDERID_TYPE_SID sets the message's sender ID to the user's security identifier (SID). Since the SID is unique for every user, there's never a chance that a message will get misidentified using this technique. The other choice is to set this value to MQMSG_SENDERID_TYPE_NONE, which means that there won't be any user identification associated with the message. Telling MSMQ that you want to attach a user identity to the message normally means that MSMQ will perform some type of validation to positively identify the person or entity that sent the message.

Sending the message is relatively easy. All you need to do is use the message object's Send() method. Notice that the queue object is provided as an argument for the Send() method, which makes sense since you have to tell MSMQ which queue to use to store the message. It's important that you open the queue for send access or you'll see an error at this point in your code (the rather ambiguous message provided by MSMQ won't really tell you much about the source of the error, so this is one place to look for possible problems).

The OnTest() method completes its work by closing the queue and uninitializing the COM environment. There are some situations in which a message you send may not appear in the queue until the queue is actually closed, so closing the queue is an important step.

As with the listener/player application, we're using the MSMQ ActiveX controls located in the MQOA.DLL file in the System32 folder. You'll need to add a reference to this file at the top of the MSMQTestDlg.CPP file, as shown here:

```
// Required for message queue ActiveX support.
#import "mqoa.dll" no_namespace
```

TESTING THE APPLICATION

Testing this application is relatively easy if you have everything set up in advance. The problem is that the MSMQ environment isn't really all that simple to set up. What should be a fairly easy application type to test actually turns out to be relatively difficult to test for several reasons, the most important of which is the interaction of the various application elements over network cabling.

The first test step is to get a message in the test queue. There are actually two parts to this test. The first is the ability of the application to create the queue if it isn't already present. The message has to have somewhere to go, which means that the queue must be in place prior to sending the message. The second part of the first test is to ensure that the message actually gets in the queue. You have to verify that the message not only gets into the queue, but that it contains the information that you expect it to. For this reason, you'll probably want to conduct initial application tests without any encryption or other security measures in place. Sending the message in plaintext will allow you to find which part of the application is responsible for any corruption much faster than if you send the message in encrypted form and can't read it in the queue.

The second test step is to ensure that the receiving application works. I built a simple application, in this case, to test the ability of the listener/player to detect the message and read its contents. You'll probably want to perform the same step in any production development situation to keep the transmission sequence simple. Once the communication path and associated queues have been tested, you can begin to add complexity to the applications involved. This means converting any listener/player into a component or service.

Checking Out the Message

It's time to perform the first phase of the testing the process. Run the MSMQTest application, type some values in each of the three data fields, then click Test. You won't see any action from the application at this point, but something should happen. Open the Computer Management MMC snap-in and find the Public Queues folder. Highlight this folder and you should see a display similar to the one shown in Figure 9-6.

Notice that the Public Queues folder shows a testqueue entry, which is the name of the text queue for our application. Also notice that this queue has a single message in it, which is what you should have if you clicked Test only once. If you look at the code in Listing 9-2, you'll notice that the test queue should have a label of Test Queue. Part of checking communication with the queue is to see if the label appears as it should.

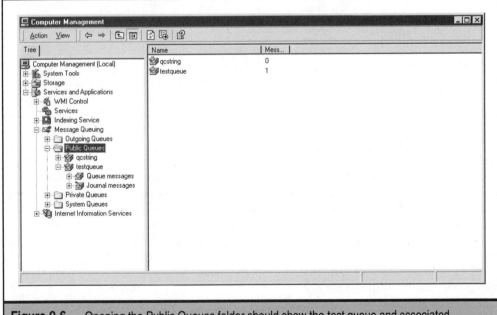

Figure 9-6.   Opening the Public Queues folder should show the test queue and associated message count

Right-click the testqueue entry, then choose Properties from the context menu. You'll see a testqueue Properties dialog box like the one shown here.

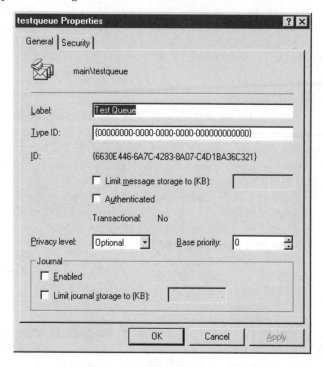

As you can see, the Label field of the testqueue Properties dialog box does indeed contain a value of Test Queue. You can change any of the other fields in this dialog box using various queue object properties, just as we set the Label field value for this example. The point is that when you create a queue from within the application, it should have all values set just as you'd set them manually when creating the queue from Computer Management.

At this point, you should generate four or five additional messages at a variety of priorities so that you can see how the queue handles messages. Highlight the Queue messages folder that's beneath the testqueue folder. Figure 9-7 shows a typical example of the results you should get from trying out various priorities. Notice that this list is in priority order—you could easily sort it by any of the other columns as well.

There are a few additional points of interest that you should consider at this point. The first thing you should see is that the Size column refers to the size of the text within the message, not the size of the entire message. This column will tell you the size of the body of the message and can help you find messages that contain more data than an application could normally handle.

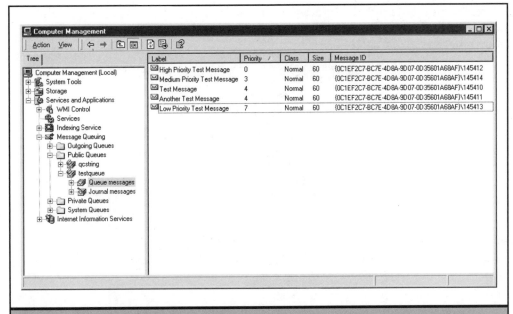

Figure 9-7. The Queue Messages folder will contain the messages that applications send to the queue

The Message ID column identifies the message in two ways. First, it tells you which machine sent the message. The GUID at the first part of the message identifies a unique machine on the network. The second half of the message ID contains the number of the message for that queue. The combination of the two identification parts gives each message a unique ID that you can sort on to determine which users are working with the queue the most.

As previously stated, all of the messages in the queue right now have a Class of Normal. That's because they were all generated by our test application. If this was a response queue, you might see other message classes, depending on the kind of message sent by either the server-side component or Queue Manager.

At this point, it might be interesting to look at one of the messages. Double-click one of the messages in the queue and you'll see a dialog box similar to the one shown here.

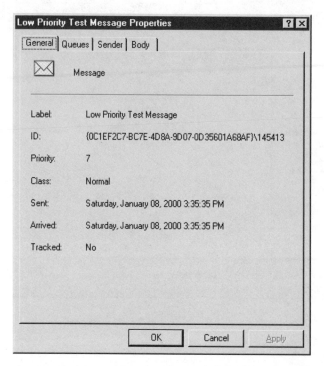

As you can see, the General tab starts out with essentially the same information as the entry in Computer Management. The Sent and Arrived fields tell you when the application sent the message and when it was received by the queue. A large difference in time here can indicate problems if the client isn't operating in disconnected mode. While the Sent and Arrived fields won't be precisely the same in some cases, they should at least be close. If they aren't, you may have some kind of latency problem with your network. The Tracked field simply tells you whether MSMQ is tracking the progress of the message as it traverses the network.

Every message will affect at least one queue—the one you're sending it to. However, messages can affect more than just the queue that the application sent them to. Look at the Queues tab and you'll see a display similar to the one shown here.

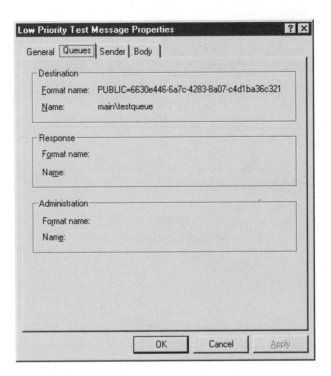

There are three queues that the message will report. The first is the queue that the application specified as a final destination. If you decide to get a response from MSMQ about the message's final destination, then this tab will also have an entry for the Response queue. Finally, any kind of tracking requires an entry in the Administration queue. We didn't tell the application to create a journal entry for this message or to track it in any way, so there aren't any entries in these two additional queue fields. Every queue entry contains the GUID for the queue, along with the fully qualified path for the queue. This allows you to determine the precise locations of all copies of the message on the network.

It's time to look at the message sender information. Click on the Sender tab and you'll see a display similar to the one shown here.

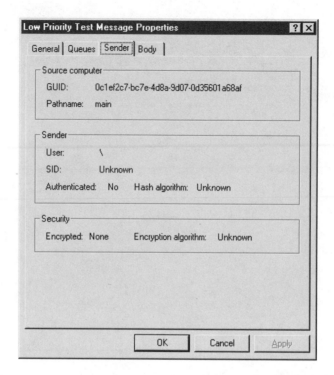

No matter how you send a message, the Source computer information will always get filled out. This information includes the GUID of the source computer, along with the source computer name. Note that the Pathname field contains the name of the computer only, it doesn't contain the fully qualified domain name for the source computer.

If you'll remember from Listing 9-2, we requested that MSMQ supply the SID of the user that sent the message. It turns out that there's a little quirk with this particular entry that isn't really explained in the Microsoft documentation. You must request message authentication before this set of values will get filled out for the message. Since we didn't specify any form of authentication, MSMQ placed the message in the queue with an unknown user. Notice that the Authenticated field is set to No and that the Hash Algorithm field is set to Unknown.

The final set of fields on the Sender tab deals with message security. Again, since we didn't include any security for this message, MSMQ hasn't filled this area out. The Security area tells you whether the message is encrypted or not and at what level. Fortunately, the entries in this section tend to be generic and don't compromise the integrity of the message in any way.

It's finally time to look at the body of the message. You'll definitely want to use plaintext for the first phase of testing so that you can see any problems with the message body before it gets encrypted. Once the message body gets encrypted, it doesn't even pay to look at the Body tab because all you'll see is gibberish. Here's a typical example of a message body in plaintext.

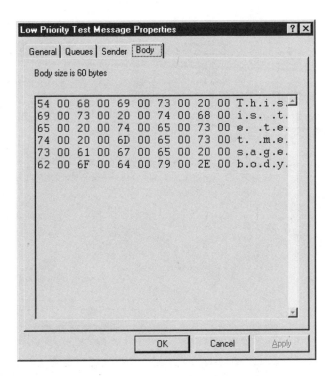

There's an interesting problem with this particular dialog box. Notice that the text gets cut off on the right side, yet there aren't any scroll bars to work with. You can reposition the text by clicking within the body text area and moving the arrow keys. At some point, the text will become visible so that you can see the contents of the message.

Viewing the Message Output

Getting the message into the queue and verifying that it's correct is actually the hard part of the testing process. What you'll want to do next is start the MSMQMon application that we created earlier. Figure 9-8 shows some typical output from the application.

There's an interesting anomaly that you should notice at this point. MSMQ gave us what is documented as the lowest-priority message in the queue to process first (priority 7). It appears from the example that priority 7 is actually the highest priority. Either the Microsoft documentation is wrong or there's something wrong with the queue setup in this example. Unfortunately, no one at Microsoft would comment about this apparent priority problem. The messages always appear to get retrieved in the opposite order, with 7 being the highest priority and 0 being the lowest priority. Needless to say, you'll want to test out potential problems like this as part of your application development process, which is one of the reasons why we ran this test application in the first place.

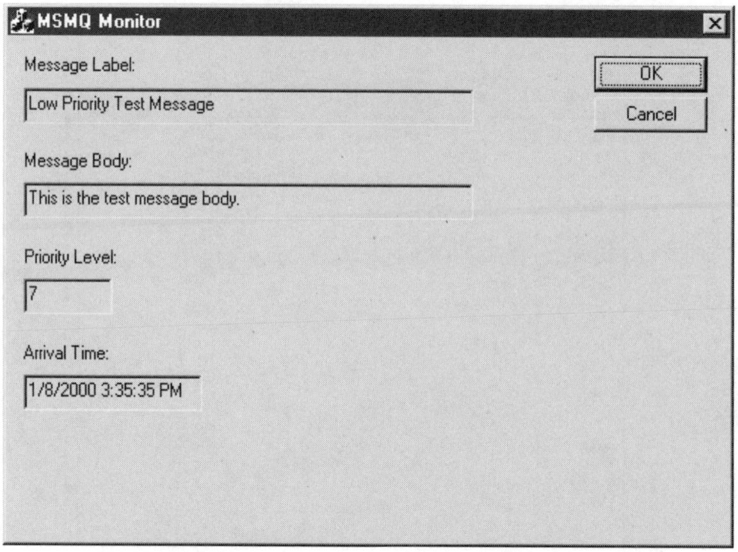

Figure 9-8. The MSMQ Monitor application will retrieve the messages placed in the queue

MSMQ ADMINISTRATIVE ISSUES

As a developer, you'll find that you need to perform certain kinds of administrative tasks, at least during the development process. We've already looked at a few of these issues throughout the chapter. For example, you need to know how to create and configure new queues as needed. It's also important to know how to read the messages that your application creates and determine if there's any problem with them. The following sections will touch on a few additional issues that you need to be aware of. None of them are earth shattering, but it's handy to know about them so that you can fully test and maintain the applications you create.

Basics of Queue Management

There are times during the course of working with a complex application that it would be nice to have some status information about the queues that you're dealing with. Unfortunately, the Computer Management MMC snap-in doesn't provide much in the way of quick documentation. However, you can create a quick overview of the queues on a certain machine using the Export List command on the context menu for the various folders in Message Queuing. Selecting this option will display a Save As dialog box that you can use to export a list of entries at that level. Here's a typical example of entries exported at the Public Queues level.

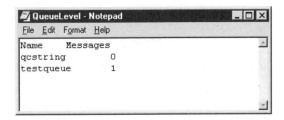

The exported list doesn't provide you with very much information, but it does provide the names of the queues that are currently in use and the number of messages that each queue contains. This is enough information, in most cases, to at least track the ebb and flow of message traffic on the network and determine if messages are moving along as anticipated. You can use this snapshot of the queue state to detect when certain events happened. For example, these snapshots could tell you when a component is getting overloaded or even stops working.

Sometimes you'll need to clean out a test queue. It might get filled with messages that you'd rather not have in place. All you need to do to clear the messages is right-click either the Queue messages or Journal messages folder and choose Purge from the context menu. Unfortunately, this is an all or nothing proposition—Computer Management doesn't provide any method for removing just one problematic message.

Some of you might be new to MMC and not know that Microsoft generally provides more display columns than you see by default. This is true of the various queues. By default you'll see the Label, Priority, Size, Class, and Message ID fields of the message. However, you can configure the display to show more than just these fields (or eliminate some of the fields if you don't want to see them). Right-click the Queue messages or Journal messages folder, then choose View | Choose Columns from the context menu. You'll see a Modify Columns dialog box like the one shown here.

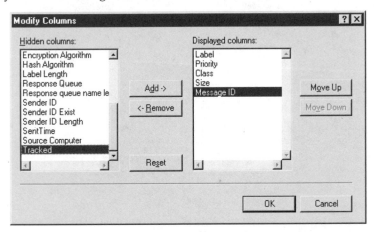

Obviously, the columns you get to choose from depend on the kinds of information presented at the level that you're looking at. The queue level is one area where you get a lot of choice. A good selection of columns at this level can definitely help your troubleshooting efforts because you won't have to open messages individually to see certain types of information.

Dead Letter Messages Queue

Checking the Dead letter messages queue (or the dead letter queue associated with your application) might seem like an obvious thing to do, but because the dead letter queue is in a different place from the main queues for your application, you might not think to do it. After a while, the dead letter queue can fill with messages and slow system performance. There are a number of false indicators that you can get when this occurs, none of which will seem very obvious at the time. For example, in one case an application reported security errors when the Dead letter messages queue overflowed with messages. In short, if you're having a weird application problem, check for some nonobvious problems with an overfilled Dead letter messages queue.

Checking the Event Viewer

COM+ doesn't always display error messages that you can use to detect problems in your application. In fact, there are several situations in which your application will appear to work just fine (no errors returned from the calls), but there will still be a problem. If you don't think to look in the Event Viewer, you might miss the information required to fix the problem. For example, there are situations when the Windows 2000 default recorder will report problems, yet you'll never see them at the application level. Here's a typical example of such a problem.

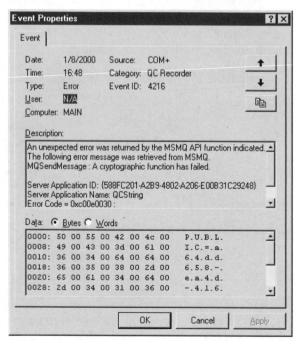

At first, you may question why Microsoft would take this approach. Consider for a moment that like the components executing on your server, Microsoft can't assume the application is still around to receive an error message. It's also in poor taste to display error messages on the server, since you can't be sure that the network administrator will find them anytime soon. As a result, the only place the Microsoft could report some types of MSMQ application errors is within the Event Viewer. The point of this whole section is that the Event Viewer will normally contain some kind of useful information in those situations where it appears the application is working, but you're not getting the desired results. It pays to check the Event Viewer when you're not sure if an application is succeeding or not.

CHAPTER 10

Working in Disconnected Mode

Today's business environment is becoming more complex and competitive by the second. In days past, it was often enough for an employee on the road to check in once a week with new sales information. Many customers today expect delivery in a week, not just the submission of the order. As a result, the road warrior has an increasing need for direct contact with the company on a daily basis and an easy method for getting orders in the company database.

Disconnected applications answer one of the most pressing needs of the road warrior—the ability to work wherever and whenever time permits, even without a connection to the company server. In times past, the road warrior was a slave to a corporate connection. Today, with a little judicious programming, the road warrior can work offline as well. No, the application won't provide complete access to everything the company has to offer with a dedicated connection, but the application can behave well enough to allow a majority of the employee's work to take place offline while on the road.

Internet Security Issues for Disconnected Applications

No matter where you turn today, someone is talking about some type of Internet security issue. Protecting your data is an extremely important consideration when working with COM+ applications. Just having the technology available for creating a disconnected application that will work whether the user has a connection to the server or not isn't the complete story—you need to consider the security of the data transferred between the client and the server as well.

Data encryption is the most commonly used method to ensure data integrity today. An encrypted message offers a secure way to transfer data between the client and server, because any tampering by a third party will be detected at the receiving end. In addition, data encryption makes it very difficult for a third party to view the information in the message containing the application data.

However, data encryption doesn't come without a price. What if the client machine has a virus? If you use complete data encryption from machine to machine, then there's little opportunity for third-party virus scanners to do their job in protecting the machine as a whole. The virus can get through without much of a challenge because a virus scanner can't see within the encrypted message. In short, it's usually too late to do anything about the virus if you send the message from "desktop to desktop" in encrypted form.

One of the ways to get around this problem is to encrypt application data at the client's desktop and decrypt it at the network firewall. Once the data reaches the firewall, there's little chance that a third party could look at the application data, making it secure from outsiders at the very least. Unfortunately, this solution isn't perfect either in some situations. For example, the threat of data tampering might be just as great within the company as without. You may want to ensure that the application data is completely protected from end to end.

Setting up a virtual private network (VPN) helps mitigate some of these concerns, but still falls short in many situations. In sum, it's important to carefully weigh the data safeguards you put in place. A solution to one problem may actually create several new ones that are harder to fix.

Fortunately, there are groups that are working on this problem as I write this. For example, the International Computer Security Association (ICSA) is working with firewall vendors in an attempt to find a solution to this problem. In addition, this group ensures that the vendors who secure their firewall product using IP Security provide the proper level of integration, reducing your reliance on a single vendor solution. You can find out more about ICSA (formerly the National Computer Security Association) at http://www.icsa.net/.

This chapter is going to look at a very simple disconnected application. We'll use the new Queued Component features offered by Windows 2000. These features are designed to allow applications to work in disconnected mode, with a maximum of application functionality retained—at least as much as can be offered by one-way communication.

The first section of the chapter will look at the disconnected application as a whole. We'll answer the question, "What makes a disconnected application functionally different from other application types you've created in the past?" It might be tempting to say that a disconnected application is simply an MSMQ application design. However, when you compare the application in Chapter 9 to the one in this chapter, you'll see that the two application types are completely different, even though they use the same underlying technology.

Once we've defined how the application will work, we'll create a server-side component in the second section of the chapter. This component isn't designed to amaze your friends—it's a very simple component. The whole object of this example is to show how to use Queued Components, rather than concentrate on the vagaries of complex component design.

Part of the creation process will be to install the component. This is one area where working with Queued Components is different than what you've done in the past. There are additional settings to make when installing the component. In addition, you'll want to look for some new MSMQ entries as the result of using the new settings. In short, at least part of the process of using Queued Components is to ensure that the application gets set up for use correctly in the first place.

The third section of this chapter will look at the application itself. We'll create a basic application that will look very much like many of the applications you've created in the past. The main difference is in the way that the application calls upon the server-side component for services. We'll be exploring a different method of accomplishing this task than the CoCreateInstance() calls that you've used in the past.

The fourth and fifth sections of the chapter will look at the two modes of testing required for this application: connected mode and disconnected mode. In a perfectly designed disconnected application, the user shouldn't see any physical application differences in either mode. The application should work the same in both environments. The major difference should be in the amount of data available to the user. In other words, the application will need to present some "data not available" messages when working in disconnected mode, nothing more.

The final section of the chapter is going to look at the various kinds of log entries that you'll see when working with a disconnected application. The point of these log entries is to help the network administrator to maintain contact with the user on the road. Unlike a standard desktop application, the disconnected application doesn't have a dedicated server connection. This means you'll have to resort to other techniques for seeing trends in application usage and for detecting potential application problems.

DEFINING THE APPLICATION

In Chapter 9, we talked about the methods required to create an MSMQ-specific application. This application would most likely work with few changes on both Windows 2000 and Windows NT (with the latest option pack installed). It relies on what have become more or less standard MSMQ ActiveX controls. We could have also created the application using standard API calls. However, that application required you to design with MSMQ from the very outset. You can't use the technique in Chapter 9 to create an application that begins as a standard COM application, then ends up using MSMQ later on.

Part of the problem with the techniques we talked about in Chapter 9 is that not every application out there will need full MSMQ support all of the time. There are a lot of applications that will begin life as a standard desktop application, then move to a laptop sometime in the future as more employees hit the road. That's the very situation that we'll address in this chapter: one where an application begins life as a standard desktop application, then moves on to become something more, something distributed.

TIP: It usually pays to have a function-by-function detailed schematic of your application before you begin the process of redesigning it for distributed use. Knowing which functions can work offline and which can't is a big plus because then you can easily analyze which application features are good candidates for offline processing. You may be surprised to find that the majority of most applications can work in an offline mode with very little loss of functionality. In addition, some application features can be redesigned in such a way that they'll easily work with a download of part of the company database to the client machine prior to severing the connection with the server. For example, you could download to the laptop a list of just the customers that the employee will visit during a road trip.

At this point, you may be saying to yourself that there isn't any way to accomplish this task because of the limitations for working with MSMQ. There aren't any magic bullets when it comes to computer work. No matter what you do, MSMQ provides one-way communication and that's it. If your application requires two-way communication for every feature, then it simply isn't a good candidate for the MSMQ way of dealing with distributed applications. In fact, it probably isn't a good candidate for any type of distributed application format because working in a distributed environment implies working in situations where there may be no connection to the server for the client to use. Working offline is one of the things that every distributed application must accommodate in some way. Fortunately, while many applications do require two-way communication to accomplish some tasks, there's usually some number of tasks (like data entry) that can be accomplished offline. As a developer, you need to separate the features of your application into those that can work offline and those that can't.

The following sections of the chapter are going to help you better understand what you'll need to know when working with Queued Components in a distributed application environment. The most important idea that we'll talk about in the sections that follow is the fact that you can convert existing desktop applications to a distributed environment with relative ease and little loss of functionality. However, these changes don't come for free—you still need to make some hard decisions on how things will work and what types of functionality loss are acceptable in a distributed environment. More importantly, you'll need to decide what kinds of data to store in a "buffer database" locally, what kinds of changes to allow to that database, and how much data to store locally.

The first section will hit the question of desktop versus distributed application development head-on. We'll talk about application conversion in general. This section will answer the major question that most of you have: Given a generic desktop application, what do you need to convert it to distributed use with Queued Components?

NOTE: This chapter assumes that many of you will be performing various types of conversions from the desktop to the distributed environment as more employees work offsite for various reasons. Using MSMQ on new applications makes sense because you can design all of the queue mechanics from the very outset of application development. However, Queued Components is a much better choice for application conversions because you can accomplish most of your goals with very little redesign. The bottom line is that using MSMQ directly is more flexible and results in applications that are better performance-tuned. On the other hand, using Queued Components shortens the development cycle and requires little in the way of up-front programming—the only things you really need to worry about are some rules in the way the functions are designed to interact with the outside world.

The second section is going to look at a very important element of the Queued Component picture—the default recorder, listener, and player provided by Windows 2000. It's because of these three components that Queued Component applications can work in the first place. You always need a recorder, listener, and player for every MSMQ application. In the past, Microsoft forced you to develop your own components to perform these tasks or include the required code within the client application (as we did in Chapter 9). It was later found that much of the recorder, listener, and playback code is the same—it doesn't vary much from application to application unless that application has some special need. That's where the idea for Queued Components comes into play. You can create many applications that rely on MSMQ without creating the three components required to work with MSMQ as long as your application follows certain rules.

The third section of the chapter is going to be very application-specific. We're going to look at application flow for the example application in this chapter. Hopefully, looking at the way this application is designed will help you design your own applications and convert others to distributed use. More importantly, comparing this application to the one in Chapter 9 should help you understand the major differences between standard MSMQ and Queued Components. You'll see that from an overview perspective, both are about the same. The real difference between the two is how communication with a queue is accomplished.

Desktop versus Distributed Development

The first thing you'll always need to consider when working with Queued Components or MSMQ is the difference between the desktop and the distributed environment—at least in the way that Windows 2000 handles things. There are some standard changes you'll need to make to any desktop application that you want to modify for distributed application use. For one thing, any function that will use Queued Component services must be designed with outgoing parameters only. This means that you can use the [in] IDL attribute, but not the [out], [out, retval], or [in, out] attributes. No matter what other kind of magic your application performs, data communication is still one-way. However, even though there will be a change from the application perspective (and the way you develop the application code), the user will likely still be in a position of not seeing much change in the way the application works.

Let's look at the method calls first. Here's a typical example of a method call to a component on the server:

```
[id(1), helpstring("method EnterItem")]
HRESULT EnterItem(
    [in] int iCustomerID,
    [in, out] int *iOrderID,
    [in, out] int *iItemNumber);
```

Normally, you'd get the customer ID as part of a previous call, so the application would know this information is correct. There isn't any reason to request the server to send the information back since there isn't much chance that it's incorrect. However, in a standard desktop application, you'd want some type of verification that the order ID and the item number are correct. This means asking the server to provide verification in some way. The distributed form of the same method would probably look like this:

```
[id(1), helpstring("method EnterItem")]
HRESULT EnterItem(
    [in] int iCustomerID,
```

```
[in] int iOrderID,
[in] int iItemNumber);
```

The application now has to assume that the order ID is correct. Perhaps the client application was issued a block of order IDs before the user left the company. The point is that there isn't any connection to the server for verification purposes, and you must pass all data by value rather than by reference. The same holds true for the item number. The local application has to assume that this item exists, at least at the time that the user is sending the order information to the local queue.

Obviously, the inability to send data both ways is going to impact how the application deals with data transfer to some extent. Consider an application feature that you normally use for order entry. In a desktop environment, you'd normally enter a customer ID, then wait for the computer to fill out the customer information onscreen using the contents of the customer database on the server. Once the customer information is filled in, the user will normally start adding items to the list of items that the customer wants to purchase. Every time the user wants to enter a new item, the item is first looked up in the catalog; then, the appropriate part number and other information are added to the customer order. Finally, the user will submit the order to the server. Since the server has been intimately involved in the data entry process, it can place the order information directly into the database without checking it for accuracy in most cases (it depends on how much freedom you give the order taker in adding new information).

The distributed version of the same function will work essentially the same if you do some preplanning. The user will still enter a customer ID. However, in this case the application first checks to see if there's a server connection. If there isn't a server connection, the application will use a local customer database that the user downloaded prior to leaving the office for the road. (The customer information download could also occur automatically as long as the company maintains a centralized appointment database—the names of the customers that the user will visit during the trip have to come from somewhere.) Obviously, since the user doesn't have access to the entire company database while on the road, there are going to be times when he or she will enter a customer ID and the computer won't be able to supply the appropriate information. In this case, the application needs to allow the user to enter the customer information manually. Obviously, this information will require some form of checking when the user uploads orders from the road or when they get back to the office.

Entering items that the customer wants to purchase comes next and this is actually the hardest part of the conversion. It's unlikely that a laptop could hold the entire catalog of most companies—unless that company sells very few items. So, what you really need to do is download a subset of the catalog to the user's machine. A good subset may include popular items that the company sells, new items that may not appear in the paper catalog, the items that the customer has ordered in the past, and items that the employee feels the customer may order based on past sales. In short, you need to cover as many of the items that have a high likelihood of getting purchased as possible without overloading the user's machine. There are still going to be situations when the user won't have the required catalog information in the local database, which means that you'll still need to allow for manual entries based on the paper catalog that the employee has hopefully taken along on the trip.

Submitting the order means placing it in the local queue, in most cases, since the employee probably won't have a live connection during order entry. This means that any instant gratification features, like getting order or fulfillment numbers, won't work. There isn't any connection to the server, so the server can't supply this information. What you may need to do is provide some type of customer feedback when the order does arrive at the company—perhaps a postcard in the mail saying the order is on the way. Another method of handling this problem is to provide a response queue for the application. The server-side component could send positive responses to the client application each time the client made contact to upload new orders.

The order will also need scrupulous checks for inconsistencies and errors. Remember that the distributed application will need to allow the user more freedom in entering the data, which means that you'll need to perform more checks before the order is entered in the company database.

Understanding the Default COM+ Recorder, Listener, and Player

One of the main features that allows Windows 2000 to provide Queued Component functionality is the use of a default recorder, listener, and player. You'll find these components on any computer that has MSMQ installed since MSMQ is a prerequisite for using Queued Components. Figure 10-1 shows how the default COM+ recorder, listener, and player appear in the COM+ Utilities folder of the Component Services MMC snap-in.

Remember that these are public components that are available to anyone to use. You can't set any security on these components or restrict their use in any way. In fact, if you open the Properties dialog box for one of these components, you'll find that there aren't any settings that you can configure. Every behavior of these components is determined in advance, which means that there's a real lack of flexibility for a given application. Unfortunately, when you think about it, these components would have to act in this fashion given the generic set of services that they provide to Windows 2000 as a whole. Part of the cost of working with Queued Components, then, is the fact that you have less control over how the various components used by your application will react and who will gain access over them.

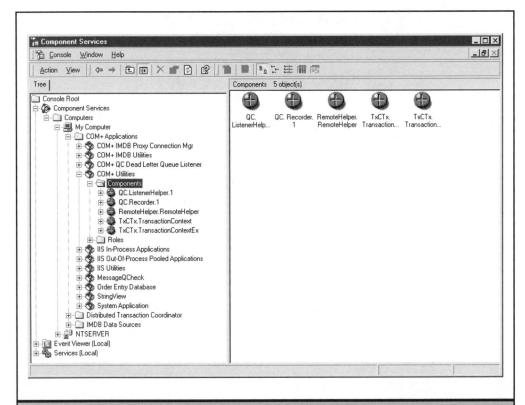

Figure 10-1.   Component Services shows some of the underlying components used for Queued
Component applications

One of the limitations you'll experience when using Queued Components is that you must use security—every message is authenticated whether you want Windows 2000 to do it or not. This particular issue can cause problems when working with a local workstation and server setup since you have to be logged in to a domain, in most cases, to get the required certificate for authentication. If you don't have a certificate, you'll see a very ambiguous message in the Event Viewer, like the one shown here.

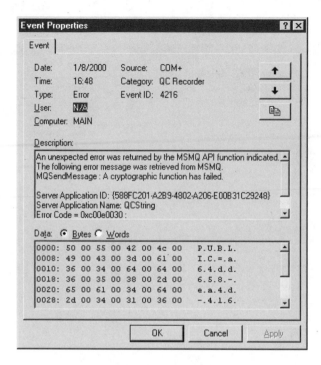

The only way to avoid this problem is to open the Message Queuing applet in the Control Panel and select the Security tab. You'll see a dialog box similar to the one shown here.

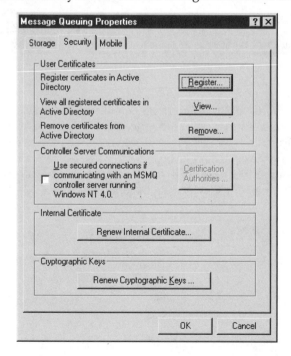

Click View. You'll see a Personal Certificates dialog box like the one shown here.

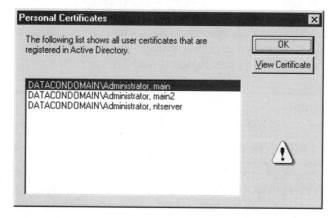

If you don't see a list of certificates, then Queued Components won't work on your machine. You'll get an error message every time. What this means is that you'll need to work with users who plan to go on the road and ensure that their machines have a certificate installed locally before they leave. You'll want to ensure that the certificate is valid by highlighting and clicking View Certificate. Here's an example of a valid certificate.

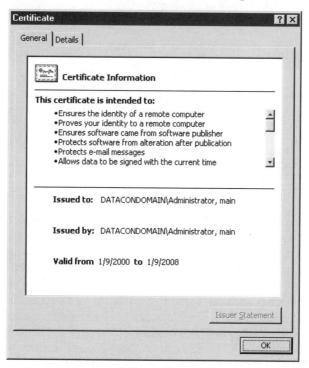

NOTE: Later in the chapter we'll create a component named QCOne that will get installed in a COM+ application named QCString. We'll access the QCString application (and the QCOne component that it contains) using the QCTest application that will also appear later in the chapter. You really don't need to know how the component and application work right now, but it's important to understand what output you should expect from them. That's why I'm talking about them now instead of waiting until we create them later.

Stopping the QCString application and viewing the messages produced by the QCTest application reveal that the user is indeed authenticated. Here's a sample message produced by QCTest.

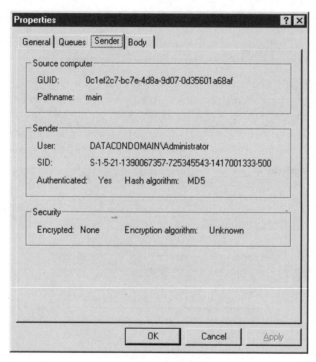

According to the Microsoft documentation, you should be able to override the authentication requirement using the AuthLevel parameter. This parameter doesn't appear to work in the current product. In short, a Queued Component application will always require authenticated messages, so you need to provide the proper certificates to make this feature work. Since the error message for this particular problem is rather cryptic, you'll want to check the security settings anytime the user has problems sending a message.

The recorder, listener, and player components do work automatically. You'll need to make special application settings to activate them, but once the settings are made, everything is very much automatic. We'll look at the required settings as the chapter progresses. For the most part, you'll find that setting up a Queued Component application requires only a little more time than a standard application requires. However, since much of the functionality of a Queued Component application is determined by application settings, you'll want to be sure that any help desk personnel know how to make the required setting changes. Otherwise, you may spend a lot of time tracking down "ghost errors" as the result of unauthorized user changes to the system configuration.

An Overview of Application Data Flow

Application data flow for this example is somewhat difficult to understand without first understanding the role of the default recorder, listener, and player. You don't specifically add support for these features anywhere in your application. In fact, as we'll see in a few moments, there isn't any mention of these components anywhere in the code. The fact remains that these three components (actually two physical entities since the listener and player are combined into one component) play an important part in getting data from one point to another on your network. Figure 10-2 shows how data flows in this example. Notice that we're not relying on a custom recorder, listener, or player for this example. Queued Components provides everything needed for us to develop an application.

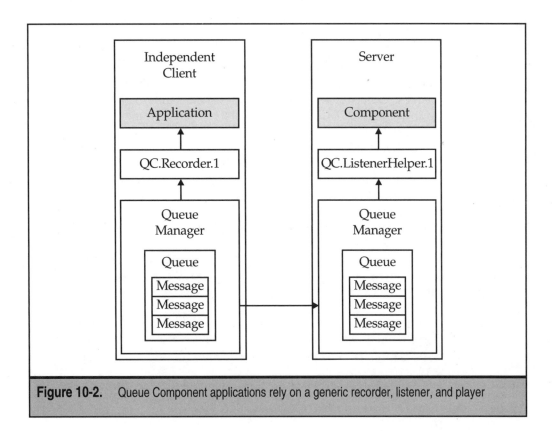

Figure 10-2.   Queue Component applications rely on a generic recorder, listener, and player

As with the Chapter 9 example, I've highlighted the elements that we'll create in the chapter. Notice that we really aren't touching anything that has to do with MSMQ. You'll find that working with Queued Components is a completely different experience from working with MSMQ when it comes to development time. All we'll need to create are an application to send the data (not the whole message, but the body of the message) and a component to receive the data. It's this fact that makes Queued Component applications such an attractive prospect for most developers.

An Overview of the Interface Definition Language (IDL) Output

Anyone who works with COM long enough will need to learn about the Interface Definition Language (IDL). Essentially, this is a method of describing the methods that make up an interface. You'll find the IDL for any component within the IDL file of the same name as the project. The Microsoft IDL (MIDL) compiler accepts the input from the IDL file and creates several output files that we'll talk about later in this sidebar.

The concept of an IDL isn't something that Microsoft came up with. It's actually part of the Open Software Foundation's (OSF) Distributed Computing Environment (DCE) specification. IDL was originally designed to meet the needs of remote procedure calls (RPCs), which should be familiar to most of you since the Distributed Component Object Model (DCOM) is based on RPC. In short, IDL isn't something new or foreign—it's actually based on a well-established standard.

The Microsoft version of IDL does contain some extensions in the form of the Object Definition Language (ODL) that were originally contained in a separate file. MIDL 3.0 combined the original IDL with Microsoft's ODL so that developers would only have one file to worry about. While IDL is concerned with interfaces, ODL is concerned with the IDispatch interface. If you declare only an interface within the IDL file, the MIDL will create the client proxy, server stub, and a header file that are required for an RPC interface. On the other hand, if you add the [object] attributed to the interface description, then MIDL will generate the files required for a COM interface.

A COM interface requires a few more files than an RPC interface. Obviously, you'll still need the proxy and stub modules. (These modules can be combined with the component if you select the required option during component creation.) You'll also get a proxy interface file (<component name>_p.C), a type definition header file (<component name>.H), an interface globally unique identifier (GUID) file (<component name>_i.C), and the proxy DLL file (DLLDATA.C). The compiled form of all of this code is the <component name>.TLB (type library) file.

CREATING AND INSTALLING THE COMPONENT

It's finally time to begin working on the component that will form one half of our Queued Component application. All that this component is going to do is receive a message string from the sending application and display it in a dialog box. Normally, you wouldn't create a component like the one we'll work with in this chapter. The whole purpose of this example is to show how simple Queued Component development can be.

The following sections divide the task of creating the component into three sections. The first section will help you create the component shell. All we'll need for this example is a small ATL component that contains a simple object. The second section will add a modicum of code to the simple component. The third section will show you how to install the component within Component Services. This is actually the meat and potatoes section because the process of defining a Queued Component application is different than other kinds of applications you may have created in the past.

Creating the Component Shell

As previously mentioned, we're going to use a very simple component for this example to ensure that the component programming doesn't get in the way of seeing the big picture. The following procedure will help you create the component shell required for this example. It assumes that you've already started Visual C++.

1. Use the File | New command to display the New dialog box shown here.

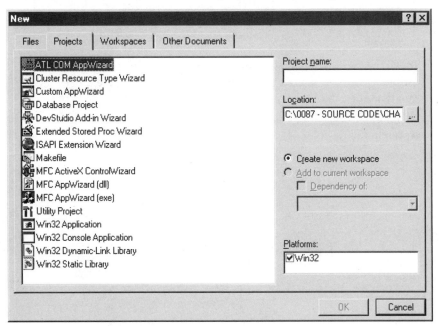

2. Highlight the ATL COM AppWizard entry. Type a name for the component. The example uses a name of QCOne, although you could use any name you desire.

3. Click OK. You'll see the ATL COM AppWizard - Step 1 of 1 dialog box shown here.

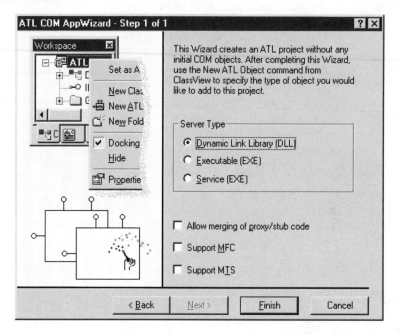

4. Check the "Allow merging of proxy/stub code" and Support MFC options. Since this is going to be a COM+ application, we'll use the Dynamic Link Library (DLL) server type.

5. Click Finish. You'll see the New Project Information dialog box shown here.

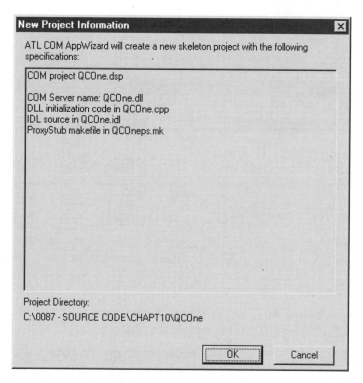

New Project Information
ATL COM AppWizard will create a new skeleton project with the following specifications:

COM project QCOne.dsp

COM Server name: QCOne.dll
DLL initialization code in QCOne.cpp
IDL source in QCOne.idl
ProxyStub makefile in QCOneps.mk

Project Directory:
C:\0087 - SOURCE CODE\CHAPT10\QCOne

OK   Cancel

6. Click OK. Visual C++ will create the new component shell for you. At this point, we'll need to add a new ATL object that will contain the code that the client application will call later.

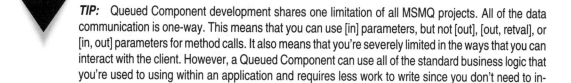

TIP: Queued Component development shares one limitation of all MSMQ projects. All of the data communication is one-way. This means that you can use [in] parameters, but not [out], [out, retval], or [in, out] parameters for method calls. It also means that you're severely limited in the ways that you can interact with the client. However, a Queued Component can use all of the standard business logic that you're used to using within an application and requires less work to write since you don't need to include either a recorder or a listener as part of the application.

7. Right-click the QCOne Classes folder found on the ClassView tab of the Workspace window, then choose New ATL Object from the context menu. You'll see the ATL Object Wizard dialog box shown here.

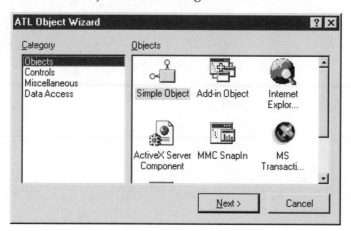

8. Highlight the Simple Object option, then click Next. You'll see the ATL Object Wizard Properties dialog box shown here.

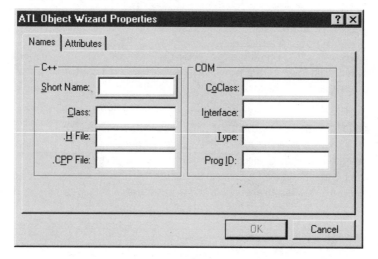

9. Type **DlgString** in the Short Name field. Visual C++ will automatically fill in the other field values for you.

10. Click the Attributes tab. Check the Free Threaded Marshaler option, and then click OK. Visual C++ will create the new object for you.

11. Right-click the IDlgString interface entry on the ClassView tab of the Workspace window, then choose Add Method from the context menu. You'll see the Add Method to Interface dialog box shown here.

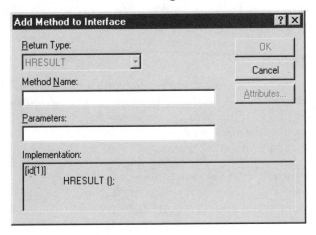

12. Type ShowString in the Method Name field. Type **[in] BSTR bstrDlgString** in the Parameters field. Click OK. At this point, the component shell is ready to go. All we need is the one method to demonstrate the power of Queued Components.

Adding Some Component Code

It's time to add some code to the one and only method for this component. Listing 10-1 shows the code you'll use to make the component functional.

```
STDMETHODIMP CDlgString::ShowString(BSTR bstrDlgString)
{
    CString oDlgString; // Converted dialog box string.

    AFX_MANAGE_STATE(AfxGetStaticModuleState())

    // Perform the string conversion.
    USES_CONVERSION;
    oDlgString = OLE2T(bstrDlgString);

    // Display the string.
    AfxMessageBox(oDlgString);

    return S_OK;
}
```

Notice that the code isn't very complicated. All that this example does is receive a BSTR as input, convert it to a CString, then display the result in a dialog box. Even though we're returning a value of S_OK, the client won't actually get to see it. Remember that what the client receives is an HRESULT value that shows the message to this component got recorded within the client-side queue—nothing else.

Installing the Component

The installation process for this component is a little different than what we've done in the past. We need to tell Windows 2000 that we want it to provide automatic Queued Component services for this COM+ application. However, as you'll see in the steps that follow, you don't have to queue all of the application—only the parts that can work in an offline mode get queued. The other parts of the application will work much as they normally would.

1. Open Component Services. Right-click the COM+ Applications folder and then choose New | Application from the context menu. You'll see the Welcome to the COM Application Install Wizard dialog box.

2. Click Next. You'll see the Install or Create a New Application dialog box shown here.

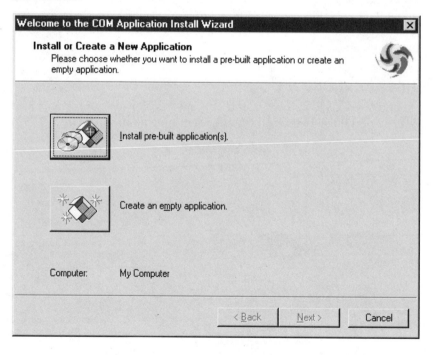

3. Click Create an Empty Application. You'll see the Create Empty Application dialog box shown here.

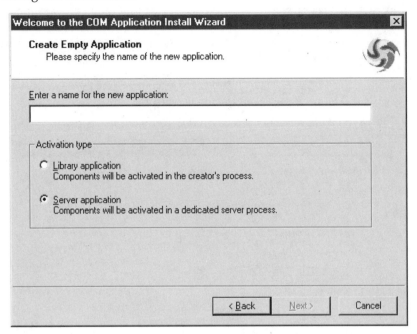

4. Type a name for the application in the "Enter a name for the new application" field. The example uses QCString for an application name.

5. Ensure that the "Server application" option is checked. We don't want the component to attempt to execute in the client environment since the client isn't guaranteed to be available when the server-side application executes.

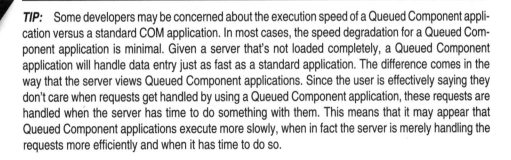

TIP: Some developers may be concerned about the execution speed of a Queued Component application versus a standard COM application. In most cases, the speed degradation for a Queued Component application is minimal. Given a server that's not loaded completely, a Queued Component application will handle data entry just as fast as a standard application. The difference comes in the way that the server views Queued Component applications. Since the user is effectively saying they don't care when requests get handled by using a Queued Component application, these requests are handled when the server has time to do something with them. This means that it may appear that Queued Component applications execute more slowly, when in fact the server is merely handling the requests more efficiently and when it has time to do so.

6. Click Next. You'll see the Set Application Identity dialog box shown here. Normally, the default user security will work fine for the application. However, this is one situation when you may want to enter a specific username and password. The reason is simple: since the client won't be available for security queries, the user can't compensate for incorrect password entries and the like. Unfortunately, the question of whether to use full security or a known good identity is a hard one to answer and should be viewed with your particular application in mind. In some cases, the security problems incurred using a known good identity just aren't worth the risks and the client request will have to be answered based upon the user's actual security.

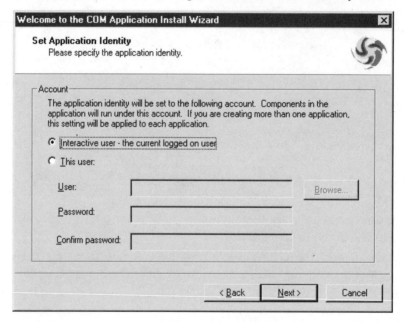

7. Click Next. You'll see a final COM AppWizard dialog box.

8. Click Finish. Windows 2000 will create the new COM+ application for you. At this point, we need to make the first Queued Component application setting.

9. Right-click the QCString entry within the COM+ Applications folder, then choose Properties from the context menu. Click the Queuing tab and you'll see some queue options like the ones shown here.

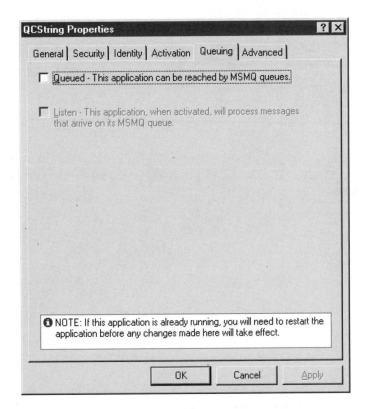

10. Check the Queued option. This represents the minimal option for working with Queued Components. It signifies that your application has been designed in such a way that it can work with queued requests. If your application also needs the services of the default listener component, then you should check the Listen option. Since our application doesn't have any listening features of its own, we'll need to check the Listen check box. It's absolutely essential that you check both boxes, or the example application won't work as anticipated.

11. Click OK. The application is now set up to use Queued Components.

How do you know that the application has been set up for Queued Component use? Open the Computer Management MMC snap-in and look at the Message Queuing entry. You should see a series of new folders like the ones shown in Figure 10-3 for the QCString application. The entry in the Public folder is where the new messages go. If a message

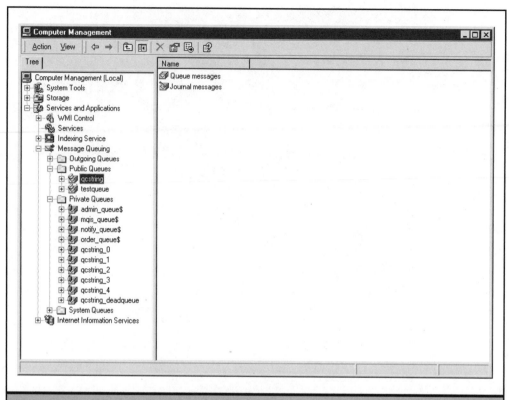

Figure 10-3.   Setting the application up for Queued Component use automatically generates the required queue folders

isn't processed for some reason, then it will get moved to the Private folder. The series of five folders here will allow COM+ to attempt to process the messages again. Each folder represents a lower level in the processing hierarchy. We've already talked about this mechanism in Chapter 5, so we won't discuss it here. However, it's nice to see the theory of Chapter 5 put into practice in this chapter.

At this point, we have an application, but we still need to add a component to the application. The next series of steps will help you install the component we created in this chapter within the QCString application, then set it up as a Queued Component application.

1. Right-click the Components folder under the QCString application in Component Services, and then choose New | Component from the context menu. You'll see the Welcome to the COM Component Install Wizard dialog box.

2. Click Next. You'll see the Import or Install a Component dialog box shown here.

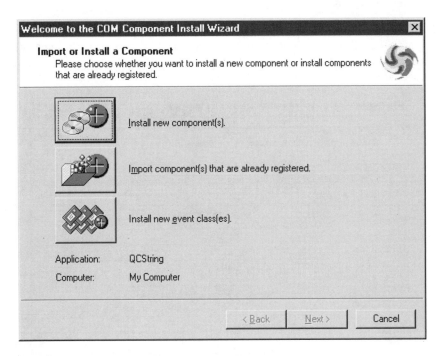

3. Click "Install new components" since we're adding a new component to this application. You'll see a Select Files to Install dialog box like the one shown here.

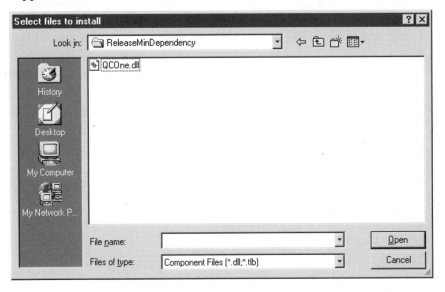

4. Locate QCOne.DLL file, highlight it, then click Open. You'll see an Install New Components dialog box similar to the one shown here. This dialog box should contain the name of the components you've defined for the module. In this case, we only have one named DlgString.

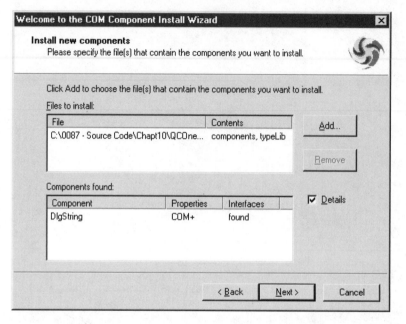

5. Click Next. You'll see a final COM Component Install Wizard dialog box.

6. Click Finish. Windows 2000 will add the new component to the QCString application for you.

7. Highlight the IDlgString interface within Component Services as shown in Figure 10-4. This is the interface that we'll be accessing in a queued mode.

8. Right-click IDlgString, then choose Properties from the context menu. Click the Queuing tab and you'll see an IDlgString Properties dialog box like the one shown here.

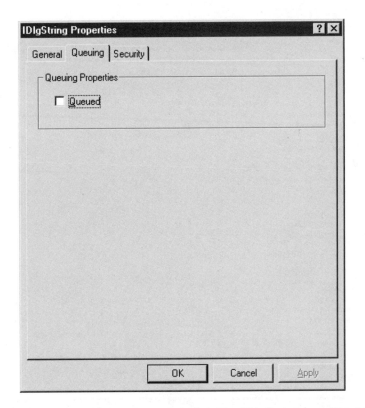

9. Check the Queued option, then click OK. The IDlgString interface is now ready for use from an application in queued mode. We need to perform one additional step—we have to start the application or it won't monitor the queue.

NOTE: If MSMQ detects that an interface contains methods that require two-way communication, it won't enable the Queued option on the Queuing tab of the interface Properties dialog box. This is the first problem to check if you think you should be able to enable queuing for a particular interface and can't. Queuing is enabled for all of an interface or none of it. You can't select specific methods, so methods that require two-way communication should appear in a separate interface. Remember that you can have mixed-mode applications where some features are queued and others aren't. Using separate interfaces for queued and nonqueued methods is one part of getting this task accomplished.

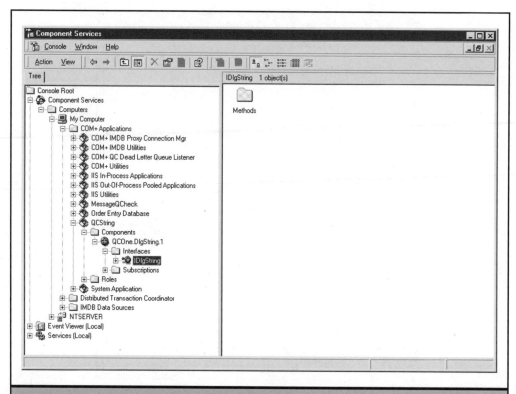

Figure 10-4.   Both the application and interfaces must be marked as queued for the Queued Component application to work properly

10. Right-click QCString, then select Start from the context menu. Let's perform one additional check to ensure that the application is actually running.

11. Highlight COM+ Applications. You should see a dialog box similar to the one shown in Figure 10-5. Look at the QCString application. The ball within the box should be rotating if the application is running. If not, recheck all of your settings, then select the QCString application again and select Start from the context menu.

CREATING A TEST APPLICATION

It's time to create the test application. Just as you had to make slight modifications to the component to make it work within a Queued Component application, you'll very likely have to make minor changes to the application as well. You won't have to make major changes to the way that the application works or any changes to the business logic that it contains. The only real difference is in how the server component gets created. Instead of using CoCreateInstance() or CoCreateInstanceEx(), you'll use the CoGetObject() function.

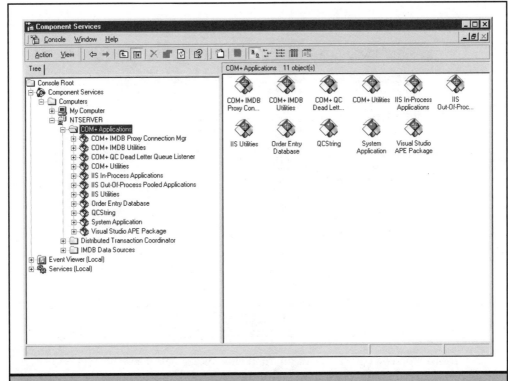

Figure 10-5.   COM+ applications look like little boxes with a ball inside—a rotating ball shows that the application has started

The CoGetObject() function is actually a little easier to use (at least from a certain perspective) than the CoCreateInstance() function, so you may find that you like using it more.

The following sections will help you create the test application. In the first section we'll create the application shell. In this case, we'll use a simple dialog-based application to do the work. The second section will show you how to create a very simple application form that we'll use to send the dialog message string to the server component. Finally, we'll add some code to make the Test button functional.

Designing the Application Shell

This is a simple dialog-based application. All we really need to do is send a message to the component so that it can display the result onscreen in the form of a dialog box. The following steps will help you create the application shell. I'll assume that you've already started Visual C++.

1. Use the File | New command to display the New dialog box.

2. Highlight the MFC AppWizard (exe) option, type QCTest in the Project Name field, then click OK. You'll see the MFC AppWizard - Step 1 dialog box shown here.

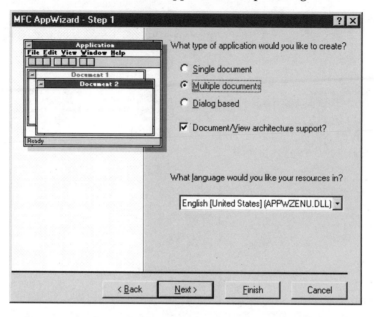

3. Choose the Dialog Based option, then click Next. You'll see the MFC .AppWizard - Step 2 of 4 dialog box shown here. This is where you choose application appearance options like the title bar text and whether the application will include an About Box.

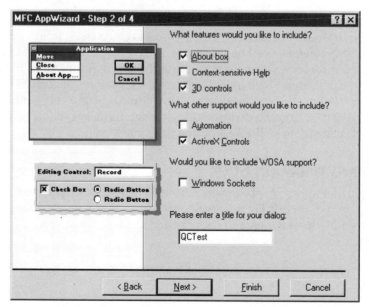

4. Uncheck the About Box option. Type **Queued Component Test Application** in the "Please enter a title for your dialog" field.

5. Click Finish. You'll see a New Project Information dialog box like the one shown here.

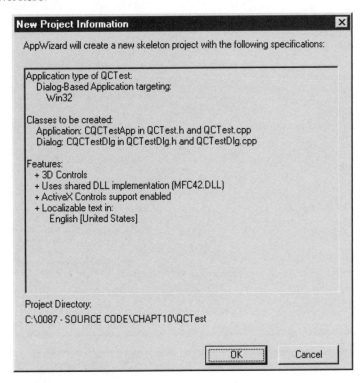

6. Click OK. Visual C++ will create the application for you and display the initial application dialog box.

Defining the Dialog Form

We'll use an extremely simple dialog box for this application. Figure 10-6 shows what it'll look like. All we need is a Test button to send a message to the component and an edit box for entering the text messages. Table 10-1 contains a list of control settings for this example. This table also contains a list of memory variables or event handlers for each control, as appropriate.

Adding Some Application Code

It's time to add some code to the OnTest() function. There really isn't anything mysterious in this code, except in the way that it creates the component. This application could be

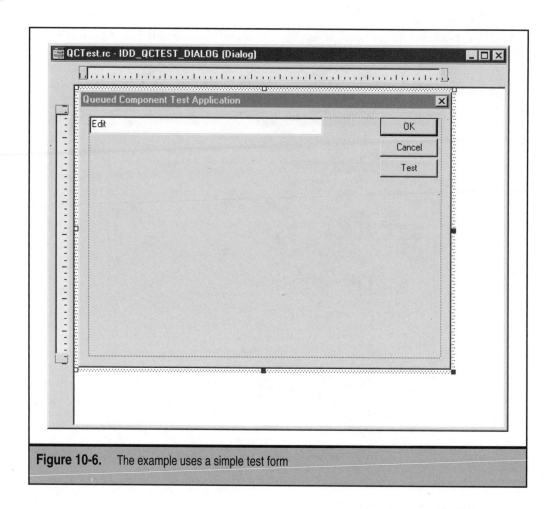

Figure 10-6. The example uses a simple test form

ID	Setting	Value	Member Variable or Event-Handler Name
IDC_DISPSTR	Size	200 × 14	m_dispStr (CEdit)
IDC_TEST	Caption	Test	OnTest()

Table 10-1. Queued Component Test Application Control Settings

used in any COM environment to send a string to a component. Listing 10-2 contains the code we'll use in this example.

```
void CQCTestDlg::OnTest()
{
    CString         oDispStr;           // Text from edit box on dialog.
    BSTR            bstrDispStr;        // Converted display string.
    IDlgString*     m_pDoTest;          // IDlgString Interface Pointer
    HRESULT         hr;                 // Result of Operations

    // Convert the first input value to a BSTR.
    m_dispStr.GetWindowText(oDispStr);
    bstrDispStr = oDispStr.AllocSysString();

    // Initialize the interface pointer.
    m_pDoTest = NULL;

    // Initialize the COM environment.
    CoInitialize(NULL);

    // Create a queued component.
    hr = CoGetObject(L"queue:ComputerName=NTServer/new:QCOne.DlgString",
                    NULL,
                    IID_IDlgString,
                    (void**) &m_pDoTest);

    // If the creation failed, exit.
    if (FAILED(hr))
    {
        if (hr == MK_E_SYNTAX)
            AfxMessageBox("The pszName parameter isn't correct.");

        if (hr == MK_E_NOOBJECT)
            AfxMessageBox("The object couldn't be found.");

        if (hr == MK_E_EXCEEDEDDEADLINE)
            AfxMessageBox("The object couldn't be created in time.");

        if (hr == MK_E_CONNECTMANUALLY)
            AfxMessageBox("The operation requires manual user input.");

        if (hr == MK_E_INTERMEDIATEINTERFACENOTSUPPORTED)
            AfxMessageBox("The object didn't support a required interface.");

        // Display the general failure message and exit.
        AfxMessageBox("Object Creation Failed");
        return;
    }

    // Send the display string to the queue.
    m_pDoTest->ShowString(bstrDispStr);
```

```
// Clean up the interface pointer.
m_pDoTest->Release();
m_pDoTest = NULL;

// Uninitialize the COM environment.
CoUninitialize();
}
```

The first task the code performs is to get the string from the dialog box and convert it into a BSTR for transmission to the component. This task involves two steps. First, the code uses the GetWindowText() method to fill out a CString. We then use AllocSysString() to convert the CString into a BSTR value.

The next two lines of code initialize the pointer to the component interface and initialize the COM environment. Any COM application would require you to perform these two steps.

The big difference from the normal COM application comes next. Notice that we're using CoGetObject() in place of CoCreateInstance() or CoCreateInstanceEx(). Unlike these other two functions, CoGetObject() relies on a string to gain the information it needs in order to create a component. There are actually two strings here that are separated by a slash (/). The first deals with the queue. You still have to tell MSMQ where to find the queue that's used to transfer data for this application. In this case, we're using a queue moniker to perform that task. The second string instructs Windows 2000 to create a new component called QCOne and gain access to the DlgString object within it. The combination of QCOne.DlgString is called the display name of the component. If you eliminated the queue string, Windows 2000 would still try to create the component for you. The queue part of the string only activates MSMQ.

Let's talk a little more about the queue moniker part of the string. Your application is automatically programmed with certain information about the queue. For example, the default queue always has the same name as the COM+ application. We saw that part of the picture earlier in the chapter when we created the COM+ application for the QCOne component. So, all you really need to do is override any default values that don't contain the correct information. In this case, we need to tell MSMQ that the QCString queue is located on a server named NTServer. There are a lot of other parameters that you can add to the queue moniker. All you need to do is separate them with commas. Table 10-2 provides a quick overview of these other parameters.

There are three additional CoGetObject() parameters. The second parameter in the list is the binding state for the component. CoGetObject() provides a default set of binding options if you don't provide any with the call. There isn't a good reason to override the default binding options when working with this kind of application, so you'll normally set this value to NULL and allow CoGetObject() to use the default binding options. The third and fourth parameters should look very familiar because they're the same parameters that you provide with any other COM call. The first is the interface ID of the interface that you want to work with. The second is a variable that will hold a pointer to the interface so that you can work with the resulting object.

Parameter Name	Functional Area	Description
AppSpecific	Message content	Allows you to add application specific information in the form of an unsigned integer to the message prior to sending it. You can use this parameter to allow for special kinds of message processing within the server-side component.
AuthLevel	Message security	Determines what level of authentication MSMQ provides for the message. An authenticated message is digitally signed and requires a user certificate. The two default values for this parameter are none and always authenticate messages. MSMQ appears to ignore this parameter in the current implementation.
ComputerName	Destination queue	Tells MSMQ the name of the machine that contains the queue for the specified object. This parameter defaults to the client machine in most cases.
Delivery	Message delivery	Determines which mode of delivery is used for the message. You have a choice between recoverable (MQMSG_DELIVERY_ RECOVERABLE) and express (MQMSG_DELIVERY_EXPRESS). The express method is faster, while the recoverable method is more reliable.
EncryptAlgorithm	Message security	Defines the method used to encrypt the message contents. The acceptable values include CALG_RC2 and CALG_RC4. MSMQ may be able to use other encryption values, depending on the capability of the underlying operating system.

Table 10-2.   Queue Moniker Parameter Listing

Parameter Name	Functional Area	Description
FormatName	Destination queue	Tells MSMQ to use a specific format name. A format name is a GUID that defines a specific queue object. You can determine the GUID for a queue by looking at the ID field on the General tab of the queue Properties dialog box.
HashAlgorithm	Message security	Defines the cryptographic hash algorithm used to encrypt the message as a whole (including the various keys sent with the message). Acceptable values for this parameter include CALG_MD2, CALG_MD4, CALG_MD5, CALG_SHA, CALG_SHA1, CALG_MAC, CALG_SSL3_SHAMD5, CALG_HMAC, and CALG_TLS1PRF.
Journal	Message delivery	Determines if a journal is used to track message flow on the various machines used to transfer it from the client to the server. The journal defaults to a setting of MQMSG_JOURNAL_ NONE, which means that MSMQ doesn't maintain a journal. You can use a value of MQMSG_DEADLETTER to track messages that get sent to the dead letter queue or MQMSG_JOURNAL to track all messages.
Label	Message content	Allows you to define a label for the message. Since a Queued Component application will attempt to process a message immediately, the usefulness of this particular feature is somewhat limited. You could, however, use it to provide special tracking information for messages that end up in the dead letter queue. The label is limited to a length of MQ_MAX_MSG_LABEL_LEN characters.

Table 10-2.   Queue Moniker Parameter Listing *(continued)*

Parameter Name	Functional Area	Description
MaxTimeToReach-Queue	Message delivery	Specifies the maximum amount of time in seconds that a message can take to reach the queue from the client. You can specify the time in seconds or use one of two default values (LONG_LIVED or INFINITE).
MaxTimeToReceive	Message delivery	Specifies the maximum amount of time in seconds that the target application can take to retrieve messages from the queue. You can specify the time in seconds or use one of two default values (LONG_LIVED or INFINITE).
PathName	Destination queue	Tells MSMQ which computer and queue to use. In this case, you must provide both a computer name and a queue name separated by two slashes (when working with C/C++). For example, PathName=MyServer\\MyQueue tells MSMQ to use the queue named MyQueue on a server named MyServer. The default is to use the default queue on the client machine.
Priority	Message delivery	Determines the message priority within the queue. You can specify any integer value between 0 and 7 inclusive. There are also default values of MQ_MIN_PRIORITY (0), MQ_MAX_PRIORITY (7), and MQ_DEFAULT_PRIORITY (3). Messages normally use the queue's default priority if you don't specify a value.
PrivLevel	Message delivery	Defines the message's privacy level. Acceptable values include MQMSG_PRIV_LEVEL_NONE, MQMSG_PRIV_LEVEL_BODY, MQMSG_PRIV_LEVEL_BODY_BASE, and MQMSG_PRIV_LEVEL_BODY_ENHANCED.

Table 10-2.   Queue Moniker Parameter Listing *(continued)*

Parameter Name	Functional Area	Description
QueueName	Destination queue	Tells MSMQ which queue to use. This parameter defaults to the queue that was created for the COM+ application on the server.
Trace	Message delivery	Determines if the message gets traced as it moves from the client to the server. Acceptable values include MQMSG_TRACE_NONE and MQMSG_SEND_ROUTE_TO_REPORT_QUEUE.

Table 10-2. Queue Moniker Parameter Listing (continued)

CoGetObject() can fail in a few ways that CoCreateInstance() can't. One of the most common failures is that the syntax of the moniker string isn't correct. Fortunately, there's a specific error number for this problem, so it's easy to determine when you've gotten things set up wrong. Since we're dealing with a distributed application, you'll also want to check for missing objects and operations that require the user to connect manually.

Once we have a pointer to the IDlgString interface, the application can send the BSTR that it created earlier. All you need to do is call the ShowString() method to perform this task.

Finally, we need to perform a little cleanup for the application. In this case, we'll release the interface and set the interface pointer variable to NULL. The last step is to uninitialize the COM environment. As you can see, there really isn't anything unusual about the way this application is put together.

Now that we've gotten the OnTest() function out of the way, there are two additional pieces of code we need to make the example work. The first is the inclusion of the header for the QCOne component. You'll add it to the top of the QCTestDlg.CPP file as shown here:

```
// Include the header for the component.
#include "..\QCOne\QCOne.h"
```

We'll also need to add the QCOne component interface description to beginning of the QCTestDlg.H file. Here's what this included code looks like:

```
// Include the test control interface information.
#include "..\QCOne\QCOne_i.c"
```

TESTING IN CONNECTED MODE

In most cases, you're going to want to test the application in connected mode first. However, because of the way that Queued Component applications work, you can actually perform the testing in two phases. First, send messages to the queue with the server-side application shut down. This will allow you to see how messages get added to the queue and can help you determine if you need to add more of the parameters shown in Table 10-2. More importantly, you can perform some analysis on various queue elements like the priority of messages that arrive from certain destinations. You may decide to handle local messages first, then those from remote locations if the queue is going to fill up during working hours.

> **TIP:**   You might initially think that the queue should remain relatively free of messages as the application runs. However, a backlog of messages isn't necessarily going to cause problems if you prioritize the messages as they arrive. Running the server 24 hours a day, even if you don't have employees who access the server at night, allows the server to work more efficiently and reduces the amount of hardware you need for message processing. Remote users are unlikely to notice if their messages get processed at night after the daytime staff has left.

Once you've checked out the queue operation, it's time to purge the queue of existing messages (so that the component doesn't have to try to process them all when you start the application). Remember that all of the queues are found in the Message Queuing folder of the Computer Management snap-in. All you need to do to purge the queue is right-click the Queue messages folder (under the QCString folder) and choose Purge from the context menu.

Start the application by right-clicking QCString in the COM+ Applications folder found in Component Services, then choose Start from the context menu. Make sure the little ball is rotating within the box. Now when you send a message using QCTest, what you'll see is a dialog box pop up on the server with the same text you typed in at the application. The point of this whole exercise is that the application really doesn't look any different than it did before and it'll be the same for the users of your application. Queued Components allow you to create applications with extended range without adding any additional functionality or really very much in the way of code.

TESTING IN DISCONNECTED MODE

Testing a disconnected application with a server connection in place only ensures that the application will work at all. It doesn't really test the application in the way that it's designed to work on the road. The problem with testing the application in disconnected mode is getting your machine in a state where it reflects what you'd expect the user on the road to have.

Up until now, we've been testing the application in a more or less direct mode. Yes, MSMQ has been involved, but we really aren't ready for disconnected testing yet. The first thing we need to do is create a proxy on the test machine that the application can send messages to. This proxy will take the place of the component on the server from the local machine's perspective. Creating a proxy is relatively easy, and the following steps will show you how:

1. Open Component Services on the server. Locate the QCString application in the COM+ Applications folder.

2. Right-click QCString, then choose Export from the context menu. You'll see a Welcome to the COM Application Export Wizard dialog box.

3. Click Next. You'll see an Application Export Information dialog box like the one shown here. This is where you'll choose the name and type of export application created. We need a proxy application, in this case, so that the installation routine will direct the QCOne requests to the server, not to the local machine.

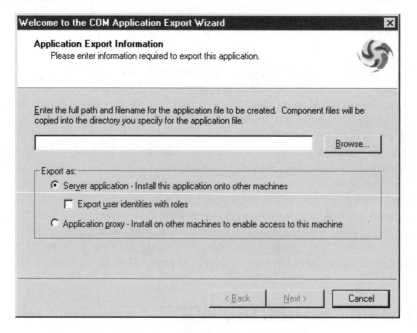

4. Click Browse. You'll see an Export Application to File dialog box like the one shown here. As you can see, I've chosen a location and name for the exported application file. (The example uses a name of QCOneInst, but you could use any name desired.) Notice that the COM Application Export Wizard automatically adds an MSI extension to the new application name.

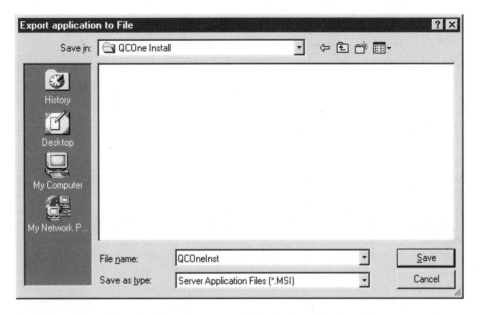

5. Click Save. You'll see the location entered in the Application Export Information dialog box.

6. Choose the Application Proxy option.

7. Click Next. You'll see a final COM Application Export Wizard dialog box.

8. Click Finish. At this point, the application you'll need is created; all you need to do is install it.

9. Locate the QCOneInst.MSI file from the client machine. Since we're installing this application to ensure that the client will work properly in disconnected mode, you must install it at the client machine.

10. Right-click QCOneInst and then choose Install from the context menu. An installation dialog box will appear for a few moments, then go away.

If you open Component Services on the client machine, at this point you'll see that there's a new application named QCString. However, this application isn't the full-fledged application found on the server—it's an application proxy. Open the QCString Properties dialog box and you'll notice that you can't change any of the application options. This application is designed to precisely replicate the server application. That's why you want to ensure that the server application is working before you create the proxy as we've done here.

There's one other small change that you'll need to make to the code for the client application. In Listing 10-2 we have several lines of code that look like this:

```
hr = CoGetObject(L"queue:ComputerName=NTServer/new:QCOne.DlgString",
                NULL,
                IID_IDlgString,
                (void**) &m_pDoTest);
```

You need to change this line of code to point to the queue on the client machine now instead of the server. All this means is removing the ComputerName parameter so that the code looks like this:

```
hr = CoGetObject(L"queue:/new:QCOne.DlgString",
                 NULL,
                 IID_IDlgString,
                 (void**) &m_pDoTest);
```

Recompile the application and ensure that it's ready to go by performing one more test with the client connected to the server. You should still see the message pop up on the server as you did before. The only thing that's changed is that the application is now ready for disconnected mode activity.

Before you begin this part of the test, you'll have to shut your machine down and disconnect any network connection. When you start the machine up again, it's going to be disconnected from the network and you'll probably see some error messages. The one message that you'll most definitely see is one that says that your machine can't be validated against the domain's list of users. This really isn't a big deal—the user on the road can't be validated either.

The first step in disconnected mode testing is to ensure that you still have access to the certificate for your machine. The way to check for this is to open the Message Queuing applet in the Control Panel. Click the Security tab. Click Register and you should still see one or more certificates. If you don't, then your machine isn't set up to work in disconnected mode and you'll have to reconnect it to the network. In short, you need to be able to support the security that MSMQ is expecting your machine to have before the test application will run. Click Cancel to close the Personal Certificates dialog box. You don't want to accidentally kill the certificate for the machine if it's installed and ready to go.

Start the QCTest application. Type a message, then click Test. It'll look like nothing has happened, but the application has stored a message locally that will get uploaded to the server when a connection is restored. Let's look at where that message got stored.

Open Computer Management, then the Message Queuing folder. You won't find the message in the Public Queues folder this time. Look in the Outgoing Queues folder (see Figure 10-7) and you'll see a queue that's used to hold the messages for our application.

There are a few things you should notice about this dialog box. The first difference between this queue folder and the folders we've used in the past is that the queue name is actually a GUID. If you compare this GUID to the GUID of the QCString queue on the server, you'll see that they're the same. The next thing you'll notice is that this queue isn't validated. That makes sense considering we don't have a connection to the server. Finally, there's a blank column called Hops. We'll see where this comes into play in a few moments.

Shut down the client machine. Reconnect the network cable. Restart the client machine again. Keep a careful eye on the server monitor. A few moments after you log back into Windows 2000, you'll see a message pop up on the server screen. The application has automatically transferred the queued message to the server and the server-side component has already acted on it. This is precisely the way a disconnected application will work in a production environment as well. The user won't see any difference in the way the application operates, and everything will happen automatically in the background.

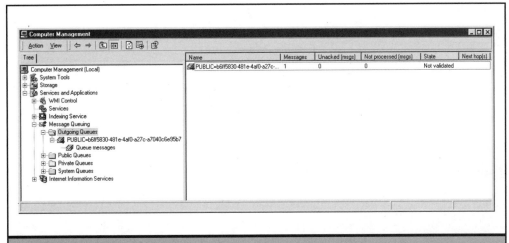

Figure 10-7. Messages that are waiting for a server connection get placed in the Outgoing Queues folder in a special folder for that application

There are a couple of final items you should look at. The first is the Outgoing Queues folder. If you look right now, you'll see that the application queue shown in Figure 10-7 is gone. Now, run the QCTest application again. Send a message to the server and look at the Outgoing Queues folder again (you may need to right-click on the dialog box and choose Refresh from the context menu to refresh the display). You'll see a new queue similar to the one shown in Figure 10-8. This is the queue that we just created with the QCTest application. However, in this case, the queue has a name in human-readable form and the Hops column will contain the IP address of the test server. Notice also that this queue is validated (connected) because we have a connection to the server.

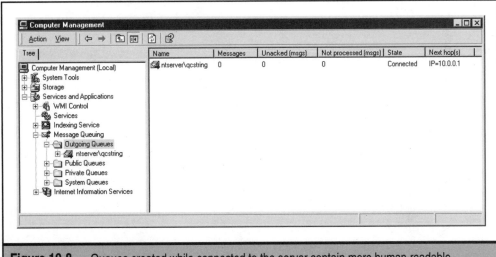

Figure 10-8. Queues created while connected to the server contain more human-readable information than those created while disconnected

GLOSSARY

This glossary has several important features you need to be aware of. First, every acronym in the entire book is listed here—even if there's a better than even chance you already know what the acronym means. This way, there isn't any doubt that you'll always find everything you need to use the book properly. The second thing you need to know is that these definitions are specific to this book. In other words, when you look through this glossary, you're seeing the words defined in the context in which they're used. This may or may not always coincide with current industry usage since the computer industry changes the meaning of words so often. Finally, the definitions here use a conversational tone in most cases. This means that they may sacrifice a bit of puritanical accuracy for the sake of better understanding.

WEB LINK: What happens if you can't find the acronym you need in the computer dictionary you just bought? Fortunately, there are at least two sites on the Internet that you can go to for help. The first is the NORUT Information Technology site at http://multimedia.itek.norut.no/ATM/atm-acronyms.html. This site is updated fairly often and provides only acronyms (another page at the same site includes a glossary). The second site is Acronym Finder. You'll find it at http://www.acronymfinder.com/. While this site isn't updated as often as the first one, it does have the advantage of providing an extremely large list of acronyms to choose from. At the time of this writing, the Acronym Finder sported 122,700 acronyms. If neither of these sites provides what you need, you may want to look at A Web of Online Dictionaries at http://www.facstaff.bucknell.edu/rbeard/diction.html. One of the interesting features of this Web site is that it provides access to more than one dictionary and in more than one language. Obviously, there are always other online solutions, many of which are free. For example, Webopedia has become one of my favorite places to visit because it provides encyclopedic coverage of many computer terms and includes links to other Web sites. You can find Webopedia at http://webopedia.internet.com/. In some cases, like Microsoft's Encarta (http://encarta.msn.com/), you'll have to pay for the support provided, but it's still worth the effort to seek these locations out to ensure that you always understand the terms used by our jargon-filled trade.

access control entry (ACE)   It defines the object rights for a single user or group. Every ACE has a header that defines the type, size, and flags for the ACE. Next comes an access mask that defines the rights a user or group has to the object. Finally, there's an entry for the user or group's security identifier (SID).

access control list (ACL)   Part of the Windows NT security API used to determine both access and monitoring properties for an object. Each ACL contains one or more access control entries (ACEs) that define the security properties for an individual or group. There are two major ACL groups: security access control list (SACL) and discretionary access control list (DACL). The SACL controls Windows NT auditing feature. The DACL controls access to the object.

access token A definition of the rights that a service or resource requestor has to the operating system. This is the data structure that tells the security system what rights a user has to access a particular object. The object's access requirements are contained in a security descriptor. In short, the security descriptor is the lock and the access token is the key.

ACE *See* access control entry

ACID An acronym commonly used to describe the four essential properties of any transaction. These properties include atomicity, consistency, isolation, and durability.

ACL *See* access control list

Active Template Library (ATL) A special set of header, source, object, and executable files created by Microsoft. The main purpose of ATL is to reduce the size and dependence of COM objects created for use in environments where memory and network bandwidth are a potential problem. For example, an ATL object won't rely on the Microsoft Foundation Classes (MFC). In many cases, the ATL executable is self-contained and doesn't rely on anything other than standard Windows core files. While ATL executable files are smaller than their MFC counterparts, they're also more complex to develop and often require the developer to write more code in order to obtain a similar result.

ActiveX Control *See* OCX

ActiveX Data Object (ADO) A local and remote database access technology that relies on OLE-DB to create the connection. ADO is a set of "wrapper" functions that make using OLE-DB and the underlying OLE-DB provider easier. ADO is designed as a replacement for DAO and as an adjunct to ODBC.

ADO *See* ActiveX Data Object

aggregate A collection of facts or figures used to create a graph. Some presentation graphic programs use these numbers to create a graph showing both the component parts and their sum. For example, the individual wedges in a pie chart represent the components; the entire pie represents their sum.

API *See* application programming interface

application programming interface (API) A method of defining a standard set of function calls and other interface elements. It usually defines the interface between a high-level language and the lower-level elements used by a device driver or operating system. The ultimate goal is to provide some type of service to an application that requires access to the operating system or device feature set.

ATL   *See* Active Template Library

AutoAbort   A new Microsoft Transaction Server (MTS) feature that automatically aborts a transaction should certain events occur (determined by the operating system and the developer). This means that a transaction is automatically rolled back (or whatever other abort logic you've provided) the instant that the connection is lost. You'd normally implement this logic within the component using the SetAbort() method.

automatic transaction enlistment   Normally, when you want to create a transactional connection to a database, you have to enlist the connection into the application's current transaction. Microsoft Transaction Server (MTS) takes care of this matter for you automatically, which reduces the amount of code required to create the application and the chance of error.

backup site controller (BSC)   This is an adjunct to the primary site controller (PSC). It maintains the current configuration information for the site, but isn't accessed unless the PSC becomes nonoperational. The BSC can also perform load balancing and other site-related tasks as an adjunct to the PSC. For example, the BSC provides load balancing for MSMQ sites with heavy message loads. While there can be only one PEC or PSC per site, you can have multiple BSCs. Each BSC will handle part of the overall message-processing load. In addition, the BSC is used for backup and recovery purposes. If a PEC or PSC goes down, then the BSC can be used to restore the current MSMQ state to a new machine.

BIN   *See* binary file extension

binary file extension (BIN)   A file that contains data or code in hexadecimal (machine code) format. This file is normally created as part of a compilation process and represents the machine form of the human-readable file.

BSC   *See* backup site controller

Causality identifier (CID)   A form of globally unique identifier (GUID) used to link the method calls between two or more machines. For example, if machine A requests that machine B activate a component, and machine B has to request that machine C activate a component first, then the calls are causally related and DCOM will generate a CID for them. The CID will remain in effect until the original call machine A created is satisfied by a return call from machine B.

CID *See* causality identifier

class ID (CLSID) A method of assigning a unique identifier to each object in the registry. Also refers to various high-level language constructs.

CLB *See* Component Load Balancing

client The recipient of data, services, or resources from a file or other server. This term can refer to a workstation or an application. The server can be another PC or an application.

CLSID *See* class ID

cluster A group of servers that are joined together in order to service the needs of a large group of clients. Access to the cluster is normally controlled through a router. Clusters are used for a wide range of activities, including load balancing.

COM *See* Component Object Model

Compensating Resource Manager (CRM) This COM+ feature allows your application to work with the Distributed Transaction Coordinator (DTC) without requiring you to create a special resource dispenser. Normally, you'd be required to create a resource dispenser for your application. Depending on the complexity of your application, the resource dispenser might not have a lot of work to do. COM+ gets rid of the extra programming requirement by providing a default resource dispenser known as the CRM. All of the "magic" required to perform resource dispenser tasks is in the special interface you add to your component. CRM accesses this interface and allows your component to vote on the outcome of a transaction based on the results of the individual transaction within the component. In short, you get all of the features of a full resource dispenser implementation without any of the work. The CRM also takes care of any recovery requirements for a failed transaction based on the log entries it makes, which means that you get automatic error recovery without any additional work.

component catalog A special-purpose database that holds descriptions of components registered on the server. An application can download these descriptions to find out more about the component and how to interact with it. In short, you no longer have to worry about where the TLB (type library) file is; your application can download the required information from a central store.

Component Load Balancing (CLB) A specialized form of load balancing that deals with the ability of COM+ applications to balance the processing load across multiple servers at the component level. CLB allows the application to perform load balancing at a finer level, which means that the processing load is better distributed across the processing elements. This also allows multiple servers to handle requests from a single client, potentially increasing data throughput by an order of magnitude.

Component Object Model (COM) A Microsoft specification for an object-oriented code and data encapsulation method and transference technique. It's the basis for technologies such as OLE (object linking and embedding) and ActiveX (the replacement name for OCXs, an object-oriented code library technology). COM is limited to local connections. Distributed Component Object Model (DCOM) is the technology used to allow data transfers and the use of OCXs within the Internet environment.

context-oriented rights A Windows security methodology that defines the way rights are assigned to component users. The rights assigned to a component flow with the context for the component. If you give a user a certain level of access to the component as a whole, then that access is provided at the method level as well unless you specifically assign the user a different set of rights at that level.

cracker A hacker (computer expert) who uses their skills for misdeeds on computer systems where they have little or no authorized access. A cracker normally possesses specialty software that allows easier access to the target network. In most cases, crackers require extensive amounts of time to actually break the security for a system before they can enter it.

CRC *See* cyclic redundancy code

CRM *See* Compensating Resource Manager

CryptoAPI *See* Cryptographic Application Programming Interface

Cryptographic Application Programming Interface (CryptoAPI)   The specification provided by Microsoft that enables software developers to add encryption technology to their applications. It uses a 128-bit encryption technology, which means that the developer can't export such applications outside the United States or Canada.

Cyclic redundancy code (CRC)   A technique used to ensure the reliability of information stored on hard drives, transported across network cabling, or others sent from one place to another. It uses a cyclic calculation to create a numeric check number. The computer performs the same calculation when it retrieves the data and compares it to the CRC. If the two match, there's no data error. Otherwise, the sending machine must either resend the data or the receiving computer must reconstruct it.

DACL   *See* discretionary access control list

DAT   *See* digital audio tape drive

data source name (DSN)   A name assigned to an Open Database Connectivity (ODBC) connection. Applications use the DSN to make the connection to the database and gain access to specific database resources like tables. The DSN always contains the name of the database server, the database, and (optionally) a resource like a query or table. OLE-DB connections may also use a DSN.

database management system (DBMS)   A method for storing and retrieving data based on tables, forms, queries, reports, fields, and other data elements. Each field represents a specific piece of data, such as an employee's last name. Records are made up of one or more fields. Each record is one complete entry in a table. A table contains one type of data, such as the names and addresses of all the employees in a company. It's composed of records (rows) and fields (columns), just like the tables you see in books. A database may contain one or more related tables. It may include a list of employees in one table, for example, and the pay records for each of those employees in a second table.

database owner (dbo)   A security entry for some database management systems (DBMSs) like SQL Server. The dbo is the person or entity that created the database originally and owns the full rights to its contents.

database pooling   A resource pooling methodology designed to increase server efficiency. When an application makes a database connection request, a preallocated connection is used from the pool. Likewise, when the database connection is severed, the connection is returned to the pool. Using connections from a preallocated pool reduces the time required to create a database connection because the resources required for the connection are already allocated.

DBMS *See* database management system

dbo *See* database owner

DCE *See* distributed computing environment

DCOM *See* Distributed Component Object Model

DDE *See* Dynamic Data Exchange

digital audio tape drive (DAT) A tape drive that uses a cassette to store data. The cassette and drive use the same technology as the audio version of the DAT drive. The internal circuitry of the drive formats the tape for use with a computer system, however. The vendor must also design the interface circuitry with computer needs in mind. DAT tapes allow you to store large amounts of information in a relatively small amount of space. Typical drive capacities range from 1.2GB to 8GB. (DDS-3 formatted drives have even higher capacities.)

Digital Signatures Initiative (DSI) A standard originated by the World Wide Web Consortium (W3C) to overcome some limitations of channel-level security. For example, channel-level security can't deal with documents and application semantics. A channel also doesn't use the Internet's bandwidth very efficiently because all the processing takes place on the Internet rather than the client or server. This standard defines a mathematical method for transferring signatures—essentially a unique representation of a specific individual or company. DSI also provides a new method for labeling security properties (PICS2) and a new format for assertions (PEP). This standard is also built on the PKCS #7 and X509.v3 standards.

disconnected applications An application that uses an intermediate storage mechanism like Microsoft Message Queue (MSMQ) to process transactions like those used for databases. A disconnected application allows the user to create one-way messages while in a disconnected state. The application automatically uploads these queued messages to the server once a connection to the server is reestablished. In all cases, disconnected applications require clients that can operate in stand-alone mode without any support from the server.

discretionary access control list (DACL) A Windows NT–specific security component. The DACL controls who can actually use the object. You can assign both groups and individual users to a specific object.

distributed authentication security service (DASS) Defines an experimental method for providing authentication services on the Internet. The goal of authentication in this case, is to verify who sent a message or request. Current password schemes have a number of problems that DASS tries to solve. For example, there's no way to verify that the sender of a password isn't impersonating someone else. DASS provides authentication services in a distributed environment. Distributed environments present special challenges because users don't log on to just one machine; they could conceivably log on to every machine on the network.

Distributed Component Object Model (DCOM) The advanced form of the Component Object Model (COM) used by the Internet. This particular format enables data transfers across the Internet or other nonlocal sources. It adds the capability to perform asynchronous as well as synchronous data transfers—which prevents the client application from becoming blocked as it waits for the server to respond. *See* COM for more details.

Distributed computing environment (DCE) A specification created by the Open Software Foundation (OSF) that defines methods for data exchange between a client and server. The remote procedure call (RPC) support built into Windows NT is compatible with the DCE specification.

Distributed interNetwork Architecture (DNA) A term used to describe Microsoft's vision of three-tier development architecture. The three tiers include the user's desktop, business logic processing on a middle-tier server, and database processing on a back-end server. DNA is used to help emphasize various features of Microsoft products like Visual Studio and to help the developer modularize large-scale applications.

distributed password authentication (DPA) A shared secret authentication method originally started by some of the larger online services like CompuServe and MSN. It allows a user to use the same membership password to access a number of Internet sites when those sites are linked together as a membership organization. In essence, this methodology replicates some of the same features that users can get when using the same password to access multiple servers on a local network. DPA relies on the

Microsoft Membership Service for membership authentication and server-specific access information.

distributed transactions The ability to create a transaction that spans servers, platform types, and even DBMS products is essential in today's programming environment. Microsoft Transaction Server (MTS) allows the programmer to create a single atomic transaction. All of the changes required to update the database are either made or rolled back. It doesn't matter where those changes are located or why the transaction failed. What this means is that the developer can create complex enterprise-wide transactions that ensure the entire company's database resource is kept up-to-date. A change that appears in one location within the company is guaranteed to appear in all other locations if you make these changes using a single transaction.

DLL *See* dynamic link library

DNA *See* Distributed interNetwork Architecture

DPA *See* distributed password authentication

drive mapping A method of assigning a drive letter to a specific volume and directory on a network drive. Drive mappings provide a quick method to access information on a network drive without worrying about the precise location of the data. Drive mappings usually range from drive G to Z (assuming you use drive F as the first network drive.)

DS directory service

DSI *See* Digital Signatures Initiative

DSN *See* data source name

Dynamic Data Exchange (DDE) The capability to cut data from one application and paste it into another application. You can cut a graphics image created with a paint program, for example, and paste it into a word processing document. After it's pasted, the data doesn't reflect the changes made to it by the originating application. DDE also provides a method for communicating with an application that supports it and requests data.

dynamic link library (DLL) A specific form of application code loaded into memory by request. It's not executable by itself. A DLL does contain one or more discrete routines that an application may use to provide specific features. For example, a DLL could provide a common set of file dialog boxes used to access information on the hard drive. More than one application can use the functions provided by a DLL, reducing overall memory requirements when more than one application is running.

encryption   *See* Cryptographic Application Programming Interface

event log file (EVT)   A file used to hold the event log entries for a particular aspect of system performance. For example, there are separate files for application, security, and system entries. Each log file can hold several different event types, including informational, warning, and error events. An application never interacts with the EVT file itself since more than one application requires access to the EVT file at one time. A well-designed application will always use the Windows API to perform this task.

EVT   *See* event log file

File Transfer Protocol (FTP)   One of several common data transfer protocols for the Internet. This particular protocol specializes in data transfer in the form of a file download. The user is presented with a list of available files in a directory list format. An FTP site may choose DOS or UNIX formatting for the file listing, although the DOS format is extremely rare. Unlike HTTP sites, an FTP site provides a definite information hierarchy through the use of directories and subdirectories, much like the file directory structure used on most workstation hard drives.

FTP   *See* File Transfer Protocol

global commit coordinator   An operating system service used to coordinate the transactions taking place on multiple machines within an *n*-tier application. There's one global commit coordinator that resides on the initiating machine. It's the object at the very root of the commit tree and ensures that all of the Transaction Managers stay in sync. The global commit coordinator's only task is to ensure that the outcome of a transaction is never in doubt. Either all of the Transaction Managers commit to a transaction or they all abort it.

globally unique identifier (GUID)   A 128-bit number used to identify a Component Object Model (COM) object within the Windows registry. The GUID is used to find the object definition and allow applications to create instances of that object. GUIDs can include any kind of object, even nonvisual elements. In addition, some types of complex objects are actually aggregates of simple objects. For example, an object that implements a property page will normally have a minimum of two GUIDs: one for the property page and another for the object itself.

graphical user interface (GUI) 1. A method of displaying information that depends on both hardware capabilities and software instructions. A GUI uses the graphics capability of a display adapter to improve communication between the computer and its user. Using a GUI involves a large investment in both programming and hardware resources. 2. A system of icons and graphic images that replace the character mode menu system used by many machines. The GUI can ride on top of another operating system (like DOS and UNIX) or reside as part of the operating system itself (like OS/2). Advantages of a GUI are ease of use and high-resolution graphics. Disadvantages consist of higher workstation hardware requirements and lower performance over a similar system using a character-mode interface.

grid A nonprinting pattern of rectangles that help you place text, pictures, or graphic objects on a page.

GUI *See* graphical user interface

GUID *See* globally unique identifier

hacker One of a group of individuals who work with computer systems at a low level, especially in the area of security. A hacker normally possesses specialty software that allows easier access to the target application or network. In most cases, hackers require extensive amounts of time to actually break the security for a system before they can enter it. There are actually two kinds of hackers, those that break into systems for ethical purposes and those that do it to damage the system in some way. The second group is actually known as crackers. Some people have started to call the first group "ethical hackers" to prevent confusion. Ethical hackers normally work for security firms that specialize in finding holes in a company's security. However, hackers work in a wide range of other computer arenas as well. For example, a person who writes low-level code (like that found in a device driver) after reverse engineering an existing driver is technically a hacker.

HTML *See* Hypertext Markup Language

HTTP   *See* Hypertext Transfer Protocol

Hypertext Markup Language (HTML)   1. A scripting language for the Internet that depends on the use of tags (keywords within angle brackets, <>) to display formatted information onscreen in a nonplatform-specific manner. The nonplatform-specific nature of this scripting language makes it difficult to perform some basic tasks such as placement of a screen element at a specific location. However, the language does provide for the use of fonts, color, and various other enhancements onscreen. There are also tags for displaying graphic images. Scripting tags for using more complex scripting languages such as VBScript and JavaScript were recently added, although not all browsers support this addition. The latest tag addition allows the use of ActiveX controls. 2. One method of displaying text, graphics, and sound on the Internet. HTML provides an ASCII-formatted page of information read by a special application called a browser. Depending on the browser's capabilities, some keywords are translated into graphics elements, sounds, or text with special characteristics, such as color, font, or other attributes. Most browsers discard any keywords they don't understand, allowing browsers of various capabilities to explore the same page without problems. Obviously, there's a loss of capability if a browser doesn't support a specific keyword.

Hypertext Transfer Protocol (HTTP)   One of several common data transfer protocols for the Internet. This particular protocol specializes in the display of onscreen information such as data entry forms or information displays. HTTP relies on HTML as a scripting language for describing special screen display elements, although you can also use HTTP to display nonformatted text.

icon   A symbol used to graphically represent the purpose and/or function of an application or file. For example, text files might appear as sheets of paper with the name of the file below the icon. Applications designed for the environment or operating system usually appear with a special icon depicting the vendor or product's logo.

IDE   *See* integrated development environment

identifier   The name used to reference a function, procedure, or variable. An identifier always begins with a character. Some systems recognize only the first ten characters of an identifier. However, other identifiers may contain any number of characters.

IID   *See* interface identifier

IMDB   *See* in-memory database

in-memory database (IMDB)   A method of storing small amounts of data that are in constant use within the server's memory rather than on disk. Storing the database in memory increases system performance and reduces the amount of disk activity that the server encounters. A good example of an IMDB candidate is a database that stores all of the ZIP codes currently in use.

in-process server   A COM object that executes within the same process as the client. An in-process server normally resides on the same machine as the client process. In-process servers will execute faster than an out-of-process server equivalent since there are no process boundaries to cross. However, an in-process server isn't isolated from the client process, which means a failure of the in-process server will also cause the client to fail in most cases.

integrated development environment (IDE)   A programming language front end that provides all the tools you need to write an application through a single editor. Older DOS programming language products provided several utilities—one for each of the main programming tasks. Most (if not all) Windows programming languages provide some kind of IDE support.

interface identifier (IID)   A unique number that identifies a particular interface within an object. The client uses the IID to gain access to an interface pointer, which will then allow access to the interface's methods.

interface pointer identifier (IPID)   Essentially a handle to a source or target component in a transaction. The IPID is used to uniquely identify the component and its interface within an apartment and can be used for things like tracing how COM executes within an application.

Internet Protocol Security Protocol (IPSec)   IETF created the IP Security Protocol Working Group to look at the problems of IP security, such as the inability to encrypt data at the protocol level. It's currently working on a wide range of specifications that will ultimately result in more secure IP transactions. For example, IPSec is used in a variety of object-based group policy schemes. Windows currently uses IPSec for network-level authentication, data integrity checking, and encryption.

Internet Server Application Programming Interface (ISAPI) A set of function calls and interface elements designed to make using Microsoft's Internet Information Server (IIS) and associated products such as Peer Web Server easier. Essentially, this set of API calls provides the programmer with access to the server itself. Such access makes it easier to provide full server access to the Internet server through a series of ActiveX controls without the use of a scripting language. There are two forms of ISAPI: filters and extensions. An extension replaces current script-based technologies like CGI. Its main purpose is to provide dynamic content to the user. A filter can extend the server itself by monitoring various events like user requests for access in the background. You can use a filter to create various types of new services like extended logging or specialized security schemes.

Internet service provider (ISP) A vendor that provides one or more Internet-related services through a dial-up, ISDN, or other outside connection. Normal services include e-mail, newsgroup access, and full Internet Web site access.

IPID *See* interface pointer identifier

IPSec *See* Internet Protocol Security Protocol

ISAPI *See* Internet Server Application Programming Interface

ISP *See* Internet service provider

JIT activation *See* just-in-time activation

just-in-time activation (JIT activation) Server resources are always scarce, so good resource management techniques are essential. The latest component resource management techniques normally include gaining access to resources only when needed, then releasing them immediately. However, older components were designed to gain access to all of the resources required to perform a task early, then hold on to those resources until no longer needed. Using JIT activation means that even if a client holds on to a component reference, Windows 2000 can still use physical resources required by that component until they're needed again by the application. Windows 2000 monitors all of the components that are marked as JIT enabled. When a certain time period has elapsed without any method calls, the component deactivates, and the resources that it's using are returned to the resource pool. As far as the application is concerned, the component is still active and the reference to it is still valid. The next time the application makes a method call to the deactivated component, Windows 2000 will reactivate it and allocate the resources that it requires. This entire process occurs in the background without any programmer input. The user is completely unaware of what has taken place.

Kerberos   This is Microsoft's primary replacement for the Windows NT LAN Manager (NTLM) security currently used to ensure that your data remains safe when using Windows. Kerberos version 5 is a relatively new industry-standard security protocol devised at MIT that offers superior security support through the use of a private-key architecture. This protocol supports mutual authentication of both client and server, reduces server load when establishing a connection, and allows the client to delegate authentication to the server through the use of proxy mechanisms. Kerberos connects to an online key distribution center (KDC) and the directory service (DS) account to obtain session tickets used for authentication purposes.

KDC   key distribution center

LAN   *See* local area network

load balancing   Refers to the ability of an individual application, group of applications, individual server, or group of servers to maintain a consistent load across all processing elements. This, in turn, provides maximum processing throughput, greater processing efficiency, and reduced user waiting time. Load-balanced systems are inherently more reliable than assigned or single systems since the load-balanced system automatically compensates for downed or overloaded servers.

local area network (LAN)   Two or more devices connected together using a combination of hardware and software. The devices, normally computers and peripheral equipment such as printers, are called nodes. A network interface card (NIC) provides the hardware communication between nodes through an appropriate medium (cable or microwave transmission.) There are two common types of LANs (also called networks). Peer-to-peer networks allow each node to connect to any other node on the network with sharable resources. This is a distributed method of files and peripheral devices. A client/server network uses one or more servers to share resources. This is a centralized method of sharing files and peripheral devices. A server provides resources to clients (usually workstations). The most common server is the file server, which provides file-sharing resources. Other server types include print servers and communication servers.

local procedure call (LPC)   A method of accessing a function that resides outside of the application's current process but within a process found on the same machine.

locally unique identifier (LUID)   Essentially a pointer to an object, the LUID identifies each process and resources for security purposes. In other words, even if a user has two copies of precisely the same resource option (like a document), both copies would have a unique LUID. This method of identification prevents some types of security access violation under Windows NT.

LPC   *See* local procedure call

LUID   *See* locally unique identifier

mail-handling service (MHS)   A method for encrypting and decrypting user mail and performing other mail management services. Most NOSs provide some type of MHS as part of the base system. Several standards are available on the Internet for providing MHS as part of a Web site. The two most notable specifications are IETF RFC1421 from the IETF and X.400 from the ITU (formerly CCITT).

MDAC   *See* Microsoft Data Access Components

MDI   *See* multiple document interface

message queuing   The act of storing a message for later processing by the client or server. Microsoft Message Queue (MSMQ) uses message queuing technology to allow a developer to create disconnected applications on independent clients. A disconnected application stores messages for the server on the local hard drive until the client establishes a connection to the server. The messages are then transferred in the background to the server's queue to await further processing by the server.

message transfer agent (MTA)   This is an X.400 standard term that refers to the part of a message transfer system (MTS) responsible for interacting with the client. For example, in an email system, the MTA delivers email to the individual users of that system.

message transfer system (MTS) A method of transferring mail from one location to another. In most cases, this requires some form of encryption along with other transport-specific issues. Most NOSs provide some types of MTS as part of their base services. However, the Internet requires special transport mechanisms. Several standards are available on the Internet for providing MTS as part of a Web site. The two most notable specifications are the IETF RFC1421 from the IETF and X.400 from the ITU (formerly CCITT).

messaging application An application that relies on messages to transfer data between the client and the server. Windows uses Microsoft Management Queue (MSMQ) to add messaging capability to applications. The addition of messages also allows the application to operate in either connected or disconnected mode (given an independent client). One of the major reasons to use messages is that they allow the server to process the data when processing capability is available. This allows the client to work faster and uses processing capability more efficiently.

method-level security The ability of a component role-based security model to assign security at the method level rather than at the component level. This allows the developer or network administrator to assign specific levels of component access based on user roles rather than by specific user name.

MFC files *See* Microsoft Foundation Class files

MHS *See* mail-handling service

Microsoft Data Access Components (MDAC) A set of components designed to make data access easier. MDAC is actually a software development kit (SDK) that includes components, sample code, headers, libraries, and other elements that allow the developer to use newer Microsoft technologies like OLE-DB.

Microsoft Foundation Class files (MFC files) The set of DLLs required to make many Microsoft applications work. These files contain the shared classes used as a basis for creating the application. For example, a push button is a separate class within these files. Normally, you'll find the MFC files in the Windows SYSTEM folder—they use MFC as the starting letters of the filename.

Microsoft Management Console (MMC) A special application that acts as an object container for Windows management objects like Component Services and Computer Management. The management objects are actually special components that provide interfaces that allow them to be used within MMC to maintain and control the operation of Windows. A developer can create special versions of these objects for application management or other tasks. Using a single application like MMC helps maintain the same user interface across all management applications.

MMC *See* Microsoft Management Console

MTA *See* message transfer agent

MTA *See* multithreaded apartment

MTS *See* message transfer system

multiple document interface (MDI) A method for displaying more than one document at a time within a parent window. The Program Manager interface is an example of MDI. You see multiple groups within the Program Manager window.

multithreaded apartment (MTA) A term that refers to the method used to write the code for a COM component. The term "apartment" is a metaphor. Just as an apartment is a single room (or set of rooms) in an entire building, a COM apartment is a single part of an entire application. The best way to think of MTA is as a common area that anyone in the apartment building can access—like a laundry. A laundry contains multiple washers and dryers (objects of different types) that anyone can access. There's only one MTA per application, and it contains all of the objects that any thread can access. This means that an MTA COM object has to be able to keep track of which thread is asking for what service.

NDR *See* network data representation

network data representation (NDR) A method for transmitting network data in a platform-independent manner. NDR determines how the various values get marshaled into data packets for network transmission. Microsoft uses NDR as part of its strategy for making the Distributed Component Object Model (DCOM) work.

network interface card (NIC) The device responsible for allowing a workstation to communicate with the file server and other workstations. It provides the physical means for creating the connection. The card plugs into an expansion slot in the computer. A cable that attaches to the back of the card completes the communication path.

Network News Transfer Protocol (NNTP) The protocol used to transfer news messages between clients and servers. This is a stream-based protocol designed to allow query, retrieval, posting, and distribution of mail messages. The specification for this protocol is found in RFC 977.

NIC *See* network interface card

NNTP *See* Network News Transfer Protocol

n-tier application An application designed to operate in a distributed environment in such a way that individual parts of the application execute on different machines. The current methodology is to use the client workstation to display data and accept user input, one or more servers to perform business rule analysis, one or more servers to interact with the database, and finally, one or more database servers.

NRA national registration authority

NTLM *See* Windows NT LAN Manager security

OBJ *See* Object

Object (OBJ) 1. An intermediate file format used to store compiled code. OBJ files aren't linked and therefore aren't executable. DOS applications store them in LIB files. You can also use OBJ files in certain Windows environments, including some C compilers and Delphi. 2. A text block, a picture block, or a graphic. You can create objects by choosing the Text tool, Picture tool, or Shape tool from the toolbar. 3. When used in the OLE sense of the word, a representation of all or part of a graphic, text, sound, or other data file within a compound document. An object retains its original format and properties. The client application must call on the server application to change or manipulate the object.

object flow rights A Windows security methodology that defines the way rights are assigned to component users. Rights flow from one object to the next. This is a requirement for multiserver *n*-tier applications since the user would require access to all of the components required to complete a particular transaction. Fortunately, you can override this default behavior to ensure that access to sensitive components is properly regulated.

object identifier (OID) A number that uniquely identifies an object class or attribute, along with the object's definition. OIDs are issued by a central agency normally called a national registration authority (NRA). Each country has its own NRA. The NRA in the United States is the American National Standards Institute (ANSI). Every entity that requests an OID receives a root OID that can be used to create additional OIDs for individual objects. For example, Microsoft has an OID of 1.2.840.113556. Microsoft has added branches to this OID for a variety of purposes within Windows. For example, there's one OID for Active Directory classes and another for Active Directory attributes. A specific OID example is the IPSEC-Data object with an OID of 1.2.840.113556.1.4.623. As you can see, branches are added using a dot syntax.

object linking and embedding (OLE) The process of packaging a filename, application name, and any required parameters into an object, then pasting that object into the file created by another application. For example, you could place a graphic object within a word processing document or spreadsheet. When you look at the object, it appears as if you simply pasted the data from the originating application into the current application (similar to DDE). The data provided by the object automatically changes as you change the data in the original object. Often, you can start the originating application and automatically load the required data by double-clicking on the object.

object linking and embedding for databases (OLE-DB) A Microsoft technology used to access databases using component technology. OLE-DB is a low-level access technology that could be augmented through various high-level access technologies. For example, the ActiveX Data Objects (ADO) technology used by Visual Basic developers relies on OLE-DB to provide low-level services. OLE-DB is also the successor to older technologies like ODBC. The main difference between ODBC and OLE-DB is that ODBC will only work with relational DBMSs. OLE-DB can work with both relational and nonrelational DBMSs.

object pooling An object management methodology where an object is simply deactivated, rather than destroyed, when a user is finished using it. When the next user needs the same object, the object properties are changed and the object is reactivated, rather than created again. Using this technique greatly reduces the time required to provide objects once the object is initially created. If an object sits for a given interval without use, the operating system destroys it to make resources available for other uses.

object remote procedure
call (ORPC)
This protocol is used by all COM objects to implement cross-apartment accesses. It's an automatic service provided as part of the COM environment to components that don't implement the IMarshall interface. If a component wishes to handle its own low-level communication, then it must implement its own version of the IMarshall interface.

OCX *See* OLE Custom eXtension

OID *See* object identifier

OLE *See* object linking and embedding

OLE Custom eXtension
(OCX)
A special form of VBX designed to make adding OLE capabilities to an application easier for the programmer. Essentially, an OCX is a DLL with an added programmer and OLE interface.

OLE-DB *See* object linking and embedding for databases

ORPC *See* object remote procedure call

out-of-process server
A COM object that executes outside of the client process in a separate process. An out-of-process server doesn't need to reside on the same machine as the client process; it can use technologies like DCOM to communicate across machine boundaries. Out-of-process servers will typically execute slower than an in-process server equivalent since there are process boundaries to cross. However, since the out-of-process server resides in a separate process, failure of the out-of-process server won't normally affect the client.

PAS *See* Preboot Authentication Service

PCT *See* private communication technology

PEC *See* primary enterprise controller

PEM *See* Privacy Enhanced Mail

PKI *See* Public Key Infrastructure

Preboot Authentication
Service (PAS)
A new technology from Intel that allows a laptop or notebook computer to verify a user's identity before it even boots the operating system. Verification takes place through various types of nonpassword technologies like a thumbprint reader.

primary enterprise controller (PEC) Refers to the server that is tasked with managing various types of configuration information at the enterprise level. For example, a PEC manages the MSMQ state information, including any database entries, for the entire enterprise. This is the main machine in your MSMQ setup and usually appears at the corporate site. The PEC is also the primary site controller (PSC) for the site at which it appears.

primary site controller (PSC) The main configuration storage server for a given site within an enterprise. For example, the PSC manages all of the MSMQ state information for a particular site. These are the machines that you'll use for administering the MSMQ setup. Any change you make to one PSC is replicated on all other PSCs through MQIS or Active Directory. The PSC is responsible for updating any BSCs attached to its site. The PSC manages local information and transmits it to the primary enterprise controller (PEC) for distribution to the enterprise as a whole.

Privacy Enhanced Mail (PEM) A multipart specification that defines how to maintain the privacy of email. It includes sections on email encryption, security key management, cryptography, and security key certification. The cryptography portion of the specification includes algorithms, usage modes, and identifiers specifically for PEM use. (*See* Distributed Authentication Security Service.)

private communication technology (PCT) This is a special level of Internet security that Microsoft and the IETF are working on together. The short version is that PCT will enable a client and server to engage in private communication with little chance of being overheard. This level of security depends on digital signatures and encryption methodologies to do its work.

ProgID *See* program identifier

program identifier (ProgID) A number or string that can uniquely identify a specific application or component within Windows. The ProgID normally appears within the registry to allow Windows to associate files and other resources with a specific application. For example, the Data Access Objects version 3.5 components have several ProgID entries within the registry. The database engine is DAO.DBEngine.35, while a field object uses a ProgID of DAO.Field.35.

protocol A set of rules used to define a specific behavior. For example, protocols define how data is transferred across a network. Think of a protocol as an ambassador who negotiates activities between two countries. Without the ambassador, communication is difficult, if not impossible.

PSC *See* primary site controller

Public Key Infrastructure (PKI) A protocol that allows two sites to exchange data in an encrypted format without any prior arrangement. The default method for initiating the exchange is to create a Secure Sockets Layer (SSL) connection. The main difference between this technology and others on the market is that it relies on a public-key system of certificates to ensure secure data transfer. The latest specification for SSL is SSL3, which the IETF is calling Transport Layer Security (TLS) Protocol. A newer addition to the mix is private communication technology (PCT). PCT still uses public-key encryption, but there are some distinct advantages to using it that we'll discuss later in this section. One of the benefits of using PKI is that there's no online authentication server required since the certificate is issued by a well-known certification authority (normally a company like VeriSign when the technology is used publicly).

QC *See* Queued Components

Queued Components (QC) The COM+ version of Microsoft Message Queue (MSMQ). This integrated product offers enhanced support for transferring components from client to server using messages. Since this version of MSMQ is also guaranteed full access to Microsoft Transaction Server (MTS), all message transfers may take place within a transaction.

RC *See* resource container file

real-time operating system (RTOS) An operating system that's capable of producing real-time processing for a specific environment. Normally, Windows isn't considered a true RTOS because it provides features like message loops, event processing, and queuing. The response time between client input and server response can vary too much for most real-time applications under Windows.

real-time processing The ability of an operating system to provide immediate response to client queries. The length of time between client query and server response is defined by the requirements of the application. For example, a computer that controls the braking system in a car has to provide a faster response to input than a computer used to maintain the inventory of a corporation. In both cases, real-time processing is required, but the acceptable response time of real-time processing varies.

REG file A special file used by the registry to hold a text version of the keys and values it contains. Some applications provide .REG files that you can use to incorporate their file associations and OLE capabilities into some programs.

remote procedure call (RPC) One of several methods for accessing data within another application. RPC is designed to look for the application first on the local workstation, and then across the network at the applications stored on other workstations. This is an advanced capability that will eventually pave the way for decentralized applications.

resource container file (RC) The special file used by some programming languages to hold application resources like icons and bitmaps. The RC file is managed by the programming language IDE. Normally, you'll only need to see the graphic contents of the RC file, not the binary details.

resource dispenser Specialized components that dispense the component resources that applications require. Any COM+ component can use resource dispensers to manage the various objects required by the component. Windows 2000 supplies a default set of resource dispensers, but you also have the option of building your own. For example, many database managers include both a Resource Manager and one or more custom resource dispensers. The resource dispenser works with nondurable data, the type that's stored in memory and lost when the computer is shut down or rebooted. None of the components handled by the resource dispenser are persisted. In short, the resource dispenser allows Windows to manage a rather large pool of temporary objects that get used for a wide variety of purposes by a number of applications.

Resource Manager An operating system service that manages durable data (the type that will get recorded on some permanent media). A Resource Manager is commonly used to save application state information and to work with database records. Contrast this with the definition of resource dispenser, which is used for nondurable data. The Resource Manager and

Transaction Manager work hand-in-hand to perform the two-phase commit required for transaction processing.

resource pooling   The act of maintaining a complex resource, like a COM object, in memory in a deactivated state until it's needed by another client. Normally, objects and other complex resources are completely destroyed and the individual simple resources made available for other purposes. Using resource pooling reduces the time required to create new objects by reallocating objects previously used by other clients.

role-based security   A method for controlling access to an object based on the requestor's job function within an organization. In other words, if the requestor has a specific job function (or role), then they're allowed to access the object. This method of maintaining security is an extension of groups. However, unlike groups, a requestor must perform a specific job function before access is granted. This security methodology is normally used with COM+ applications.

router   A device used to connect two LANs together. The router moves signals from one LAN to the other.

RPC   *See* remote procedure call

RTOS   *See* real-time operating system

S/WAN   *See* Secure Wide Area Network

SACL   *See* security access control list

SCM   *See* Service Control Manager

script   Usually associated with an interpreted macro language used to create simple applications, productivity enhancers, or automated data manipulators. Windows currently supports a variety of scripting languages at the operating system level. You'll also find scripting capability in many higher-end applications like Web browsers and word processors. Scripts are normally used to write small utility-type applications rather than large-scale applications that require the use of a compiled language. In addition, most script languages are limited in their access of the full set of operating system features.

SDK   *See* software development kit

Secure Socket Layer (SSL) A digital signature technology used for exchanging information between a client and a server. Essentially, an SSL-compliant server will request a digital certificate from the client machine. The client can likewise request a digital certificate from the server. These digital certificates are obtained from a third-party vendor like VeriSign who can vouch for the identity of both parties.

Secure Wide Area Network (S/WAN) This is an initiative supported by RSA Data Security, Inc. The IETF has a committee working on it as well. RSA intends to incorporate the IETF's IPSec standard into S/WAN. The main goal of S/WAN is to allow companies to mix and match the best firewall and TCP/IP stack products to build Internet-based virtual private networks (VPNs). Current solutions usually lock the user into a single source for both products.

security access control list (SACL) One of several specialized access control lists (ACL) used to maintain object integrity. This list controls Windows' auditing feature. Every time a user or group accesses an object and the auditing feature for that object is turned on, Windows makes an entry in the audit log.

security descriptor A reference to the level of security assigned to an object. This is the data structure that tells the security system what rights a user needs to access the object. The user's rights are contained with an access token. In short, the security descriptor is the lock and the access token is the key.

security identifier (SID) The part of a user's access token that identifies the user throughout the network—it's like having an account number. The user token that the SID identifies indicates which groups the user belongs to and what privileges the user has. Each group also has a SID, so the user's SID contains references to the various group SIDs that he or she belongs to, not a complete set of group access rights. You'd normally use the User Manager utility under Windows NT to change the contents of this access token.

server An application or workstation that provides services, resources, or data to a client application or workstation. The client usually makes requests in the form of OLE, DDE, or other command formats.

Service Control Manager (SCM) The SCM is part of the load-balancing technology used by Windows servers. When a client makes a DCOM call to the load-balancing router, it's the SCM that actually receives the request. The SCM looks up the component in the load-balancing router table, then makes a DCOM call to one of the servers in the application cluster to fulfill the request. The server in the application cluster creates an instance of the request object, then passes the proxy for it directly to the client. At this point, the server and the client are in direct communication; the router is no longer needed.

SID   *See* security identifier

Simple Network Management Protocol (SNMP)   A network protocol (originally designed for the Internet) to manage devices from different vendors.

Simple Object Access Protocol (SOAP)   A Microsoft-sponsored protocol that provides the means for exchanging data between COM and foreign component technologies like Common Object Request Broker Architecture (CORBA) using XML as an intermediary.

single-threaded apartment (STA)   A method of defining how object methods get executed. STAs include three restrictions not found in multithreaded apartments (MTAs). The first is that an STA contains one, and only one, object. This ensures that once a component is instantiated, the resulting object doesn't share memory space with any other object, which could result in corruption. The second restriction is that one, and only one, thread can enter the apartment to interact with the object inside. The reason for this restriction is obvious. A single-threaded object can only handle the requests of one thread at a time, which means that COM must protect the object from access by more than one thread. Ensuring that only one thread can enter the apartment at a time is the easiest way to accomplish this task. Finally, a thread can execute only one object method at a time. This restriction ensures that there won't be any data corruption due to shared variables within the object. As a result of these restrictions, a single process could contain multiple STAs—one for each STA object that the application instantiated.

SNMP   *See* Simple Network Management Protocol

SOAP   *See* Simple Object Access Protocol

software development kit (SDK)   A special add-on to an operating system or an application that describes how to access its internal features. For example, an SDK for Windows would show how to create a

File Open dialog box. Programmers use an SDK to learn how to access special Windows components such as OLE.

SSL *See* Secure Socket Layer

STA *See* single-threaded apartment

synchronization object There are two considerations for this term. Objects are simply instantiated components within the Windows environment. Each object has a life of its own. However, there are times when you want to allow the data within a group of objects to interact in such a way that the end result is a composite of the data contained within all of the objects. For example, you might want to synchronize the data within the appointment, contact, email, and task objects of a groupware package. In this case, you need to create a synchronization object in place of a standard object. The synchronization object differs from the standard object in one important way—it maintains a database of changes since the last synchronization. In this way, a synchronization object can compare the updates from a group of objects quickly, find conflicts, and then do something about those conflicts. There are also examples of operating-system-specific synchronization objects like semaphores. A semaphore restricts access to shared resources to a predetermined number of threads. In short, it synchronizes data access within an application.

thread One executable unit within an application. Running an application creates a main thread. One of the things the main thread does is display a window with a menu. The main thread can also create other threads. Background printing may appear as a thread, for example. Only 32-bit applications support threads.

thread-neutral apartment (TNA) A new apartment type for Windows 2000 that's specifically designed to meet the needs of COM+ developers. Like the multithreaded apartment (MTA), there's at most one TNA within a process. One of the things that differentiates TNA from the single-threaded apartment (STA) and MTA apartment types is that it contains objects only; no threads are allowed within this apartment. Instead of executing within the TNA, when a thread requests access to a TNA object, it receives a lightweight proxy that switches to the object's context without the penalty of a thread switch. MTA threads can request this access directly, while STA threads will need to create a new thread-neutral object.

TLB *See* type library file

TLS *See* Transport Layer Security Protocol

TNA *See* thread-neutral apartment

Transacted Shared Property Manager (TSPM) A new programming interface of the COM+ Shared Property Manager (SPM). This interface creates a cache that allows the client synchronized access to application-defined shared properties across multiple process boundaries. There are quite a few subtle differences between TSPM and SPM due to the *n*-tier application orientation of this interface. However, the main difference is that TSPM allows synchronized access across multiple process boundaries, while SPM only works across a single process boundary. You'd normally use this feature for *n*-tier applications where the client and server locations may not be known at design time. For example, this is a good mechanism to use for Web-based applications or online transaction processing (OLTP) situations that require sharing or management of the Internet client session state.

transaction A single exchange of data or resources between a client and server. The transaction serves to document the data or resource transfer so that the process can be reviewed or reversed later.

Transaction Manager An operating system service that determines the outcome of application transactions based on the votes of the individual components within the application. The Transaction Manager ensures that every data element or object within the transaction is transmitted at least once, but only one time. The Transaction Manager works with the Resource Manager to perform the two-phase commit required for transactional data transfers.

transparent database access A Microsoft Transaction Server (MTS) feature that allows the developer to gain transparent access to databases on a number of platforms, including: Windows NT/2000, UNIX, IBM AS/400, IBM MVS, and Tandem. Microsoft is also working on other platform support, which may be available at the time you read this. MTS makes it possible to transparently access database resources on a wide range of platforms through the use of an Open Database Connectivity (ODBC) data source name (DSN), which specifies the name and location of the database.

Transport Layer Security Protocol (TLS) The transport layer is where error detection and correction occur. It ensures that the data sent by the client is received correctly by the server, and vice versa. TLS ensures that the data transmitted between client and server remains private. This may mean using a combination of digital certificates and data encryption to make it difficult to crackers to gain access to the data.

TSPM *See* Transacted Shared Property Manager

type library file (TLB) This file contains interface information for a specific component (usually with the same filename). The TLB file is used by programming languages like Visual Basic to allow the developer to see the various interfaces provided by a component. In addition to interfaces, the developer will also see the methods and properties (and, when available, a list of acceptable property values) associated with the component.

UI thread *See* user interface thread

UNC *See* universal naming convention

uniform resource identifier (URI) *See* uniform resource locator (the two terms are used interchangeably)

uniform resource locator (URL) A text representation of a specific location on the Internet. URLs normally include the protocol (http:// for example), the target location (world wide web or www), the domain or server name (mycompany), and a domain type (com for commercial). It can also include a hierarchical location within that Web site. The URL usually specifies a particular file on the Web server, although there are some situations when a default filename is assumed. For example, asking the browser to find http://www.mycompany.com would probably display the default.htm file at that location.

universal naming convention (UNC) A method for identifying network resources without using specific locations. In most cases, this convention is used with drives and printers, but it can also be used with other types of resources. A UNC normally uses a device name in place of an identifier. For example, a disk drive on a remote machine might be referred to as "\\AUX\DRIVE-C." The advantage of using UNC is that the resource name won't change, even if the user's drive mappings do.

URI *See* uniform resource identifier

URL *See* uniform resource locator

user interface thread (UI thread) The use of threads allows applications to perform more than one task at a time using multiple instruction execution paths. As the name suggests, user interface (UI) threads are normally created to provide some type of user interface functionality within an application. You'll derive the UI thread from the CWinThread class instead of using a function, as with the worker thread function. The InitInstance() method is the one CWinThread method that you must override because it's the first one called after the thread is created. The InitInstance() method should contain all of the code required to initialize your thread. Obviously, this means displaying a main dialog box for the thread, if necessary. Terminating a UI thread is much the same as terminating a worker thread. However, a UI thread requires a little special handling if you want the caller to retrieve the exit code for the thread. First, you need to set the m_bAutoDelete data member to FALSE, which prevents the CWinThread object from deleting itself. Second, you'll need to manually delete the thread and release any memory that it uses.

virtual private network (VPN) A special setup that Windows 2000 and Windows 98 SE provide for allowing someone on the road to use the server at work. This is where the virtual part comes in—the connection isn't permanent, you're using it for a short time. The reason that this connection has to be private is that you don't want anyone else to have access to your company's network. What you do is call into your ISP using dial-up networking. Now that you have access to the Internet, you can use dial-up networking to make a second connection to the server using Point-to-Point Tunneling Protocol (PPTP). The setup is very secure because it actually uses two levels of data encryption—digital signing of packets and encrypted passwords.

VPN *See* virtual private network

W3C World Wide Web Consortium

WAN *See* wide area network

wide area network (WAN) An extension of the LAN, a WAN connects two or more LANs together using a variety of methods. A WAN usually encompasses more than one physical site, such as a building. Most WANs rely on microwave communications, fiber-optic connections, or leased telephone lines to provide the internetwork connections required to keep all nodes in the network talking with each other.

Windows NT LAN Manager security (NTLM) A security scheme based on a challenge/response scenario. The server challenges the client, which must then provide an appropriate username and password. If the username and associated password are found in the server's security list for the service that the client has requested, then access to the service is granted. This security scheme is relatively easy to break and has been replaced by more reliable security schemes like Kerberos in later versions of Windows.

worker thread The use of threads allows applications to perform more than one task at a time using multiple instruction execution paths. Worker threads are normally used for background tasks that require no or minimal user interaction. They're implemented as a function that returns a UINT result and accept one argument of the LPVOID data type. A worker thread normally returns a value of 0, which indicates that it successfully completed whatever task it was designed to perform. You can return other values to indicate either errors or usage counts.

Index

#

#import directive, 378
#include directive, 301, 333
#pragma statement, 378

A

Abort logic, CRM, 100-101
Aborted message, in an endless loop, 147
About Box, 428-429
Absolute data integrity, 58
Absolute security descriptor, 82
Access control entries (ACEs), 83, 85
Access control lists (ACLs), 82-83, 85, 128
Access token privileges, 81
Access tokens, 78-79, 81-82
Access-allowed ACE, 83, 85
Access-denied ACE, 83
Accessor class, 233, 246
Accessor class methods, SQL Server, 246
ACE headers, types of, 83
ACEs (access control entries), 83, 85
ACID acronym (MTS transactions), 97-98
Ack message property, 141
ACL (access control list), 82, 128
 ACEs in, 85
 contents of, 83
 types of entries in, 83
Action tab, for an alert, 344-345
Activate() method (IObjectControl), 57
Activation, component, 60, 106
Active Directory, 7, 23, 33, 120, 148-152, 160
Active Directory catalog, 9
Active Document applications, 160
Active queue, moving a message from, 147
Active Template Library (ATL), 170, 223
ActiveX components, 160
 creating, 227
 in-process, 16
ActiveX control environments, 36-37
ActiveX control interfaces, 34-40
ActiveX controls
 communications, 35
 MFC and, 226
 Microsoft standards for, 36
 MSMQ, 377, 386
ActiveX technologies, 160
Add Member Function dialog box, 275-276
Add Member Variable dialog box, 273
Add Method to Interface dialog box, 230, 417
AddCustomer() method (IOrderModify), 232
AddDocTemplate() method, 302
Adding a Class dialog box, 287
AddItem() method (IOrderModify), 231
AddOrder() method (IOrderModify), 231
AddRef() interface method, 35, 40
AdjustTokenPrivileges() function, 82

Administration queue, 138, 391
Administrative services (COM+), 9
Administrative services (MTS), 10
Administrative tools, ADMINPAK.MSI file, 357
Administrator group, 214
Administrator role, 258-259
ADMINPAK.MSI file, 357
AdminQueueInfo message property, 141
AfxEndThread() function, 48
AfxGetApp() function, 329
AfxMessageBox() function, 307
Aggregation, 33-34, 264, 268
Alert counter, 342-344
Alert Properties dialog box, 342
AllocateAndInitializeSID() function, 81
AllocSysString() function, 432
Allow merging of proxy/stub code, 226, 262
ANSI NULL values, 204
Apartment types, predefined, 50
Apartment types and assignments, 49-52
Apartments, 14, 47, 49-52
Apartment-threading values, Windows 2000-supported, 51
APE (Application Performance Explorer), 179
AppID concept, 33
AppID key of HKEY_CLASSES_ROOT registry hive, 43
Application cluster, using, 24
Application cluster machine load, 24
Application component scalability, 99
Application event log, 321
Application Export Information dialog box, 438
Application flexibility, 200
Application hierarchy levels, 106
Application identifier (AppID) concept, 33
Application log, 322-323
Application modules, DNA, 199
Application Performance Explorer (APE), 179
Application programming, data-driven, 4
Application schematic, function-by-function, 402
Application types, 159-182
Applications design, ease-of-use issues, 3
AppSpecific property (message), 142, 433
AppTest application, 280-303
AppTest application code, 294-302
AppTest.CPP files, 301
AppTest.H file, 295
AppTestView.CPP file, 296
AppWizard (MFC), 269-283, 370-372, 428-429
Array of result structures, 268
ArrivedTime message property, 143, 377
Artificial intelligence (AI), 339

Asynchronous communication, 121-136, 155
Asynchronous data transfer, 155
ATL (Active Template Library), 170, 223
ATL COM AppWizard, 223-236, 262-264, 414-417
 configuration options, 226
 first dialog box, 226
ATL component, creating and installing, 413-426
ATL component code, 417-418
ATL object property values, On/Off button, 229, 264
ATL Object Wizard, 263
ATL Object Wizard dialog box, 227, 233, 416
ATL Object Wizard Properties dialog box, 228, 233-234, 236
ATL objects, database project, 232-236
ATL-based MTS component, creating, 223-245
Atomic transaction, MTS, 112
Atomicity (MTS transactions), 97
Attribute mask, access token privileges, 81
Attribute-based programming model, 100
Attributes, COM+, 165
Auditing, in role-based security, 88
Authentication, 368, 392, 407, 410
 MSMQ, 132-133
 and role-based security, 89
 shared secret, 76
Authentication method, choosing, 193-194
Authentication over HTTP, Windows 2000, 76-77
Authentication structure, in client component, 267
Authenticode, Internet Explorer, 75
AuthLevel property (message), 142, 433
AutoAbort feature, MTS, 102
AutoComplete feature, MTS, 102
Automatic error recovery, 55
Automatic transaction enlistment, 109
Automation, COM+ and, 56-60

B

Back Office, Visual Studio 6.0 Enterprise Edition, 186
Back-end processing tier, 200, 202
Background queue, moving a message to, 147
Backup, OrderEntry database, 216-219
Backup device file, 219
Backup Devices folder, 217
Backup expiration date, 218
Backup folder, 217
Backup Now, 219
Backup and restore REGDB, 63
Backup scheduling, 219
Backup Site Controllers (BSCs), 150
Backup Volume Label, 218
Backward compatibility, 107-108

Balancing server load. *See* Load balancing
Base component, 33
Base priority setting (message), 368
BIN file, 324
Binary component reuse, 34
Binding state for a component, 432
Bluetooth specification, 180
Body message property, 141
Body tab, Test Message Properties dialog box, 393
BodyLength message property, 141
Bookmarks, for moving to next/previous records, 246
Browsers, exporting data from, 67
BSTR data type values, 278, 376-377
   conversion to CString, 243, 279, 418
   DBTIMESTAMP values converted to, 245
   TCHAR values converted to, 244
Bugs, divide and conquer method of finding, 280
Built-in security, Windows 2000, 75, 77-86
Business ATL object, 227-229
Business logic tier, 200-201
Business object classes, 223
Business object methods, 230-232
Business object/database object pair, 309

▼ **C**

C++ language, with MSMQ, 121
C++ object, defined, 78
CALG_RC4 stream encryption, message body, 131
CALG_RC2 block encryption, message body, 131
CanBePooled() method (IObjectControl), 58
Catalog Manager (COM+), 23, 104
Catalog table (order entry system example), 203, 205
   test dialog box controls, 273
   testing access to, 269-280
Catalog test application
   creating, 269-280
   dialog box design, 271-272
   event handlers, 275-276
   member variables, 273-274
CatalogTestDlg.CPP file, 278
CatalogTestDlg.H file, 278
Catastrophic failures, 317, 320
CChildFrame class, 302
CComCompositeControl class, 37
CComControl class, 37
CDatabase class OpenEx() method, 112
Cell Directory Services (CDS), 25
Centralized database, 166
Certificate-Based Key Management (PEM2), 72
Certificates for authenticated messages, 76, 133, 407, 409-410
CFormView class, 282
Char arrays, 329
Char type database field, 204-205
Checked fields, 211
Choose Components to Import dialog box, 256-257
Class identification (CLSID), 34, 178
Class message property, 142
Classes
   created by Visual C++, 233

creating COM+, 287-288
   load-balanced, 93
   and queries, 223
ClassWizard (MFC), 274, 300
CLB (Component Load Balancing), 8, 56, 91-94, 164, 169, 312
Client ATL object, 263-264
Client component code, 265-269
Client component methods, 264
Client components, 163
Client configuration, failures from, 318-319
Client queue setups, MSMQ, 123
Client and server connection, DCOM, 19-21
Client and server setup, 185, 199, 221-222
Client and server situation, 6
Client setup, MSMQ, 124
Client table (order entry system), 203-204, 291
Client tier, 200-201
Client view (AppTest), 284-287
   code, 295-300
   control settings, 286-287
Client-managed states, 166
Clients
   explained, 15
   satellite offices as, 180
Client-side component shell, 262-264
Client-side components
   creating, 261-280
   vs. library applications, 178
   range- and value-checking, 310
Clipboard, copying dialog box contents to, 337
CloseEventLog() function, 322
CLSID entry in HKEY_CLASSES_ROOT registry hive, 42
CLSID key, 34, 178
CLSID_CoClass, 378
Cluster of servers, 105
CoCreateInstance() function, 28, 32, 378
CoCreateInstanceEx() function, 104, 221, 267-268, 346, 349
Code reuse, component, 16, 33-34
CoGetObject() function, 426, 432, 436
CoGetObject() function parameters, 432
CoInitialize() function, 50, 280
CoInitializeEx() function, 50
COM
   vs. COM+, 5-9, 108, 161-173
   and DCOM, 107-108
COM Application Export Wizard, 438
COM Application Install Wizard, 418-426
COM Component Install Wizard, 252-257
COM environment
   initializing, 267
   uninitializing, 280, 377
COM interface, vs. RPC interface, 412
COM runtime, 19
COM technology, 13-52
COM Web site, 14
COM+ (*see also* COM+ Applications)
   accessing components at method level, 164
   as a wrapper for technologies, 7
   attribute-based programming model, 100
   attributes, 165
   and automation, 56-60
   benefits of, 163-164
   vs. COM, 5-9, 108, 162, 166-203
   and connectivity, 3

consolidation, 54, 56
context, 59-60, 165
default recorder and player, 406, 411
design goals, 5-6
diagnosing complex problems, 348
domains, 57
equipment costs, 175
event sinks, 55, 62
extended functionality and range, 161
features, 3-5
interfaces in, 170-172
introduction to, 2-3
learning curve for, 175
library applications, 177-178
and messages, 6-7
MSMQ with, 6-7, 181-182
MTS and, 54, 99-102, 114, 181-182
performance issues, 174-175
preinstalled applications, 178-179
and the programmer, 4
programming issues, 173-176
programming methodology, 169
proxy applications, 178
resource management, 108
role of resource pooling, 10-11
security, 175-176
server applications, 177
state maintenance, 165
transaction handling, 114
transactions and, 6
types of security, 79
unique features of, 53-94
unique services of, 7
updated technologies, 160
use of memory, 175
and the user, 3-4
and the user interface, 4
whether to use, 221
and Windows 2000, 175
COM+ Application folders, Component Services, 178-179, 251-253
COM+ Applications (*see also* COM+)
   adding components to, 251-257
   vs. COM, 5-9, 108, 161-173
   creating, 247-251
   definition requirements, 198
   diversification, 160
   execution speed, 419
   flexibility, 200
   levels of security, 175-176, 214
   new/updated elements, 166-203
   packages as, 105-106
   reliability, 106-107
   security for, 257-261
   testing, 302-303
   with three minimum components, 311
   types of, 176-179
COM+ Catalog, 62-63
COM+ Catalog Manager, 23
COM+ components. *See* Components (COM+)
COM+ objects. *See* Objects
COM+ 1.0 services, 101
COM+ services, 7-9, 101-102
COM+ Utilities folder, Component Services, 406
COM+ Web site, 97
Combo box, 380-381

Common Object Request Broker
  Architecture (CORBA), 174
Communication, overview of, 358-369
Communication paths, DCOM, 20-21
Communications, asynchronous MSMQ,
  121-136. *See also* MSMQ
Compatibility, backward, 107-108
Compatibility issues, 314
Compatibility requirements, Windows
  2000, 309
Compensating message, 147
Compensating Resource Manager (CRM), 8,
  55, 61-62, 100-101
Complexity, application reliability and, 319
Component attributes, COM+, 9
Component catalog, 55
Component Checker (MDAC), 313-316
  Choose Analysis Type dialog box,
    313-314
  Detail views, 316
Component context interface, 59-60
Component creation failures, 306
Component event interfaces, 44
Component interactions, failures from, 311
Component Load Balancing (CLB), 8, 56,
  91-94, 164, 169, 312
Component programming, COM+, 168-170
Component properties dialog box, 260-261
Component registration, database project,
  247-261
Component registry entries, 40-47
Component resources. *See* Resource
  dispensers; Resources
Component reuse, 16, 33-34
Component scalability, 99
Component Services MMC snap-in, 63, 96,
  106, 115 170, 247,259
  administrative tools, 87
  Queued Component applications, 407
  rotating ball, 427
  window, 248, 255-256
Component shell
  ATL object, 413-417
  client-side, 262-264
  database project, 223-236
Component technologies
  and the GUI, 4-5
  introduction to, 2-3
  maintenance reductions, 99
  working with several, 174
Component testing, 269-280
Component transactions, declarative, 60
Component version number checks, 313
Component-level security, 88, 176
Components (COM+)
  adding to COM+ Applications, 251-257
  as descriptions of objects, 15
  binding state for, 432
  categorizing, 15-16
  code reuse, 16, 33-34
  creating and installing, 413-426
  debugging, 34
  detecting failed, 308
  developing for server use, 5
  introduction to, 2-3
  MSMQ, 140, 144-146
  placing in context, 100-101
  potential places to activate, 106
  queued, 7-8

registry requirements, 40-47
  in separate server processes, 106, 308
  server queue for active, 122-123
  transactional, 60
  viewing in context, 57
Components folder, 252
Composite ActiveX control environment, 37
Computer Associates (CA) Ingres II, 110
Computer Management MMC snap-in, 137,
  341-342, 366-367
  Message Queueing folder, 437
  Outgoing Queues folder, 440-441
  Public Queues folder, 387
ComputerName property (message), 433
Computing power, real vs. perceived,
  162-163
Concurrency, 50, 260
Configuration errors, failures from, 318
Connected mode application failures, 307
Connected transaction failures, 310-316
Connection errors (server), finding, 268
Connection failure, transactions and, 98-99
Connection losses, Internet, 98
Connection optimization, 22
Connection tab, Data Link Properties dialog
  box, 235
Connection test, 236
Connectionless applications, and MSMQ, 12
Connection-oriented data flow
  optimization, 21-22
Connections
  how DCOM creates and manages,
    19-21, 31
  live vs. disconnected, 6
  transactions and, 98
  typical out-of-process, 18-25
Connectivity, COM+ and, 3
Consistency (MTS transactions), 98
Consolidation, COM+, 54, 56
Consumer, database, 233
CONTAINER_INHERIT_ACE
  constant, 83
Containers, 251
  access flow rights for, 81
  explained, 15
  in-process servers and, 16
  for runtime objects, 33
Containment, 33-34
Context
  COM+, 59-60, 165
  placing components in, 100-101
  Windows 2000, 101
Context-oriented rights, 115
Control Panel, Message Queuing applet, 440
CopySID() function, 81
COrderModify class, 222
COrderRequest class methods, 221
CorrelationId message property, 142
COSERVERINFO data structure, 32, 104, 268
Cost of updating to Windows 2000, 174
CoUninitialize() function, 51, 377
Crackers, 64-65
Create Empty Application dialog box,
  249-250, 419
Create New Data Source dialog box
  (Database Project), 192
Create New Data Source to SQL Server
  dialog box, 193-195

Create() method (queue information
  object), 376
CreatePrivateObjectSecurity() function, 86
CreateThread() function, 47
Creator process, component activation, 106
CRM Clerk, 62
CRM (Compensating Resource Manager), 8,
  55, 61-62, 100-101
CRM Compensator, 62
CRM Worker, 62
Cross-context calls, 60
Cryptographic algorithms, 131
Cryptography API (CryptoAPI), 75
CString conversions, 243, 279, 377, 418
CString label, 376
CString object, 332
CString pbstrProductID value, 243
CTime class, 377
CTime object, 377
CURRENCY value, conversion to BSTR, 279
Current connected state of an application, 6
Current object context, obtaining, 243
Current record
  defining, 271-272
  getting, 279
Cursors, for moving to next/previous
  records, 246
Custom vs. Dual interface for MTS
  components, 229
CustomerID database field, 211-212
CustomerID field index, 220
CWinThread class, 48-49
CWinThread object, 48
Cyclic redundancy code (CRC), 311

D

DACL (Discretionary access control list),
  82, 84
Daily backups, 216
DAT file, 219
Data backups, 216
Data encryption, 12, 129-131, 400
Data encryption and decryption keys, 130
Data entry, failures from, 312, 317-318
Data entry keystrokes, reducing number
  of, 294
Data flow optimization,
  connection-oriented, 21-22
Data integrity, 58, 184, 400
Data in a known good state, 98
Data Link Properties dialog box
  Connection tab, 235
  Provider tab, 234
Data overruns, failures from, 318
Data in a production system, value of, 216
Data structure
  passing a pointer to, 48, 52
  setting up, 267-268
Data transfer sequence, MSMQ application,
  355, 366
Data view, choosing, 282
Data View tab, Workspace window, 196
Database access, on disk vs. in-memory, 8
Database access rights, 191
Database application. *See* OrderEntry
  database
Database ATL objects, 232-236

Database Backup/Restore dialog box, 218
Database class, 233
Database connection, noOdbcDialog option, 112
Database connection pooling, 109
Database connection test, 269-280
Database design process, 207
Database Devices folder, 208
Database diversity, 109
Database features, MTS, 109-112
Database file, sizing, 209
Database management, 202
Database management systems (DBMSs), 2, 108-111
Database Manager, 22
Database modeling, 197
Database object classes, 223
Database owner (dbo), 214
Database programming with MTS, 112-113
Database project (*see also* OrderEntry database)
    client-side component, 261-280
    component code, 237-245
    component registration, 247-261
    component shell, 223-236
    n-tier view of, 221-222
Database Project (Visual C++), 191-198
Database records, moving to next and previous, 246
Database tables, levels of access to, 236
Databases
    MSMQ, 149
    server-side component, 222-261
    that don't support ODBC, 113
    transactions and, 108-114
Databases folder, 210
Data-driven application programming, 4
DBMS (database management system), 2, 108-111
DBTIMESTAMP data type, converting to a BSTR, 245
DCE RPC network protocol, 18, 20, 26
DCOM call to load-balancing router, 93
DCOM Configuration Tool, 33
DCOM connection, 18-21, 31
DCOM (network protocol), 18-34, 176
    and aggregation, 268
    based on RPC, 412
    and COM, 107-108
    and COM+, 54
    in detail, 25-31
    discussion list group, 348
    implementing, 31-33
    load balancing, 22-25
    vs. messaging applications, 122-123
    SORF_NOPING flag, 31
    types of load balancing with, 22-24
    within DCE environment, 26
DCOM Wire Protocol, 25-26
DDE server, 86
DDEImpersonateClient() function, 86
Deactivate() method (IObjectControl), 57
Dead letter queue, 137-138, 340-345, 396
Dead letter queue message problems, 342
Debugging components, 34
Declarative component transactions, 60
Declarative security, 107
Default column, 211

Definitions of terms used in this book, 443-475
Delete permission, 214
Delivery guarantees, MSMQ, 11, 126-127
Delivery property (message), 143, 433
Dependent client message queues, 124, 139
Dependent services, listing, 187
DeregisterEventSource() function, 322-333
Design goals of COM+, 5-6
Desktop vs. distributed development, 404-406
Desktop object inheritance, 84
DestinationQueueInfo message property, 141
Developer's Readiness Kit, Windows 2000, 190
Diagnostic component, creating on the server, 347
Diagnostic and query aids, 185
Diagram pane (Local Query), 197
Dialog box contents, copying to the clipboard, 337
Dialog form, creating, 372, 380-381, 429
Dialog program shell, creating, 269-271
Dialog-based applications, 269-280, 369-386, 427-429
Digital certificates, 75, 129
Digital Signature Initiative (DSI), 69
Digital signatures, 75-76
Directory Service (DS) account, 76
Directory structure, COM+ application, 251-252
DisableCommit() method (IObjectContext), 103
Disconnected applications, 179-181
    concept of, 6
    Internet security for, 400-401
    message queues for, 139-140
    messaging and, 123
    response queue and, 337-339
    using MSMQ, 11-12, 156
Disconnected mode, working in, 399-441
Disconnected mode application failures, 307
Disconnected transaction failures, 316-319
Discretionary access control list (DACL), 82, 84
Disk access, MSMQ, 124-125
Disk backup device, 217
Disk setup, and MSMQ performance, 153-154
Diskdump default backup device, 218
Distributed application development, 5
Distributed applications
    data security for, 10
    development, 404-406
    Queued Components in, 403
Distributed Authentication Security Service (DASS), 71
Distributed Computing Environment (DCE), 18, 25
Distributed vs. desktop development, 404-406
Distributed File Service (DFS), 25
Distributed interNetwork Architecture (DNA), 6, 24, 177, 199
Distributed part of MS-DTC, 117
Distributed Password Authentication (DPA), 76

Distributed Time Service (DTS), 25
Distributed Transaction Coordinator (DTC), 58, 186-187, 189, 312
Distributed transactions, MTS, 112
Divide and conquer method of finding bugs, 280
DlgString object, 432
DLL applications, 414-426
DLL files, 15
DLL interactions, 312-316
DLL projects, 226
DLL server option, 262
DLL servers. *See* In-process servers
DLLs (dynamic link libraries), 15-16, 226, 414-426
Document class, 302
Document object, 302
Document template strings, 288-290
Domain accounts (Windows 2000), 7
Domains, COM+, 57
DOS programming, 3-4
Downed servers and routers, 94
Downloads, as security holes, 66-67
Drop-down list box, sizing, 381, 383
DSI (Digital Signature Initiative), 69
DTC (Distributed Transaction Coordinator), 58, 186-187, 189, 312
Dtcsetup program, 189
Dual application setup, 180
Dual vs. Custom interface for MTS components, 229
Dual string array, 31
DuplicateHandle() method, 48
Durability of MTS transactions, 98
DWORD values, 329-330, 335
Dynamic link libraries (DLLs), 15-16, 226, 414-426
Dynamic linking, explained, 14
Dynamic load balancing, 23-24

E

Ease-of-use issues (applications design), 3
Edit boxes, 272, 380
Edit control, 278
EditCustomer() method (IOrderModify), 232
EditItem() method (IOrderModify), 231
EditOrder() method (IOrderModify), 231
Efficiency of COM+ Applications, 167
Email queries, 339
EnableCommit() method (IObjectContext), 103
EncryptAlgorithm property (message), 142, 433
Encrypted data, 12, 129-131, 400
Encryption, two-step MSMQ process, 130
Encryption algorithms, 131
Encryption and decryption keys, 130
Encryption technologies, Windows 2000, 129
Endless loop, aborted message in, 135, 147
Enterprise applications, 5
Errant data entry, failures from, 317-318
Error codes, interpreting, 346-347
Error detection
    flexible, 313
    programming techniques, 345-346
    two phases of, 319-320
Error event entries, 332
Error events, 322

Error handling, MSMQ, 144, 147-148
Error message display, and event log entries, 307
Error messages, 308, 350
Error overload handling, 347-348
Error recovery, automatic, 55
Error severity levels, 350
Error source detection, 319-346
Error trapping, 268, 278, 281
ERROR_CALL_NOT_IMPLEMENTED, 78
Error-detecting macros, 349, 351
Error-proof application myth, 313
Error-recovery methods, 55, 319-351
Event entries, types of, 332
Event handle, getting, 332
Event handlers, for catalog test application, 275-276
Event log entries, 308, 339-340
and error message display, 307
generating, 325-337
Event log error number, 334
Event log example, 325-337
Event Log Generation Check dialog box, 326, 328
Event log messages, 323-325
Event log numbers, 323
Event log types, 321-322
Event logs, using, 320-337
Event log-specific functions, 322-323
Event Properties dialog box, 336-337, 397
Event Properties dialog box buttons, 337
Event sinks, 55, 62, 112
Event Viewer, 320, 323, 335-336, 396-397
EventCheck application, 325-337
EventCheck.CPP file, 326
EventCheckDlg.CPP file, 330, 333
EventCheck.RC2 file, 334
Event-logging registry key, 329
EventMsg.BIN file, 334
EventMsg.H file, 332-333
EventMsg.RC file, 334
Events
object, 15
transaction, 103-104
types of COM+, 7
EVT files, 322
EXE files, 15, 226
EXE servers. *See* Out-of-process servers
Executable service objects, 84
Execution context, 268
Execution environments (Windows), 49-50
Execution speed, COM+ applications, 167
ExitInstance() method, 49
Export Application to File dialog box, 438-439
Export List command, 395
Express delivery mode, performance penalties, 152-153
EXtensible Markup Language (XML), 174
External transactions, MSMQ, 126, 133-136

 F

FAILED macro, 351
Failed network connection, 310-311
Failure recognition, 308-309
Failure scenarios, 307-319
Failure status, for interfaces, 268

Failures
catastrophic, 317
unforeseen, 312-313
Fault tolerance
maintaining, 106, 308
and separate server processes, 309
Faulty message, in an endless loop, 135
File extensions (HKEY_CLASSES_ROOT), 41
File server, security descriptor attached, 86
File system security under Windows 2000, 84
FinalClientRetry() method, 147-148
FinalServerRetry() method, 147-148
Fingerprint reader, 181
Firewalls, 400-401
FLAGS registry key, 46
Flat-file database, 202
Foreign keys, database table, 205, 207, 211-213
Form name, setting, 287
FormatName property (message), 434
FoxPro, MTS support in, 111
FoxPro Component Wizard, 170
Frame class, 302
Function-by-function application schematic, 402

 G

Generic Security Service API (GSS-API), 71
GetACE() function, 84
GetBuffer() method, 279
GetCatalogItem() method (IOrderModify), 231, 243, 265, 279
GetCustomer() method (IOrderModify), 232, 245
GetDeactivateOnReturn() method (IContextState), 59
GetExitCodeThread() function, 48
GetFileSecurity() function, 84
GetItem() method (IOrderModify), 231
GetKernelObjectSecurity() function, 84
GetMyTransactionVote() method (IContextState), 59
GetObjectContext() method, 104
GetOrder() method (IOrderModify), 231
GetProperty access, MSMQ, 129
GetSecurityDescriptorDACL() function, 84
GetTokenInformation() function, 81-82
GetTransaction() method (IObjectContextInfo), 59
GetUserObjectSecurity() function, 78, 84
GetWindowText() method, 432
Global Commit Coordinator, 117
Global Directory Services (GDS), 25
Globally unique identifiers (GUIDs), 41-44, 140, 389, 391-392, 440
Glossary of terms used in this book, 443-475
Graphical user interface (GUI), programming for, 4
Graphics, programming for, 4
Graphics libraries, 17
Grid pane (Local Query), 197
Group SIDs
ordering of, 85
security descriptor, 82
Groups/Users hierarchy, 214
Group/Users folder, 214

GSS-API C-bindings, 71
Guaranteed communication (MSMQ), 11
GUIDs (globally unique identifiers), 41-44, 140, 389, 391-392, 440

 H

Hackers, 64-65
Handler class ID, 31
Hard drive failure, 317
Hard drive space, failures from, 318
Hardware drive striping, 154
Hardware limitations, failures from, 311-312
Hash values, message authentication, 132
HashAlgorithm property (message), 142, 434
HELPDIR registry key, 46
Hierarchical database view, 196
HKEY_CLASSES_ROOT registry hive, 16, 40, 290
AppID key, 43
CLSID entry, 42
entries, 32
keys, 44
typical display, 41
HKEY_LOCAL_MACHINE registry hive, 329
Hops column, Outgoing Queues Folder, 440-441
Hosting, MSMQ, 149-151
HPFS security, 84
HRESULT value (hr), 155, 268, 278, 345-346, 349-350, 418
HRESULT value macros, 349, 351
HTML <A HREF> tag, 66
HTML ActiveX control environment, 37
HTML <OBJECT> tag, 70
HTTP, Windows 2000 authentication over, 76-77

I

IBM DB2, MTS support in, 110
ICatalog interface, 105
ICatalogCollection interface, 105
ICatalogObject interface, 105
I<Class> interface, 36-37
ICOMAdminCatalog interface, 63
IComponentUtil interface, 105
IConnectionPointContainer interface, 38
Icons, programming for, 4
IContextState interface, 59-60
ICrmCompensator interface, 62
Id message property, 142
IDataObject interface, 38, 40
IDD_FORMVIEW dialog type, 287
IDD_ORDER_FORM dialog box, 291
IDispatch interface, 37-38, 412
IDL (interface definition language) output, 412
IDlgString interface, 424-425
IDlgString Properties dialog box, 424-425
IETF (Internet Engineering Task Force), 70
IETF working groups, 70
IGetAppData interface, 172
IID_Interface, 378
IMarshal interface, 52
Immediate backup, 219

Impersonation, 346
Import or Install a Component dialog box, 252, 254, 422-423
Importing MSMQ ActiveX controls, 377
Independent client message queues, 139
Independent client setup, MSMQ, 124
Index Build, 220
Index field, 220
Indexes
    OrderEntry database, 219-220
    primary key, 220
Information event entries, 332
Information events, 321, 332
Informational messages, 350
Informix, MTS support in, 110
InitDialog() method, 333
Initialize Device option, 218
InitInstance() method, 49, 301, 326
In-memory database (IMDB), 8, 169
In-process servers, 16-17, 161, 226
    and containers, 16
    in DLL files, 16
    fast and easy programming, 17
    file extensions, 15
    local calls, 16
    marshaling requirements of, 52
    vs. out-of-process servers, 15
InprocServer32 key, 43
Insert Database Item dialog box (Database Project), 197
Insert permission, 214
Insert Resource dialog box, 284-285
Install or Create a New Application dialog box, 248-249, 418
Install new components dialog box, 255, 424
Install pre-built applications, 248
Instantiation, 15
INSTCAT.SQL script, 189
Int type database field, 204-205
Interactive user option, 250-251
Interception, 60
Interceptors, operating system, 100-101
Interface attributes, 171
Interface definition language (IDL) output, 412
Interface GUID file, 412
Interface methods, calling, 34-40
Interface pointer, 267, 269
Interface pointer identifier (IPID), 26, 31
Interface pointer initialization, 267
Interface Properties dialog box, 171
Interface support for ActiveX control types, 37-38
Interfaces, 14, 34-40, 170-172, 268, 426
Internal transactions, 126, 133, 135-136
International Computer Security Association (ICSA), 401
International Standards Organization (ISO), 116
Internet, an unstable media, 98
Internet application development, 3
Internet Component Download, security holes, 66-67
Internet Explorer
    Authenticode, 75
    Favorite Places, 67
Internet Protocol Security Protocol (IPSec), 69
Internet security for disconnected applications, 400-401

Internet security standards, 68-74
Intranets, 3
IObjectContext interface, 59, 102-103
IObjectContext methods, 102-103
IObjectContextActivity interface, 60
IObjectContextInfo interface, 59
IObjectControl interface, 57-58, 229
IOleControl interface, 38
IOleInPlaceActivateObject interface, 39
IOleInPlaceObjectWindowless interface, 39
IOleObject interface, 39
IOrderAccess interface, 300
IOrderModify interface, 230-232
IOrderModify methods, 231-232
IP address of test server, 441
IP Security, 401
IPackageUtil interface, 105
IPersistStorage interface, 39
IPersistStreamInit interface, 38
IPID (interface pointer identifier), 26, 31
IPlaybackControl interface, 147
IProvideClassInfo interface, 40
IProvideClassInfo2 interface, 40
IQuickActivate interface, 40
IRemoteActivation interface, 26
IRemoteComponentUtil interface, 105
IRoleAssociationUtil interface, 105
IsAuthenticated message property, 142
ICallerInRole() method (IObjectContext), 59, 103
ISecurityCallContext interface, 60, 87, 89-91
ISecurityCallContext methods, 90-91
IS_ERROR macro, 351
IsInTransaction() method (IObjectContext), 103
IsInTransaction() method (IObjectContextInfo), 59
ISO standard, 116
Isolation
    MSMQ transaction, 135
    MTS transaction, 98
ISpecifyPropertyPages interface, 38
IsSecurityEnabled() method, 59, 103
ISupportErrorInfo interface, 264
IT managers, important issues for, 184
Item List view (AppTest), 284, 293
    code, 300-301
    control settings, 295
Item table (order entry system), 203, 205-206, 245
Item table schema, 206
ItemID database field, 211
Itoa() C function, 279, 377
IUnknown interface, 35-36, 40, 169, 378
IUnknown methods, 40, 378
IViewObject interface, 39
IViewObjectEx interface, 39
IViewObject2 interface, 39

J

JEPI (Joint Electronic Payments Initiative), 72
Journal folder, 368
Journal property (message), 141, 434
Journal messages, 137-138, 141, 340
Journal Messages folder, 138, 395
Journal queue, 138
Journals, explained, 368
Just-in-time (JIT) activation, 56-58

K

Kerberos, 69, 76, 175
Key Certificate Services (PEM4), 73
Key Distribution Center (KDC), 76
Keystrokes (user), reducing number of, 294

L

Label property (message), 142, 434
Laptop computer innovations, 180-181
LastName index, 220
Legacy applications and code, 8, 49, 107-108
Library applications (COM+), 177-178, 249
    vs. client-side components, 178
    vs. server applications, 249
Lightning storms, 313
Lightweight components, 223
Limit journal storage to (KB) option, 368
Limit message storage to (KB) option, 368
Listener component, COM+ default, 124, 156, 354, 406, 411
Listener/player application, creating, 369-377
Listener/player application playback code, 372-377
Listener/player application shell, 370-372
Listener/player test application, 379-386
Listener/player test application code, 382-386
Listener/player test application shell, 379-380
Lite Composite ActiveX control environment, 37
Lite HTML ActiveX control environment, 37
Live connection, as old technology, 6
Load balancing, 5, 8
    class level, 93
    goals of, 92
    how it works, 92-94
    implementing COM+, 24
    MTS, 105-106
    types of DCOM, 22-24
    within DCOM, 22-25
Load Balancing Service, 93-94
Load-balanced COM+ classes, creating, 93
Load-balancing router, 24, 93
Load-balancing setup, 93
Local client queue, MSMQ, 123
Local message queue, 6
Local procedure call (LPC), 18
Local Query window panes (Database Project), 197
Local queue, MSMQ, 123
Locally unique identifier (LUID), 81-82
LookupPrivilegeValue() function, 82
Loosely coupled events, 169
Lotus Notes, MTS support in, 110
Low Priority Test Message Properties dialog box, 390-393
LPC (local procedure call), 18
LPCSTR variable, 279, 332
LPVOID data type, 48, 333
LUID, 81-82

M

Macro substitutions, 325, 333-334
Macros, in ICOMAdminCatalog interface, 63

Maintainability of COM+ applications, 168
Maintenance reductions of component
    technology, 99
MakeAbsoluteSD() function, 82
MakeSelfRelativeSD() function, 82
Malicious scripts, 66
Manage Groups dialog box, 214
Manage Indexes dialog box, 219-220
Manage Tables dialog box, 211-213
Manage Users dialog box, 214-215
Marshaling, requirements of, 52
MaxTimeToReachQueue property
    (message), 143, 435
MaxTimeToReceive property (message),
    143, 435
MC utility, 324-325
MedVision Inc. case study, 134
Member variables, for Catalog test
    application, 273-274
Memory leaks, 280
Memory-mapped files, 125
Menu object inheritance, 84
MEOW signature, 30-31
Message authentication, 132-133
Message body, 365
Message body and label, 385
Message body in plaintext, 392-393
Message boxes, removing for production
    system, 243
Message categories, 325
Message category numbers, 325
Message Compiler (MC) utility, 324-325
Message data properties, 141
Message delivery modes
    MSMQ, 127
    and performance penalties, 152
Message dequeuing, 135
Message Encryption and Authentication
    (PEM1), 72
Message file
    compiling, 324
    source code for, 324
Message ID, 389
Message label, 365
Message object Send() method, 386
Message output, viewing, 393-394
Message priorities, 368, 385-386, 393
Message priority numbers, 368
Message properties, 141-143, 365
Message queue types, 137-139
Message Queuing applet, Control Panel, 440
Message Queuing dialog box, 58, 137, 189,
    395, 408
Message Queuing folder, Computer
    Management, 437
Message Queuing Properties dialog box,
    125, 408
Message queues, 11-12, 121, 388-389, 395.
    See also MSMQ
    closing, 377
    for disconnected applications, 139-140
    local, 6
    overview of, 136-140
    types of, 137-139
Message recovery data, 125
Message resource, creating, 323-324
Message security, 392
    Queued Components, 407
    over a network connection, 130-132

Message security properties, 142
Message Sent and Arrived times, 390
Message size, and performance, 154
Message store, 125
Message tampering, forms of, 132
Message text size, 388
Message time tracking properties, 143
Message transmission failure, 366
Message type, defining, 365-366
MessageID, 325
MessageIDTypedef entry, 325
Messages (see also Message queues; MSMQ)
    administrative and application, 136
    advantage to using, 121, 123
    altering content, 132
    and COM+, 6-7
    damaged, 132
    disadvantage of using, 122
    management and propagation, 136
    masquerading as from a known entity, 132
    moving between queues, 147
    parts of, 140-143
    in plaintext, 386
    positive and negative acknowledgments,
        365-366
    reading, 132
    receiving, 376
    receiving vs. sending, 385
    reducing size of, 154
    storage of, 125
    supporting multiple threads, 154
    that abort, 147
    that failed authentication, 133
    that passed authentication, 133
    using default settings for, 154
    ways to handle errant, 147
Messaging application, vs. DCOM, 122-123
Method attributes, modifying, 172
Method calls, 404
Method-level security, 115
Methods, 15, 173
    granting access to, 173
    overriding, 49
    tabs of configuration information, 172
MFC AppWizard, 269-283, 370-372, 428-429
MFC ClassWizard, 274, 300
MFC (Microsoft Foundation Classes), 170, 226
Microsoft Access, MTS support in, 111
Microsoft Cluster Server (MSCS), 94
Microsoft COM+ Web site, 97
Microsoft Data Access Components
    (MDAC), 55, 313-316
Microsoft Data Engine (MSDE) for Visual
    Studio 6.0, 190
Microsoft Distributed interNetwork
    Architecture (DNA), 6, 24, 177, 199
Microsoft distributed transaction
    coordinator (MS DTC), 60, 115-117
Microsoft Foundation Classes (MFC), 170, 226
Microsoft FoxPro, MTS support in, 111
Microsoft FoxPro Component Wizard, 170
Microsoft IDL (MIDL) compiler, 412
Microsoft Installation (MSI) database file, 357
Microsoft Internet Explorer
    Authenticode, 75
    Favorite Places, 67
Microsoft Knowledge Base, 306, 313
Microsoft Management Console (MMC)
    snap-ins, 9-10, 16, 80

Microsoft Membership Service, 76
Microsoft OLE DB Provider for SQL Server,
    234-235
Microsoft OLE2 SDK, 36
Microsoft SQL Enterprise Manager
    window, 208-209
Microsoft SQL Server. See SQL Server
Microsoft TechNet MSMQ case studies, 134
Microsoft Transaction Server. See MTS
MIDL 3.0, 412
MInterfacePointer data type, 30
Mixed-mode applications, online and
    offline, 358
MMC interface, 10
MMC snap-ins, 9-10, 16, 80
Modify Columns dialog box, 395
Modular applications, 99
Modularity, importance of, 200
Moniker strings, 436
MQBeginTransaction() function, 364
MQCloseCursor() function, 362
MQCloseQueue() function, 360
MQCreateCursor() function, 362
MQCreateQueue() function, 360
MQDeleteQueue() function, 360
MQ_ERROR_NO_DS value, 139
MQFreeMemory() function, 359
MQFreeSecurityContext() function, 129, 363
MQGetMachineProperties() function, 360
MQGetOverlappedResult() function, 359
MQGetPrivateComputerInformation()
    function, 360
MQGetQueueProperties() function, 361
MQGetQueueSecurity() function, 128, 363
MQGetSecurityContext() function, 129, 364
MQHandleToFormatName() function, 361
MQInstanceToFormatName() function, 361
MQIS (MSMQ Information Service)
    database, 12, 120-121, 148-152
MQLocateBegin() function, 363
MQLocateEnd() function, 363
MQLocateNext() function, 363
MQMSG_AUTHENTICATION_REQUEST
    ED value, 133
MQMSG_CLASS_ACK_REACH_QUEUE
    value, 365
MQMSG_CLASS_ACK_RECEIVE value, 365
MQMSG_CLASS_NORMAL value, 365
MQMSG_LEVEL_ALWAYS value, 133
MQMSG_PRIV_LEVEL_NONE value, 131
MQMSGPROPS data structure, 133
MQMSG_SENDERID_TYPE_NONE
    value, 386
MQMSG_SENDERID_TYPE_SID value, 386
MQOA.DLL file, 358, 377, 386
MQOpenQueue() function, 129, 152, 361
MQPathNameToFormatName() function, 362
MQReceiveMessage() function, 135, 359
MQRegisterCertificate() function, 364
MQSendMessage() function, 129, 134, 359
MQSetQueueProperties() function, 362
MQSetQueueSecurity() function, 128, 364
MQ_SINGLE_MESSAGE option, 126
MS-DTC, 60, 115-117
MsgClass property, 365
MSMQ ActiveX controls, 377, 386
MSMQ APIs, 358-365
MSMQ application, data transfer sequence,
    355, 366

MSMQ application elements, 140
MSMQ application errors, in Event Viewer, 397
MSMQ C functions, table of, 359-365
MSMQ case studies, 134
MSMQ configurations, storage of, 125
MSMQ database installation, 149
MSMQ development time, vs. Queued Components, 412
MSMQ information resources for error handling, 348
MSMQ Information Services (MQIS), 12, 120-121, 148-152
MSMQ message fields, 372, 380
MSMQ message fields display, 372
MSMQ message properties, 141-143
MSMQ (Microsoft Message Queue), 2, 11-12, 58, 119, 354-397. *See also* Message queues; Messages
  ActiveX control API, 358-359, 365
  administrative issues, 394-397
  asynchronous communication for, 121-136
  authentication, 132-133
  C function call API, 358-365
  C++ language with, 121
  COM components, 144-146
  in COM+, 6-7, 54, 181-182
  complete messages only, 155
  data by value, 155
  default queue folders and queues, 137
  defining message type, 365-366
  delivery guarantees, 126-127
  diagram for disconnected, 355
  digital certificate use, 129
  discrete components, 12
  disk setup and performance, 153-154
  encrypted data on client and server, 12
  error handling, 144, 147-148
  failures, 316
  features, 11-12
  host machines, 149-151
  hosting, 149-151
  interactive messaging, 156
  interactive messaging diagram, 356
  internal performance, 152-154
  load balancing, 150
  message body encryption, 131-132
  message delivery modes, 127
  message queues, 136-140
  and MTS, 133-136
  newsgroups for, 138
  objects secured at three levels, 129
  overview of, 119-157
  performance, 152-157
  processing limitations, 154-157
  programming information Web site, 121
  routing, 122-124
  security, 128-133
  state information, 150
  three-transaction approach, 126-127
  transaction types, 126, 133
  transactional message support, 109
  transactional queues, 127-128
  types of disk access, 124-125
  whether to use, 122
  Windows 2000 methods for using, 140, 144
MSMQ Monitor application, 394
MSMQ 1.0

  vs. MSMQ 2.0, 151
  registering a certificate, 151
MSMQ Tips Web site, 348
MSMQ transactions, internal vs. external, 135
MSMQ 2.0
  in mixed environments, 148, 151
  vs. MSMQ 1.0, 151
MSMQApplication, 144
MSMQCoordinatedTransactionDispenser, 144
MSMQEvent, 145
MSMQGPROPS data structure, 131
MSMQMessage, 145
MSMQMonDlg.CPP file, 377
MSMQQuery, 145
MSMQQueueInfo, 146
MSMQTest application, 379-392
MSMQTest application code, 382-386
MSMQTest application shell, 379-380
MSMQTestDlg.CPP file, 386
MSMQTransaction, 146
MSMQTransaction object, 126
MSMQTransactionDispenser, 146
MSSQL directory backup, 217
MTA (Multithreaded Apartment), 51, 113, 376
MTS catalog interfaces, Visual C++, 105
MTS components
  creating, 223-245
  Dual vs. Custom interface, 229
MTS Explorer, security roles, 107
MTS (Microsoft Transaction Server), 2, 6, 9-11. *See also* Transactions
  application reliability, 243
  AutoAbort feature, 102
  AutoComplete feature, 102
  and COM+, 54, 99-102, 114, 181-182
  and COM+ services, 101-102
  component administration, 115
  context wrappers, 59
  data integrity, 243
  database features, 109-112
  database programming with, 112-113
  and DTC, 58
  levels of security, 114
  load balancing, 105-106
  monitoring performance of, 112
  and MSMQ, 133-136
  newsgroups, 97
  and ODBC drivers, 113
  overview of, 95-117
  prerelease versions, 113
  for reliable data transmission, 306
  and remote execution, 104-105
  resource management, 100
  resource pooling, 11
  security, 7, 9, 96
  support in various DBMSs, 110-111
  transactions, 96-102
  two-phase commit, 116
MTS objects, overview of, 102-103
MTS SDK, 112
MTS services, 9-10
MTS support in various DBMSs, 110-111
MTS-enabled components, 202
MTSTest test application, 221
MTXREREG utility, 247
MTXStop utility, 247
Multicast events, 7
Multiple document interface (MDI) application, 281

Multiple server load. *See* Load balancing
Multiple servers, with multiple components, 199
MULTI_QI (results) data structure, 268
Multithreaded Apartment (MTA), 51, 113, 376
Multiuser environment, 5

N

Named pipes, 86
NavEx, 67
NDR (network data representation) format, 30
Netscape bookmarks, 67
Network bandwidth, 175
Network connection, failed, 310-311
Network firewalls, 400-401
Network resource name request, 31
Network sniffer, 30
Network traffic, COM+ applications, 168
Network traffic reduction, 175
Networked programming environment, 3
Network-level security, 176
New Alert Settings dialog box, 341-342
New Backup Device dialog box, 217
New Class dialog box, 287-288
New Database Device dialog box, 208
New Database dialog box, 210
New dialog box, 191, 224, 370, 413
New Project Information dialog box, 225-226
New Windows Message and Event Handlers dialog box, 275
Newsgroups, for MSMQ, 138
Next button, coding, 276-280
Next and previous records, getting, 279
Nonvolatile registry key, 329
NTFS security, under Windows 2000, 84
N-tier architecture, 6, 199, 221-222
NULL device, dumps sent to, 218
Nulls
  vs. ANSI NULL values, 204
  vs. not checked values, 203
Nulls column, 211

O

Object containers, 15, 33-34, 251
  access flow rights for, 81
  inheritance, 83
  in-process servers and, 16
  for runtime objects, 33
Object creation methods (remote objects), 19
Object Definition Language (ODL), 412
Object events, 15
Object identifier (OID), 31
Object inheritance, 83-84
Object methods. *See* Methods
Object Permissions dialog box, 215-216
Object pooling, 55, 58, 61, 63, 169, 174, 229
Object properties, 15
Object protection, vs. user rights, 78
Object queues, creating, 376
Object reference data structure types, 31
Object references, 30-31
Object remote procedure call (ORPC), 20, 26
Object resources. *See* Resources
Object state, maintained across transactions, 166

Object-based security, 64, 78-80, 86-88
Objects
  creating, 15-34
  defined, 15, 78
  elements of, 15
  uses for, 14
  within application memory space, 16
Objects folder, 211
OCX files, 15-16
OCXExmpl component, 44
ODBC, 109
ODBC Direct, 112
ODBC drivers, 113, 192-193
ODBC Microsoft SQL Server Setup dialog
  box, 195
ODirection variable, 301
Offline applications, 179-181
Offline communication, 179
OLE applications, vs. out-of-process
  servers, 17
OLE DB features of Visual C++, 221
OLE Transactions (specification), 60
OLEAUT32.DLL, 279
OLE/COM Object Viewer (Visual C++),
  46-47
OleInitialize() function, 50
OLE1 registry entries
  (HKEY_CLASSES_ROOT), 41
OLE32 remote object creation methods, 19
OLE2 registry entries
  (HKEY_CLASSES_ROOT), 41
OLE2 specification, 36
OLE2T() function, 243
OleUninitialize() function, 51
OnClick() method, 37
One to many relationship, 207
OnIdle() method, 49
OnInitDialog(), 372
OnInitialUpdate() method, 299-300
OnNext() method, 296
ON/Off button, ATL object, 229, 264
OnPrevious() method, 296
OnRefresh() method, 296, 300
OnTest() method, 330, 333, 382, 386, 429
Open database connectivity (ODBC), 109,
  113, 195
Open Software Foundation (OSF), 18, 25, 412
Open Systems Interconnect Transaction
  Processing Format and Protocol (OSI-TP
  FAP), 116
OpenEventLog() function, 322-323
OpenProcessToken() function, 81
Oracle RDB, MTS support in, 111
Order entry application, desktop vs.
  distributed, 405
Order entry system. *See* OrderEnty database
Order view (AppTest), 284, 291
Order view (AppTest) code, 300-301
Order view (AppTest) control settings, 292
OrderAccess component, adding objects to,
  233-236
OrderAccess file classes, 222
OrderEntry application folders, 251-253
OrderEntry database, 202-220
  adding tables to, 210-213
  backup, 216-219
  defining, 208-210
  indexes for, 219-220
  overview of, 202

tables, 202-220
tables list, 203, 213
task overview, 201-202
security for, 214-216
OrderForm.CPP file, 300
OrderID database field, 211
Orders table (order entry system), 203,
  205-206, 291
Orders table schema, 206
OSF (Open Software Foundation), 18, 25, 412
OSI-TP FAP, 116
Outgoing Queues folder, 138, 440-441
Out-of-process connections, typical, 18-25
Out-of-process server calls, forms of, 18
Out-of-process servers, 18, 161, 177, 226
  file extensions, 15
  vs. in-process servers, 15
  marshaling requirements for, 52
  vs. OLE applications, 17
  uses for, 17
Overriding methods, 49
Ownership rights, 191
OXID, 31

P

Packages, COM+ Applications as, 105-106
Pass by value vs. pass by reference, 405
Passing a pointer, 279
PathName parameter (queue), 435
PCT (Private Communication Technology),
  70, 76
Performance
  COM+, 174-175
  MSMQ, 152-157
Performance Logs and Alerts folder, 341
Permissions
  assigning to database tables, 215
  failures from lack of, 311
  message handling, 369
Per-object state management, 166
Persistent store (database), 166
Personal Certificates dialog box, 409
Plaintext message, 386, 392-393
Platform SDK, Windows 2000, 170, 185, 247
Player component, COM+ default, 124, 354,
  406, 411
Pointer, passing, 48, 52, 279
Pointer to a structure, 48, 52
Pooling objects, 55, 58, 61, 63, 169, 174, 229
Preboot Authentication Service (PAS), 181
PreTranslateMessage() function, 49
Previous button, implementing, 246,
  276-280
Previous record method, 279
Price field, 205
Primary Enterprise Controllers (PECs),
  149-150
Primary header elements (from #import), 378
Primary key field name, 212
Primary keys, 211-213
  creating for tables, 220
  database table, 205, 207
Primary Site Controllers (PSCs), 150
Priorities, message, 368, 385-386, 393
Priority property (message), 142, 377, 435
Privacy constants, MSMQ message, 131
Privacy Enhanced Mail Part I (PEM1), 72

Privacy Enhanced Mail Part II (PEM2), 72
Privacy Enhanced Mail Part III (PEM3), 73
Privacy Enhanced Mail Part IV (PEM4), 73
Privacy levels for encrypted messages,
  131, 368
Private Communication Technology (PCT),
  70, 76
Private folder, 422
Private key encryption, 130
Private queues, 138, 140, 340-341
Private Queues folder, 138, 341
Privileges, changing, 82
Privileges for roles, revoking, 173
PrivLevel property (message), 143, 435
Processes, 49, 106-107
Processing power, for user interface vs.
  business needs, 162-163
ProcessWndProcException() function, 49
ProductID value, 278-279
Production system data, value of, 216
Program identification (ProgID), 43, 178
Programmers, COM+ and, 4
Programming failure modes, 307
Programming methodology, COM+, 169,
  173-176, 345-346
Project creation process, client-side, 262
Projects tab, New Visual C++ project, 191
Properties, object, 15
Property page GUIDs, 42-43
PROPID_M_AUTHENTICATED value, 133
PROPID_M_AUTH_LEVEL value, 133
PROPID_M_ENCRYPTION_ALG, 131
PROPID_M_PRIV_LEVEL value, 131
PROPID_M_SECURITY_CONTEXT data
  structure, 129
Protecting data. *See* Security
Protocol stack, 21
Protocols, for transactions, 6
Provider, database, 233-234
Provider tab, Data Link Properties dialog
  box, 234
Proxy, 19, 438-439
Proxy applications, 178
Proxy DLL file, 412
Proxy interface file, 412
Proxy and stub modules, 412
Proxy/stub mechanism, 17-18, 45, 226
ProxyStubClsid key, 45
Public folder, 421
Public Key Cryptography Standards
  (PKCS), 75
Public Key Infrastructure (PKI), 129, 175
Public queues, 138-139, 395
Public Queues folder, 138, 367, 387
Pushbuttons, 380
  coding, 276-280
  defining, 272
  event handlers, 275-276
Pvoid interface pointer, 269

Q

QCOne component interface, 436
QCString application
  component code, 417-418
  creating and installing, 413-426
  testing in connected mode, 437
  testing in disconnected mode, 437-441

QCString properties dialog box, Queuing tab, 421
QCTest application, creating, 426-436
QCTest application code, 429-436
QCTest application control settings, 430
QCTest application shell, designing, 427-429
QCTestDlg.CPP file, 436
QCTestDlg.H file, 436
Queries
  and classes, 223
  creating, 197
QueryInterface() function, 35
QueryServiceObjectSecurity() function, 84
Queue globally unique identifier (GUID), 140
Queue information object, creating, 376
Queue management, 319, 394-396
Queue Manager (MSMQ), 12
Queue Messages folder, 138, 388-389, 395
Queue moniker, 432
Queue moniker parameter listing, 433-436
Queue Name dialog box, 367
Queue operation failure, 139
Queue Properties dialog box, 367
Queue security, setting, 368-369
Queue setups, MSMQ, 123
Queue state, snapshot of, 395
Queue strings, 432
Queued Component services, automatic, 418
Queued Components (QC), 7-8, 58, 160, 169, 340, 407
  data flow, 411-412
  development time vs. MSMQ, 412
  in a distributed application, 403
  execution speed vs. COM application, 419
  private queues, 340-341
  security, 407
  test application control settings, 373-374, 382
QueueName property (message), 436
Queues on a machine, viewing, 395
Queues required by an application, creating, 366-369
Queues tab, Test Message Properties, 390-391
Queuing exception class for a component, 147
Queuing tab, QCString properties dialog box, 420

R

Range-checking application code, 310
RC (resource) file, 324
RC2 (resource) file, 334
Read committed isolation level, 135
Receive() method (queue information object), 376
Reconnection strategy, 24
Record numbers, 272
Record pointer, 244
Recorder component, COM+ default, 124, 354, 406, 411
Recoverable delivery mode (MSMQ), 127, 152-153
Recovery, staging, 348-351
Recurring backup, 219
Reentrancy, 50
Reference counter, incrementing/decrementing, 40

Referral component technique, 23
Refresh button, coding, 276-280
Refresher course in COM technology, 14
RegCloseKey() function, 329
RegCreateKeyEx() function, 329
REGDB, backup and restore, 63
RegGetKeySecurity() function, 84
REG_OPTION_BACKUP_RESTORE value, 329
RegisterEventSource() function, 322, 332
Registering an event with the event log, 332
Registry Editor, 47
Registry entries, 34
Registry keys, 43, 84, 329
Registry requirements of COM components, 40-47
Registry (Windows), 14, 34
RegSetKeySecurity() function, 84
RegSetValueEx() function, 329-330
RegSetValueEx() function arguments, 330
Release() method, 35, 40
ReleaseBuffer() method, 279-280
Reliability
  and application complexity, 319
  of COM+ applications, 106-107, 167
  server, 18, 164
Reliable delivery method, MSMQ, 127
Remote development and debugging, SQLServer, 190-198
Remote execution, MTS and, 104-105
Remote execution host, determining, 104
Remote object creation methods, 19
Remote procedure calls (RPCs), 18, 25, 86, 176, 412
Remote server name (RemoteServerName), 178
RemoteActivation() method, 26-30
RemoveCustomer() method (IOrderModify), 232
RemoveItem() method (IOrderModify), 232
RemoveOrder() method (IOrderModify), 231
Report queue, 138
ReportEvent() function, 323, 333
Resource allocation failures, 312
Resource dispensers, 55, 60-61, 113, 135
Resource entry, document object, 302
Resource management, 11, 61-62
  COM+, 108
  MTS, 9, 100
  vs. transaction flexibility, 136
Resource Manager, 61, 113, 116, 135
Resource objects, 55
Resource pooling, 9-11, 57, 61, 108
Resource status levels, 10-11
Resources
  allocating and deallocating, 10
  in enlisted inventory, 10
  in enlisted use, 10-11
  marking allocated, 10
  releasing, 377
  returned to the resource pool, 57
  in unenlisted inventory, 10
  in unenlisted use, 10
Response messages, 157, 366
Response queues, 138, 337-340, 358
ResponseQueueInfo message parameter, 141, 366
Result structures, array of, 268

Results pane (Local Query), 197
ResumeThread() method, 48
Retry queues, 147
Reusing components, 16, 33-34
Rights, assigning, 78, 81, 85, 115, 191, 311
Robust error handling, 346
Role Administrator, 257
Role privileges, revoking, 173
Role-based security, 55-56, 63-91, 172-173, 257, 259
  advantages of, 87-88
  auditing in, 88
  authentication and, 89
  introduced, 64
  vs. object-based security, 86-88
Roles, creating, 257-258
Roles folder, 252
Rolled back transactions, 61, 307
Routers, 93
  downed, 94
  load-balancing, 24
  server access through, 8
Routing (MSMQ), 12, 122-124
RPC interface, vs. COM interface, 412
RPC specification (DCE), 18
RPC_E_WRONG_THREAD error message, 50
RPCs (remote procedure calls), 18, 25, 86, 176, 412
RSA web site, 68
Run() method, 49
Runtime object, container for, 33

S

Satellite offices as independent clients, 180
Scalability
  COM+ Applications, 105, 166, 168
  component, 99
  Windows NT, 99
Schedule Backup dialog box, 219
SCODEs (status codes), 351
SDI (single-document interface) application, 281
Secondary header (from #import), 378
Secure Sockets Layer (SSL), 70, 76-77
Secure transactions
  in COM+ and Windows 2000, 115
  MTS, 96-102
Secure/Multipurpose Internet Mail Extensions (S/MIME), 73
Secure/Wide Area Network (S/WAN), 74
Security (see also Role-based security)
  COM+, 7, 79, 175-176
  COM+ Application, 167, 257-261
  COM+ types of, 79
  commercial view of, 68
  ensuring a consistent level of, 77
  file system, 84
  importance of, 184
  Internet, 400-401
  message, 392
  MSMQ, 12, 128-133
  MTS, 7, 9, 96
  object-based, 64, 78-80
  in OrderEntry database, 214-216
  in Queued Components, 407
  server, 18, 86, 176
  setting for a queue, 368-369

standard Windows 2000, 64-86
transaction, 96
Windows 95/98, 77-78
Windows 2000 built-in, 77-86, 115
Security access control list (SACL), 82
Security administration control, MSMQ, 128
Security boundary, explained, 88
Security call context collection, 90
Security context, MSMQ, 128
Security descriptor flags, 82
Security descriptors, 82-85
  access steps, 85
  classes of, 83-84
  explained, 78-79
  types of, 82
Security holes, 65-68
Security identifier (SID), 78-83, 132, 386, 392
Security isolation, 107
Security levels
  MTS, 114
  server, 176
  Windows 2000, 75-77
Security options, choosing, 235
Security providers, 19
Security roles, 7, 107
Security standards
  for the Internet, 71-74
  latest information on, 68
  overview, 68-75
  vendor, 70
Security tab (for messages), 440
Security tab (for methods), 172
Select Counters dialog box, 343-344
Select Data Source dialog box (Database Project), 192
Select Database Table dialog box, 236
Select files to install dialog box, 254, 423
Select permission, 214
Select Users or Groups dialog box, 258
Self-relative security descriptor, 82
SE_LOCK_MEMORY_NAME privilege, 82
Send() method, message object, 126, 386
Sender identification type, 385-386
Sender tab (messages), 391-392
SenderCertificate message property, 143
SenderId message property, 143
SenderIdType message property, 143
Sending messages and COM objects, 353-397
SentTime message property, 143
Serializable isolation level, 135
Serialization, 10
Server access through a router, 8
Server applications (COM+), 177, 249-250
Server clusters, 105
Server connection errors, finding, 268
Server loads, unanticipated, 311-312
Server name, UNC format server, 267
Server queue for active components, 122-123
Server queue setups, MSMQ, 123
Server view of messaging, 140
Server-based component properties, 230
Server-based components, 163-164, 230
Servers
  choosing, 235
  component registration on, 247-261
  downed, 94
  impersonating clients, 86

in-process, 15-17, 52, 161, 226
in-process vs. out-of-process, 15
out-of-process, 15, 17-18, 52, 161, 177, 226
  protecting, 86
Server-side components, database, 222-261
Server-side processing, stopping to view a message, 366
Service Control Manager (SCM), 19, 26, 93
Service (EXE) projects, 226
Service objects, executable, 84
Service Pack 5a, SQL Server 6.5, 186, 188
Service Pack 4, Microsoft Windows NT 4.0, 190
Service Pack 3, Visual Studio, 170, 188
Services, COM+, 7-9
Services MMC snap-in, 186
SE_SYSTEM_PROFILE_NAME privilege, 82
Set Application Identity dialog box, 250-251, 420
SetAbort() method (IObjectContext), 102-104, 244
SetComplete() method (IObjectContext), 102-104, 244
SetFileSecurity() function, 84
SetKernelObjectSecurity() function, 84
SetSecurityDescriptorSACL() function, 85
SetServiceObjectSecurity() function, 84
SetUserObjectSecurity() function, 84
Severity levels of errors, 350
Shared Property Manager, 166
Shared secret authentication, 76
Shared transient state, 166
ShowString() method, 436
SHTTP (Secure Hypertext Transfer Protocol), 74
SID-related API calls, 81
SIDs (security identifiers), 78-83, 132, 386, 392
Signature (MEOW), 30-31
Signed hash value, message authentication, 132
Simple Object Access Protocol (SOAP), 174
Single Threaded Apartment (STA), 51-52
Single threaded object, 51
Single-document interface (SDI) application, 281
Single-machine application test, 221
Smart application downloads, 157
Smart pointer declarations, 378
S/MIME, 73
SORF_NOPING flag (DCOM), 31
Source component reuse, 34
SourceMachineGuid message property, 143
Sp_dboption stored procedure, 198
Specify Table Name dialog box, 212
Sp_stored_procedures, 198
SQL Enterprise Manager window, 208-209
SQL pane (Local Query), 197
SQL Server
  backup methods, 217
  current revision level, 188
  diskdump default backup device, 218
  lack of remote diagnostic aids, 185
  movement limitations, 246
  MQIS and, 148
  with MSMQ, 12
  MTS support in, 111
  remote development and debugging, 190-198
  Service Pack 5a, 186

stored procedures, 198
SQL Server services, stopping, 217
SQL Server 7.0, upgrading to, 184
SQL Server 7.0 Developer Edition, 190
SQL Server 6.5, upgrading from, 184, 190
SQL Server 6.5 Developer Edition, 185-189
SQL Server 6.5 Developer Edition installation, 186-189
SQL Server 6.5 Service Pack 5a, 186, 188
SQLSetConnectionAttr() function, 113
SSL (Secure Sockets Layer), 70, 76-77
SSL3, 76
Standard object reference, 31
Standardized access, 36
Standards-based security, 68
StartQuest StarSQL Pro, MTS support in, 111
State information
  with COM+, 165
  storing in a database, 166
State maintenance, component, 165
State management, per-object, 166
State management component, 200
Static load balancing, 22-23
Storage tab, Message Queuing Properties dialog box, 125
Stored procedures, 198
String Properties dialog box, 289
String Table resource, 288-289
Strings
  removing leading and trailing spaces, 243
  separated by a slash, 432
Stub, 21. See also Proxy/stub mechanism
SUCCEEDED macro, 351
Success messages, 350
Sybase PowerBuilder, MTS support in, 111
SymbolicName entry (message), 325
Symmetric-key encryption, 130
System administrator (sa) account, 210
System audit ACE, 83

 T

Tandem NonStop SQL, 111
Tape backup device, 217
TCHAR m_productID values, 243
TCHAR values converted to BSTR values, 244
Template string resource, 290
Terms used in this book, glossary of, 443-475
Test application (AppTest), 280-303
Test application (QC), 426-436
Test pushbutton, 330, 333, 380, 429
Test connection, 236
Test queue
  and associated message count, 387
  cleaning out, 395
Test queue Properties dialog box, 388
This user option, 250
Thread affinity, 113
Thread safe execution environment, 50
Thread safe ODBC driver, 113
Thread safe resource dispenser, 113
Thread types, 47-49
Thread-Neutral Apartment (TNA), 51-52
Threads, 14, 47-52
Three-component application minimum, 311
Three-machines COM+ application, 311-312
Three-tier approach, extension to, 199-200

Three-transaction approach, MSMQ, 126-127
Thumbprint reader, 181
Timing failures, 312
TOKEN_ADJUST_PRIVILEGES privilege, 82
TOKEN_QUERY privilege, 81
Tokens, explained, 81
TokenUser class, 82
ToolBoxBitmap32 key, 43
Trace property (message), 141, 436
Transaction costs, 174
Transaction driven application example, 183-303
Transaction events, 103-104
Transaction failures, 305-351
    connected transactions, 310-316
    disconnected transactions, 316-319
Transaction flexibility, vs. resource management, 136
Transaction logs, 125
Transaction management from other vendors, 116
Transaction Manager, 116-117
Transaction processing, 58
Transaction sequence, 102-106
Transaction steps, 104
Transaction technology, 6
Transaction voting code, 243-244, 306
Transactional context, 100
Transactional delivery mode, 127, 153
Transactional queues, MSMQ, 127-128
Transactional Shared Property Manager (TSPM), 169
Transactions, 56, 96-102. *See also* MTS
    ACID acronym for, 97-98
    for both MSMQ and SQL Server, 135
    from the COM perspective, 115
    and COM+, 6
    and data recovery, 99
    and databases, 108-114
    in DBMSs, 96
    environmental factors, 98
    fault tolerance, 98
    internal vs. external MSMQ, 135
    and LAN connections, 98
    MSMQ-supported, 126, 133
    point of stability, 98
    rolled back, 61, 307
    under MTS, 9
Transparent database access, 112
Transport Layer Security (TLS) protocol, 76
True application types, 176
Try...catch structure, 346-347, 349, 376-377
T2BSTR() function, 244
Two-machine (client and server) setup, 185, 199, 221-222
Two-phase commit, MTS, 116
Type definition header file, 412
Type libraries, 44-45, 47, 55
TypeLib registry key, 44-45

U

Unbound events, 7
Unicast events, 7
Unique ID key, 211
Universal Naming Convention (UNC) format, 267, 322
Universal Resource Identifiers (URI), 74

Update permission, 214
Updates, installing components for, 253
UPS monitoring, 84
User access tokens, 78-82
User input, failures from, 312, 317-318
User interface threads, 48-49
User interfaces
    COM+, 4, 173
    defining, 284-294
    designing, 280-281
User Manager utility, Windows 2000, 81
User permissions
    assigning to database tables, 215
    failures from lack of, 311
    message handling, 369
User privileges
    changing, 82
    revoking, 173
User rights, 78, 81, 85, 115, 191, 311
User role, 257, 259
User-level security, 176
User-preferred formats, for data entry, 294
Users
    beginning, 3
    COM+ and, 3-4
    out of the office (remote), 4
    retraining, 175
USES_CONVERSION macro, 243
Utility methods, ICOMAdminCatalog interface, 63

V

VarBstrFromCy() method, 279
Variables, for moving to next/previous records, 246
Variant data ype, 376-377
Veridicom BIOS eXtension (VBX) development kit, 181
Verification, 181
VeriSign, 129
Version number of a control, 44, 46
Version number registry key, 44, 46
VFAT file system security, 84
Views
    designing and creating, 284-294
    making accessible, 301
Virtual private networks (VPNs), 3, 161, 176, 401
Viruses, 400
Visual C++
    aggregation, 33
    classes created by, 233
    Database Project, 185, 191-198
    MTS catalog interfaces, 105
    OLE DB features, 221
    OLE/COM Object Viewer, 46-47
    Service Pack 3 update, 170, 188
    source component reuse, 34
Visual Studio APE Package, 179
Visual Studio Installer, 190
Visual Studio Interoperability Studio, 177
Visual Studio Service Pack 3 installation, 188
Visual Studio 6.0 Enterprise Edition Back Office, 186
Visual Studio 6.0 Microsoft Data Engine (MSDE), 190
Visual Studio 6.0 Plus Pack, 190

Volatile registry key, 329
Volumn name, 218
Voting on transactions, 243-244, 306

W

Warning events, 322, 332
Warning messages, 336, 350
Win32 registry keys, 46
Window station, 84
Windows execution environments, 49-50
Windows 95/98 security, 77-78
Windows NT
    lack of scalability, 99
    authentication method, 193
    LAN Manager (NTLM) security, 76, 175
    Service Pack 4, 190
Windows registry, 14, 34
Windows 3.x programming environment, 3-4
Windows 2000
    authentication over HTTP, 76-77
    built-in security features, 77-86
    Challenge/Response, 77
    and COM+, 175
    COM+ application directory structure, 251-252
    compatibility requirements, 309
    configuring interfaces, 170
    cost of updating to, 174
    cryptographic algorithms, 131
    Developer's Readiness Kit, 190
    domain accounts, 7
    encryption technologies, 129
    features, 114
    file system security, 84
    Internet security standards, 68-70
    levels of security, 75-77
    management interface, 114
    methods for using MSMQ, 140, 144
    monitoring everything, 68
    object inheritance, 84
    Platform SDK, 170, 185, 247
    secure transactions, 115
    Security API, 75
    security tools, 64
    standard security, 64-86
    User Manager utility, 81
WinError.H file, 349
WinVerifyTrust, 66
Wire protocol, DCOM, 25-26
Wireless network connections technology, 180
Worker threads, 48
World Wide Web Consortium (W3C), 70, 174

X

X.509 digital certificates, 129
XML (EXtensible Markup Language), 174

Z

ZIPCode index, 220